Human Biology

for AS

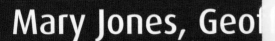

Mary Jones, Geoff

PUBLISHED BY THE PRESS SYNDICATE OF THE UNIVERSITY OF CAMBRIDGE

The Pitt Building, Trumpington Street, Cambridge, United Kingdom

CAMBRIDGE UNIVERSITY PRESS

The Edinburgh Building, Cambridge CB2 2RU, UK

40 West 20th Street, New York, NY 10011-4211, USA

477 Williamstown Road, Port Melbourne, VIC 3207, Australia

Ruiz de Alarcón 13, 28014 Madrid, Spain

Dock House, The Waterfront, Cape Town 8001, South Africa

http://www.cambridge.org

First published 2004

Printed in the United Kingdom at the University Press, Cambridge

Typefaces Berthold Akzindenz Grotesk, ITC Legacy, Dax, Swift   *System* QuarkXPress®

A catalogue record for this book is available from the British Library

ISBN 0 521 54891 8   paperback

Produced by Geoff Jones

Front cover photograph: red and white blood cells (computer artwork); copyright Roger Harris/Science Photo Library

Contents

Acknowledgements   iv

Introduction   v

AS Unit 2856: Blood, circulation and gaseous exchange

1   Observing the blood   1
2   Investigating blood chemistry   20
3   Blood clotting   46
4   Heart disease   68
5   Monitoring circulation   86
6   Maintaining a healthy heart   105
7   The lungs   119

AS Unit 2857: Growth, development and disease

8   Stem cells and DNA   140
9   Cell division   159
10   Foetal development   183
11   Infant development   209
12   Infectious disease   218
13   Controlling infectious disease   235

Answers to self-assessment questions   264

Glossary   281

Index   291

Acknowledgements

We are grateful to the following for permission to reproduce photographs:

John Adds 4 all, 7t, 27, 127, 129, 164, 199; Alamy 137 (Janine Wiedel Photolibrary), 196 (Popperfoto); Bubbles Photolibrary 17 (Jonathon Chappell), 40 (Jennie Woodcock), 135 (Lucy Tizard); Corbis 20 (Duomo), 35 (Kevin R. Morris), 119 (Les Stone), 218 (Bettmann), 235 (Picimpact), 243 (Ariel Skelley), 251 (Reuters); Food Features 259; Greenpeace 170; Geoff Jones 7b, 14, 115, 118, 233, 260, 261, 262; PA Photos 80; Photofusion 140 (Bob Watkins); Roche Diagnostics Ltd, Lewes 38; Science Photo Library 2 (Antonia Reeve), 11 (Dr Gopal Murti), 15 all (Dr Jeremy Burgess), 46 (Pascal Goetgheluck), 48 (Prof. P.M. Motta, G. Macchiarelli, S.A. Nottola), 54 (Du Cane Medical Imaging Ltd), 64 (Sotiris Zafeiris), 83 (Simon Fraser), 86 (Simon Fraser/Coronary Care Unit, Freeman Hospital Newcastle), 88 (AJ Photo/Hop Americain), 97 (Biophoto Associates), 103 (Sheila Terry), 105 (Mauro Fermariello), 133 (Manfred Kage), 138 (Prof. S.H.E. Kaufmann & Dr J.R. Golecki), 143 (James King-Holmes), 145 (SPL), 152 (Lawrence Livermore Laboratory), 159 (Mauro Fermariello), 167 (James Stevenson), 176t (CNRI), 176m (SPL), 176b (Camal, ISM), 177t (Alfred Pasieka), 177m (Mehau Kulyk), 177bm (National Cancer Institute), 179 (Peter Menzel), 183 (Lea Paterson), 187 (Ruth Jenkinson), 188 (Ian Hooton), 192 (Adam Hart-Davis), 194tl (Jesse), 194tr (SPL), 202 (Saturn Stills), 205 (Dept. of Clinical Cytogenetics, Addenbrookes Hospital), 209 (Biophoto Associates), 210t (Simon Fraser), 210m (Saturn Stills), 224 (Jim Patrico/Agstock), 239 (A. Crump, TDR, WHO), 241l (Dr P. Marazzi), 241m (Dr Kari Lounatmaa), 241r (Cliff Moore), 245 (SPL), 247 (Hank Morgan), 249 (Saturn Stills), 257 (Biophoto Associates); Wellcome Photo Library 3.

Picture research: Vanessa Miles

We have made every effort to trace copyright holders, but if we have inadvertently overlooked any we will be pleased to make the necessary arrangements at the earliest opportunity.

Introduction

This book provides complete coverage of Module 1 (Unit 2856) and Module 2 (Unit 2857) of the OCR Human Biology AS specification. Chapters 1 to 7 cover Module 1, *Blood, Circulation and Gas Exchange*, while Chapters 8 to 13 cover Module 2, *Growth, Development and Disease*. This book has been endorsed by OCR as providing complete coverage of these two Modules of the AS specification.

The book is designed to be accessible to readers who have achieved at least a grade CC or C grade in a GCSE course in double award Science or Biology, or their equivalent (for example, IGCSE or O level). However, descriptions and explanations of biological facts and concepts are introduced carefully, ensuring that forgotten – or perhaps misunderstood – material from earlier studies is briefly dealt with before moving on to something new. Full colour and informative illustrations throughout will help you to understand facts and concepts.

Within each Chapter, text printed in black relates directly to the content of the Module. In general, this follows the same sequence as in the specification. There are a few exceptions to this: for example, learning outcome 5.1.1.1(g) is dealt with in Chapter 2 rather than Chapter 1, because its coverage builds on an understanding of the structure of proteins which is also in Chapter 2. If you read, understand and learn all of the materials printed in black, you will have thoroughly covered every one of the learning objectives in the AS specification for these two Modules.

Some Chapters contain Activities and Procedures, which are boxed and contain text printed in black. These deal with learning outcomes from the specification. You should try to carry out all of the Activities yourself, as this will help you to succeed in your examinations. Most of the Procedures cover techniques carried out in hospitals, or at the scene of an accident, and you are not expected to do these yourself – although in some cases you may be able to. You need to learn these Procedures, as they are all listed in the specification and may be tested in your examination papers.

Self Assessment Questions, SAQs, appear in every Chapter. These are designed to help you to think about and to use the information within that Chapter. Some of them require only short answers, while others require writing in more continuous prose. Some of them involve the handling and interpretation of data. You should try to do all of these questions, as they enable you to check your understanding of that topic. There are answers to almost all of the SAQs on pages 264 to 280.

Each Chapter begins with a real-world Case Study, putting the material that follows into context. Most Chapters also contain further Case Studies. These are all based on real incidents and situations, although the names of people involved have been omitted or changed unless they are already well-known. The Case Studies are boxed and the text is printed in blue.

For example:

> John Taylor had been worrying for a few days now. His interview for promotion in his job at the bank was very important to him. Normally ...

There are also Just for Interest boxes. These take the material a little further, sometimes by delving deeper into a particular concept, and sometimes by looking at a wider field of interest related to the specification. These are also printed in blue.

So anything printed in blue will probably make interesting reading for you, but you do *not* need to learn it because it is not part of the OCR specification.

The SAQs and Case Studies will help you to develop skills that you will need in your examination for Unit 2858/01, the Case Studies paper, and Unit 2858/2, the Investigative Skills coursework.

Human Biology for AS contains a large vocabulary of technical terms. You need to be able to use these terms appropriately when you write answers in your examinations. Each new term is explained as you meet it in the text. The Glossary on pages 281 to 290 provides brief definitions or explanations of most of these terms.

Observing the blood

John Taylor had been worrying for a few days now. His interview for promotion in his job at the bank was very important to him. Normally he walked to the bus stop, but on the day of the interview, February 10th, he jogged instead. Nearing the bus stop, he found he was having to breathe very rapidly and his heart was racing. He felt weak and could hardly stand upright. A person at the bus stop thought Mr Taylor was having a heart attack, and called an ambulance.

At the hospital, a blood sample was taken, to help to determine what was wrong with Mr Taylor. Various tests were carried out on the blood samples in the hospital's pathology laboratories and a heart attack was ruled out. But the results of these and other tests suggested that he had a hereditary disease, called sickle cell anaemia. The pain and breathlessness were indications that he was having a 'sickle cell crisis'. The medical staff were very surprised that he had not had a crisis before, but he would not be the first person to live for many years with this condition, not knowing that he had it.

Testing blood samples

Testing blood samples often plays a major part in helping to provide information about a person's health and in diagnosing medical conditions. In this chapter, we will look at how some of these tests are carried out and what information they can provide.

Most of these tests will be done in the pathology laboratories in a hospital.

The tests explained in this chapter involve making a slide of blood and then observing it using a microscope. In Chapter 2, we will look at other investigations which require chemical tests on the blood sample. Both types of tests can usually be done quite quickly and can often give very useful information about a person's health.

The people who handle blood in a pathology laboratory need to take great care not to come into direct contact with it. They treat all blood samples as potentially hazardous, because blood can contain disease-causing agents such as the human immunodeficiency virus, HIV, which causes AIDS.

Taking a blood sample

If you find yourself in Accident and Emergency with some as yet undiagnosed symptoms, one of the first things that is likely to happen is that a nurse will take a blood sample from you. The blood sample will be split into many smaller samples, each of which will have a different test carried out on it. These may help to decide whether you are really ill or not, and to diagnose what is wrong with you. The blood sample will also be used to determine your **blood group**, which will go into your medical record in case you need a blood transfusion in the future.

1 Sterile equipment is used, so that bacteria or viruses cannot be introduced into the patient's blood.

2 The person collecting the sample wears disposable gloves, to avoid any bacteria or viruses in the patient's blood getting into his own blood.

3 The skin is swabbed with alcohol, which is allowed to dry before the skin is punctured.

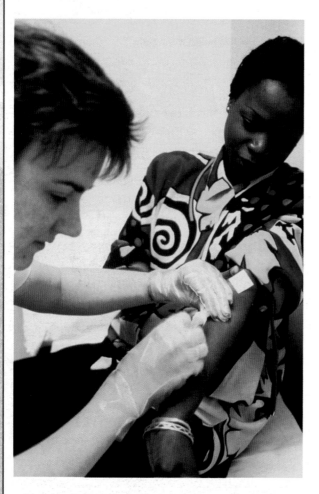

A blood sample being taken in a hospital's Accident and Emergency Department.

A tourniquet pulled around the arm can make the veins stand out more.

4 Normally, blood is taken from a vein. A fine needle is inserted into the vein, and blood is withdrawn slowly into a syringe.

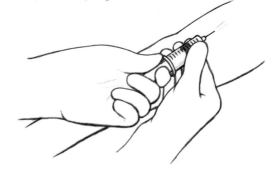

SAQ

1.1 Suggest why the skin is swabbed with alcohol when taking a blood sample.

1.2 Suggest why the sample is taken from a vein and not an artery.

PROCEDURE 1.2

Making a blood film

Some of the tests that are done on a blood sample involve looking at the appearance of the blood. For these tests, the blood is spread onto a microscope slide, making a **blood film**. A bit of practice is needed to get the blood film just right – too thick and you cannot see individual cells, too thin and there are not enough cells to see.

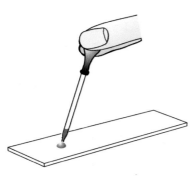

1 A small drop of blood is placed in the centre of a very clean and dry microscope slide.

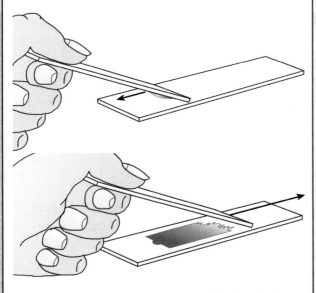

2 A spreader is used to spread the blood back along the slide.

3 The slide is immediately labelled with the date and the patient's name. In some hospitals, bar-codes are used.

PROCEDURE 1.3

Staining a blood film

Blood contains two major types of cells. By far the most common are the **red cells**, also called **erythrocytes**. These are easily visible under the microscope. The second type are the white cells, also called **leucocytes**. There are many different kinds of these, and to be able to see them clearly and tell them apart they need to be **stained**. This involves adding a dye to them, which is taken up by some kinds of leucocytes more than others, and by some parts of each cell more than other parts.

The stains used are **Romanowsky stains**. There are several different kinds of them that the pathology staff may use. One kind of Romanowsky stain is called **Leishman's stain.**

In Leishman's staining, the blood film is first allowed to dry and then fixed (preserved and sterilised) with methanol. The stain is then poured over the slide (this is called flooding). After 2 minutes, water is added and then left for another 5–7 minutes. Finally, the slide is washed until the blood film looks pale pink to the naked eye.

In pathology laboratories, this process is normally automated, so that many blood films can be stained in a short period of time.

A blood film being spread. After this it is stained. A label is already attached to the slide. This label has unique codes identifying the sample and patient.

3

Examining a blood film

Examination of a stained blood film under a microscope often plays a major part in diagnosing illness. The shapes, sizes and relative numbers of the different kinds of blood cells can indicate the state of a person's health and also give clues to the presence of a particular disease (see Fig 1.1 and page 7).

Below and to the right are photographs of four types of white cell, each with red cells around them.

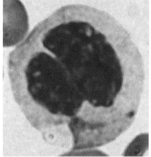 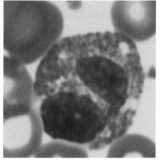

Macrophage (monocyte) (×2200)   Eosinophil (×2200)

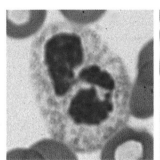 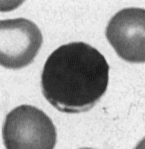

Neutrophil (×2200)   Lymphocyte (×2140)

1 Collect a prepared slide of mammalian blood. Look at it with the naked eye, and choose an area where there seems to be a fairly even film of blood. Place the slide on the microscope stage with your chosen area over the hole.

2 Swivel the objective lenses until the smallest one (low power) is over the slide. Look down the eyepiece and turn the focussing knob until the cells come into focus.

> **! Care !** As you use the focussing knob to move the objective lens closer to the slide, watch from the side so that you can stop before the lens crashes into the slide. This is particularly important for the higher power (longer) objectives. (The oil immersion objective, if you have one, has a sprung lens which reduces the chance of breakage.)

3 Search the slide to find an area where you can see at least two white blood cells. Then swing the high power objective lens into position and focus using the fine focus.
(If you have an oil immersion objective, add a drop of oil to the slide and focus.)

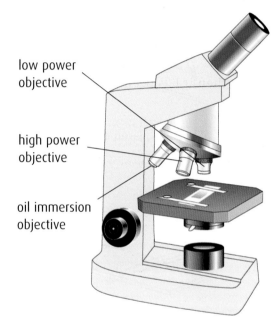

low power objective

high power objective

oil immersion objective

4 Make a drawing of at least two different types of white blood cells. Use the photographs above to help you to identify and label them. Move to an area of the slide where the red cells are spread thinly and draw a few red cells.

5 Change back to the low power objective. Find an area of the slide where the red cells seem to be fairly thinly distributed. Keeping the slide completely still, count all the red cells and all the white cells in your field of view. Repeat in at least two other areas of the slide. Use your counts to calculate approximately how many more red cells there are than white cells in the blood film.

Magnification

Most people have red blood cells with a diameter of about 6.0 to 8.5 μm. The symbol **μm** stands for **micrometre**. One micrometre is one millionth of a metre. Another way of writing this is to say that one micrometre equals 1×10^{-6} metres.

$$1\,\mu m = 1 \times 10^{-6}\,m$$
$$1\,m \ = 1 \times 10^{6}\,\mu m$$

The **magnification** of a photograph or a drawing is how many times bigger it is than the real object. If a red blood cell has a real diameter of 6.0 μm, but is shown as 6 mm in a micrograph, then it has been magnified 1000 times.

For example, imagine that you make a drawing of a spider. The actual length of the spider is 10 mm. Your drawing of the spider is 30 mm long.

 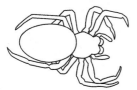

$$\text{magnification} = \frac{\text{size of the picture}}{\text{real size of the object}}$$

For the spider example:

$$\text{magnification} = \frac{30}{10} = \times 3$$

Sometimes, you know the magnification and the size of the picture, and you want to know the real size of the object. To work this out, you need to turn the formula around:

$$\text{real size of the object} = \frac{\text{size of the picture}}{\text{magnification}}$$

SAQ

1.3 A person makes a drawing of an incisor tooth. The width of the actual incisor tooth is 5 mm. The width of the tooth in the drawing is 12 mm. Calculate the magnification of the drawing.

1.4 The magnification of the photograph of a neutrophil in Activity 1.1 is ×2200.
   a Measure the maximum diameter of the neutrophil in the photograph, in mm.
   b Convert your measurement to μm. (There are 1000 μm in 1 mm, so you need to multiply your measurement by 1000.)
   c Use this formula to calculate the real size of the white blood cell.

$$\text{real size of object} = \frac{\text{size of object in picture}}{\text{magnification}}$$

1.5a Reorganise the equation in question 1.4 so that it can be used to calculate magnification.
   b What is the magnification of the diagram below, if the real diameter of the red blood cell is 7 μm?

1.6 The magnification of the diagram of the white cell below is ×2770. Copy the diagram and draw a 10 μm scale bar appropriate to the diagram.

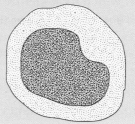

The functions of blood cells

Red blood cell or erythrocyte

Erythrocytes transport oxygen (see page 25) and carbon dioxide.

The cell is very small, to allow it to travel through tiny capillaries and so get very close to cells in body tissues (see pages 95 and 96).

There is no nucleus, to make more room for haemoglobin.

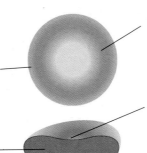

The cytoplasm is packed with a protein called haemoglobin, which temporarily combines with oxygen or carbon dioxide.

The biconcave shape provides a relatively large surface-area-to-volume ratio (see page 128), which increases the amount of oxygen and carbon dioxide which can pass into and out of the cell in a certain period of time (see page 30).

Neutrophil

Neutrophils are normally the most common type of leucocytes (white cells). They destroy bacteria and other foreign material by phagocytosis (see page 225).

multilobed nucleus

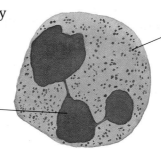

The cytoplasm contains small granules. Some of these granules are lysosomes which contain enzymes for digesting bacteria, whilst others are glycogen stores.

Macrophage (monocyte)

Macrophages, like neutrophils, destroy bacteria and other foreign material by phagocytosis. They are larger than neutrophils. They are found in tissues such as the lungs and lymph nodes, as well as in the blood (see pages 129 and 225).

Lymphocyte

B lymphocytes secrete antibodies, which destroy bacteria. The blood also contains T lymphocytes, which look identical to B lymphocytes but have different functions (see pages 227 and 228).

Platelet

Platelets are specialised fragments of cells. They are involved in blood clotting (see page 47).

Fig 1.1 Blood cells.

6 µm

Unusual blood films

On the right are photographs of blood films in which the red blood cells are abnormal. Red blood cells carry oxygen. An illness in which they cannot do this effectively – perhaps because there are not enough of them, or because there is something wrong with the haemoglobin they contain – is called **anaemia**. Symptoms of anaemia include tiredness and shortness of breath, caused by the lack of oxygen supply to the tissues.

The uppermost blood film is from someone with sickle cell anaemia. You can see that some of the red blood cells are an unusual shape – thin and curved (sickle shaped) instead of the normal biconcave disc. This is what John Taylor's blood would have looked like during his sickle cell crisis.

Sickle cell anaemia is caused by a faulty gene for the production of haemoglobin. A person with one copy of this faulty gene and one normal copy has enough normal haemoglobin for there to be few, if any, problems. But in a person with two faulty copies, all the haemoglobin is abnormal. This haemoglobin reacts oddly in conditions of low oxygen concentration (for example, when someone is exercising hard and the muscles are using up oxygen rapidly), forming insoluble fibres inside the red cells and pulling them out of shape. The sickled cells get stuck in blood capillaries, causing intense pain. In some people, there are no symptoms when they are relatively inactive, but in others they may have all the signs of anaemia – such as tiredness, pale skin and shortness of breath.

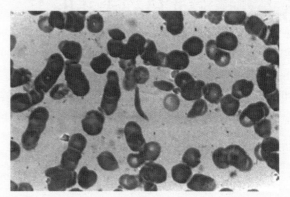

A blood film from a person with sickle cell anaemia.

The blood film below is from a person with a completely different kind of anaemia. This person has nothing wrong with their genes, which code in the normal way for making normal haemoglobin. However, this person has a shortage of iron in the body, and iron is an essential component of haemoglobin. He or she is suffering from iron deficiency anaemia.

A trained medical laboratory worker would recognise that the red blood cells in this blood film do not contain as much haemoglobin as they should. Some of the cells are smaller and some paler than usual. Both of these features can be indications of other kinds of anaemia, so further tests need to be done to be certain that iron deficiency is the cause of these problems.

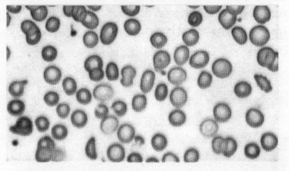

A blood film from a person with iron deficiency anaemia.

Counting red blood cells

One of the tests done on a blood sample is checking whether the numbers of red and white cells are within the normal range. This is called a **blood cell count**. Normally, you would expect to find that there are around 5.2 million red cells mm^{-3} in a male adult, while women have about 4.8 million red cells mm^{-3}.

In a pathology laboratory red cell counting is automated using a machine such as a Coulter counter.

This is very quick, and can process many blood samples in a very short time. White cell and platelet counting is also automated for routine samples. However, the pathology lab technicians can use a special microscope slide called a haemocytometer for non-routine counts of white cells. Though this haemocytometer could also be used to do a red cell count it is not accurate enough for it to be used in a hospital.

1 A 1 in 200 dilution of the blood sample is made. For example, 0.1 cm^3 of well-mixed blood is added to 19.9 cm^3 of diluting fluid.

2 The haemocytometer is prepared. This is a special microscope slide with two sets of ruled grids in the centre, with deep grooves either side. Between the grooves, the surface of the slide is 0.1 mm lower than elsewhere. This platform is called the counting chamber.

3 A special coverslip is placed over the counting chamber. It must be slid on firmly but carefully.

   ! Care ! Only press down in the areas shown in the diagram – or the expensive coverslip will break.

   Look out for 'interference' colours appearing where the coverslip overlaps the slide on each side of the counting chamber. These are called Newton's rings. Only when you see these will the distance between rulings and coverslip be exactly 0.1 mm. This does take some practice!

4 Now the diluted blood sample is mixed and some is taken into a fine pipette. It is carefully introduced into the space between the coverslip and the platform. The blood needs to cover the platform completely, but not spill over into the grooves. Then the haemocytometer is placed onto the stage of a microscope and the low power objective is used to find and focus on one of the central ruled grids.

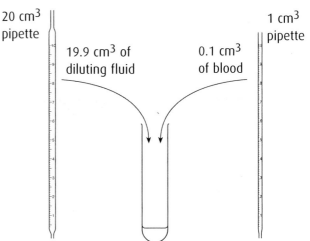

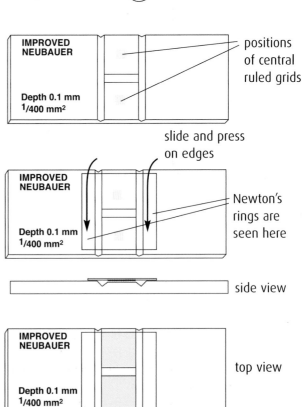

continued ...

5 Next the ×40 objective is used, to focus on the central block of squares. The number of red cells in the 5 blocks of 16 small squares (shown as 1 to 5 on the diagram) is counted. If a red cell is on a boundary line at the top or on the left it is counted. If it is on the boundary at the bottom or on the right, it is ignored.

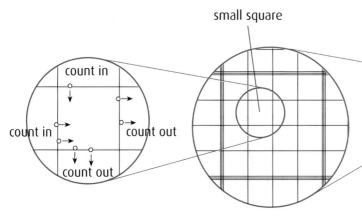

small square

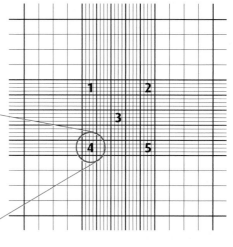

Improved Neubauer counting chamber rulings

Calculations

All the information is now collected to be able to calculate the number of red cells in 1 dm^3 of blood. This is how it is done.

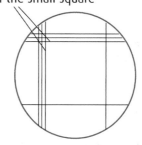

inner lines mark edge of the small square

Look at the diagram at bottom right. Each small square has sides of 0.05 mm. The depth of the blood sample is 0.1 mm.

Therefore the volume of blood over one small square is $0.05 \times 0.05 \times 0.1 = 0.00025$ mm^3.

Cells were counted in 80 of these small squares.

Therefore the total volume of the blood in which you counted the cells is $80 \times 0.00025 = 0.02$ mm^3.

Say you count N cells in total.

There are 10^6 mm^3 in 1 dm^3.

If there are N cells in 0.02 mm^3 then there are $N \times 10^6 \div 0.02$ cells in 1 dm^3.

But the blood had been diluted by a factor of 200.

So the number of cells in 1 dm^3 of undiluted blood is $200 \times N \times 10^6 \div 0.02$ cells dm^{-3}.
This is the red cell count for the sample.

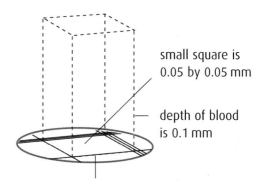

small square is 0.05 by 0.05 mm

depth of blood is 0.1 mm

volume of blood over one small square is 0.00025 mm^3

Summary

1. A blood sample is taken from a vein using a sterile needle, after the skin has been swabbed with alcohol to kill any microorganisms present.

2. A small drop of blood is spread on a slide to make a blood film. The film is then stained to help the cells to show up clearly. A commonly-used stain is Leishman's stain.

3. Blood contains leucocytes (white cells), erythrocytes (red cells) and platelets. There are far more erythrocytes than leucocytes.

4. Erythrocytes have no nucleus. Their cytoplasm is full of a red pigment called haemoglobin, which transports oxygen around the body. Their biconcave shape provides a large surface area to volume ratio, which increases the rate at which oxygen can diffuse in and out.

5. There are several different types of leucocyte – neutrophils, macrophages and lymphocytes. They all have a nucleus.

6. Neutrophils have a multilobed nucleus. They destroy bacteria by phagocytosis.

7. Macrophages also destroy bacteria by phagocytosis. They are larger than neutrophils.

8. Lymphocytes have a large, round nucleus which almost fills the cell. Some of them make antibodies, which destroy bacteria.

9. Platelets are cell fragments which help in blood clotting.

10. A haemocytometer is a slide that is used to count blood cells. The slide has accurately marked areas and known depth. The number of blood cells per dm^3 of blood is calculated.

Cell ultrastructure

Using a light microscope, you can see stained blood cells well enough to pick out the nucleus of a leucocyte. However, the cytoplasm of leucocytes and most other human cells contains many other smaller structures, called **organelles**. Most organelles cannot be seen with a light microscope. A much more powerful kind of microscope, called an **electron microscope**, is needed. This shows us the **ultrastructure** of the cell.

It is rare for cell ultrastructure to be used in diagnosis of illness. This is partly because the fine structure of a cell doesn't help in most diagnoses. There are also more basic reasons: electron microscopes are expensive, and it takes a long time to prepare a specimen in the appropriate way to be able to see its ultrastructure in the microscope.

The ultrastructure of a leucocyte

Fig 1.2 is a photograph taken through an electron microscope, called an **electronmicrograph**. Fig 1.3 is a diagram of the structure of a leucocyte as it might appear using an electron microscope.

Cell surface membrane

All cells are surrounded by a thin layer made up of protein and lipid molecules. This membrane is known as the **cell surface membrane**. There are also other membranes inside the cell.

The cell surface membrane controls what enters and leaves the cell. Substances such as water and oxygen can easily diffuse through it into the cell. However, many other substances can only enter or leave the cell through special **transporter proteins** in the cell surface membrane.

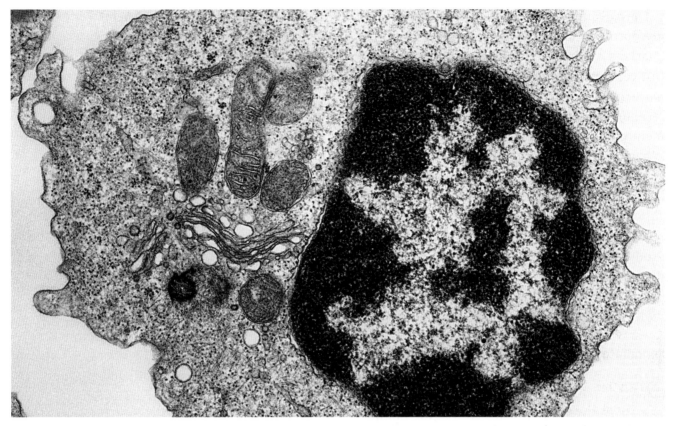

Fig 1.2 Electronmicrograph of a leucocyte.

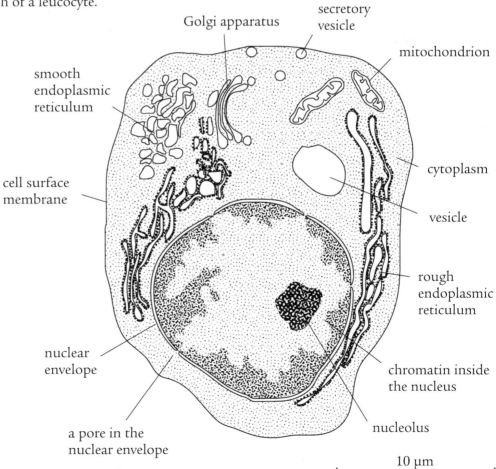

Fig 1.3 Drawing of a leucocyte. This is a lymphocyte which is making and secreting antibodies.

Golgi apparatus

secretory vesicle

mitochondrion

smooth endoplasmic reticulum

cytoplasm

cell surface membrane

vesicle

rough endoplasmic reticulum

nuclear envelope

chromatin inside the nucleus

a pore in the nuclear envelope

nucleolus

10 μm

The cell surface membrane also contains **glycoproteins** and **glycolipids**. They act as 'markers' so that other cells can recognise that this cell belongs here, and is not a foreign cell. Most cells, including leucocytes, also have **receptor molecules** in their cell surface membranes to which other chemicals can bind. When this happens, it often affects the behaviour of the cell. For example, if harmful bacteria get into your body, they may produce substances which bind with a lymphocyte's receptors. The lymphocyte reacts to this by producing and releasing antibodies which can destroy the bacteria (see page 226). You can find out more about cell membranes, and the molecules they are made from, in Chapter 2.

Endoplasmic reticulum and Golgi apparatus

In the cytoplasm of the leucocyte, there is an extensive network of membranes called the **endoplasmic reticulum** (Fig 1.3). The membranes enclose spaces called **cisternae**.

On some parts of the endoplasmic reticulum, called **rough endoplasmic reticulum (RER)**, there are darkly-staining structures called **ribosomes**.

This is where the cell makes proteins. For example, a leucocyte might respond to contact with a bacterium by making proteins called **antibodies**. As soon as they have been made, the antibodies enter the cisternae. The cisternae break up to form small membrane-enclosed 'bags' called **vesicles** (Fig 1.4).

The vesicles are then moved towards a stack of curved cisternae called the **Golgi apparatus**. Here the finishing touches are made to the antibodies, and they are 'packaged' into another set of vesicles. These are then carried from the Golgi apparatus to the cell surface membrane, from where the antibodies can be released outside the cell (secreted) to do their work of destroying bacteria.

Not all of the endoplasmic reticulum has ribosomes on it. Endoplasmic reticulum with no ribosomes is known as **smooth endoplasmic reticulum (SER)**. This can have a variety of functions, which are different in different kinds of cells. For example, in some of the cells in the ovaries and testes, steroid hormones such as oestrogen and testosterone are made on the smooth ER. In liver cells, toxins are broken down on smooth ER.

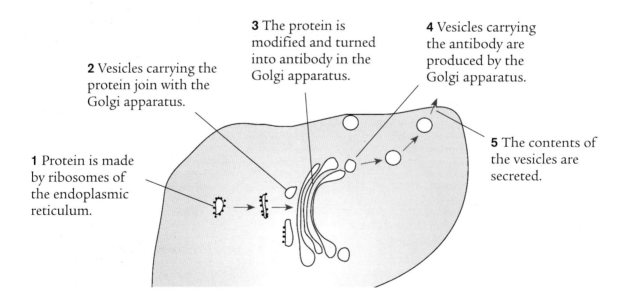

2 Vesicles carrying the protein join with the Golgi apparatus.

3 The protein is modified and turned into antibody in the Golgi apparatus.

4 Vesicles carrying the antibody are produced by the Golgi apparatus.

1 Protein is made by ribosomes of the endoplasmic reticulum.

5 The contents of the vesicles are secreted.

Fig 1.4 Steps in the production and secretion of antibodies.

Mitochondria

Mitochondria can be quite large organelles – sometimes up to 10 μm long – and you can just about see large ones if they are stained and you are using a good light microscope. However, an electron microscope is needed to see their internal structure (Fig 1.5).

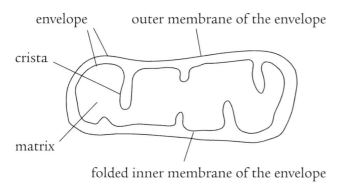

Fig 1.5 A mitochondrion.

Mitochondria have two membranes surrounding them. The two membranes are sometimes called an **envelope**. These membranes help to isolate the contents of the mitochondria from the rest of the cell. This allows chemical reactions to take place inside a mitochondrion without interference.

Mitochondria are the site of **aerobic respiration**. This happens in the matrix and on the inner membrane, where there are enzymes which catalyse the reactions involved. In respiration, glucose molecules are broken down and used to make **adenosine triphosphate** (**ATP**) molecules (see page 149). During this process, chemical energy in the glucose is transferred to chemical energy in **ATP**. The ATP leaves the mitochondrion and can then be used by other parts of the cell when energy is needed. For example, muscle cells use ATP to contract. Phagocytes use ATP to provide energy for movement.

Nucleus

Almost all cells found in animals contain a fairly large, densely-staining structure within the cytoplasm, called a **nucleus**. Red blood cells are an exception to this, but all leucocytes contain a nucleus.

The nucleus is surrounded by an envelope of two membranes. There are gaps in the envelope, called **nuclear pores**. The nucleus contains the hereditary material, **DNA**, in the form of long strands called **chromosomes** (see page 146). These are not normally visible, but when the cell is about to divide they become more compact and dense and can then be seen (if they are stained) with a light microscope. The nucleus of a leucocyte, like most cells in the human body, contains two sets of 23 chromosomes – that is, 46 in all. The nuclear envelope ensures that the chromosomes are kept together inside the nucleus.

There is usually an especially darkly-staining area inside the nucleus, and this is called the **nucleolus**. Here, some of the DNA is used as a template for making a substance called **RNA**. The DNA contains information which the cell needs to ensure it makes the right proteins. This information is copied onto RNA, which can leave the nucleus through the nuclear pores and travel to a ribosome. Here, the information is used in protein synthesis.

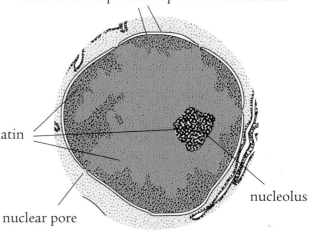

Fig 1.6 A nucleus.

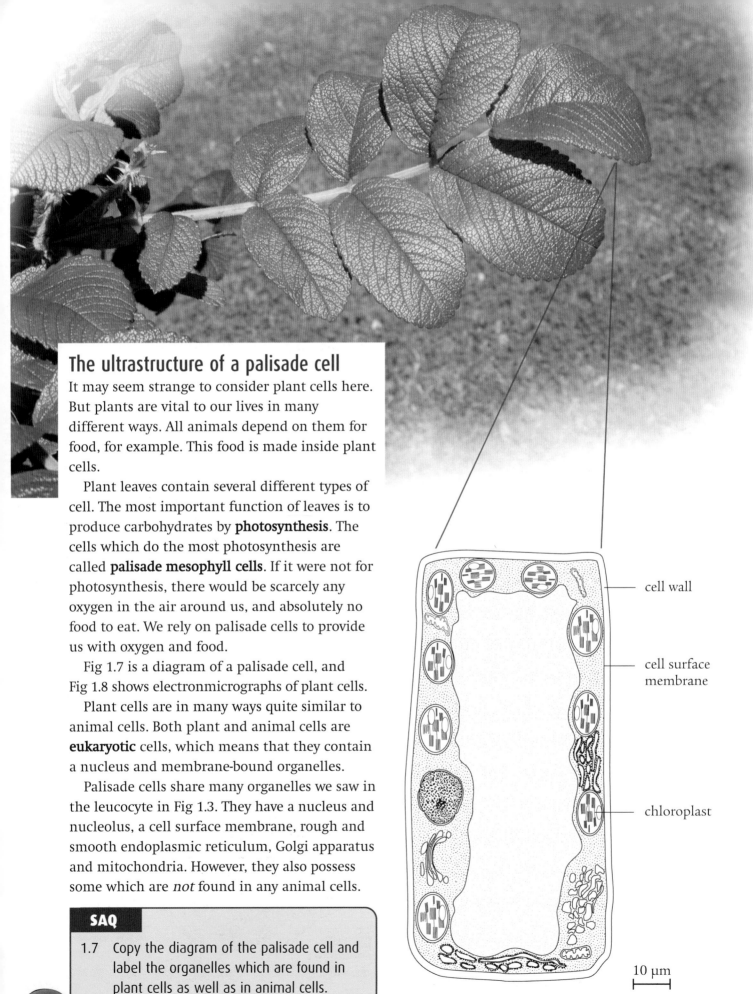

The ultrastructure of a palisade cell

It may seem strange to consider plant cells here. But plants are vital to our lives in many different ways. All animals depend on them for food, for example. This food is made inside plant cells.

Plant leaves contain several different types of cell. The most important function of leaves is to produce carbohydrates by **photosynthesis**. The cells which do the most photosynthesis are called **palisade mesophyll cells**. If it were not for photosynthesis, there would be scarcely any oxygen in the air around us, and absolutely no food to eat. We rely on palisade cells to provide us with oxygen and food.

Fig 1.7 is a diagram of a palisade cell, and Fig 1.8 shows electronmicrographs of plant cells.

Plant cells are in many ways quite similar to animal cells. Both plant and animal cells are **eukaryotic** cells, which means that they contain a nucleus and membrane-bound organelles.

Palisade cells share many organelles we saw in the leucocyte in Fig 1.3. They have a nucleus and nucleolus, a cell surface membrane, rough and smooth endoplasmic reticulum, Golgi apparatus and mitochondria. However, they also possess some which are *not* found in any animal cells.

cell wall

cell surface membrane

chloroplast

10 μm

SAQ

1.7 Copy the diagram of the palisade cell and label the organelles which are found in plant cells as well as in animal cells.

Fig 1.7 Palisade cell at electron microscopic detail.

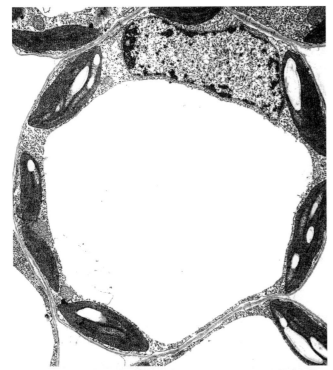

Fig 1.8 Electronmicrographs of plant cells. The top photograph shows a complete mesophyll cell. Below is one chloroplast inside a mesophyll cell. The chloroplast has been coloured green and blue.

Chloroplasts

Chloroplasts are only found in plant cells which can photosynthesise. Like mitochondria, they are surrounded by two membranes (an envelope), which isolate the reactions inside the chloroplast from the cytoplasm.

Inside the chloroplast, there are stacks of membranes known as **grana** (singular: granum). These membranes contain **chlorophyll**. This is a green pigment which traps energy from sunlight. The energy is then used to make water and carbon dioxide react together to form carbohydrates and oxygen.

If more carbohydrate is made than is required by the plant, it is converted to **starch** and stored as grains inside the chloroplast.

Cell wall

All plant cells have a layer of **cellulose** outside their cell surface membrane. This is called the **cell wall**. The cellulose forms long, strong fibrils which form layers. The cell wall also contains **pectin**, which helps to hold the cellulose fibrils in position.

When a plant cell absorbs water, it swells. The contents of the cell push outwards against the tough cell wall, which is strong enough to resist the pressure. The cell becomes tight and firm, and is said to be **turgid**. Animal cells don't have a cell wall, so if they absorb a lot of water the cells burst.

Unlike the cell surface membrane, the cell wall does not control what passes through it. A cell wall is therefore said to be **fully permeable**, while the cell surface membrane is **partially permeable**.

SAQ

1.8a Make a table to compare the ultrastructure of a leucocyte and a palisade mesophyll cell.

b Some leucocytes, such as neutrophils, crawl around actively. Would you expect them to have more, fewer or the same number of mitochondria as a palisade cell? Explain your answer.

c Explain the difference between the terms in each of these pairs:
• cell wall and cell membrane;
• chloroplast and chlorophyll.

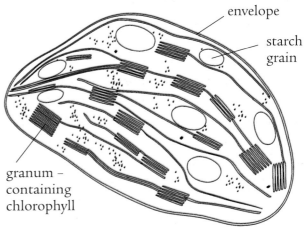

Fig 1.9 A chloroplast.

1.9 Name and describe the functions of the structures labelled A–J in this diagram. Present the information as a table.

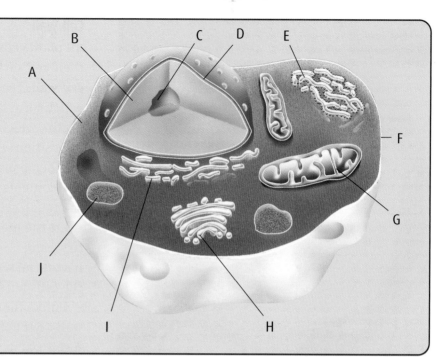

Summary

① Animal and plant cells are eukaryotic cells, which means that they contain a nucleus and membrane-bound organelles.

② All cells are surrounded by a partially permeable cell surface membrane. This is responsible for controlling what goes in and out of the cell and also for cell recognition. There are also membranes inside the cell, which help to form compartments whose contents are not allowed to mix with the rest of the cell.

③ The endoplasmic reticulum is a network of interconnecting membranes forming compartments called cisternae.

④ Rough endoplasmic reticulum has ribosomes, where proteins are synthesised. These may be transported in vesicles to the Golgi apparatus, where they are modified and packaged before being secreted out of the cell.

⑤ Smooth endoplasmic reticulum is responsible for making steroid hormones.

⑥ Mitochondria are relatively large organelles bounded by an envelope (two membranes). ATP is produced by aerobic respiration inside mitochondria.

⑦ The nucleus contains DNA in the form of chromosomes. Inside the nucleus there is a nucleolus where some of the information coded in DNA is transferred to RNA.

⑧ Plant cells are always surrounded by a cell wall, which animal cells never have. The cell wall is made of cellulose fibres and helps to stop the cell from bursting when it takes up a lot of water.

⑨ Some plant cells, such as palisade mesophyll cells, contain chloroplasts. These have an envelope and also membranes within them on which chlorophyll is held. Photosynthesis occurs here.

Blood groups

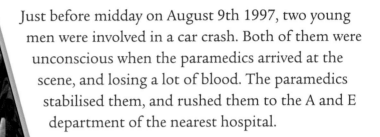

Just before midday on August 9th 1997, two young men were involved in a car crash. Both of them were unconscious when the paramedics arrived at the scene, and losing a lot of blood. The paramedics stabilised them, and rushed them to the A and E department of the nearest hospital.

The trauma team at the hopital knew the men were coming, and were ready to receive them. A rapid assessment was made of the two unconscious patients. It was obvious that both needed blood transfusions and immediate surgery if they were to survive. Their blood was quickly tested to find their blood groups. One was blood group O and the other AB. Even before they reached the operating theatre, a member of the trauma team rapidly picked up two packs of blood from the cooled cabinet where it was stored.

As surgeons worked on the men in the operating theatre, it became clear that one of them was extremely ill. He was given blood continuously – four packs in all. Then, two hours after he had reached the hospital, he died. The other injured man, also given blood, survived surgery and eventually recovered fully.

Very shortly after the man's death, it was realised that he had not died from his injuries, but because the medical staff had given him the wrong type of blood. A member of the trauma team had confused the identities of the two men. The group O blood had been given to the man whose blood group was AB, while the group AB blood had been given to the man with blood group O. It was this man who had died.

Blood group antigens and antibodies

In the case study on page 17, why did one man die and the other survive, even though they were both mistakenly given blood which did not match their blood group?

When someone is told they are blood group A, it means that they have A **antigens** on the surface of their red blood cells. These antigens are one of the cell markers found in the cell surface membrane of red blood cells. There are two different kinds of them – A and B – which produce the ABO system of blood groups. This gives four possible blood groups, depending on whether you have both of these antigens on your red blood cells, only one of them, or neither of them.

Table 1.1 Blood group antigens.

Antigens on red blood cells	Blood group
A	A
B	B
AB	AB
none	O

In your blood plasma, you may have **antibodies** relating to these antigens. The antibodies you have are the exact opposite of your blood group.

Table 1.2 Blood group antigens and plasma antibodies.

Antigens on red blood cells	Antibodies in blood plasma
A	anti-B
B	anti-A
AB	none
none	anti-A and anti-B

Blood transfusions

In the case study, the man who died had blood group O. So he had no antigens on his red blood cells, and both anti-A and anti-B in his blood plasma.

When he was mistakenly given group AB blood, his anti-A and anti-B antibodies immediately bound to the A and B antigens on the foreign red blood cells he was being given. This caused the cells to clump together (**agglutinate**). The clumps of red blood cells could not get through his blood vessels. It was this that killed him, not his injuries.

So why was the other man not killed? He, too had been given blood which did not match his blood group. However, because he was blood group AB he had no anti-A or anti-B antibodies in his plasma. He could safely have been given blood with any blood group. No matter what antigens the transfused blood contained, the red cells in it would not have agglutinated.

This table summarises the types of blood which can safely be given to people with a particular blood group.

Table 1.3 Compatible transfusion recipients.

Donor	Recipient (who can safely be given this blood)
A	A and AB
B	B and AB
AB	AB
O	A, B, AB and O

SAQ

1.10a Which blood group is known as the 'universal donor'? Explain your answer.
   b Which blood group is known as the 'universal recipient'? Explain your answer.

The Rhesus antigen

As well as A and B antigens, red blood cells may also have a different protein, called the **Rhesus antigen**, in their cell surface membranes. If you have this antigen, you are said to be Rhesus positive; if you don't, you are Rhesus negative. However, unlike the ABO blood groups, no-one automatically has anti-Rhesus antibodies in their blood plasma. The antibodies are only produced if some Rhesus positive blood is mixed with Rhesus negative blood. If that happens, then the blood may agglutinate.

This is a danger to a woman and her developing baby if she if Rhesus negative and the unborn child is Rhesus positive. (This could happen if the father was Rhesus positive.) As the embryo develops in her uterus, the blood of the baby and the mother come very close to each other, in the placenta, but do not mix.

In the placenta, many substances diffuse between the mother and her baby. Red cells are normally far too big to pass through the barrier between the mother's blood and the baby's. However, if some of the baby's red cells, carrying the Rhesus antigen, do somehow get into the mother's blood, then she will develop anti-Rhesus antigens against it. This does not normally happen during pregnancy, so there is unlikely to be a problem. But during childbirth, the baby's blood will certainly contact the mother's blood and she is said to be **sensitised**.

So, if she then becomes pregnant with a second Rhesus positive baby, her ready-made anti-Rhesus antibodies can cross the placenta, and get into the baby's blood. Here they can cause the baby's red cells to clump together, which may be fatal.

To prevent this taking place, all pregnant women are tested. If a woman is Rhesus negative she is given an injection of anti-Rhesus antibodies at childbirth. This may sound strange, but it fools the body into thinking it is already making anti-Rhesus antibodies. So, even if some Rhesus blood from the baby contacts the mother's blood, it does not stimulate the mother to make anti-Rhesus antibody of her own. She is not sensitised to Rhesus antigen. The antibody given by injection soon breaks down.

Summary

1. Red blood cells may have antigens in their cell surface membranes. In respect of the ABO blood grouping system, there are two kinds of antigen – A and B.

2. A person with A antigens on the red cells has blood group A. If they have B antigens they have blood group B. If they have both antigens they have blood group AB and if they have neither they are blood group O.

3. A person's blood plasma can contain antibodies to one, both or neither of these antigens. A person with blood group A has anti-B antibodies. A person with blood group B has anti-A antibodies. A person with blood group AB has neither, while a person with blood group O has both kinds of antibodies.

4. If red blood cells are introduced into the body of someone who has antibodies against them, the antibodies will bind with the antigens on the red cells and make them clump together (agglutinate).

5. Red blood cells may also carry Rhesus antigen. If such red cells get into the blood of a person who does not have this antigen, the white cells will, after some time, produce antibodies against them. This can be dangerous if a Rhesus negative woman has a second Rhesus positive baby.

CHAPTER 2

Investigating blood chemistry

At the 1984 Olympic Games, held in Los Angeles, American cyclists won medals for the first time in 72 years. More surprisingly, no fewer than *four* won medals. It emerged that they had used a technique called 'blood doping' to enhance their performance.

Over the next few years many athletes used this technique. Several months before the competition, $1\,dm^3$ of blood was taken from the athlete and frozen. As the athlete continued in his or her training, their blood level would slowly return to normal. Then, a few hours before the competition, their red cells were thawed and transfused back into their body.

Blood doping raised the quantity of haemoglobin in the athlete's blood. This meant that the blood could carry more oxygen, so the muscles were able to carry out aerobic respiration more quickly. This especially helped athletes taking part in endurance sports, such as cycling and cross-country skiing. It could give a 17–30% increase in performance.

By 1998, there was a simpler way of achieving the same effect. This used a hormone called erythropoietin, or Epo for short. Epo is produced by the kidneys and increases the rate at which new red blood cells are produced. Some cyclists who took part in the Tour de France in 1998 had injected this hormone.

These techniques are now officially banned. They are seen as being unfair, and can be very dangerous. Blood doping increases the risk of blood clots developing in blood vessels, and it is thought that several European cyclists died from this between 1987 and 1990. But still people used it. In March 2002, at the Salt Lake City Winter Olympics, discarded blood transfusion equipment was found where the Austrian skiing team had stayed. Investigations found that three of the skiers had received blood transfusions just before the competition.

Blood doping is very difficult to detect. However, tests are now available that can distinguish between the Epo that is naturally produced in the body and the Epo which can be bought and injected. Another test which is very useful is to measure the haemoglobin concentration in the blood. If this is well above normal, then blood doping is suspected.

Haemoglobin

A haemoglobin molecule. Each red blood cell contains about 300 000 000 of them (3×10^8).

Haemoglobin is a **protein** found inside red blood cells. It is a pigment – that is, a coloured substance – that looks red. It carries oxygen around the body, which is used for respiration. Haemoglobin is therefore described as a **respiratory pigment**. Its name can be abbreviated to Hb.

The structure of haemoglobin

Like all proteins, haemoglobin is made up of many smaller molecules linked together end to end. These are called **amino acids**.

Amino acids and peptide bonds

Fig 2.1 shows the structure of an amino acid molecule.

All amino acids have a central carbon atom. Carbon atoms have four bonds which can hold them firmly to other atoms. In an amino acid, the central carbon atom forms one bond with a **carboxyl group**, −COOH, another bond with a

Fig 2.1 The basic structure of all amino acids.

hydrogen atom, and a third bond with an **amino group**, −NH$_2$. The fourth bond, however, can be to any one of a whole range of different groups. The letter **R** is used to show this group. In animals such as humans, there are about 20 different amino acids, each with different R groups.

Like all proteins, haemoglobin is made on the ribosomes inside a cell. Here, separate amino acids are brought close together and bonded together. Fig 2.2 shows how this is done. The bond which is formed is called a **peptide bond**.

As the peptide bond is formed, two hydrogen atoms from one amino acid and one oxygen atom from the other join together to form a water molecule. Reactions where this happens are called **condensation reactions**.

On the ribosomes, a long chain of amino acids is formed, all linked together by peptide bonds. This chain is called a **polypeptide**.

SAQ

2.1 The amino acid glycine is the simplest amino acid. Its R group is a single hydrogen atom. How many atoms are there altogether in a molecule of glycine?

Two atoms of hydrogen and one of oxygen are lost – they form a molecule of water.

The two amino acids are joined at this point by a peptide bond.

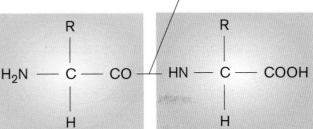

Fig 2.2 The formation of a peptide bond by a condensation reaction.

The haemoglobin molecule

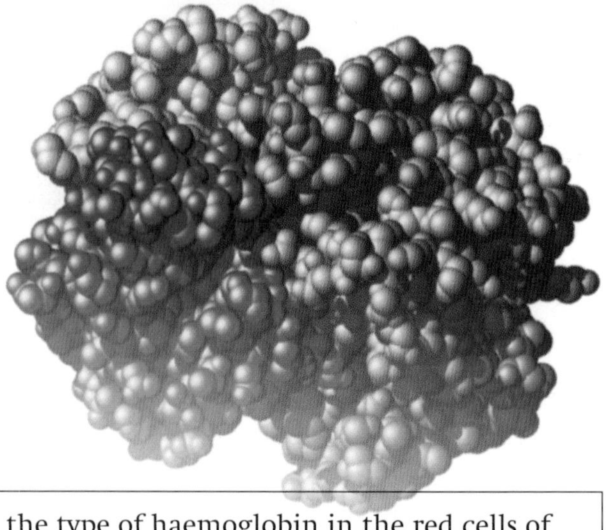

Many proteins are just a single polypeptide chain. However, a haemoglobin molecule is made up of four polypeptide chains, all wound round each other in a very precise pattern.

To describe and understand this structure, we need to imagine unravelling this tangle and looking at the individual chains.

Primary structure If we look at the different amino acids in the polypeptide chains, and the sequence in which they are linked together, we find that – for a particular kind of polypeptide – they are always exactly the same. This sequence is called the **primary structure** of the molecule.

In the type of haemoglobin in the red cells of humans, there are two types of chain, known as α-chains and β-chains (Fig 2.3). The amino acid sequences – that is, the primary structure – of these chains are slightly different from each other.

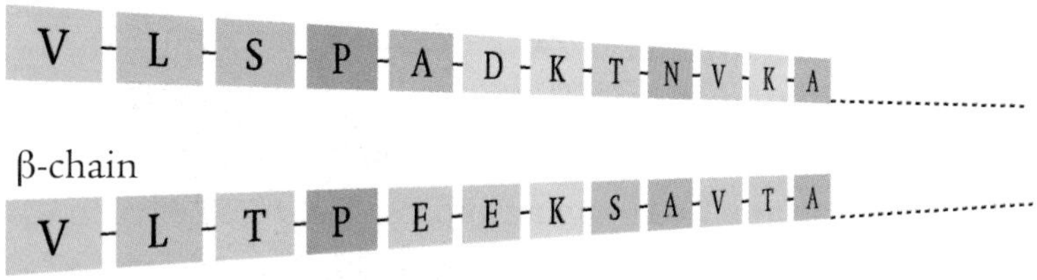

α-chain

V - L - S - P - A - D - K - T - N - V - K - A

β-chain

V - L - T - P - E - E - K - S - A - V - T - A

Different amino acids can be represented by a one-letter or three-letter abbreviation. For example, V or Val represents the amino acid valine.

Fig 2.3 The first 12 amino acids of the primary structure of the α- and β-chains of Hb. The total length of each chain is 141 amino acids.

Secondary structure Each part of a polypeptide chain tends to form a particular shape. For example, some parts twist into a spiral known as an α-**helix** (Fig 2.4). The way a particular part of a chain twists is always exactly the same. This is called the **secondary structure** of the protein.

The shape is maintained by hydrogen bonds, as described on page 62.

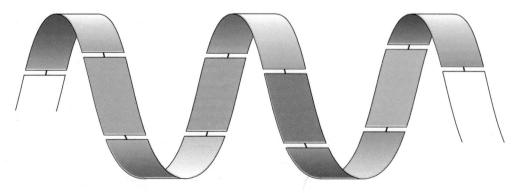

Fig 2.4 An example of a secondary structure – the α-helix.

Tertiary structure This twisted chain can now twist even more. The overall shape formed by this is called the **tertiary structure** of the protein. Imagine a curly cable attached to a telephone. The regular coils are equivalent to the secondary structure. If you then twist the coil around into a particular shape, this is the equivalent of the tertiary structure of a protein. This is held by means of hydrogen bonds, disulphide bonds and hydrophobic bonds (see page 62).

Each of the polypeptide chains winds itself around a little group of atoms with an **iron ion** at the centre. This is called a **haem group** (Fig 2.5).

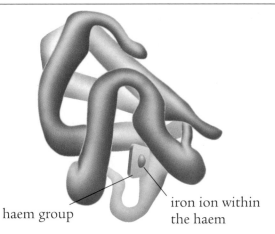

haem group

iron ion within the haem

Fig 2.5 Tertiary structure of one β-chain of haemoglobin.

Quaternary structure But there is still one more level of complexity to come. We mentioned earlier that a haemoglobin molecule is made of four polypeptide chains. These four chains fit together to make the complete haemoglobin molecule. The shape that they produce is called the **quaternary structure** of the protein (Fig 2.6). This shape is also held by bonds, as with the tertiary structure.

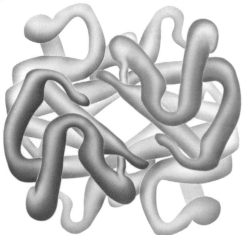

Fig 2.6 Quaternary structure of a haemoglobin molecule. The two β-chains are shown brown and the two α-chains blue (– the four haems are not shown).

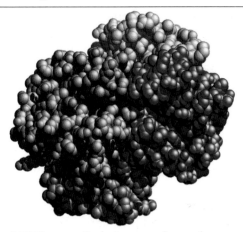

Fig 2.7 The two β-chains are shown brown and the two α-chains blue in this 'space-filled model' of the haemoglobin molecule. Each 'blob' within this diagram represents an atom of carbon, oxygen or nitrogen. Hydrogen atoms have not been shown.

You can see from Fig 2.7 that the complete haemoglobin molecule is shaped roughly like a ball. Proteins whose molecules have this kind of shape are called **globular proteins**. There are other kinds of protein that don't curl into balls, instead forming long, thin shapes. They are called **fibrous proteins** (see Chapter 3).

SAQ

2.2 Match each term with its definition.
   Terms:
   primary structure
   secondary structure
   tertiary structure
   quaternary structure

Definitions:
- The three-dimensional shape of a complete polypeptide chain.
- The arrangement of two or more polypeptide chains that associate together to form a protein molecule.
- The sequence of amino acids in a polypeptide or protein.
- The regular shapes taken up by parts of a polypeptide chain e.g. an α-helix.

Measuring the concentration of haemoglobin in the blood

The haemoglobin content of someone's blood is measured if there is concern that they may be anaemic. It may also be done if an athlete is suspected of using blood doping. Normal values are about 150 g of haemoglobin dm^{-3} in a man, and 135 g dm^{-3} in a woman.

This test is automated in most pathology laboratories. However, manual methods may still be used in certain instances.

The World Health Organization recommends the use of the **haemiglobincyanide** method. This involves adding a special reagent to the blood sample. All of the haemoglobin in the blood combines with cyanide from the reagent to form haemiglobincyanide (**HiCN**). This produces a stable red solution. The intensity of the colour can be measured using a colorimeter, and compared against a standard sample with a known concentration of haemoglobin.

1 A dilution of approximately 1 in 200 of blood is made by adding 20 mm^3 of blood to 4 cm^3 of the special reagent, in a test tube. The tube is stoppered and then tipped upside down several times.

2 The tube is left at room temperature for at least 5 minutes, to give time for all the haemoglobin to be converted to HiCN.

3 Liquid with no haemoglobin (the blank) is placed in the colorimeter sample tube, called a cuvette, and its absorbance is set to 0 in the colorimeter. A colorimeter measures how much light of a particular colour is absorbed by the liquid in the tube in comparison to the blank. HiCN is red, so it allows red light to pass through it and absorbs yellow-green light. So in this case, yellow-green light is used at all stages.

4 The test sample is then placed in the colorimeter in place of the blank. The greater the concentration of HiCN, the greater the absorbance of the yellow-green light.

5 The test sample is then removed and a standard solution (known concentration) of HiCN is placed in the colorimeter. (These standards can be bought and kept for many years without deteriorating.) The results using this standard can be compared to the results with the unknown sample, allowing the concentration of haemoglobin in the test sample to be calculated.

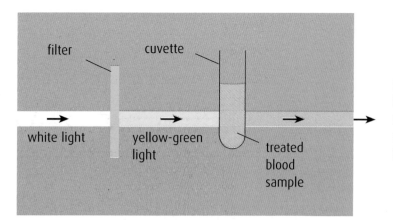

filter   cuvette

white light   yellow-green light   treated blood sample

In the colorimeter the light intensity is measured relative to the blank, giving a value for light absorbance by the sample.

The path of light through filter and cuvette in a colorimeter.

How haemoglobin transports oxygen

Almost all the cells in the body require constant supplies of oxygen. The blood picks up oxygen as it passes through the lungs, and then gives it up again when it reaches respiring cells.

It is the haemoglobin, inside the red cells, which carries out this role. Haemoglobin molecules have the ability to pick up oxygen where there is a lot of it and then, equally importantly, to release it where oxygen levels are low.

As the blood flows through capillaries in the lungs, the red cells are brought close to the air inside the air sacs. Oxygen from this air diffuses through the wall of each air sac and into the red blood cells (Fig 2.8). Here, it combines with the haem groups in the haemoglobin molecules.

Haemoglobin in which this has happened is called **oxyhaemoglobin**. It is bright red. If you cut yourself, the haemoglobin in your escaping red cells combines with oxygen in the air, which is why this blood is always red.

As the blood travels around the body, it passes through capillaries in tissues where respiration is happening. As the cells in these tissues are respiring, they are using up oxygen, which makes the concentration of oxygen in these areas quite low. In these circumstances, oxygen leaves the haemoglobin molecules and diffuses into the tissues.

Haemoglobin which does not have oxygen combined with it is called **deoxyhaemoglobin**. It is a much more bluish colour than oxyhaemoglobin. You may be able to see this colour if you have veins close to the surface of the skin somewhere – perhaps on the inside of your wrist.

So, we can see that the structure of a haemoglobin molecule, with its four haem groups which can take up and then release oxygen, makes it ideal as an oxygen-transporting molecule. Another feature of haemoglobin which helps it to carry out this role is that it is **soluble** in water. The curled-up, globular shape has **hydrophilic** (water-liking) R groups sticking out all around it. These are attracted to water molecules in the cytoplasm, so the haemoglobin molecules mix in with the water very easily.

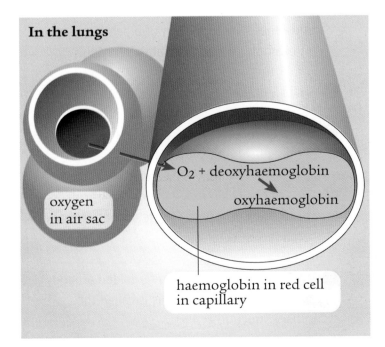

In the lungs

oxygen in air sac

O_2 + deoxyhaemoglobin
oxyhaemoglobin

haemoglobin in red cell in capillary

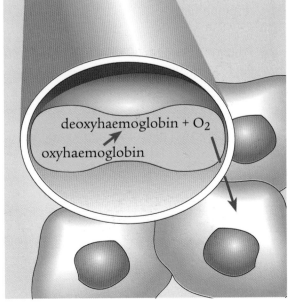

In the tissues

deoxyhaemoglobin + O_2
oxyhaemoglobin

Fig 2.8 Uptake and release of oxygen by haemoglobin.

2.3 Zack was asked to explain how the structure of haemoglobin helped it to carry out its function. He wrote:
'Haemoglobin is shaped like a biconcave disc. This gives it a large surface-area-to-volume ratio, so it can take up and release oxygen very quickly.

a Zack was obviously confused. What has he confused haemoglobin with?

b Write a correct answer to the question which Zack answered.

2.4 An investigation was carried out to see if blood doping could improve athletes' performances. Several volunteers had their haemoglobin concentration measured, and also the time for which they could run on a treadmill. They then had 2 dm³ of their blood removed and kept frozen. After two months, the red cells from this blood were thawed and infused back into the athletes. The same tests were then carried out on the athletes again. Means for each set of results were calculated. The results are shown in the table.

	Before infusion	After infusion	Difference	Percentage difference
haemoglobin concentration / g 100 cm^{-3}	13.8	17.6	3.8	+27.5
treadmill run time /seconds	793.0	918.0	125.0	

a Calculate the percentage difference in treadmill run time.

b Explain the results for the haemoglobin concentration.

c Explain the results for treadmill run time.

d Suggest why it is very difficult to detect this type of blood doping.

Summary

1 Red blood cells are filled with a protein called haemoglobin. This is a respiratory pigment which carries oxygen between the lungs and respiring tissues.

2 Proteins are made up of about 20 different kinds of smaller molecules, called amino acids.

3 The basic structure of an amino acid is:

$$H_2N — \underset{\underset{H}{|}}{\overset{\overset{R}{|}}{C}} — COOH$$

4 Amino acids differ in their R groups.

5 Amino acids can be linked together by forming peptide bonds. This takes place on the ribosomes. The formation of a peptide bond is an example of a condensation reaction.

6 A chain of amino acids is called a polypeptide.

7 The sequence of amino acids in a polypeptide is called its primary structure.

8 Parts of the chain may take on a particular shape, such as a helix. These shapes are called secondary structures.

9 The coiled chain may then be folded around into a particular shape. This is called the tertiary structure.

continued ...

Summary continued

10 More than one polypeptide may fit together to form a protein molecule. This is called the quaternary structure.

11 There are four polypeptides in a haemoglobin molecule. Two are identical and are called α-chains, while the other two are called β-chains. Each chain has a haem group in its centre, containing an iron ion.

12 Haemoglobin is a globular protein – in other words, the molecule is roughly ball-shaped.

13 The shape of the haemoglobin molecule ensures that the hydrophobic (water-liking) R groups are on the outside of the ball. This enables the protein to dissolve in the watery cytoplasm in the red cell.

14 The haem groups in haemoglobin pick up oxygen where it has a relatively high concentration, and release it where there is little oxygen.

The red blood cell surface membrane

All living cells are surrounded by a cell surface membrane. This membrane controls the substances which pass in and out of the cell.

Fig 2.9 The cell surface membrane of the red blood cell keeps haemoglobin inside but allows other substances, such as oxgygen, to pass through it.

Red cell ghosts

Red blood cells are among the very simplest of all cells. They have no nucleus, no mitochondria and no membrane-bound organelles. They are really just bags of haemoglobin.

The red blood cell membrane has been studied intensively. It is relatively easy to make red blood cells burst, by placing them in a very dilute solution. They take up water and burst, leaving empty 'shells' of just their membrane. These are called red cell 'ghosts'.

As there are no other membranes in the cell, you can be sure that the membranes you are studying are indeed cell surface membranes.

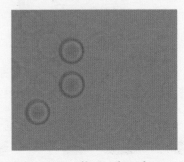

The three distinct cells in the photograph above are intact red cells, but around them you can just make out red cell ghosts.

JUST FOR INTEREST

The structure of the red cell surface membrane

Fig 2.10 shows the structure of the cell surface membrane of a red blood cell. A very similar structure is found in most other cells.

Phospholipids

The membrane is formed from a double layer of molecules called **phospholipids**. These molecules have a head which contains a phosphate group, and two tails made up of **fatty acids**.

The phosphate groups are attracted to water. They are said to be **hydrophilic**. The fatty acid tails are repelled by water. They are said to be **hydrophobic**. In watery environments, such as those found inside and outside a red blood cell, the phospholipid molecules arrange themselves so that their hydrophilic heads are in the water, while the hydrophobic tails are kept away from the water. This arrangement produces a double layer of phospholipid molecules, called a **bilayer**.

Cholesterol molecules are also found as part of this bilayer. Cholesterol is lipid-soluble; it can combine with fatty acids to form lipids.

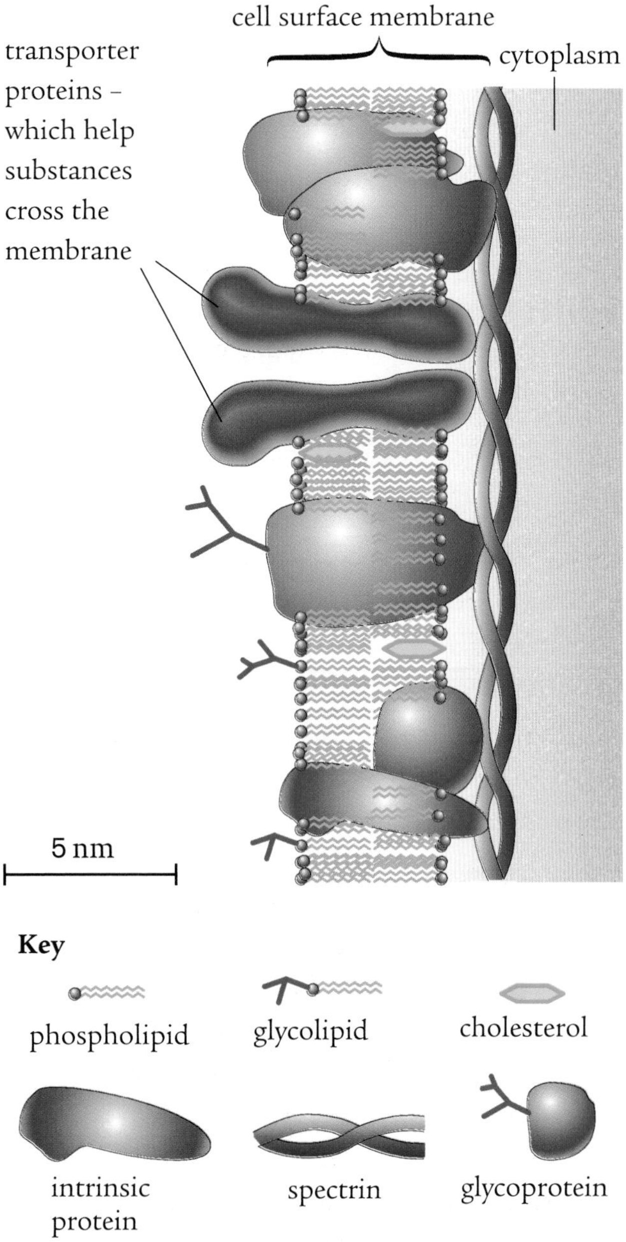
cell surface membrane
transporter proteins – which help substances cross the membrane
cytoplasm
5 nm
Key
phospholipid
glycolipid
cholesterol
intrinsic protein
spectrin
glycoprotein

Fig 2.10 Structure of a cell surface membrane.

JUST FOR INTEREST

Rattlesnakes and ice cream

The venom of rattlesnakes and cobras contains an enzyme called phospholipase. This enzyme attacks the tails of the phospholipids in cell surface membranes. The product of this reaction is a substance called lysolecithin.

Lecithins behave like detergents – they help fatty substances to form tiny droplets that mix easily into water. Substances which do this are called emulsifiers. You may have noticed lecithin listed as an ingredient on food labels. For example, it is often used in ice cream and mayonnaise.

However, having lysolecithin injected into your blood by a rattlesnake is not quite such a pleasant experience as eating ice cream. You will remember that cell surface membranes contain phospholipids. Lysolecithin dissolves the cell surface membranes of red blood cells. The cells rupture, causing intense pain and sometimes death, unless an anti-venom is administered.

Proteins, glycoproteins and glycolipids

Many **protein molecules** are found associated with the bilayer. Many of them lie in the membrane, often protruding on both sides. These are known as **intrinsic proteins**. Some of these proteins form channels though which ions such as sodium or chloride can pass into or out of the cell. Many of the intrinsic proteins have short chains of **carbohydrate** attached to them, normally on the outer surface of the membrane. They are called **glycoproteins**. Lipid molecules may also have these chains and are called **glycolipids**. These molecules act as receptors. In red cells, some of these glycolipids form the A, B or Rhesus antigens which determine the blood group.

There are also proteins which lie on the surface of the membrane. They are called **extrinsic proteins**. In a red blood cell, all the extrinsic proteins are on the *inner* surface of the membrane, next to the cytoplasm. Other cells may have extrinsic proteins on the outer surface as well.

In red blood cells the extrinsic proteins are linked up to one another by a protein called **spectrin**. This forms a strong framework, known as the **membrane skeleton**, which helps to hold the red blood cells in their distinctive biconcave shape.

The structure of cell membranes is often described as being a **fluid mosaic**. The membrane is 'fluid' because the molecules from which it is made can float around. However, they usually can't change layers – they can only move within their own layer. The membrane is a 'mosaic' because, if viewed from above, this is how it might look (Fig 2.11).

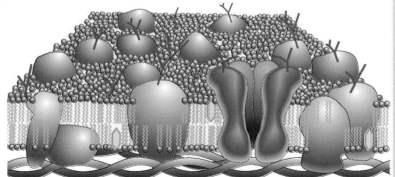

Fig 2.11 Fluid mosaic structure of the membrane.

Cell membrane abnormalities

Red blood cells have a hard life. They are constantly being pushed around the body, being squeezed through tiny capillaries which are only just big enough for them to get through. Their membrane skeleton helps them to survive this harsh treatment. Nevertheless, even well-formed red blood cells only live for around 120 days – but that's still about 10 million heartbeats.

The precise shape and form of the proteins in the cell surface membrane, just like all other proteins, is coded for by DNA. There are people in whom this coding is incorrect, so that the red cells are not able to function correctly. This often results in a **haemolytic anaemia** – a condition in which the red cells easily break open (lyse).

For example, the proteins which hold the inner skeleton to the cell surface membrane may be abnormal. This causes the cells to become spherical, rather than biconcave, as there is not a proper skeleton to hold them in shape. These cells are very fragile and easily break apart. People with this hereditary illness may need regular blood transfusions.

There are also some rare illnesses involving the intrinsic proteins which form the channels allowing ions to pass through the cell surface membrane. One such disease affects the channels for sodium ions. These may open when they should not, allowing sodium ions to rush into the cell. This causes water to follow, and can result in the cell bursting.

Passive movement through the membrane

Cell membranes help to prevent important substances inside the cell from being lost. They also prevent unwanted substances from getting in. However, there are numerous substances which *can* pass in and out of a cell through its cell surface membrane. For example, a red blood cell should allow oxygen and carbon dioxide to pass in and out easily, while keeping the haemoglobin inside the cell.

Many substances are simply allowed to pass through passively (Fig 2.12). This means that the cell does not use any energy to make them move. This passive movement happens because molecules or ions are always moving around randomly, hitting into each other and bouncing off in different directions.

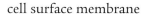

cell surface membrane

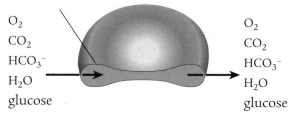

O_2	O_2
CO_2	CO_2
HCO_3^-	HCO_3^-
H_2O	H_2O
glucose	glucose

Fig 2.12 Some substances which diffuse passively into and out of a red blood cell.

Diffusion

Oxygen diffuses easily through the red cell membrane. As a red cell passes through the capillaries in the lungs, the oxygen concentration outside the cell is higher than inside. There is a **concentration gradient** across the cell membrane. This means there are more oxygen molecules outside than inside. As the oxygen molecules move randomly around, some will bump into the cell membrane and go through it. As there are more outside than inside, more will go in than go out. This is **diffusion**. In diffusion, particles of gas, solvent or solute move from an area of high concentration to an area of low concentration – that is, down a concentration gradient (Fig 2.13).

Molecules of gases and liquids bounce off each other.

A substance, represented by the brown molecules, will diffuse from an area where it is at a high concentration to an area where it is at a lower concentration. This is the path that one molecule might take.

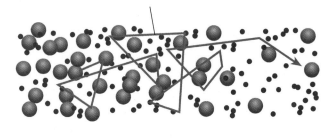

Direction of falling concentration of the brown substance – its concentration gradient.

Fig 2.13 Diffusion.

In a similar way, oxygen will diffuse out of the red cell when it is in conditions where the concentration of oxygen is higher inside than outside, such as when the cell passes through capillaries in a respiring muscle.

The kinds of substances which can easily diffuse through the membrane must be soluble in lipids, or have small molecules. Water, like oxygen, has small molecules and can diffuse freely through the phospholipid bilayer. The movement of water through cell membranes is so important that it is given a special name – **osmosis**. This is described in detail on pages 31–32.

SAQ

2.5 Make a simplified copy of Fig 2.8. Add the labels 'high concentration of oxygen' and 'low concentration of oxygen'. Also add arrows to show oxygen concentration gradients, labelled 'falling oxygen concentration'.

Facilitated diffusion

Oxygen and water have small molecules and can easily pass through the phospholipid bilayer. However, other molecules or ions may be too big, or too highly charged, to do this. The fatty acids in the centre of the membrane repel anything with a charge. For example, chloride ions, Cl^-, have an electrical charge and so cannot pass freely through the bilayer.

Cells therefore need special pathways through the cell membrane that will allow such substances to pass through. These pathways are provided by **transport proteins**. These proteins form a hydrophilic channel through the membrane. This allows substances such as chloride ions to pass through, moving down their concentration gradient (Fig 2.14). This process is called **facilitated diffusion**. It is just like ordinary diffusion, except that the molecules or ions only get through the membrane if they meet a channel.

For example, red cell membranes contain a transport protein which allows hydrogencarbonate ions (HCO_3^-) and chloride ions (Cl^-) to pass through easily. There are also channels through which glucose can diffuse.

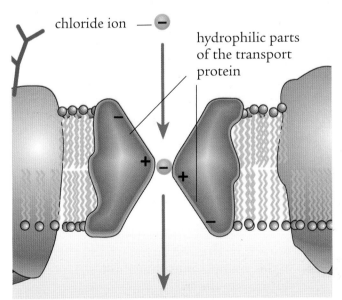

Fig 2.14 Facilitated diffusion of chloride ions.

Each channel formed by the proteins will allow only a specific molecule or ion to pass through. The proteins can change their shape, making the channel either open or closed and therefore controlling when substances can pass through.

SAQ

2.6 The rates at which glucose and water can diffuse through two types of membrane were compared. The table shows the results.

Type of membrane	Rate of diffusion of glucose molecules / arbitrary units	Rate of diffusion of water molecules / arbitrary units
containing only phospholipids and no protein	4×10^{-10}	5×10^{-3}
membrane of red cells	2×10^{-5}	5×10^{-3}

a Which value is larger, 4×10^{-10} or 2×10^{-5}?
b Explain the results for glucose.
c Explain the results for water.

Osmosis

Water, like oxygen, is able to pass easily through the phospholipid bilayer. It therefore diffuses through, down a concentration gradient. However, we don't usually talk about the 'concentration' of water. Instead, the term **water potential** is used (see Fig 2.15).

The water potential of a solution is a measure of how much water it contains in relation to other substances, and how much pressure is being applied to it. A solution containing a lot of water, and under pressure, is said to have a **high water potential**. A solution containing a lot of dissolved substances (solutes) and little water, and not under pressure, has a **low water potential**. You can think of water potential as being the tendency of water to leave that solution.

By definition, pure water at normal atmospheric pressure is given a water potential of 0. The more solute you dissolve in the water, the lower its water potential gets. Therefore, a solution of sugar has a water potential which is less than 0 – that is, it has a negative water potential.

Just as we don't normally talk about the 'concentration' of water, we don't normally use the term 'concentration gradient' for it, either. Instead, we talk about a **water potential gradient**. Water tends to move down a water potential gradient, from where there is a lot of water to where there is less of it. It diffuses out of a dilute solution (a lot of water – high water potential) and into a concentrated solution (a lot of solute – low water potential).

Why is this so important? The cells in your body are surrounded by watery fluids. Red blood cells, for example, float in blood plasma. Water can flow freely through the cell surface membrane, but most of the substances dissolved in it cannot. If there is a water potential gradient between the contents of a red cell and the blood plasma, then water will move either into or out of the cell. If a lot of water moves like this, the consequences can be dangerous.

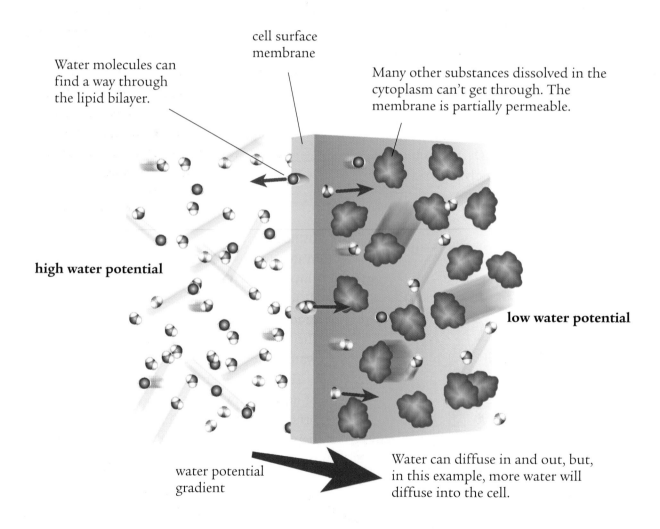

cell surface membrane

Water molecules can find a way through the lipid bilayer.

Many other substances dissolved in the cytoplasm can't get through. The membrane is partially permeable.

high water potential

low water potential

water potential gradient

Water can diffuse in and out, but, in this example, more water will diffuse into the cell.

Fig 2.15 The diffusion of water in osmosis. In this example, the cell is surrounded by pure water.

2.7a What would happen to a red blood cell if it was placed in pure water? Explain your answer.

 b Would the same thing happen to a plant cell? Explain your answer.

 c What would happen to a red blood cell if it was placed in a concentrated salt solution? Explain your answer.

Active transport across the membrane

So far, we have looked at three ways in which substances can move down a concentration gradient from one side of the cell surface membrane to the other. The cell doesn't have to do anything to make this happen, which is why these methods are all said to be **passive**.

However, there are many instances where a cell needs to take up, or get rid of, substances whose concentration gradient is 'the wrong way round'. This is usually the case with **sodium ions** and **potassium ions**. Most cells need to contain a higher concentration of potassium ions, and a lower concentration of sodium ions, than the concentration outside the cell. To achieve this, the cells constantly pump sodium ions out and potassium ions in, across the cell surface membrane, up their concentration gradient. This requires energy, so it is called **active transport**.

Active transport is carried out by **transporter proteins** in the cell surface membrane, working in close association with ATP. An ATP molecule is broken down to form ADP and phosphate (see page 149). This releases energy, which is used to cause a shape change in the transporter protein. The shape change moves three sodium ions out of the cell and two potassium ions in. This is going on all the time in most of your cells, and is called the **sodium-potassium pump** (Fig 2.16). It is estimated that more than a third of the ATP generated by respiration in a person's cells is used for the sodium-potassium pump.

Fig 2.16 The sodium-potassium pump. To see what is happening, start at step 1 for each ion in turn, and work your way round clockwise.

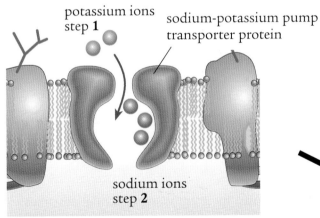

potassium ions
step **1**

sodium-potassium pump transporter protein

sodium ions
step **2**

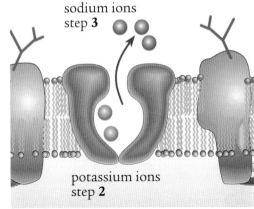

sodium ions
step **3**

potassium ions
step **2**

The breakdown of ATP provides energy for the proteins to change shape and allow the ions to move.

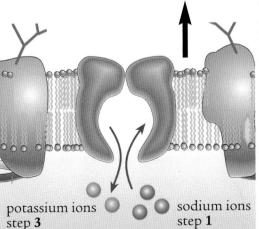

potassium ions
step **3**

sodium ions
step **1**

2.8 Some cells were placed in a solution containing two solutes, A and B. The concentration of both solutes was 2 μg dm⁻³. The cells did not contain any of either solute. The concentration of the solutes inside the cells was measured over a period of 2 hours. The results are shown in the graph.

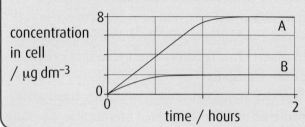

a Explain what is meant by the term 'solute'.

b What was the maximum concentration of A inside the cells? At what time was this maximum concentration reached?

c What was the maximum concentration of B inside the cells? At what time was this maximum concentration reached?

d How do these concentrations relate to the original concentrations of A and B outside the cells?

e Suggest how (i) A and (ii) B were entering the cells. Explain your answers.

Summary

1 All cells are surrounded by a cell surface membrane. This membrane is made of a double layer of phospholipid molecules, all arranged with their hydrophilic heads pointing outwards and their hydrophobic tails pointing inwards. Cholesterol molecules are dotted amongst them.

2 Protein molecules float amongst the phospholipids. Some, such as transporter proteins, lie within the membrane and are called intrinsic proteins. Some, such as the 'membrane skeleton' proteins in red blood cells, are loosely attached to one surface of the membrane, and are called extrinsic proteins.

3 Lipid molecules and protein molecules often have short chains of sugars (carbohydrates) attached to them. They are then known as glycolipids and glycoproteins.

4 One major function of the cell surface membrane is to control the passage of substances into and out of the cell. It is said to be partially permeable.

5 Small molecules, such as water and oxygen, are able to pass freely through the phospholipid bilayer. Larger molecules, or ions (which carry an electrical charge), cannot get through the phospholipid bilayer easily, and are allowed in and out by passing through transporter proteins.

6 Substances may pass across the membrane down their concentration gradient. This is passive transport. Diffusion, facilitated diffusion and osmosis involve passive transport.

7 In osmosis, the term water potential describes the tendency for water to move out of a solution. Dissolved solutes reduce water potential. Pressure on the solution increases water potential. Pure water under normal atmospheric pressure has a water potential of 0. Water moves passively down its water potential gradient.

8 The cell can use energy to force substances to move up their concentration gradient across the membrane. This is called active transport. It uses energy, supplied by ATP.

Body fluids

Jockeys who ride thoroughbred racehorses often have a huge struggle to keep their weights down. The less weight a racehorse carries, the better the chance of winning the race. In many races, a particular weight is specified for the horse to carry. Many professional jockeys must maintain a body weight which is well below their natural weight. For example, a person who is 1.68 m tall has an ideal body weight of 64 kg. A jockey of this height may need to keep his or her weight down to 51 kg. Similar problems often occur for boxers, who may need to rapidly shed some weight before a fight.

In a recent study of jockeys working in Australia, nearly half of those questioned said that they had problems keeping their weight down. Most said they skipped meals, and ate very little in the 24 hours before riding in a race. Such necessity to reduce food intake to well below normal levels over long periods of time often leads to eating disorders such as bulimia.

However, the most rapid way for a jockey to lose weight is to lose water from the body. About 60% of a person's total body mass is made up of water. Jockeys get rid of water by sweating for up to three hours in a sauna, usually in the morning of the race day. They may also take drugs called diuretics ('water pills') which make the kidneys expel more water in the urine. It is possible to lose up to 2 kg in a sauna and up to 3 kg by taking diuretics.

Such massive loss of water from the body can be highly dangerous. Dehydrated jockeys may feel 'muzzy-headed', tired and headachy. Concentration is affected, and coordination reduced. There is some concern that, over time, it may increase the risk of developing kidney disease.

What can be done? In present circumstances, jockeys will go on finding whatever way they can to lose weight, because if they don't they will not be given any rides and so can't earn a living. The use of diuretics by sportspeople has now been banned in the UK. But this doesn't do anything about the root of the problem. One suggestion is that the weights carried by horses should be increased, which would allow jockeys to maintain a more realistic body weight, but many people in the racing industry are against this.

Water in the body

We have seen in the case study on page 35 that around 60% of body mass is made up of water. So if a person's body mass is 75 kg, their body contains about 45 dm^3 of water. This water has a mass of 45 kg. Approximately two thirds of this is inside the cells. Of the remaining one third, about 5 kg of it is in the blood and the rest (10 kg) is in between the body cells. Why do we have so much water in our bodies?

Water is an amazing substance, which we take absolutely for granted. Yet, without it, there could be no life. Investigations and questions about whether there could be life on Mars revolve around whether there has ever been liquid water on the planet or not. If there is no sign of liquid water, then there can't be life. If liquid water is found on Mars – even if it lies deep below the surface – then we could hope to find some form of life there.

There are many reasons why we need such a lot of water in the body. Here are some of them.

Water is a solvent. This means that many things will dissolve in it. This is important for:
• transporting substances around the body. Blood plasma contains all kinds of substances dissolved in water which are being transported from one part of the body to another.
• allowing chemical reactions to take place inside cells. Many of the molecules inside cells are in solution in water. This enables them to react with each other. If the water content of a cell drops too low, then these reactions slow down or stop.

Water has a high specific heat capacity. This means that you have to put a large amount of heat into water to make its temperature change by very much. So being mostly water helps us to keep our body temperature almost constant. Even if the temperature around us is very low or very high, the water in our bodies does not quickly change its temperature.

Water has a high latent heat of evaporation. This means that a lot of heat is needed to make liquid water change to gaseous water (water vapour). We make use of this by sweating. Sweat is mostly water. When sweat lies on hot skin, some of the heat from the skin is used to change the liquid water into water vapour. So the evaporation of sweat takes heat from our bodies and cools us down.

Types of body fluid

The fluids present in large amounts in the body are called **body fluids**. There are three of them: blood plasma, tissue fluid and lymph. They are shown in Fig 2.17.

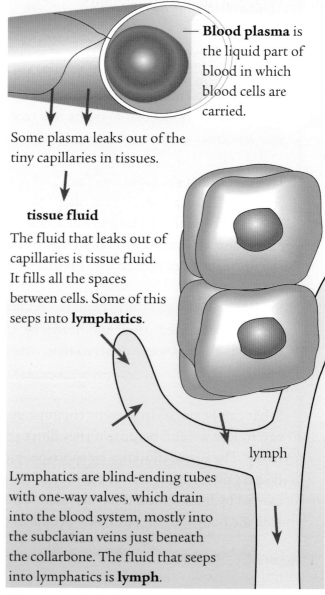

Blood plasma is the liquid part of blood in which blood cells are carried.

Some plasma leaks out of the tiny capillaries in tissues.

tissue fluid
The fluid that leaks out of capillaries is tissue fluid. It fills all the spaces between cells. Some of this seeps into **lymphatics**.

lymph

Lymphatics are blind-ending tubes with one-way valves, which drain into the blood system, mostly into the subclavian veins just beneath the collarbone. The fluid that seeps into lymphatics is **lymph**.

Fig 2.17 Body fluids.

Composition of body fluids

Blood plasma, tissue fluid and lymph are all very similar in composition. This is not surprising as they are all in continuous contact with each other. However, there are some differences between them.

Blood plasma carries a huge number of different substances in solution. Fig 2.18 lists the most important of these.

Tissue fluid is very like blood plasma. However, large protein molecules do not readily leak out of capillaries, so there is only about a third of the amount of protein as there is in blood plasma.

Lymph has a composition which is very similar to tissue fluid. It is therefore similar to blood plasma, but with generally only a third of the amount of protein as plasma. But the lymph which drains from some organs, such as the liver, will contain a little more protein.

Concentrations of solutes in the blood

If a red blood cell was placed in pure water or in a concentrated solution, the consequences would be disastrous. In pure water the cell would burst, whilst in a concentrated solution it would lose water and shrivel up.

To avoid a lot of water moving into or out of cells by osmosis, the water potentials of body fluids must be the same as the water potential of cytoplasm inside cells. This requires the concentrations of the main solutes in blood plasma being kept within a narrow range, especially those of sodium and potassium ions, glucose and protein.

For example, if you eat a meal containing a lot of sugar, the concentration of glucose in your blood plasma could increase. This would decrease the water potential of the blood plasma. There would be a water potential gradient between the cytoplasm of the red and white blood cells, and the plasma in which they float. Water would move down this gradient out of the cells and into the plasma.

In a healthy person such variations are small, but there are some diseases where the variations in water potential are so great that they cause problems. For example, in some people blood glucose levels can rise to dangerously high levels, as in diabetes mellitus.

To help diagnose this disease, blood glucose concentration has to be measured. And frequent measurement is also necessary in managing the disease (see page 38).

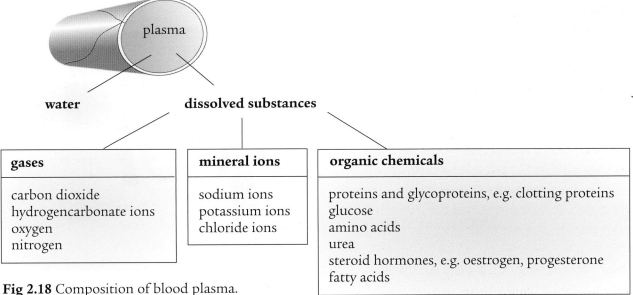

Fig 2.18 Composition of blood plasma.

gases	mineral ions	organic chemicals
carbon dioxide hydrogencarbonate ions oxygen nitrogen	sodium ions potassium ions chloride ions	proteins and glycoproteins, e.g. clotting proteins glucose amino acids urea steroid hormones, e.g. oestrogen, progesterone fatty acids

Measuring the concentration of glucose in the blood

This is an important diagnostic tool and an aid to self-management of the concentration of glucose in the blood, especially for people who suffer from diabetes mellitus.

Blood glucose can be measured at home or by a health professional, using a glucose test meter. But monitoring of blood glucose at home is particularly useful with diabetes mellitus, as this is where most food is eaten. Immediate dietary changes can then be made in the light of the results of the measurement.

Most blood glucose testing is now done using a **biosensor**. A test strip is used that has been impregnated with an immobilised version of the enzyme **glucose dehydrogenase**. When this strip is in contact with a blood sample the enzyme converts the glucose in the blood into gluconolactone. The reaction produces a small electric current, which is picked up by an electrode (the transducer) on the test strip. This current is read by a meter which produces a reading for blood glucose concentration in approximately 30 seconds.

1 Place the biosensor strip in the meter, leaving the area for the blood sample exposed. It is clear which end has the electrode on it and which has the area for the blood sample. Unused test strips must be immediately resealed in their container with an airtight stopper.

2 Place the lancet in the pen designed to obtain a blood sample.

3 Wash your hands and disinfect the skin with alcohol.

4 Place the pen on a soft area of skin at the tip of any finger and press the button. This causes the sterile lancet to prick the skin. The force of the pricking process can be adjusted.

5 If the sample of blood is drawn up into a syringe care should be taken to ensure that the blood is at room temperature for the testing step.

6 Place enough blood at the edge of the strip to allow it to be drawn up to completely cover the area for the sample.

7 After 25–30 seconds the blood glucose concentration will appear on the screen of the meter. This value will be stored in the memory of the meter to provide a continuing record of blood glucose concentration.

Normal blood glucose levels are described as being 3.89–5.83 mmol dm^{-3}. However, as with other measurements, there is some variation between people in terms of values that are normal to them.

pen containing the lancet that pricks the finger

meter which measures the current and records blood glucose concentration

test strip with attached glucose dehydrogenase at one end and electrode at the other

control solutions

Accu-Chek Advantage Blood Glucose System

2.9 This table shows the concentration of some ions in the tissue fluid which surrounds a group of cells, and in the cytoplasm of the cells.

Substance	Concentration / arbitrary units	
	Outside cells	Inside cells
sodium ions	142	10
potassium ions	4	140
chloride ions	103	4
hydrogencarbonate ions	28	10

a Use the data to suggest which substances are taken into the cells by active transport. Explain your answer.

b Use the data to suggest which substances are moved out of the cell by active transport. Explain your answer.

c The concentration of glucose in the tissue fluid was 900 mg dm^{-3}, whereas the concentration inside the cells was only 200 mg dm^{-3}. Remembering that all cells respire, explain this difference in concentration.

d The concentration of proteins inside the cells was 160 g dm^{-3}, whereas the concentration outside was 20 g dm^{-3}. Remembering where proteins are made, suggest a reason for this difference in concentration.

e Explain how the structure of the cell surface membranes of the cells prevents any of these substances moving in or out passively, by diffusion.

Geoff had been asked if he would run in the 1500 metre race at the school sports day, though he preferred to run cross-country races in winter. It was a hot and humid July day and he ran as best he could but only came fourth. After school he had promised to speak at a meeting in the local town, so he had to ride quite quickly on his bicycle to get there on time.

The meeting went well, but afterwards, when he and several of the group went to a cafe, he began to find his fingers curling inwards into the palms of his hands. He had a cake in one and was surprised to find that he had crushed it completely. He then began to feel a tightness on his chest and breathing became difficult. By then his friends had begun to worry. They noticed that he had gone very quiet and pale – not to mention what he was doing to the cake.

Geoff thought he had better explain that something strange was happening and that he felt fine, just very hungry, though the tight finger grip hurt. But now the muscles in his face had contracted, closing his lips and only strange noises came out! The friends called a taxi and he was taken home. There the muscle contractions began to wear off.

He was studying A level biology at school and was able to work out what had happened, but his mother made him visit the doctor next day. He gave an explanation to the doctor, who was much amused to be told both symptoms and medical reasons for them, but agreed with his diagnosis.

He would have benefited from a sports drink after the race. What do you think had happened?

Sports drinks

During exercise, or whenever there is a danger of a person's core (internal) temperature going much above 37 °C, we sweat. Evaporation of the water in sweat takes heat from the skin, and so cools the body down.

Sweat is formed from blood plasma, and its composition is therefore very like blood plasma. It contains many different inorganic ions, including sodium, potassium, calcium and chloride. It also contains urea and lactic acid.

A person doing strenuous exercise for a long period of time may lose large volumes of sweat from their body. If fluid is not replaced quickly, then the body may become so dehydrated that performance is impaired. Excessive sweating can also cause an imbalance between sodium and potassium in body fluids which affects the muscles. Muscles need the correct balance of ions to contract at the right time, which is why muscle cramps are a common feature of the recovery period after strenuous exercise.

Fluids are replaced by drinking. Drinking plain water is fine if only water needs to be replaced. But if inorganic ions (sometimes called **electrolytes**) have also been lost, then it is better if a liquid is drunk which also contains these.

Moreover, during exercise, the muscles will be using glucose as a fuel for respiration. If the exercise is very strenuous, a person can be using as much as 4 g of glucose per minute. The body does have some stores of carbohydrate (see page 43), but if hard exercise continues for more than a couple of hours, it may well have used up all of these stores. So an athlete may also want to replace glucose used up by the muscles, as well as water and electrolytes lost in sweating.

Isotonic drinks contain water, inorganic ions and glucose. The prefix 'iso-' means 'the same'. An isotonic drink has approximately the same water potential (that is, concentration) as blood plasma. The drink will help restore the water potential and correct ion balance of the blood and body fluids derived from them.

Summary

1. The body contains three types of body fluid – blood plasma, tissue fluid and lymph.

2. All body fluids are mostly water, with a variety of substances dissolved in them. About 60% of body mass is due to water. Blood plasma contains about 5 kg of water while tissue fluid contains about 10 kg.

3. Having so much water in the body helps it to maintain a constant temperature. This is because water has a high specific heat capacity. Water is an excellent solvent, important for transporting substances in solution, and also for allowing chemical reactions to take place. It has a high latent heat of vaporisation, which helps to cool the body when sweat evaporates from the skin.

4. Blood plasma carries many different substances in solution, including gases, mineral ions and various organic substances.

5. Blood plasma, tissue fluid and lymph are very similar, but tissue fluid and lymph contain a lot less protein than plasma.

6. Isotonic drinks can be used to replace fluids lost by sweating. They contain just the right concentration of electrolytes (inorganic ions) and glucose to ensure that they have the same water potential as body fluids. The glucose in them can help to replace glucose which has been used in respiration. The inorganic ions in them help restore the balance of ions in body fluids.

Carbohydrates

Glucose is an example of a **carbohydrate**. Carbohydrates include sugars – for example, glucose and sucrose – and also starch, glycogen and cellulose. They form an important part of the diet. Their main functions in the body are to:

- provide energy when they are respired inside cells;
- act as cell markers when used in the structure of cell surface membranes. Carbohydrate chains are attached to proteins to form the glycoprotein cell markers.

Glucose and other sugars

Sugars are carbohydrates with relatively small molecules. They are all soluble in water, and they taste sweet. Glucose is perhaps the most important carbohydrate in our bodies, because it is used by cells as a **respiratory substrate**. This means that it is gradually broken down, inside cells, to release energy.

Fig 2.19 shows the structure of a molecule of **glucose**. You can see that it contains carbon, hydrogen and oxygen atoms. This is true for all carbohydrates.

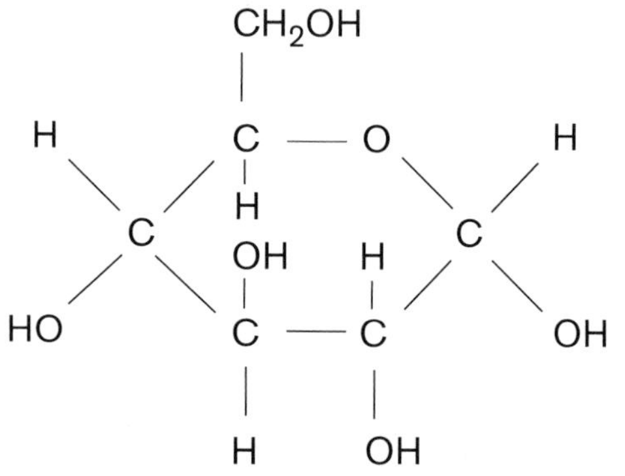

Fig 2.19 The structure of a glucose molecule.

Glucose is a **monosaccharide**. This means that its molecules are made up of one sugar unit. In the glucose molecule, there are six carbon atoms, twelve hydrogen atoms and six oxygen atoms. The molecular formula for glucose is therefore $C_6H_{12}O_6$.

42

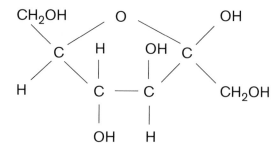

Food for thought

Glucose is the only fuel which brain cells are able to use. Even when you are not thinking hard, a great deal of activity is going on in your brain cells. Much of this energy is involved in the transmission of nervous impulses, both along axons and across synapses (the tiny gaps between one neurone and another). For an adult man it is estimated that the brain uses around 120 to 150 g of glucose per day. When you think that the whole body uses the amount of energy equivalent to 700 g of glucose per day, you can see that the energy demands of brain cells represent a high proportion of our total energy requirements.

Cardiac muscle cells, on the other hand, tend to use a different fuel – fatty acids. Muscle cells also tend to use fatty acids when resting, turning to glucose only when they are working hard.

Glucose is a hexose sugar, which means that it contains six carbon atoms. All hexose sugars have the formula $C_6H_{12}O_6$, but there are several different ways in which these atoms can be arranged. For example, a molecule of fructose has the structure shown in Fig 2.20.

Fig 2.20 The structure of a fructose molecule.

There are also monosaccharide sugars which contain different numbers of carbon atoms. In Chapter 8, you will meet a sugar called deoxyribose. This sugar has five carbon atoms, so it is a pentose sugar. Deoxyribose is part of DNA.

In Fig 2.19, the carbon atom on the right of the diagram has a hydrogen atom pointing upwards and an OH group pointing downwards. Glucose molecules with this structure are known as **alpha glucose (α glucose)**. If the H and OH groups are 'swapped over', then the molecule is known as **beta glucose (β glucose)**.

There are also several different sugars in which two sugar units are linked together. These sugars are called **disaccharides**. For example, the disaccharide **maltose** can be made when the carbon atom of one glucose is joined to another glucose molecule (Fig 2.21).

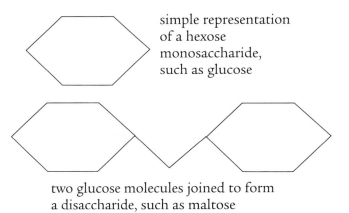

simple representation of a hexose monosaccharide, such as glucose

two glucose molecules joined to form a disaccharide, such as maltose

Fig 2.21 Monosaccharides and disaccharides.

Polysaccharides

'Poly' means 'many', so polysaccharides are carbohydrates made of many monosaccharide units linked together.

Fig 2.22 shows the structure of part of a molecule of **glycogen**.

Glycogen is a polysaccharide made from hundreds of glucose molecules. We store glycogen in liver cells and in muscle cells. A 70 kg male athlete may have about 90 g of glycogen in his liver and 400 g in his muscles. A 60 kg female athlete will have less than this, perhaps 70 g in the liver and 300 g in the muscles.

These glycogen stores are a short-term energy reserve that the body can draw on when muscle cells are working hard and respiring quickly. The glycogen molecules can easily be broken down to their consituent glucose molecules. These stores don't last long if a person is exercising hard. After they are used up, the body turns to using fat as an energy source instead.

Why do our liver and muscles store glycogen, and not glucose? One reason is that glucose, like all sugars, is soluble in water. If there was a lot of glucose inside a cell, it would decrease the cell's water potential. This could make it liable to gain water by osmosis, which could upset the workings of the cell. Glycogen, on the other hand, consists of large molecules which can't dissolve in water. Glycogen molecules form a compact energy store which won't affect the water potential of the cell. However, it is very easy to break them down into glucose when this is needed. This is done at the ends of the chains. Each glycogen molecule has a lot of ends.

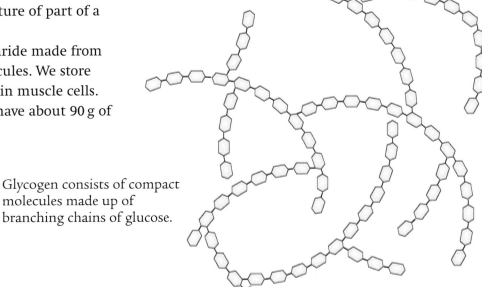

Glycogen consists of compact molecules made up of branching chains of glucose.

Fig 2.22 The structure of part of a glycogen molecule.

Glycosidic bonds

If we have too much glucose in the blood, the liver and muscles take some of it into their cells and turn it into glycogen for storage. This reaction involves the formation of **glycosidic bonds** between the individual glucose units (Fig 2.23). This reaction, like the one in which amino acids are linked together to form proteins, is a **condensation reaction** – that is, it involves the removal of water (see page 21).

How the carbon atoms are numbered in glucose

α form of glucose

How a glycosidic bond is formed

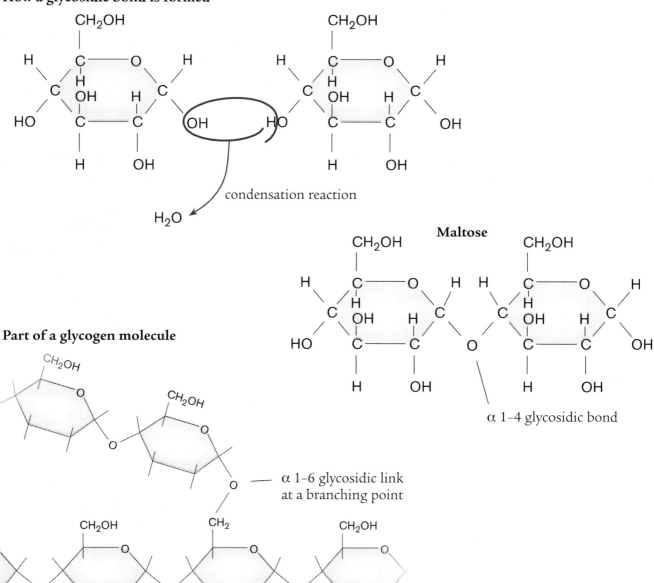

condensation reaction

H_2O

Maltose

α 1–4 glycosidic bond

Part of a glycogen molecule

α 1–6 glycosidic link at a branching point

Fig 2.23 Glycosidic bonds.

2.10   Copy and complete this table.

	Glucose	Glycogen
type of carbohydrate	monosaccharide	
where it is found in the body		
functions		

2.11a Where in a cell are amino acids linked together to make protein molecules?
   b In which organs of the body are glucose molecules linked together to make glycogen molecules?
   c How are these two reactions similar to one another?

2.12 Many athletes drink isotonic drinks during or after exercise. At the top of the next column is a recipe for a home-made isotonic drink.

200 cm³ of orange squash (undiluted)
800 cm³ of water
a pinch of salt

a Which of these ingredients contains glucose?
b Explain why taking in glucose can be beneficial to an athlete.
c Glucose is absorbed into the blood from the small intestine by active transport. Explain what is meant by 'active transport'.
d Which of the ingredients contains sodium ions?
e Explain why a person may need to take in sodium ions after they have been exercising.
f Explain why a person needs to take in water after exercising.
g When sodium ions and glucose have been taken into cells, this causes water to enter by osmosis. Explain why this happens.
h Use your answer to (g) to explain why drinking an isotonic sports drink can rehydrate you faster than drinking plain water.

Summary

❶ Carbohydrates are substances whose molecules contain carbon, hydrogen and oxygen. They include sugars such as glucose and polysaccharides such as glycogen.

❷ Glucose is a hexose sugar, so its molecular formula is $C_6H_{12}O_6$.
In the ring form, the molecule looks like this:

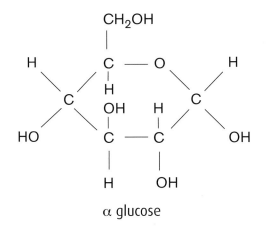

α glucose

❸ Glucose is the respiratory substrate for many parts of the body. It is also the form in which carbohydrate is transported in blood.

❹ Disaccharides have molecules in which two sugar units are joined together. Maltose is a disaccharide made up of two glucose molecules.

❺ For storage, many glucose molecules can be linked together by glycosidic bonds to form polysaccharides. In humans, the storage polysaccharide is glycogen, and it is stored in liver cells and muscle cells.

❻ Glycogen is an ideal storage substance because it has large, compact and insoluble molecules. It can easily be broken down to glucose again when required.

Blood clotting

The leech moved gently over Andrew's skin, humping its dark, moist, slippery body forward. It clearly knew exactly where it was going, and within seconds had arrived at the swollen mass that had once been Andrew's thumb. Gently, it bit into the blood-filled tissue with its three-jawed mouth and settled down to feed on Andrew's blood.

"OK", said Andrew's doctor. "That's the first one. We'll put around three on altogether, I think."

Amazingly, in the 1960s, the age-old practice of using leeches in medicine was resurrected. Leeches were used for at least 2000 years as a way of 'blood-letting' – removing blood from a person's body. Blood-letting was almost a universal remedy for whatever disease the unfortunate patient had, and it probably did at least as much harm as good in most cases. But by the late 1800s, the use of leeches had practically died out, being seen as old-fashioned as well as repulsive. It was not until the 1960s that surgeons began to think again about their possible benefits.

When leeches begin to feed, they first inject an anaesthetic, so the person being bitten feels nothing at all. They then sink their jaws into the flesh, and inject an anti-coagulant called hirudin to stop the blood clotting and to help it flow freely. A leech will normally feed for about 30 minutes, in which time it can increase its body weight by up to 10 times.

This is why leeches have begun to prove useful once more. When a surgeon tries to replace part of the body which has been lost – for example an accidentally-chopped off ear, or Andrew's severed thumb – he or she attempts to reconnect the ends of the major blood vessels. This is relatively easy to do with the arteries, because they have thick, strong walls. But the walls of the veins are thin and flimsy, and it is practically impossible to sew their cut ends back together again. So, while blood is still flowing into the repaired tissue as normal, it can't flow back out again. The tissue becomes engorged with blood, making it swell and decreasing the likelihood that it will heal again. The leeches act as substitute veins after tissue replacement surgery, helping to remove excess blood, preventing it from clotting and keeping it flowing smoothly as the body repairs itself.

How blood clots

Skin makes a very effective protective layer over our bodies. If the skin is broken, it becomes all too easy for harmful microorganisms (**pathogens**) to get into the tissues beneath. One form of defence against this is the formation of a blood clot, which seals the opening and stops pathogens getting in. It also helps to stop too much blood getting out.

While it is clearly important that blood clots (coagulates) when it meets a wound, it is equally important that it clots *only* in these circumstances. There is a very fine balance between blood which doesn't clot enough and blood which clots too easily. Blood that clots inside a blood vessel can be very dangerous indeed.

The formation of a blood clot

Fig 3.1 shows the pathway of events that leads to the formation of a blood clot. The signal for this to begin is usually that damage has been done to a blood vessel wall, or to other tissues around it.

There are many different substances which contribute to the formation of a blood clot. They come from three areas:

1 Damaged tissue This contains a mixture of proteins and other substances called **thromboplastin**, with which the blood comes into contact when the tissues are broken and damaged.

2 Platelets These are activated by the damaged tissue. They become sticky and release chemicals which promote clotting, for example **calcium ions**.

3 Blood plasma This contains fibrinogen, more calcium ions and also a protein called **prothrombin**.

The thromboplastin from the damaged tissues causes the prothrombin in the blood plasma to change into an **enzyme** called **thrombin**. This can only happen if calcium ions are present. Thrombin then catalyses a reaction in which fibrinogen is changed to **fibrin**. This also requires the presence of calcium ions.

What is needed to start blood clotting

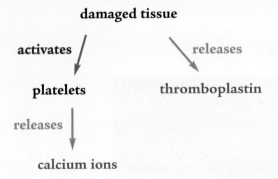

blood plasma
contains

fibrinogen   calcium ions   prothrombin

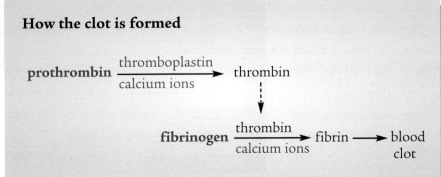

Fig 3.1 Blood clotting.

Fibrinogen is a large, soluble, globular protein. Thrombin breaks four small polypeptides (peptides) from each fibrinogen molecule. The remaining fragment is called a **fibrin monomer**. Many of the fibrin monomers link to form long, insoluble molecules of fibrin.

Fibrin is an example of a **fibrous** protein, which means that its molecules are long and insoluble. The molecules do not curl up into a ball as globular proteins do. The fibrin molecules form threads which get tangled up with one another, and with red blood cells. The fibrin, the sticky platelets and the blood cells form a tangled mass in the damaged tissues, called a **blood clot** (Fig 3.2).

Just a few minutes after the clot has formed, it starts to shrink. The fluid within the clot is squeezed out onto the surface of the skin, so the clot itself becomes drier. This fluid, which is blood plasma without the clotting proteins, is called **serum**. As some of the fibrin molecules are attached to the edges of the wound, these edges are pulled closer together as the clot retracts. The dried, shrunken clot is called a **scab**.

Beneath the scab, cells at the edges of the wound begin to divide over and over again, producing new cells which gradually form new tissue. The wound slowly heals. Eventually, once the wound is completely healed underneath it, the scab falls away.

A closer look at thrombin – an example of an enzyme

Thrombin is an enzyme. Enzymes are protein molecules which catalyse metabolic reactions – that is, chemical reactions taking place in a living organism. So enzymes are a type of **catalyst**.

By definition, a catalyst changes the rate of a chemical reaction, but is not used up during the reaction. So we can define an enzyme as follows.

> An **enzyme** is a protein which alters the rate of a metabolic reaction, but is not used up during the reaction.

Every different metabolic reaction taking place inside a person has a particular enzyme which catalyses it. We have seen that the reaction catalysed by thrombin is:

$$\text{fibrinogen} \xrightarrow{\text{thrombin}} \text{fibrin}$$

Fibrinogen is said to be the **substrate** of this reaction, and fibrin is the **product**.

damaged tissues, releasing thromboplastin proteins

platelets, attached to surfaces

fibrin – the fibrous protein trapping blood cells

Fig 3.2 A scanning electron-micrograph of a blood clot just starting to form. The photograph has been enhanced and coloured to show the different components clearly.

Fig 3.3 shows the shape of an enzyme molecule. Enzymes are always globular proteins. The long chains of amino acids from which they are made curl up into a very precise shape. This shape includes a place where there is a kind of 'dent' on the surface. This is called the **active site** of the enzyme, because it is here that the reaction takes place.

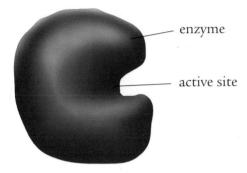

Fig 3.3 Active site of an enzyme.

The active site of an enzyme is exactly the right shape for its substrate to fit into. So, the active site of a thrombin molecule is a perfect fit for a fibrinogen molecule making an enzyme–substrate complex (Fig 3.4). Not only this, but the R groups of thrombin's amino acids at the active site are placed in exactly the right positions to form temporary bonds with the fibrinogen molecule.

Imagine some blood plasma containing thrombin molecules and fibrinogen molecules.

These are both soluble in the watery plasma. All the molecules are doing what molecules in solution always do – moving around randomly and bumping into each other. Each time a fibrinogen molecule bumps into the active site of a thrombin molecule, bonds are immediately formed between the two molecules. As these bonds form, the fibrinogen molecule is pulled out of shape – so much so that it actually breaks apart into several pieces (Fig 3.5). One of these is the fibrin monomer which will then react with other fibrin monomers to form the long fibrin threads necessary for the formation of a blood clot.

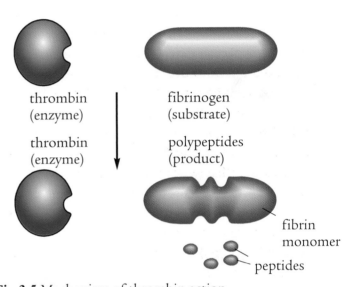

Fig 3.5 Mechanism of thrombin action.

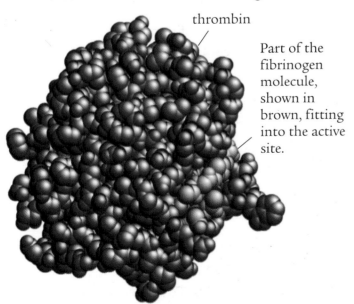

Fig 3.4 The enzyme–substrate complex formed by thrombin and fibrinogen.

thrombin

Part of the fibrinogen molecule, shown in brown, fitting into the active site.

SAQ

3.1 Most enzymes are only able to affect one kind of substrate. For example, the enzyme thrombin catalyses the conversion of fibrinogen to fibrin but it will not catalyse the breakdown of starch to maltose. Using what you know about the structure of an enzyme molecule and how enzymes work, explain why enzymes are so specific to a particular substrate.

Activation energy

If no thrombin is present, the fibrinogen molecules in the blood plasma will just stay as fibrinogen molecules. They will not undergo the chemical reaction in which they change to fibrin. How is it that thrombin can make this happen?

To answer this, we need to think about **energy changes**. Fibrin molecules possess less energy (called chemical potential energy) than fibrinogen molecules. However, to get fibrinogen to change into fibrin, the fibrinogen molecules have to be given some extra energy. This is called **activation energy** (Fig 3.6).

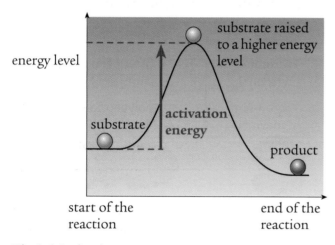

Fig 3.6 Activation energy.

One way of giving substances extra energy is to heat them up. You have probably done this on many occasions in a laboratory. For example, you can put some glucose and Benedict's reagent into a test tube at room temperature, and they will sit there for ever doing nothing at all. However, if you heat them up, then a reaction occurs. By heating them, you have provided activation energy to make the reaction happen.

Heating things up isn't a good way of making metabolic reactions happen inside a living organism, for obvious reasons. Enzymes solve this problem by reducing the **activation energy** needed for a particular reaction to take place (Fig 3.7).

The substrate can be changed into product much more easily, and at normal body temperature. Thrombin reduces the activation energy required for fibrinogen to be changed into fibrin.

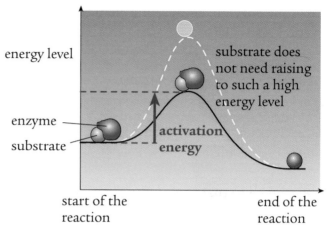

Fig 3.7 Reduction of activation energy by an enzyme.

Enzyme and substrate concentrations

If you look back at Fig 3.5, you can see that, after the fibrin fragments have left the active site of the thrombin molecule, the thrombin is completely unchanged. It is ready to deal with the next fibrinogen molecule which happens to bump into it. The rate at which all this can happen is so fast that it is practically impossible to comprehend. In just one second thousands of substrate molecules can slot into the active site, change into product and then leave the active site.

In a solution containing enzyme molecules and a set number of substrate molecules, it is easy to see that the more enzyme molecules there are, the more substrate molecules can be processed per minute. In other words, the greater the concentration of enzyme, the faster the rate of reaction. This is true unless there are so many enzyme molecules that some of them are 'waiting' for a substrate molecule to slot into their active sites. If this is the case, then the reaction won't go any faster no matter how many extra enzyme molecules are added (Fig 3.8).

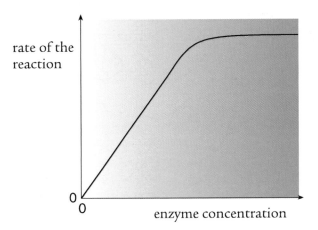

Fig 3.8 How enzyme concentration affects the rate of reaction.

Now imagine that the solution contains a set number of enzyme molecules and we alter the number of substrate molecules. With a low concentration of substrate, many of the enzyme molecules will be working nowhere near as fast as they could – they spend a lot of time 'waiting' for one of the few substrate molecules to bump into their active site. If we increase the substrate concentration, then the enzymes won't wait so long. More substrate molecules will bump into an active site each minute, and so the reaction will take place faster. Increasing the substrate concentration increases the rate of reaction – until there are so many substrate molecules that every enzyme is working flat out. Adding even more substrate molecules won't affect the rate of reaction, and the curve flattens out (Fig 3.9).

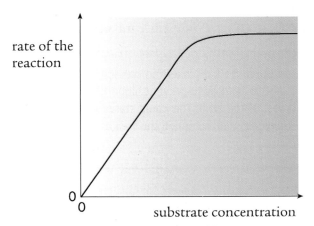

Fig 3.9 How substrate concentration affects the rate of reaction.

Blood clotting deficiency

The effects of enzyme and substrate concentration on the rate of reaction are illustrated by some illnesses in which blood does not clot when it should.

For example, some people do not have enough prothrombin in their blood, and so not enough thrombin is formed. This greatly reduces the rate of the reaction in which fibrinogen is changed to fibrin.

The usual cause of a deficiency of prothrombin in the blood is liver disease. Prothrombin, like most blood proteins, is made by the liver. A diseased liver does not make enough prothrombin, so only a low concentration of thrombin will be produced when a blood vessel is damaged. The concentration of fibrinogen will also be much lower than normal, because this too is formed by the liver. So liver disease often results in a person's blood taking much longer to clot than usual, because both enzyme and substrate concentration are lower than they should be.

SAQ

3.2 Copy and complete these sentences, using the following words. You may use each word once, more than once or not at all. Try doing it without looking anything up.

fibrin, platelets, plasma, carbohydrate, fibrinogen, active, insoluble, clot, tissue, destroyed, substrate, globular, calcium, catalyst, thrombin, fibrous, unchanged, specific, product

Enzymes are .... proteins which act as .... They speed up the rate of conversion of .... to .... The enzyme is .... at the end of the reaction. An enzyme molecule has an .... site into which the .... fits. Each enzyme is .... for a particular substrate. One example of an enzyme is .... It speeds up the reaction in which .... is converted to ....

Preventing blood loss

When a blood vessel is damaged, a chain of chemical reactions is brought into play which results in the formation of a blood clot. But if the wound is large, or if an artery is cut, then it is not possible for a blood clot to stem the blood loss. In such cases, medical help is needed to stop excessive loss of blood.

Here are the rules about what you should do if you find yourself in the position of caring for a person who is bleeding profusely.

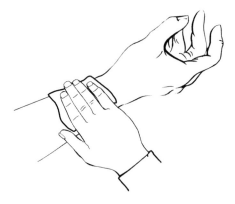

1 Stay calm. Assess the situation carefully, and then act.

2 If possible, obtain help from a doctor or a qualified first-aider.

3 If you can, put on sterile gloves. This protects you from potential infection from the patient's blood, and also helps to stop a wound being infected from bacteria on your skin.

4 Remove or cut clothing to expose the wound.

5 Check the site of the wound. Is there an object (e.g. glass) in it? This affects how you deal with the wound.

6 If there is no object in the wound, place a clean piece of cloth over it and press down firmly with the fingers or the palm of the hand. This will reduce the rate of blood loss.

7 If there is an object in the wound, press at the sides of the wound, pushing its edges together.

8 If the wound is in a limb, and if possible without risking further harm to the patient, raise the limb to a higher level. Expect the patient to be feeling sick or faint as this is a natural reaction to shock. So you should ensure that he or she can sit or lie down.

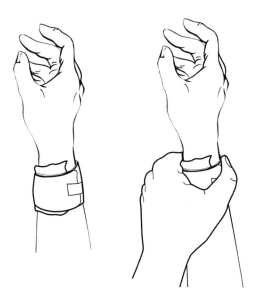

9 Use a bandage to keep the dressing on the wound. Do keep exerting pressure on it, but not so hard as to prevent blood flow to the rest of the limb. This could starve tissues of oxygen, which can kill the tissues.

Summary

1. Blood normally clots when a blood vessel is damaged, which helps to prevent pathogens entering the body, and also prevents too much loss of blood.

2. When tissue is damaged, thromboplastin from the tissue causes prothrombin in the blood plasma to change into thrombin. This reaction requires the presence of calcium ions.

3. Thrombin is an enzyme which catalyses a reaction in which fibrinogen is changed into fibrin. This reaction also requires the presence of calcium ions.

4. Platelets help in blood clotting. When they meet damaged tissue they release calcium ions and become sticky.

5. Prothrombin, thrombin and fibrinogen are all globular, soluble proteins. Fibrin is an insoluble, fibrous protein. It forms a network of fibres across the wound.

6. Within minutes of its formation, the blood clot retracts, losing liquid and shrinking to form a scab. This helps to draw the edges of the wound together.

7. An enzyme, for example thrombin, is a protein which acts as a catalyst.

8. Enzymes are globular proteins which have an active site where substrate molecules can temporarily bind.

9. Enzymes help reactions to happen by lowering activation energy.

10. Enzymes are specific – that is, each enzyme can only bind with one substrate (or at least very few different substrates).

11. The greater the concentration of substrate, the greater the rate of reaction. For a set concentration of enzyme, this is true until all enzyme molecules are working flat out, beyond which the rate will not change.

12. The greater the concentration of enzyme, the greater the rate of reaction. For a set concentration of substrate, this is true until some enzymes are 'waiting' for a substrate molecule, beyond which the rate will not change.

13. Thrombin and fibrinogen are made in the liver. Liver disease may result in too low a concentration of the enzyme thrombin in the blood, reducing the rate at which fibrinogen is changed to fibrin, so blood clotting takes longer than usual. Liver disease also reduces the concentration of the substrate fibrinogen, which has the same effect.

14. Blood loss from an open wound can be stemmed by applying pressure to the wound, after checking for the presence of objects in it.

Preventing blood clotting

We have seen that blood clotting is extremely important in preventing too much blood being lost, and in protecting the body from invasion by pathogens through the open wound. If blood doesn't clot, even the smallest wound can be dangerous. But the opposite is also true. If blood clots when it shouldn't, a person's health may be harmed. In some cases, it can be fatal.

Kate had a huge amount of work to do. As head of the maths department in her school, she had somehow got behind with producing the scheme of work for her department. With an inspection due to begin on Monday, she needed to work right through the weekend if she was to be able to feel confident of showing her department in a good light. Early on Saturday morning, she settled at her computer. And there she stayed, hour after hour, all through Saturday until late in the evening. She was back at the computer early on Sunday morning, working right through until the early hours of Monday.

She didn't feel too well on Monday morning, but thought it was just a case of having a run of late nights, and the stress she was under. Her legs felt stiff, and the right leg was a bit painful, but she put this down to sitting in the same position for so long – she had not been out of the house all weekend. But as she taught her first class of the day, she began to feel very ill indeed. There was suddenly a tremendous, crushing pain in her chest, and she could hardly breathe. She collapsed onto the floor. Her class quickly alerted a teacher in the next door classroom. An ambulance was called and Kate was taken to hospital.

There she was diagnosed as suffering from acute pulmonary embolism. 'Acute' means a short-term illness (as opposed to a 'chronic' one, which lasts for a long time). 'Pulmonary' means to do with the lungs, and an 'embolism' is a blood clot which is carried along in the blood. Kate had a blood clot in her lungs, stopping blood from flowing through them correctly (the orange area in the photograph).

Deep vein thrombosis

Although Kate's life-threatening embolism was in her lungs, the problem had actually started in her legs.

Blood is pumped at high pressure out of the heart into the aorta. This large vessel gradually divides into many other arteries, which eventually deliver blood into tiny capillaries which take the blood close to individual cells. The capillaries gradually join up to form veins. By the time blood reaches the veins, it has lost most of its pressure and is travelling slowly. To help the blood to make its way back to the heart, veins contain valves which only allow the blood to flow towards the heart, not away from it. Moreover, they are often positioned so that they are surrounded by muscles. This is true of the leg veins. As you walk, contracting and relaxing the leg muscles, they squeeze inwards on the veins, pushing the blood through the valves and back towards the heart.

If, however, you are stationary for long periods of time, this doesn't happen. With no leg movement, blood can stagnate in the leg veins. When blood is moving very slowly, clotting can quite often happen. This is because small quantities of many of the chemicals required for blood clotting are always being formed. If the blood is not moving, then the concentrations of these chemicals may build up to a high enough level to get the blood clotting process under way. Once it starts, the process builds up of its own accord.

In one of Kate's legs, the blood in one of the deep-lying veins had formed a clot. This is called a **thrombosis**. Kate had suffered from a dangerous incident of **deep vein thrombosis**, otherwise known as **DVT**.

The thrombosis in her leg had not caused much trouble – just some stiffness and soreness which she had not thought were important. However, as she moved around on Monday, the blood clot had shifted. It came loose inside the leg vein, and was carried along with the flowing blood. It entered her heart, and was pumped onwards to the lungs. Up until now, the blood vessels through which it passed were large ones, but in the lungs the clot got stuck in one of the smaller blood vessels providing blood to the air sacs of a part of the lung. Blood pressure in the lungs and heart rapidly built up, causing the intense pain and collapse.

Risk factors for deep vein thrombosis

It is not at all easy to predict who might suffer from DVT. However, several factors seem to greatly increase the risk. Allowing blood flow to become slow, having damaged tissues or being old all seem to increase the chance of DVT.

In the UK, there is about 1 case of DVT per every 2000 people per year. For those under 40, only about 1 in 3000 have an incident of DVT, whilst for those over 80 the risk is 1 in 500.

Between 90 – 95% of cases of DVT or pulmonary embolism are in people with at least one of the risk factors listed below.

Table 3.1 DVT risk factors.

DVT – risk factors	Lower the risk!
Keeping still for long periods e.g. on long plane flights	Move or walk around at intervals
Having an operation especially on the hips or knees	Keep moving limbs – even in bed
Being old	Keep active and fit
Being pregnant, recently giving birth, taking the contraceptive pill or being on hormone replacement therapy (HRT)	Be aware of the risk and keep active

The best thing to do is to make sure you don't sit still for long periods of time. If you are on a long flight, get up and walk around when you can. If you have to stay seated, bend and straighten your legs every now and then. Drink plenty of water (so that blood-clotting factors won't get too concentrated in your blood). Avoid alcohol (as this causes dehydration). Don't take sleeping pills, as being asleep will make you inert for a long period of time.

Wearing 'flight socks' can also help. These socks exert pressure on your legs, higher pressure near to the foot and lower pressure higher up. This pressure gradient helps to persuade blood to flow upwards, keeping it moving towards the heart.

Taking an aspirin tablet may help. Aspirin reduces the ability of blood to clot. However, aspirin should be avoided by people with stomach ulcers.

Treating DVT

DVT itself is not especially dangerous, although if left untreated it can cause long-lasting and painful damage in the leg veins. The real danger comes when the blood clot breaks off and blocks the vessels in the lungs.

Where a pulmonary embolism has been diagnosed, medical staff will usually give the patient a 'clot-busting' drug. This will probably be administered through a drip.

One of these drugs is the enzyme **streptokinase** – one of the many toxins produced by *Streptococcus pyogenes*. Once in the blood, streptokinase causes the production of a protein called **plasmin**. Plasmin attacks fibrin in blood clots, breaking it down and so making the clot disappear. However, streptokinase is not ideal, because it can cause damage to other tissues. Also, streptokinase is recognised by the body's immune system as a foreign antigen, so the immune system may react against it. Now there are newer drugs available, some of them produced by genetic engineering, which are much better at breaking down blood clots. But streptokinase is still widely used, because the new drugs are very expensive.

Antithrombin – an enzyme inhibitor

It is obviously important that blood should not clot at the wrong time or in the wrong place. To help to prevent this from happening, the blood contains a protein called **antithrombin**. This, like most blood proteins, is made in the liver.

Antithrombin combines with thrombin, partially covering its active site (Fig 3.10). This prevents thrombin combining with fibrinogen, so no fibrin can be formed. Antithrombin is therefore an **enzyme inhibitor**. It slows down, or even stops, the rate of action of the enzyme thrombin.

Antithrombin effectively mops up any thrombin left over once the blood clot has formed. It stays combined with it for the next 15 to 20 minutes. By this time, the clotting process will have run its course, and no further thrombin will be being made.

Like most enzyme inhibitors, antithrombin is a **reversible inhibitor**. It eventually leaves the enzyme, allowing it to start functioning again. However, there are some enzyme inhibitors which are irreversible. For example, some heavy metals, such as mercury, may bind permanently with enzyme molecules, preventing them from ever working normally again.

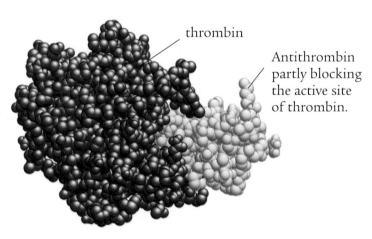

thrombin

Antithrombin partly blocking the active site of thrombin.

Fig 3.10 Antithrombin bound to thrombin.

Clot-busters

In 1994, the British media decided to home in on stories of 'deadly flesh-eating bugs'. There had been a small cluster of incidences of an illness whose correct name is necrotising fasciitis. But 'flesh-eating' had a much more headline-grabbing sound. The name has stuck.

Flesh-eating bug takes another life

Hospital investigates death

A DEADLY flesh-eating bug has taken the life of a young wom

In fact, this disease is nothing new. The bacterium which causes it, *Streptococcus pyogenes*, is very common. It is the usual cause of sore throats and tonsilitis. It can also cause the illness known as puerperal fever – an often fatal infection of women after childbirth which was quite common up until the 20th century. Infection began as the bacterium entered the body through the unprotected tissues of the uterus lining after the placenta had been expelled.

It still isn't really understood what makes *S. pyogenes* sometimes behave as a potentially lethal 'flesh-eater'. The infection always begins at the site of a wound, but this doesn't have to be large. Sometimes people pick up the infection while they are in hospital, especially if they are recovering from an operation. Many of us have the organism in our throats.

The first symptoms of necrotising fasciitis are redness, swelling, fever and pain, which can easily be confused with 'normal' slight infection of a wound. However, very quickly it becomes apparent that something much more dangerous is going on. The tissues around the wound begin to die – a process called necrosis. The infection and death of tissues spreads rapidly. The patient feels extremely ill and, despite intensive treatment in hospital, often dies.

The damage is all caused by poisonous substances, called toxins, produced by the bacteria. There are several different toxins produced, which between them cause a whole range of unpleasant symptoms.

One of these toxins makes blood clots break down. This may help the bacterium to spread through tissues by breaking through the tissues' attempts to protect themselves with a blood clot. This toxin is streptokinase. As is so often the case with this kind of toxin, ways have been found to make use of it in medicine. Streptokinase is now used to break down blood clots in cases of thrombosis or embolism.

Competitive and non-competitive inhibition

Fig 3.11 shows two different ways in which enzymes can be inhibited.

Some inhibitors have molecules with similar shapes to the enzyme's substrate. Like the substrate, they can slot into the enzyme's active site. Imagine all three kinds of molecules bumping around – enzyme, inhibitor and substrate. Both the inhibitor and the substrate may slot into the active site of the enzyme. The more substrate there is compared to inhibitor, the more likely it is that a substrate molecule will hit the enzyme. Inhibitors that behave like this are therefore called **competitive inhibitors**. They 'compete' with the real substrate for the enzyme's active site. The number of active sites occupied by the inhibitor, and therefore the degree of inhibition, depends on the relative concentrations of the inhibitor and the substrate.

Other inhibitors bind to the enzyme and stay there for some time, preventing the real substrate from binding at all. Some of these inhibitors (like antithrombin) may bind to the active site, or at least to part of it. Others may bind to a completely different part of the enzyme, which causes its shape to change so that the real substrate no longer fits into the active site. In either case, once the inhibitor has bound, that is it – the enzyme is switched off. It makes no difference how much substrate there is – there are no active sites to bind to. Inhibitors that behave like this are called **non-competitive inhibitors**.

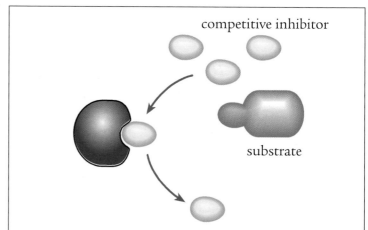

... this would be the effect of a competitive inhibitor

The more of the competitive inhibitor there is, the more likely that it will bind for a while to the active site and inhibit the breakdown of the normal substrate.

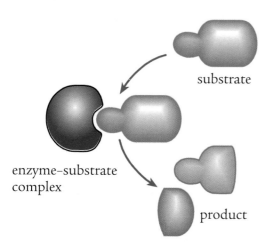

If this is the way the substrate is normally broken down to product ...

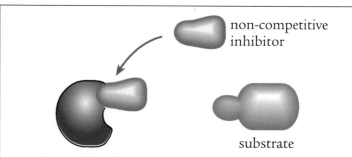

... and this the effect of a non-competitive inhibitor.

Once the non-competitive inhibitor binds, it stays there, so the enzyme does not work.

Fig 3.11 Competitive and non-competitive inhibition.

Preventing blood clotting

Once the immediate danger of a pulmonary embolism caused by DVT is over, thought must be given as to how to stop the same thing happening again.

People who are at a very high risk of a thrombosis developing can be given drugs which slow down the blood clotting process. Some of these drugs work as enzyme inhibitors – but in a rather more complicated way than the action of antithrombin on thrombin.

The first drug that a person is likely to be given is **heparin**. This is given by injection directly into a vein. Heparin works by binding to antithrombin. This causes the shape of antithrombin to change in such a way that it binds even more easily and effectively than usual to thrombin. This happens almost immediately, so heparin is good for very quickly slowing down the tendency for someone's blood to clot.

The patient may be prescribed **warfarin**. This can be taken by mouth – it doesn't need to be injected.

Warfarin actually works in the liver, not in the blood. Warfarin slows down, or stops, the formation of prothrombin in liver cells. If there is no prothrombin being made, then there won't be any thrombin formed in the blood, so fibrinogen won't be changed into fibrin.

The formation of prothrombin involves vitamin K. Vitamin K has to bind with some proteins in the liver cell in order for prothrombin to be made. Warfarin competes with vitamin K for these binding sites.

Warfarin takes longer to work than heparin – often around 7 days – but it has a much longer-term effect.

Yet another anti-clotting agent is the substance injected by leeches when they begin feeding. This is called **hirudin**. Hirudin is an inhibitor of thrombin, binding with part of its active site. Studies have been undertaken to see if hirudin could perhaps be used instead of heparin, to prevent inappropriate blood-clotting.

SAQ

3.3   The graph shows the monthly differences in the number of people admitted to hospital in France with DVT or pulmonary embolism.

a   Describe the pattern of variation shown in the graph.

b   Using your knowledge of how DVT and pulmonary embolism are caused, put forward a hypothesis which could explain this pattern.

c   Suggest how your hypothesis could be tested.

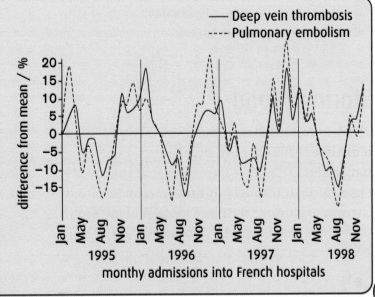

monthy admissions into French hospitals

Summary

1. Deep vein thrombosis is a blood clot which develops in a deep-lying vein, usually in a leg.

2. The risk of DVT is increased by lack of movement for extended periods of time. It is also more common in people who have just had surgery and in women who are pregnant, have just given birth or are on HRT. The risk also increases with age.

3. The risk of DVT is considerably lowered by maintaining movement, avoiding dehydration, taking aspirin or wearing 'flight socks'.

4. If a blood clot is carried to the lungs, acute pulmonary embolism may occur, which can be fatal if not treated quickly.

5. Clot-busting drugs, such as streptokinase, may be given to destroy the clot.

6. To lessen the risk of future problems caused by inappropriate blood clotting, patients may be treated with substances which directly or indirectly inhibit this process. Heparin is often given first, as this has immediate action. Warfarin has a longer-term effect.

7. A substance which slows or stops enzyme activity is known as an inhibitor.

8. Competitive inhibitors have a shape which resembles the enzyme's substrate. They compete with the substrate for the active site of the enzyme. The degree of inhibition depends on the relative concentration of inhibitor and substrate.

9. Non-competitive inhibitors bind either with the active site or with another part of the enzyme. Once bound, they normally remain in position. The degree of inhibition is not affected by the relative concentration of inhibitor and substrate.

10. Antithrombin is an example of a non-competitive inhibitor. It binds with thrombin and remains firmly bound for many minutes. This helps to ensure that the blood-clotting process does not escalate out of control.

Storing blood

Blood collected from donors is usually stored for some time before it is eventually used in blood transfusions. It is very important that the blood remains fresh throughout this time, and that no chemical changes take place in it. You have seen that when blood remains stationary it is likely to clot, and this must be avoided in stored blood. The type of blood products which are stored, and the conditions in which they are stored, are carefully chosen to ensure that no clotting or other change takes place.

The effect of temperature on enzyme activity

Clotting, as we have seen, involves a number of different chemical reactions, all controlled by enzymes. By choosing a suitable temperature at which to store blood for transfusion, these reactions can be avoided.

Fig 3.12 shows how temperature affects the rate of a metabolic reaction controlled by enzymes.

At low temperatures, the reaction is usually very slow, and indeed may not happen at all. This is because molecules only move around slowly at low temperatures – in other words, their kinetic energy is low. As temperature increases, so does their kinetic energy. They move around faster and collide with each other more often and with more energy. Substrate molecules will bump into an enzyme's active site more frequently, and they will do so with more energy. This increases the likelihood that the substrate will be changed into product. The rate of reaction therefore increases as temperature increases.

However, once the temperature reaches a certain level, the story is not quite so straightforward. Enzymes are globular proteins. Their function depends on their precise three-dimensional shape; if this alters, then the shape of the active site alters, and the substrate will no longer fit into it.

The three-dimensional shape of a protein – its tertiary structure – is held in shape by chemical bonds between the R groups of amino acids. Some of these bonds, called **hydrogen bonds**, are not very strong, and they tend to break at high temperatures. In most human proteins this starts to happen at around 40 °C. At just below this temperature, the reaction is taking place at its maximum rate, and this is known as the **optimum temperature** for the reaction. As temperature increases above the optimum, some of the enzyme molecules begin to lose shape, and are no longer so good at binding with the substrate. The enzyme molecules are said to be **denatured**. The rate of reaction is therefore slower at temperatures above the optimum. The higher the temperature above this value, the more enzyme molecules have been denatured, and the slower the reaction will be. At a temperature of 50–60 °C, all enzyme molecules are completely denatured, and the reaction does not take place at all.

If we want to store blood for a long period of time, then, it needs to be kept at a temperature where no enzyme activity takes place. It would obviously not be sensible to keep it at a very high temperature, as this would denature proteins in the blood which we want to function – haemoglobin, for example. Nor do we want to freeze it, as freezing would produce ice

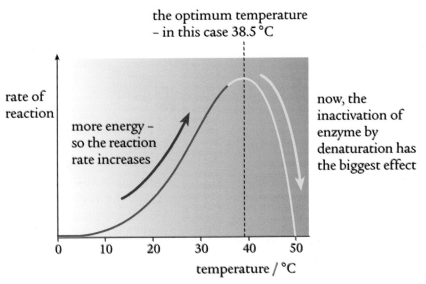

Fig 3.12 How the rate of an enzyme-catalysed reaction is affected by temperature.

crystals which would tear through cell membranes and destroy the cells. The ideal temperature has been found to be 4 °C.

Blood for transfusion is stored in a special refrigerator, known as a blood bank. The temperature is kept at a constant 4 °C, never falling or rising more than 2 °C from this value. If the temperature should drift outside this range, an alarm will immediately sound to alert staff. The alarm is battery powered, so even if the electricity supply fails it will still go off.

Bonds holding the 3-D shape of proteins

Protein molecules are formed from long chains of amino acids. The amino acids are linked to each other by peptide bonds. These bonds are very strong. However, the three-dimensional shape of a protein molecule is held in shape by other types of bonds. These are shown in Fig 3.13.

ionic bond

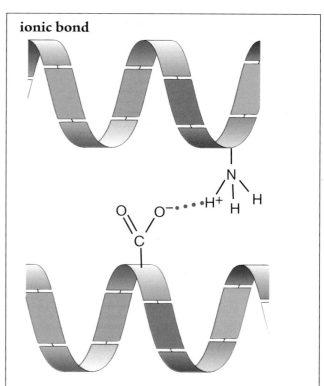

An ionic bond forms between an R group with a full negative charge and one with a full positive charge. This bond is much stronger than a hydrogen bond. It can be broken by changes in pH.

hydrogen bond

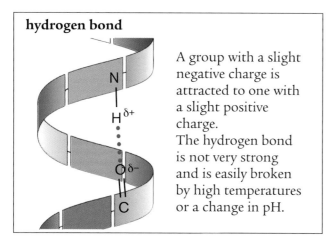

A group with a slight negative charge is attracted to one with a slight positive charge.
The hydrogen bond is not very strong and is easily broken by high temperatures or a change in pH.

hydrophobic bond

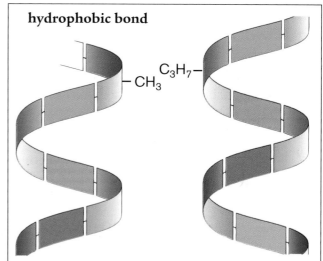

R groups which contain only carbon and hydrogen atoms will be hydrophobic. As water is nearly always present around a protein and in between its chains, hydrophobic R groups will tend to be found together. This slight attraction between them is the hydrophobic bond and is quite a weak bond.

disulphide bond

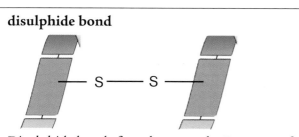

Disulphide bonds form between the R groups of the amino acid cysteine. They are very strong bonds, but can be broken by reducing agents. They are often important in holding together the different polypeptide chains in the quaternary structure.

Fig 3.13 Bonds holding protein molecules in shape.

The effect of pH on enzyme activity

We have seen that high temperatures can cause the shape of enzyme molecules to change. Another factor which can have this effect is a change in **pH**.

pH is a measure of how acidic or alkaline a solution is. A solution of pH 7 is neutral. A solution with a pH below 7 is acidic, and one with a pH above 7 is alkaline.

Most protein molecules, including most enzymes, have their most stable three-dimensional shape at a pH around neutral. If the pH falls, this may cause hydrogen bonds and ionic bonds between the R groups of its amino acids to break. There will be a similar effect if the pH rises. So, on either side of the optimum pH, the enzyme molecules will become increasingly denatured and less able to catalyse a reaction (Fig 3.14).

Moreover, pH changes can sometimes cause globular proteins to completely unravel. The molecules may become entangled with each other so that they are no longer able to dissolve in the watery plasma. They form insoluble lumps, or coagulate.

It is therefore important that the pH within stored blood does not change. A phosphate **buffer** is therefore added to the blood. A buffer is a substance which prevents the pH from changing.

Enzyme cofactors

Many enzymes can only convert substrate to product if another substance is present. This is called a **cofactor**.

For example, if you look back to page 47, you will see that two of the reactions which take place during blood clotting require the presence of **calcium ions** as a cofactor (Fig 3.1) These are normally present in blood plasma, and they are also released by platelets during the blood clotting process. If we can remove calcium ions from blood, this completely prevents it from clotting. One way of doing this is to add a substance which binds with calcium ions and keeps them 'locked up'.

There are also other ways in which blood can be prevented from clotting. Chemicals that prevent blood clotting are **anti-coagulants**. Two commonly-used anti-coagulants are **sodium citrate** and **heparin**.

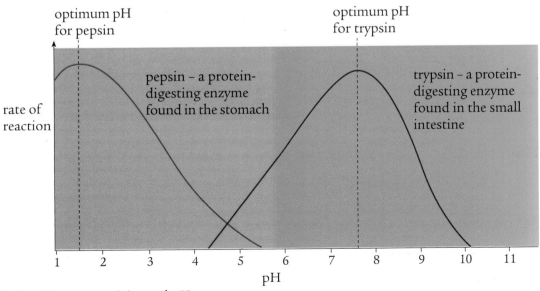

Fig 3.14 Enzyme activity and pH.

Types of stored blood product

Blood collected from a blood donor is not only needed for transfusion. There are a range of different forms in which it is stored (Fig 3.15).

Whole blood is blood containing all the usual components – plasma, red cells and white cells. This may be used to give to a patient who is losing a lot of blood, for example, during an operation. Whole blood is not used much now.

Packed red cells (red cell concentrate) are also used for transfusions. The red cells are separated out from the rest of the donated blood. When it is to be transfused, the concentrate is diluted with a solution containing sodium chloride, adenine, glucose and mannitol (SAGM). Red cell concentrate contains no white cells or platelets, which can sometimes cause problems when whole blood is transfused. In any case, very often people only need a transfusion because their blood cannot carry enough oxygen. Using concentrate, you can ensure that the total blood volume of people being given a transfusion for anaemia does not rise too high.

Fresh frozen plasma is made by centrifuging whole blood within a few hours of its being collected. It is blood without any red or white cells in it. It can be stored for up to a year. It is used for the treatment of people who have blood clotting disorders and need to be provided with all the blood clotting enzymes and cofactors.

Serum is made by allowing blood to clot and then separating off the clear liquid which is left behind. Serum is therefore blood plasma minus all the clotting factors. It is stored frozen, like plasma. It is used to obtain antibodies for the treatment of a few diseases.

Fig 3.15 A photograph of some shelves in a blood bank refrigerator. The shelves of the blood bank and the blood packs are labelled with the different blood groups (A, B, AB, O, and Rhesus positive or Rhesus negative) of the red cell concentrate in each pack.

SAQ

3.4 Explain why plasma and serum can be stored frozen, whereas whole blood is kept at 4 °C.

Table 3.2 Types of stored blood product.

Types of stored blood product	Used for
whole blood	transfusion
packed red cells (red cell concentrate)	transfusion
fresh frozen plasma	treatment of people who have blood clotting disorders
serum	to obtain antibodies for disease treatment

Screening blood products

Receiving blood from a blood donor may be a life-saver, but it can also be a life-taker if the donated blood contains harmful substances, for example, viruses.

The disease **AIDS** first appeared in the late 1970s. At first, no-one knew how it was caused. As more and more people began to show the symptoms of AIDS, intensive research finally showed that it was caused by a virus, now known as the **human immunodeficiency virus, HIV**.

During the late 1970s and early 1980s, many people were unwittingly given blood which contained HIV. As a direct result, most of them became ill with AIDS and many died.

Two other viruses, both of which cause hepatitis, have also been transmitted in this way. 'Hepatitis' means 'inflammation of the liver'. **Hepatitis B** and **hepatitis C** are unpleasant illnesses and may in some cases be fatal. (There is also a hepatitis A, but this is spread by contamination of food or water with faeces, not by blood transfusion.)

To lessen the risk of harmful viruses being present in donated blood, potential donors are asked not to give blood if there is any chance that their blood may contain these viruses. They cannot give blood if they have ever had a blood transfusion, as this increases the risk that their blood could contain harmful viruses. The first time a new donor arrives at a blood donation clinic, they will have an extensive interview to estimate their suitability as a donor. They will be asked questions about their lifestyle as well as their health, and fill in a tick-box questionnaire. Once accepted they will be allowed to give blood on that visit, and also on future occasions.

As well as these measures, all blood intended for transfusion is now **screened** to ensure that none of these three viruses is present. If the person has been in contact with any of the viruses, their blood will contain antibodies that their immune system has produced against them. A blood sample is therefore added to the antigens for these diseases. If there is a reaction, this indicates that the virus may be present and the blood will be disposed of immediately. The screening process is done automatically, by machine.

SAQ

3.5 A survey was carried out to find out what proportion of people in England and Wales had acquired hepatitis B from blood transfusions, between 1991 and 1997. The table shows some of the results.

Year	Number of people reported with hepatitis B	Number of people who acquired the disease through blood transfusion
1991	572	5
1992	531	3
1993	629	5
1994	631	3
1995	613	5
1996	581	2
1997	628	1

a Is any overall trend shown by these results? Explain your answer.

b Calculate the percentage of hepatitis B cases that were acquired through blood transfusion, for each year from 1991 to 1997 inclusive.

c Suggest how, despite the screening measures which were introduced in the early 1970s, a few people still acquired hepatitis B through transfusion.

Haemophilia and blood-borne infections

Haemophilia is an inherited disease in which blood does not clot effectively. The cause is usually the absence of one of the substances which play important roles in the chain of events leading to the formation of a blood clot – blood clotting factors. The blood clotting process shown in Fig 3.1 on page 47 is actually a highly simplified version of the process involving more blood clotting factors than are shown in that diagram.

In haemophilia A, factor VIII is missing. In haemophilia B, factor IX is missing. There are around 11 000 people in the UK with one of these diseases. They are all men, as the genes responsible for the production of these factors are carried on the X chromosome. Haemophilia is a sex-linked disorder.

There is not usually much danger to a haemophiliac from an external wound such as a cut, though it will take much longer to form a clot and scab. The main danger arises when small blood vessels are damaged within the body – for example, at a joint. This is very, very painful and can cause irreparable damage to the joint.

Since the early 1950s, blood products have been given to people with haemophilia, to lessen the symptoms of their illness. Haemophiliacs do not require whole blood, as they already have a normal number of red cells. What they do need are the clotting factors. During the 1970s, a method was found of pooling blood taken from many donors, to produce a 'factor concentrate' which could be transfused into the patient's blood. Up to 30 000 donations of blood might contribute to a single batch of factor concentrate.

When this treatment was first introduced, AIDS was only just beginning to become apparent, and HIV had not yet been found, let alone identified as the cause of the disease. People with haemophilia were being given regular blood transfusions, each one collected from a very large number of different people. Their chances of being given blood containing HIV were therefore extremely high. Many have also been given the viruses which cause hepatitis B and hepatitis C.

It is thought that nearly 5000 people with haemophilia acquired hepatitis C through transfusion, of whom 1200 also picked up HIV. It is estimated that 800 have died from AIDS. Many, however, are now living not only with haemophilia, but also with AIDS and hepatitis. Both kinds of hepatitis can lead to serious illness, but many people carry the viruses without showing any symptoms.

Summary

1. Enzyme-controlled reactions happen fastest at an optimum temperature, usually around 37–39 °C for human enzymes. The rate is slower at lower temperatures because the enzyme and substrate have little kinetic energy, so collisions are less frequent and less energetic. The rate is slower at higher temperatures because enzyme molecules are increasingly denatured as the temperature rises. They lose their shape, so the substrate no longer fits in the active site.

2. The rate of enzyme-controlled reactions is at its highest at a particular pH. Above or below this value, the enzyme begins to become denatured as the change in pH causes bonds between its R groups to break.

3. Many enzyme-controlled reactions require the presence of another substance, called a cofactor. Calcium is a cofactor in two of the reactions involved in blood clotting.

4. Blood for transfusion is therefore kept at 4 °C, with a buffer added to prevent pH changes, and with the calcium ions removed.

5. Blood may be stored as:

   • whole blood, useful for transfusions where the patient has lost a lot of blood;

   • packed red cells, useful for transfusions, especially for people who are suffering from anaemia;

   • frozen plasma, which can be given to people who are short of one or more of the blood clotting factors;

   • serum, which may be used to provide antibodies to people at risk from viral infection.

6. Blood collected from donors is screened to check that there are no antibodies for HIV, hepatitis B virus or hepatitis C virus. This is done by adding some of the blood to the antigens that are produced by these viruses. If there are antibodies to any of these viruses in the donated blood, they will react with the antigens.

Heart disease

3rd Decem[...]

World's first heart transplant

Dramatic new operation

Yesterday a human heart was transplanted for the first time into Louis Washkansky who had been dying of hea[...]

"On Saturday, I was a surgeon in South Africa, very little known. On Monday, I was world renowned."

These were the words of Dr. Christiaan Barnard, years after the events in 1967 when he carried out the first human heart transplant. He remained famous, even infamous, throughout the rest of his life, carrying out other attention-grabbing operations – such as transplanting two hearts into a patient. Even in 1991, just four years before his death, he was considering using cloning to supply organs for transplantation.

Back in 1967, the transplantation of the heart was controversial, much more so than now. Partly, this was because the heart was held in special regard by people, but there were also other concerns. The donor, Denise, had a severely fractured skull from a car accident, but her heart was still beating just before it was removed, so was she really dead? Denise was not responding to light or pain. A brain surgeon had declared that Denise was 'brain dead'. South African law did not use a beating heart as a definitive sign of life. This gamble with medical ethics established brain stem death as the criterion for death, which was to become accepted around the world.

Dr. Barnard had turned off Denise's ventilator, which was supplying oxygen to her body. He waited for the heart to stop beating before removing it. We now know that this probably weakened the heart, as it needed electric shocks to restart it. The recipient, Louis Washkansky, only lived for another 18 days. Indeed, life expectancy remained poor for transplant patients throughout the 1960s and 1970s. This improved, however, in the early 1980s with the development of better immunosuppressant drugs that prevented rejection of the heart but were not likely to kill the patient. Currently, about 50% of heart transplant patients are expected to survive for 10–12 years.

Heart structure and function

We naturally think of the heart as being one of the most important organs in the body. We use expressions such as 'getting to the heart of the matter', a 'heartfelt plea' and 'knowing in my heart.' This last one implies that people have thought of the heart as an organ that we think with. This belief was indeed held long ago, but now everyone knows that we think with our brains, not our hearts. All the same, when Christiaan Barnard gave the first heart transplant operation in 1967 many people were deeply shocked – even though kidney transplants had been carried out since 1954.

Illnesses affecting the heart are a major health problem in the twenty-first century. Coronary heart disease is the major cause of death in the United Kingdom amongst older people. Much advice, some of it conflicting, about reducing your chances of suffering from a heart attack is given in the media. This chapter looks at what coronary heart disease is and how it can be treated. First, though, we need to look at how a healthy heart functions.

The structure of the heart

You can see in Fig 4.1 that the heart has four chambers – a left and right **atrium** at the top, and a left and right **ventricle** beneath. The right side is completely separated from the left side by a **septum**. The walls of the heart are made almost entirely of a special kind of muscle, called **cardiac muscle**. It is the regular contraction and relaxation of these muscles which produces the pumping movement of the heart.

The atria on each side of the heart are separated from the ventricles by valves. These are the **atrio-ventricular valves (AV valves)**. The one on the left is often known as the **mitral** valve, or alternatively the **bicuspid** valve (because it has two flaps). The one on the right is the **tricuspid** valve. These valves are pushed shut when the ventricles contract, so that blood can't flow back into the atria.

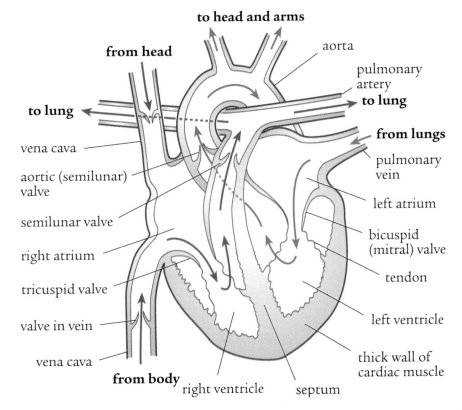

Key
→ deoxygenated blood
→ oxygenated blood

Fig 4.1 Internal structure of the human heart.

On the outside of the heart, blood vessels can be seen (Fig 4.2). These are called the **coronary arteries**, and they deliver oxygenated blood to the heart walls. It may seem odd that the heart, which is full of blood, needs to have more of it delivered to the cells in its walls. But the wall of the heart is so thick, especially around the left ventricle, that the muscle near the outside of the wall is too far away from the blood inside the ventricle to be able to obtain oxygen from it.

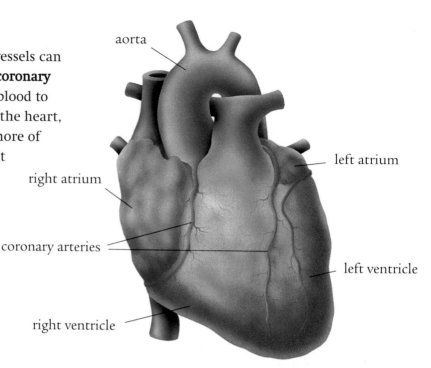

Fig 4.2 External features of a human heart.

The cardiac cycle

The cardiac cycle is the sequence of events which take place in the heart during one heart beat (Fig 4.3).

First, the atria contract. This is called **atrial systole**. As the muscles in the atria walls contract, they squeeze inwards on the blood in the atria, raising its pressure and pushing it down through the atrio-ventricular valves into the ventricles.

Next, the ventricles contract. This stage is called **ventricular systole**. Their muscular walls are thicker and stronger than the ones in the atria, so they can produce a much greater pressure. The blood is squeezed up into the aorta (from the left ventricle) and the pulmonary artery (from the right ventricle). The pressure of the blood in the ventricles pushes upwards on the atrio-ventricular valves, pushing them shut. So, if the valves are working properly, no blood can go backwards, into the atria.

Next, the muscles in the atria and ventricles all relax. This is called **diastole**.

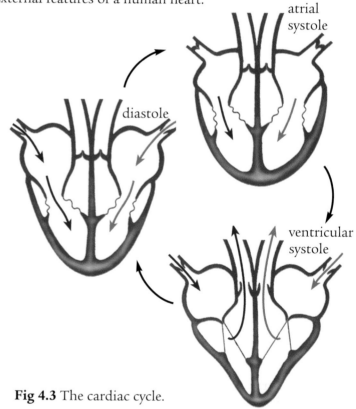

Fig 4.3 The cardiac cycle.

Pressure changes during the cardiac cycle

We have seen that contraction of the muscles of the atria and ventricles causes changes in the pressure in the various chambers of the heart. The pressure changes in the left side of the heart are shown on the graph in Fig 4.4.

You can see that the pressure in the atria rises at the start of the cycle, as they contract. Shortly after this, the ventricles contract, creating a very big increase in the pressure of the blood inside them. As they relax, the pressure inside them decreases, as does that in the atria.

It is very obvious from the graph that the pressure in the ventricles rises much higher than that in the atria. This is what we would expect, knowing that the ventricle walls are so much thicker than the atrial walls. Notice,

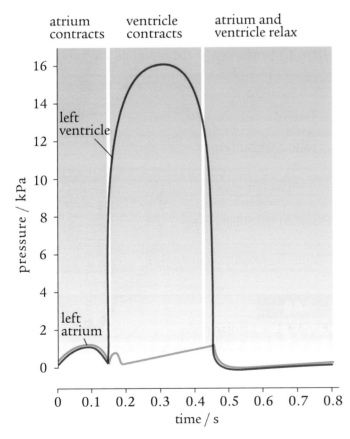

Fig 4.4 Pressure changes in the left atrium and left ventricle in one complete cardiac cycle. The pressure changes in the right atrium and ventricle follow the same pattern, but the maximum pressure is less than in the left ventricle.

though, that the pressure in the atria does go up whilst they are relaxing and the ventricles are contracting. This is caused by an increase in the quantity of blood inside them, as it flows in from the large veins which deliver blood to the heart.

We can use the graph in Fig 4.4 to pick out the moment when the atrio-ventricular valves close. These valves are little flaps of tissue which behave like swing doors. They will move in whichever direction the blood pushes them. During atrial systole the pressure in the atria is greater than that in the ventricles. So the valves are pushed downwards by the higher pressure of the blood in the atria. But during ventricular systole, the pressure in the ventricles quickly rises above that of the atria, so now the valves are being pushed upwards. As they are anchored by the tendons holding them to the heart wall, (see Fig 4.3) they can't flap past the opening and up into the atria. They can be pushed upwards just enough to seal the holes between the atria and ventricles, so closing them off and ensuring that the blood can't go back the way it came.

The atrio-ventricular valves therefore open when the pressure in the atria is greater than that in the ventricles. They close when the pressure in the ventricles is greater than the pressure in the atria. These moments are shown on the graph when the 'atrial pressure' line crosses the 'ventricular pressure' line.

The sound of the two AV valves shutting at the same time produces the first sound of a heart beat. The second sound, shortly after the first, is due to the semilunar valves shutting. The two sounds are rather like 'lub-dup'. When counting heart rate, the two sounds make one 'heart beat', so there is one beat per cardiac cycle.

SAQ

4.2 Fig 4.4 shows one complete cardiac cycle, lasting 0.8 s. Calculate the heart rate in beats per minute. Show your working.

4.3 Make a copy of this graph, which shows pressure changes in the left atrium, left ventricle and aorta.

a Mark on your graph the three stages of the cardiac cycle: atrial systole, ventricular systole, diastole.
b On your graph mark the times at which the atrio-ventricular valves open and close. Label each one and note the time at which it takes place after the start of the cycle.
c Mark on your graph the period of time during which blood flows from the left ventricle into the aorta.
d What information in the graph explains why blood flows from the atria into the ventricles?

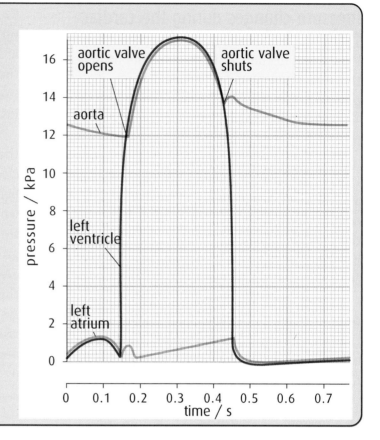

Cardiac output

The volume of blood leaving the left ventricle per beat is known as the **stroke volume**.
Cardiac output is the volume of blood leaving the left ventricle per minute. So:

cardiac output = stroke volume × heart rate

Both stroke volume and heart rate increase to supply extra oxygen to the muscles during exercise.

Extensive athletic training causes the heart to develop a higher stroke volume in all situations. As a result of this training the heart rate does not need to rise as high to achieve the same cardiac output needed for a particular level of exercise.

Table 4.1 Stroke volume and heart rate during exercise.

	Stroke volume / cm³	Heart rate / beats min⁻¹
resting non-athlete	75	75
max. for non-athlete	110	195
resting marathon runner	105	50
max. for marathon runner	162	185

4.4a Make a copy of the table above, but add another column at the end labelled 'cardiac output / cm³ min⁻¹'. Calculate the cardiac outputs for the values in the table.
b Explain why having a higher stroke volume may help to make an athlete more successful.
c Suggest what changes would occur in the body during extensive training that could result in an increased stroke volume.

Summary

1. The heart is made of cardiac muscle, which contracts and relaxes rhythmically to push blood out of the heart. The muscle is supplied with blood via the coronary arteries.

2. Oxygenated blood from the lungs flows into the left atrium, and is pumped out of the left ventricle into the aorta.

3. Deoxygenated blood from the body flows into the right atrium, and is pumped out of the right ventricle into the pulmonary artery.

4. The valve separating the left atrium from the left ventricle is called the bicuspid or mitral valve. The valve separating the right atrium from the right ventricle is called the tricuspid valve.

5. These valves are pushed open when the pressure of the blood in the atria is higher than that in the ventricles. They are pushed shut when the pressure of the blood in the ventricles is higher than that in the atria.

6. During one cardiac cycle, the atria contract, then the ventricles, and then the whole heart relaxes. The contraction phase is known as systole, and the relaxation phase as diastole.

7. A graph of pressure changes during one cardiac cycle shows that the pressure in the ventricles rises greatly during ventricular systole, forcing blood out of the ventricles. The pressure changes in the atria are much smaller, as their contraction only forces blood down into the ventricles.

8. Cardiac output is the volume of blood pumped out of the left ventricle in one minute. It is calculated by multiplying the stroke volume by the heart rate.

Coronary heart disease

Coronary heart disease, usually abbreviated to **CHD**, is a major cause of death in developed countries. In the United Kingdom, around 3–4% of men between the ages of 35 and 74 die each year as a direct result of CHD. For women, the risk is only around half of this figure. It is the single most common cause of death – 30% of all deaths amongst men, and 22% of those amongst women, are caused by CHD. Every year, 156 000 people in England and Wales die from CHD.

CHD is not the only cause of a poorly-functioning heart. Some people have valves in their heart which do not close properly, or they may have a 'hole in the heart' – a hole in the septum which allows oxygenated and deoxygenated blood to mix. The autoimmune illness rheumatic fever can also cause major damage to the heart. In this disease, a person's white blood cells attack their own tissues, including valves and muscle in the heart.

Atherosclerosis and CHD

The ability of the cardiac muscle to contract depends on it receiving a constant supply of oxygen. The muscles use the oxygen for aerobic respiration, which provides the energy that they use in contraction. If the oxygen supply fails, then the muscle cannot contract. Heart muscle lacking oxygen quickly dies.

This happens if coronary arteries which supply the heart muscle are blocked. Usually the blockage is due to the build-up of material inside the artery walls, which makes the space through which blood can flow – the **lumen** – much narrower. This condition is called **atherosclerosis**. Atherosclerosis also occurs in other arteries, such as those supplying the brain.

Atherosclerosis develops slowly, and people do not normally show any symptoms until they are at least 40 years old. It occurs naturally as part of the ageing process. However, in some people it progresses more rapidly and this can be due to a variety of things that tend to damage the lining of arteries. These include high blood pressure (see page 115), or the presence of harmful chemicals such as those in tobacco smoke, or low density lipoproteins (LDLs,

described on pages 111–112). The artery lining reacts by attempting to repair itself. There is a build-up of tissue and chemicals in the artery wall. These deposits are known as an **atheromatous plaque** (Fig 4.5).

Once the plaque has reduced the lumen of the artery by 50% or more, the flow of blood through the artery cannot keep up with the oxygen requirements of the heart muscle during exercise. The person experiences pain when exercising, known as **angina**. The pain is often in the left shoulder, chest and arm, but for some people in their neck or the left side of the face.

Blood clots can form on and around the plaque. Such a blood clot is called a **coronary thrombosis**. This happens because platelets in the blood come into contact with collagen (a fibrous protein) in the artery wall.

The blood clot narrows the artery. Over time, it may close the artery off completely. Sometimes, a clot breaks away to produce an embolus which travels along the artery and blocks arterioles downstream. Either of these events may prevent blood flowing to a particular part of the heart muscle. This part of the heart therefore stops beating, and some of the muscle cells may die. This is known as a **myocardial infarction** and is an extremely dangerous condition.

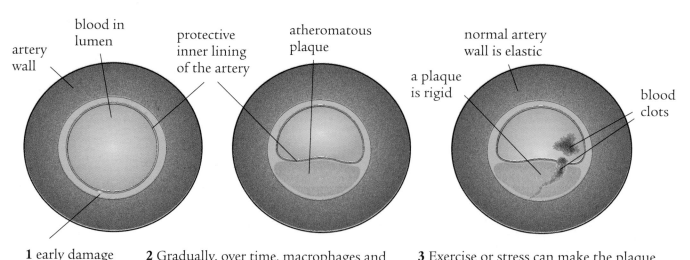

1 early damage

2 Gradually, over time, macrophages and lymphocytes (see page 6) migrate to the damaged area, muscle cells divide in the artery wall and there is a build-up of lipids.

3 Exercise or stress can make the plaque break. Blood enters the crack. Platelets in the blood are activated (see pages 47–48) and a clot forms. Part of the clot may break off.

Fig 4.5 The development of an atheromatous plaque.

Myocardial infarction

'Myo' means 'muscle', and the myocardium is the muscular wall of the heart. 'Infarction' is a term describing the loss of sufficient blood flow to a tissue to allow it to carry out its normal activity. Around 90% of instances of myocardial infarction are caused by a coronary thrombosis.

What happens during a myocardial infarction? It partly depends on how much of the heart muscle is affected. If the infarction involves a large amount of muscle, then the person may die almost immediately. Others may experience such severe pain that they call for help straight away. If less muscle is affected,

then the pain may be less severe, and the patient may wait several hours before contacting a doctor. Some, unwisely, ignore it.

The pain felt during an acute myocardial infarction is usually in the centre of the thorax (chest region), behind the sternum (breastbone), felt as 'tightness', 'crushing' or 'bursting'. Sometimes the pain extends down the left arm or into the jaws. The patient may feel sick.

The commonest time of day for acute myocardial infarction is first thing in the morning, when the patient has just got up. There is another peak around 5 pm. Friday is the commonest day of the week for a myocardial

---

PROCEDURE 4.1

Heart attack – what an untrained person can do to help

Recognise heart attack symptoms

Recognising a heart attack can be quite difficult, as the symptoms described here can all be caused by other things. Only an ECG can provide definitive evidence (see page 87).

What to do if the person is conscious

1 Calm them. Make them comfortable in a half-sitting position. Keep bystanders away. Blood circulation may not have stopped completely, so keeping quiet means that less oxygen is needed to stay alive. Raising the heart above the abdomen and legs makes it easier for it to push the blood around the body.

2 Dial 999, telling the operator you suspect a heart attack. Rapid attention is vital for survival.

3 Give immediate medication.
   If the person carries medication for angina, help or allow them to use it. If not, ask them to slowly chew an aspirin tablet. These medications help to prevent another heart attack occurring immediately, which may kill.

4 Monitor.
   Encourage rest and monitor the victim's pulse, alertness and breathing.

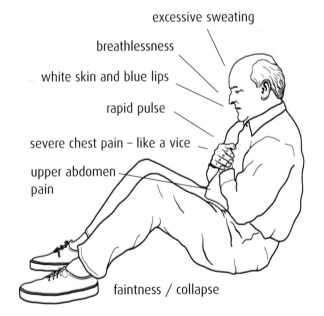

excessive sweating

breathlessness

white skin and blue lips

rapid pulse

severe chest pain – like a vice

upper abdomen pain

faintness / collapse

What to do if the victim is unconscious

Dial 999, telling the operator you suspect a heart attack and the victim is unconscious and not breathing.

If the victim is unconscious, this probably means that the blood circulation has effectively stopped and there will be no sign of breathing. Immediate cardio-pulmonary resuscitation (CPR) is required (see Procedure 4.2). If you haven't been trained to do this, see if a trained person can be quickly found.

infarction, and there are fewer at weekends. Stress or excitement may be involved. This could cause a rise in blood pressure which may rupture a plaque in a coronary artery.

Another factor which influences the frequency of deaths from myocardial infarction is the temperature. Deaths increase a day or two after an especially cold day. Heat waves also tend to increase mortality from coronary thrombosis.

Cardiac arrest

We have seen that severe myocardial infarction may cause the heart to stop beating. This is called **cardiac arrest**. No pulse can be felt, and the victim rapidly loses consciousness. The face loses its colour, becoming white or grey and lips go blue.

Although severe myocardial infarction is the main cause of cardiac arrest, it is not the only one. Other causes of cardiac arrest include those described below.

Drug overdose

Several drugs, including medicinal ones, can cause cardiac arrest if taken in excess. Paracetemol, for example, first causes liver damage if an overdose is taken but cardiac arrest may occur on around the third day after the overdose was taken if no treatment is given.

Hypothermia

Hypothermia is defined as having a deep-body temperature of below 35 °C. It can be caused by exposure of the body to extreme cold, such as falling into very cold water. Most people who are immersed in icy water for 20 to 30 minutes suffer cardiac arrest and die.

Hypothermia can also occur in elderly people sitting still in unheated rooms in cold weather for long periods of time.

Electric shock

The surge of electrical energy which flows through the body during an electric shock from lightning or power cables, for example, can cause great damage to the nervous system. It may upset the way in which the heart muscle receives its signals to contract, carried as electrical impulses through the heart (see page 89).

Toxin

The bites and stings of some animals inject toxins into the body. Some, such as sea snake venom, may cause death by stopping the heart from beating. In Australia, the stings of box jellyfish have caused numerous fatal cardiac arrests. An anti-venom to this venom is manufactured and kept ready for rapid administration to victims.

SAQ

4.5 There are many medical terms associated with heart disease, which can be confusing. Try to sort them out by matching each of these terms with their definitions.

Terms:
cardiac arrest, myocardial infarction, angina, atherosclerosis, coronary thrombosis, atheromatous plaque, coronary heart disease

Definitions:
- A rigid area in the wall of an artery, formed from a build-up of tissues and lipids.
- A term used to refer to disease affecting the coronary blood vessels in the heart wall.
- A blood clot in one of the coronary arteries.
- The complete stoppage of heart beat.
- A loss of sufficient blood flow to some of the cardiac muscle, often caused by a coronary thrombosis, and one of the main causes of cardiac arrest.
- Pain felt during exercise, a symptom of the narrowing of the coronary arteries.
- A condition in which the lumen of an artery becomes narrower, and its wall less elastic, as a result of the build-up of atheromatous plaques in its wall.

Cardio-pulmonary resuscitation (CPR)

! Care ! This requires training to carry out safely and successfully. You may be able to try it out safely on a life-size dummy.

There are, however, many cases of untrained people saving lives using CPR.

The victim should be lying on their back. Take a few seconds to check for any sign of breathing, airway blockage, chest movement or pulse. If there are no signs of circulation begin CPR immediately.

1 Locate the lowest rib on the side of the victim's body by which you are kneeling. Move your fingers to find where the rib joins the sternum (breastbone).

2 Find the position to apply pressure by placing the heel of your other hand right next to your fingers, so that the hand is over the sternum. Put the heels of both hands on top of each other at this position.

3 Lean over and press on the sternum, lowering it by about 4 cm, then release the pressure, but not removing the hands. Press at the rate of about 100 per minute for about 15 times.

4 Tilt the head back and give two rescue breaths in the following way. Pinch the soft part of the nose. Take a deep breath and place your lips around the victim's mouth to seal it. Blow steadily to inflate the lungs. Take your mouth off and let the air come out.

5 Continue to alternate chest compression and rescue breaths, occasionally checking for any sign of breathing and pulse. If a pulse returns but no breathing, continue rescue breaths. If breathing starts, move the body into a recovery position.

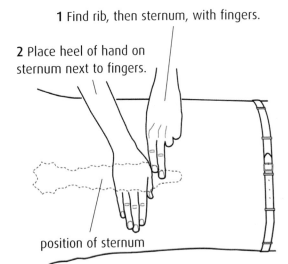

1 Find rib, then sternum, with fingers.

2 Place heel of hand on sternum next to fingers.

position of sternum

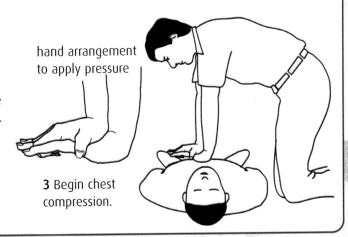

hand arrangement to apply pressure

3 Begin chest compression.

Hospital treatment for heart attack victims

In the ambulance, if the victim has no pulse, **defibrillation** will be used to restart the heart (see Procedure 4.3, Using a defibrillator).

A patient who has a pulse and is breathing will be given morphine to relieve the pain. The pain relief enables them to relax more, which puts less strain on the heart. They will be given oxygen to breathe, as this means that more oxygen can get to the cells with less effort from the heart.

The patient will also be given aspirin, which stops the platelets carrying out their role in the clotting process. They will probably also be given a clot-busting drug such as streptokinase, to help to dissolve the blood clot which is causing all the trouble. The use of streptokinase and aspirin can halve the chance of a person dying after a heart attack.

Using a defibrillator

When a heart attack has stopped the blood circulation and caused the victim to become unconscious, this is usually because the heart has an abnormal 'fluttering' rhythm, known as ventricular **fibrillation**. If a fibrillating heart is given a large electric shock the normal rhythm can sometimes be restored. The machine that gives the shock is a defibrillator.

1 The defibrillator is switched on and the electrode connections checked. Any chest hair is shaved and the skin is dried, if needed, where the electrode is to be placed.

2 The self-adhesive electrode pad is attached to the chest in the correct position.

3 The defibrillator measures the heart rhythm and breathing and will advise if and when a shock is to be applied. It will also advise on chest compression and rescue breaths.

4 Electric shocks are given, as instructed by the defibrillator.

5 If breathing starts, the victim should be moved to the recovery position.

Summary

1 Coronary heart disease, abbreviated to CHD, is a disease involving the coronary arteries which supply oxygen to the cardiac (heart) muscle.

2 Atherosclerosis is a condition in which an artery wall becomes thicker and stiffer. This narrows the lumen – the space through which blood can flow – and lessens the elasticity of the artery wall.

3 The development of atherosclerosis is part of the natural ageing process, but is speeded up by numerous factors including high blood pressure, smoking or large amounts of LDLs in the blood (see pages 11–112). Atherosclerosis in a coronary artery may cause pain, known as angina, during exercise.

5 Atherosclerosis increases the risk of a thrombosis (blood clot) forming in the artery. If this happens in a coronary artery, it is known as a coronary thrombosis.

6 If blood is prevented from passing through a coronary artery, the muscle which it supplies may stop beating (cardiac arrest) or even die. This event is called a myocardial infarction.

7 Although most instances of cardiac arrest are caused by myocardial infarction, other causes include drug overdose, hypothermia, high voltage electric shock or being bitten or stung by venomous animals.

8 The use of cardio-pulmonary resuscitation, CPR, can save the life of a person whose heart and breathing have stopped. A defibrillator may be able to restart the normal rhythm of heart beat. Giving aspirin to reduce blood clotting, and clot-busters such as streptokinase to dissolve clots, helps to reduce the risk of further blockages in the coronary arteries which may be the cause of cardiac arrest.

Aspirin

For thousands of years some people have known that chewing willow bark can help to reduce pain. However, it was not until the eighteenth century that anyone really began to look at this property from a scientific point of view. The Reverend Edmund Stone, who lived in Chipping Norton in Oxfordshire, wrote about how it could help to reduce fever and pain, and this drew aspirin to the attention of several chemists and physicians.

When the active chemical in willow bark was discovered, it was named salicin, because the Latin name for willow is *Salix*. In the body, salicin is converted to salicylic acid. However, taking salicin or salicylic acid can cause major problems with bleeding in the stomach. It was found that there were far fewer problems if the drug was taken in the form of acetylsalicylic acid. This drug was first marketed in 1899, under the trade name Aspirin®.

chemical formula of aspirin

We know quite a bit about how aspirin relieves pain. In 1970, the British scientist Dr. John Vane found out what aspirin does. He was awarded a Nobel Prize for his work.

When a part of the body is damaged, the damaged tissues produce chemicals called **prostaglandins**. These are produced from a substrate called arachidonate (a fatty acid), in a reaction catalysed by the enzyme cyclooxygenase (COX). The arachidonate is fed into the active sites in the enzyme from the endoplasmic reticulum.

Prostaglandins cause inflammation in the area of damage, which can help to heal it. However, the inflammation also causes pain, partly because the prostaglandins increase impulses from pain receptors to the brain. Aspirin stops the production of prostaglandins by adding an acetyl group (CH_3CO-) to an amino acid close to the active site of COX. This prevents the substrate from binding, so the reaction which produces prostaglandins is stopped.

Another effect of prostaglandins is to make platelets stick together. So aspirin can reduce the ability of the blood to clot. Many people who are at risk from DVT or coronary thrombosis take aspirin on a regular basis, usually 75 mg per day.

Aspirin does have some unwanted side effects. In particular, it inhibits the action of a different variety of the COX enzyme in the stomach, which reduces the protection of the wall from being damaged by the hydrochloric acid which is present. This can increase the risk of developing a stomach ulcer. The search is on for a drug that inhibits one kind of COX and not the other.

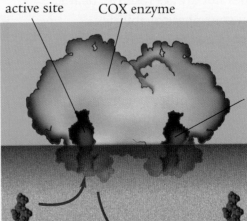

active site   COX enzyme

The active sites can be inhibited by aspirin.

endoplasmic reticulum

arachidonate   prostaglandin

Heart surgery

CASE STUDY

In November 2003 Sir Ranulph Fiennes and Dr. Mike Stroud completed a record-breaking series of seven marathons in seven days in seven continents. Remarkable though this would be for anyone, Sir Ranulph was 59 years old, had suffered a heart attack and undergone immediate triple heart bypass surgery five months before.

Sir Ranulph suffered his heart attack boarding a flight from Bristol to Edinburgh in June 2003. The well-trained flight attendants were able to give immediate aid and he was rushed to hospital. There it was confirmed he had suffered a heart attack and that it was necessary to carry out bypass surgery. And then ... back to his old ways ...

In 1982, Sir Ranulph had become one of the first men to reach both the North Pole and the South Pole on his Trans-Globe Expedition. Eleven years later, he and Mike Stroud became the first men to cross the Antarctic, unsupported, on foot. Sir Ranulph has survived gangrene at the North Pole and bullets in the Middle East. He has trekked across the Andes and canoed up the Amazon.

"Many of our adventures were only enjoyable in retrospect, but I can honestly say this was enjoyable from day to day," he said after finishing his seventh marathon.

Sir Ranulph Fiennes' exploits show that having a heart attack does not always result in death, nor even a loss in your physical abilities. However, he is not a 'normal' person, in the sense of normal physical achievements!

A heart attack is a very dangerous event. If a person has angina or other symptoms of coronary heart disease, everything possible should be done to improve the health of their heart and its blood supply. Reducing body weight and taking regular steady exercise are both very helpful. And a patient may be helped by changing their diet. For a few people this helps to prevent further deterioration of their coronary arteries (see Chapter 5).

SAQ

4.6a Suggest how reducing body weight could reduce someone's chance of suffering a heart attack.

b Playing squash once a week, but not taking any other significant exercise, might actually increase someone's chance of a heart attack. Suggest an explanation for this.

However, such lifestyle changes often do not solve the underlying problems. Moreover, coronary heart disease is not the only way a person's heart may be damaged. For example, many people are born with structural defects in their hearts, such as faulty valves or a hole in the septum between the right and left sides of the heart. These problems are very difficult to treat in any way other than by surgery.

Heart surgery can be done in many different ways. Some defects can be dealt with using surgical techniques such as **angioplasty**, where there is no need to open the chest cavity. Others may require 'open heart surgery', in which the chest is opened to allow access to the heart. As a last resort, a heart transplant may be considered.

Angioplasty

Angioplasty is a surgical technique which may be used to improve the health of a patient who has angina, and in whom other treatments have not been successful. It is also used for patients who have had coronary bypass surgery (see page 82) and whose coronary vessels need to be opened up again.

Angioplasty is a much less 'invasive' procedure than open heart surgery. The patient is given a general anaesthetic. A little balloon is then threaded into the partly blocked coronary artery, through a tube called a catheter, where it is inflated (Fig 4.6). As the balloon expands, it presses against the atheroma (the built-up tissue in the wall) and makes one or two tears in it. This allows the artery wall to be pushed outwards by the pressure of the blood, which restores the lumen to something like its normal width. The balloon is deflated and removed. Sometimes the balloon is used to push a metal mesh, called a stent, against the wall. The stent is left in place when the balloon and catheter are removed, helping to keep the artery open.

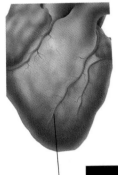

These drawings are based on X-rays of a person's heart while she was being treated by angioplasty.

coronary artery

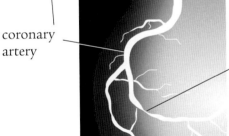

1 Before treatment the lumen of a coronary artery had been narrowed greatly by a plaque.

2 A catheter (tube) brings a balloon on a guide wire to the correct place.

3 The balloon is inflated and forces the artery open.

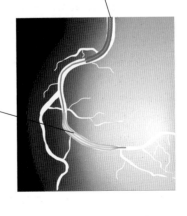

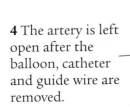

4 The artery is left open after the balloon, catheter and guide wire are removed.

Fig 4.6 Angioplasty.

Open heart surgery

Angioplasty can be done without opening the chest cavity at all – the surgeon can thread the device through a blood vessel to get it into the right place. However, many operations on the heart can only be done if the surgeon has access to the heart itself. These involve **open heart surgery**. This terms refers to the fact that the chest cavity is opened. (The 'open' part of the name refers to the open chest, not necessarily to an open heart.)

A surgeon cannot usually operate on a heart which is beating. Delicate procedures can only be carried out if the heart is still. So, during open heart surgery, the blood is passed through a **heart-lung machine**, which contains a pump to keep the blood moving around the body, and also supplies the blood with oxygen. Usually, the machine also adds anaesthetic to the blood.

Coronary bypass surgery

Coronary bypass surgery is used when a person's coronary arteries are blocked so badly that insufficient blood can pass through them to supply the heart muscle with oxygen. The 'bypass' is an extra blood vessel which provides an alternative route for the blood to the heart wall, bypassing the coronary arteries (Fig 4.7).

Surgery for 'hole in the heart'

The term 'hole in the heart' refers to a hole in the septum dividing the right hand side from the left hand side. Normally, oxygenated blood from the lungs enters and leaves the left hand side of the heart, while deoxygenated blood enters and leaves the right hand side of the heart. This means that the blood which is pumped around the body from the left ventricle is oxygenated blood. However, if a person has a small hole in the septum, then the oxygenated and deoxygenated blood can mix. The blood pumped around the body therefore has less oxygen in it than it should.

In fact, everyone has a 'hole in the heart' when they are a foetus in the uterus. The hole is between the right and left atria, and it is called the **foramen ovale**. It is useful to have such a hole at that stage, because in a foetus it is actually the *right* hand side of the heart which contains oxygenated blood. This happens because, in a foetus, the blood is oxygenated as it flows through the placenta, rather than through the lungs.

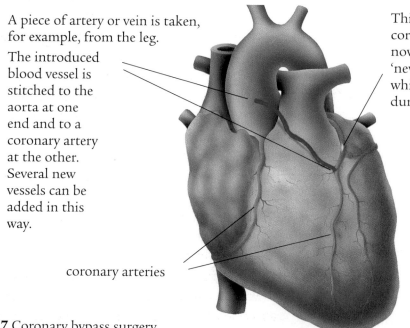

A piece of artery or vein is taken, for example, from the leg.

The introduced blood vessel is stitched to the aorta at one end and to a coronary artery at the other. Several new vessels can be added in this way.

This partly blocked coronary artery is now bypassed by the 'new' blood vessel, which was added during the surgery.

coronary arteries

Fig 4.7 Coronary bypass surgery.

The foramen usually closes at birth. However, in some people the hole does not completely close (Fig 4.8). Most of these people seem to have no symptoms at all, so they will probably never know that they have a small 'hole' in their heart. There is some evidence that these people may be at a slightly greater risk of suffering from deep vein thrombosis, a heart attack or stroke, but in general their health does not appear to be affected.

However, in some young children the hole is large enough to be a real threat to their health. And some adults may begin to show symptoms as they reach middle age. These holes used to be repaired using open heart surgery, but now new procedures have been developed.

The new procedures are a bit like angioplasty (see page 81). A tiny incision is made in the groin, and a catheter (tube) containing a little 'umbrella-like' device is threaded into a vein. This catheter is gradually threaded through the leg vein, through the vena cava and into the right hand side of the heart. Once it is manoeuvred into position, the 'umbrella' is inflated in such a way as to close the hole.

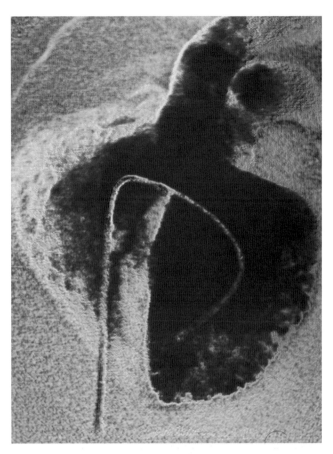

Fig 4.8 An angiogram of a heart with a foramen ovale – 'hole in the heart'. The position of the hole is highlighted by the bent catheter which passes through the hole between the two sides of the heart.

Surgery for valve repair

Some babies are born with malformed heart valves, which can mean that the blood has a tendency to just move back and forth in the heart as it beats, rather than flowing into the atria and being pumped out of the ventricles. Heart valves may also become damaged later in life. Most of the problems involve the valves between the atria and ventricles.

The repair of defective heart valves normally involves open heart surgery. The surgeon may be able to repair the faulty valves by cutting or sewing them, or it may be necessary to implant replacement valves. These may be taken from a human body, or another organism, or they may be made from metal. If these artificial heart valves are used, the patient will need to take anti-coagulant drugs for the rest of their life, to stop the blood clotting when it contacts the metal.

SAQ

4.7a Make a simple diagram showing the internal structure of the heart of a person with a 'hole in the heart'.

b On your diagram, using coded shading for oxygenated and deoxygenated blood, show how the two types of blood flow into the heart and mix.

c A 'stroke' is an event where part of the brain stops receiving blood. It can be caused by a blood clot carried in the blood (an embolus) getting stuck in an artery supplying blood to the brain.
A blood clot in a leg vein can be carried to the lungs and get stuck there, causing a pulmonary embolism. Using your diagram, explain why, in a person with a 'hole in the heart', it could cause a stroke instead.

Heart transplant

A heart transplant is only undertaken after all else fails, because it carries much more risk and is a long and expensive operation. It has taken a long time for the operation to become reasonably successful. Moreover, there are very few hearts that can be used for transplant. At any one time, about 3000 people in the UK would probably benefit from it but only about 300 transplants take place a year. (10 million were registered as organ donors in 2002. It is hoped this will be 16 million by 2010.) Hearts can only be used from people who had a healthy heart when they died, and will not be used if the person has HIV or abused drugs such as cocaine. Relatives of a dead person can prevent organs being removed if there is no donor card or the person has not registered as a donor.

The patient due to receive the heart will be given **immunosuppressant** drugs, which prevent the immune system from attacking and destroying the foreign tissue of the donated heart. The heart recipient will continue to take these drugs for the rest of their life, which increases the risk of suffering from infectious diseases and cancer.

SAQ

4.8 In 1999, a study was carried out in a hospital in Australia into the number of 'unexpected' cardiac arrests amongst patients in the hospital who had been admitted for some other reason. In 1999, a specialist 'medical emergency team', consisting of two experienced doctors and one senior intensive care nurse, was set up in the hospital. Up until then, there was no such team in place. The study compared the incidence of, and death rate from, unexpected cardiac arrests in the hospital in 1996 and 1999.

The emergency team attended patients in the hospital who had been identified as 'clinically unstable'. This meant that the patients had shown a deterioration in breathing or circulation. The medical emergency team were called to any such patient, whom they treated immediately using drugs or resuscitation equipment.

These are some of the data which emerged:
- In 1996, a total of 19 317 people were admitted to the hospital. In 1999, 22 847 patients were admitted.
- In 1996, there were 73 cases of unexpected cardiac arrest amongst these 19 317 patients. In 1999, there were 47 cases.
- In 1996, 56 patients died as a result of their unexpected cardiac arrest. In 1999, the equivalent figure was 26.

a Design a results chart which makes these results really easy to see. You should calculate percentages as well as showing the 'raw' results. (Think about which percentages you need to calculate. Why should you do this?)

b What conclusions can you draw from these results?

c The researchers carrying out the study could not control most variables.

i State any variables which were not controlled.

ii Explain why it is almost impossible to control most variables in this type of study.

Table 4.2 Pros and cons of different treatments for severe heart disease.

	Used for	Symptom relief	Outlook	Follow-up
angioplasty	• people with angina, when other treatments haven't cured it • people who've had coronary bypass surgery and now need vessels opening up again	better than continued non-surgical treatment	slightly increased risk of myocardial infarction (about the same as for a coronary bypass)	needs more medical treatment afterwards than coronary bypass
coronary bypass surgery	• people whose activity and enjoyment of life is prevented by angina and normal medical treatment is not helping • people who have all of their coronary vessels partially blocked	good – 90% are free of angina one year after surgery; 60% still free after 10 years	slightly increased risk of myocardial infarction	very little required
heart transplant	people with potentially fatal heart disease, for whom all other treatment has failed	excellent to begin with, but half will have developed coronary disease in the transplanted heart in 5 years (their immune system attacks the artery walls)	this new coronary disease may be fatal because there are no nerves connected to the new heart so no pain is felt and the first warning is myocardial infarction	• lifelong use of immunosuppressant drugs • the risk of suffering from gastric ulcers • the only treatment for new coronary disease is another transplant

Summary

1 Heart surgery is normally only carried out if all other treatments fail, as it is very expensive and carries some risk of failure.

2 Angioplasty is used to open partially blocked coronary arteries. A catheter is threaded into a blood vessel, and then guided into the damaged artery. A balloon is inflated in the artery, widening its lumen.

3 Open heart surgery involves opening the thorax to give access to the heart.

4 A coronary bypass operation may be carried out if there is a blockage in the coronary arteries which cannot be opened using angioplasty. It involves sewing a blood vessel, taken from elsewhere in the body, to the heart so the blood can flow from the aorta to the heart muscle, bypassing the damaged coronary artery.

5 A 'hole in the heart' is usually an opening between the left and right atria. If the hole is large, it may need to be closed by surgery. This may involve open heart surgery, or the use of a catheter and 'umbrella' device to block the hole.

6 Damaged or faulty atrio-ventricular valves can be repaired using open heart surgery.

7 Heart transplants are only done after all other treatment fails. The operation has a high success rate, but too few donor hearts are available. The patient needs to take immunosuppressant drugs for the rest of their life, to prevent their own immune system attacking the heart.

CHAPTER 5

Monitoring circulation

James arrived in the hospital A and E department protesting "I don't need a doctor". He had not been seen for days – then a neighbour had banged on the door of his flat until he appeared. She rang 999 saying he "was talking nonsense". An ambulance arrived at his home and he was whisked to hospital.

His left foot smelt appalling. A nurse removed a disintegrating sock from it, and the smell was even worse. A doctor diagnosed gangrene. Gangrene is caused by bacteria infecting open wounds and needs conditions of low oxygen concentration. As there was no obvious wound, this suggested that his blood system was not delivering enough oxygen to his feet, a diagnosis supported by the fact that no pulse could be detected in his legs below the knee. He had a raised temperature. He said that, yes, his foot did hurt and he didn't feel too good, but he was OK and he wanted to go home.

James was quickly put onto an antibiotic drip to try to bring the foot infection under control. Another nurse asked James a raft of questions to try to find out his medical history. She discovered that he was 59 years old, and had smoked regularly, about a pack a week, and had been smoking since he was 12. James had never heard of any of his relatives having problems with their heart or circulatory system. He wasn't registered with a GP and had never been in hospital before.

Now he was given a chest X-ray and then an electrocardiogram (ECG) was made. The X-ray revealed that his heart looked normal. However, the ECG suggested that there was a major problem. The medical team diagnosed recent myocardial infarction. Further tests revealed a blood clot in a coronary artery supplying the left ventricle.

So much tissue was dead in his left foot that it had to be amputated, in order to stop the gangrene from spreading up James's leg, despite an operation being dangerous for someone with a recent myocardial infarction. He remained in hospital for several weeks, while his leg healed and treatment was given to improve the function of his heart.

The heart's electrical activity

An **electrocardiogram**, usually shortened to ECG, measures the electrical activity going on in the heart as it beats. It is a quick and really important way of collecting information to diagnose problems affecting the heart.

An ECG is usually displayed on a computer screen. A printout can also be made. It is like a graph showing time on the bottom (x) axis and electrical activity on the vertical (y) axis (see page 88).

PROCEDURE 5.1

Recording an electrocardiogram

In the case study, James had an electrocardiogram recorded soon after arriving at hospital. Like many worried patients, he asked "Does it hurt?" "No, not a bit", was the reply. This is the procedure that was carried out.

The person is asked to lie on a bed and is given time to relax. Electrodes are attached to the chest, wrists and ankles using sticky pads. To pick up the electrical activity, a good electrical contact is needed, so a special gel is used with the pads.

When the heart muscle contracts, the area outside the cells becomes negatively charged. This can be detected by electrodes stuck onto the skin. As the wave of contraction spreads across the heart, so the area of negative charge moves. Blood and tissue fluid are electrically conducting and so the heart and the rest of the circulatory system allow the electrical effect to be detected on the surface of the body.

You can pick up an ECG with just two electrodes in different places. However, many more electrodes are used and these produce different recordings. These different ECGs can reveal useful information.

Three different recordings can be made from connections between the two wrists and one ankle.

In addition, six electrodes can be attached across the chest over the heart, which produce slightly different recordings.

James' ECG showed an abnormality which was a type of heart block. An example of this is shown on page 90.

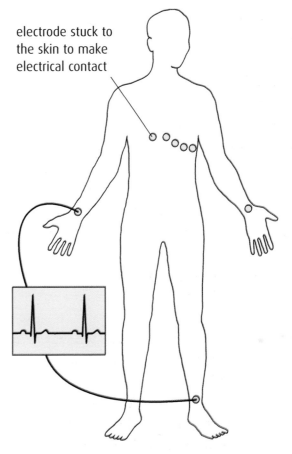

electrode stuck to the skin to make electrical contact

Only some of the electrodes that are used to record ECGs are shown here.

What an electrocardiogram shows

Fig 5.1 shows an electrocardiogram being recorded and Fig 5.2 shows an electrocardiogram for a healthy heart.

The ECG shows the electrical activity which takes place in the heart muscle as the heart beats. This activity is related to the electrical impulses which pass through the heart. Fig 5.3 shows how the different parts of the ECG correspond to the events during one heart beat.

If you look carefully at Fig 5.3, you will see that the ups and downs in the ECG happen before the ups and downs in the pressure graph. For example, the P wave on the ECG comes before the pressure rise in the left atrium. This is because the ECG records the electrical impulses which are spreading over the heart, and these electrical impulses *cause* the contraction of the muscle in the heart walls. So the P wave in the ECG represents the wave of electrical activity spreading through the walls of the atria (Fig 5.4), which is quickly followed by the rise in pressure in the atria as they contract.

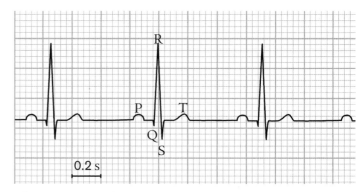

Fig 5.2 A normal ECG.

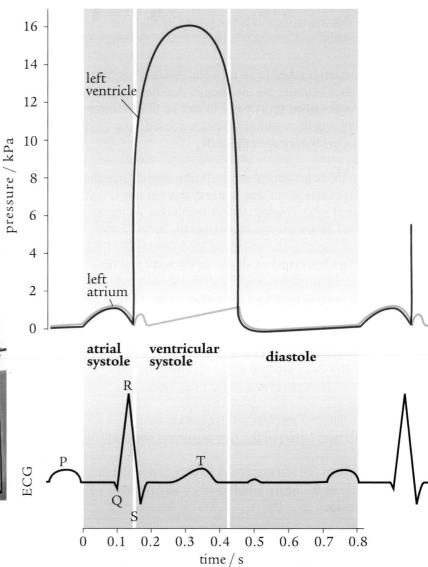

Fig 5.3 How an ECG relates to the cardiac cycle.

Fig 5.1 An electrocardiogram being taken during a fitness test. Electrodes attached to his chest record the electrical activity which is displayed on the monitor. (The blue cuff on the arm is measuring blood pressure.)

1 Each cardiac cycle begins in the right atrium. There is a small patch of muscle tissue in the right atrium wall, called the **sino-atrial node (SAN)**, which automatically contracts and relaxes all the time. It doesn't need a nerve impulse to start it off, so it is said to be **myogenic** – that is, 'started by the muscle'.

The SAN is often called the **pacemaker**, because it sets the pace at which the whole heart beats.

However, the pacemaker's rate can be adjusted by nerves transmitting impulses to the pacemaker from the brain.

2 As the muscle in the SAN contracts, it produces an electrical impulse which sweeps through all of the muscle in the atria of the heart. This impulse makes the muscle in the atrial walls contract. The impulse shows up on the ECG as the P wave. So the P wave represents the electrical activity just before atrial systole.

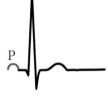

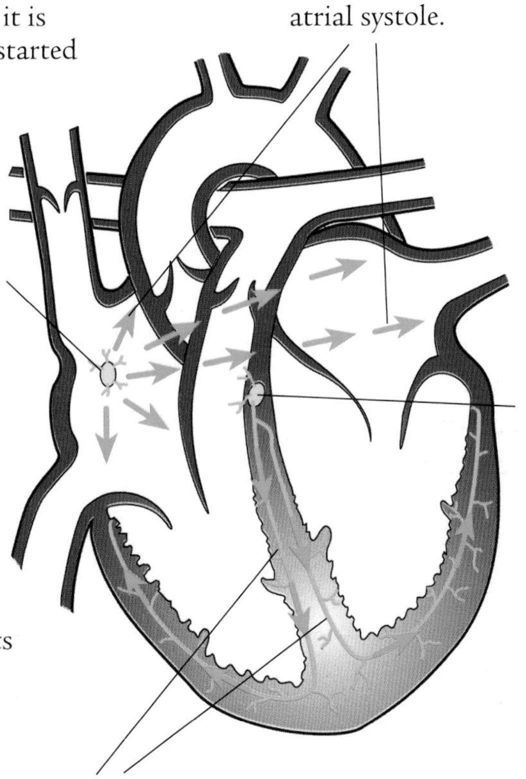

5 The ventricles then relax, indicated by the T wave. Then the muscle in the SAN contracts again, and the whole sequence runs through once more.

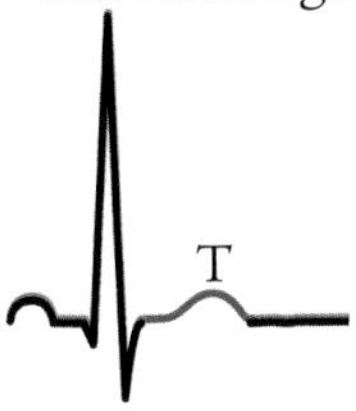

3 The impulse sweeps onwards and reaches another patch of cells called the **atrio-ventricular node (AVN)**. This node is the only way in which the electrical impulse can get down to the ventricles. The AVN delays the impulse for a fraction of a second, before it travels down into the ventricles. This delay means that the ventricles receive the signal to contract *after* the atria.

4 The impulse moves swiftly down through the septum of the heart, along fibres known as **Purkyne tissue**. Once the impulse arrives at the base of the ventricles it sweeps upwards, through the ventricle walls. This is shown by the Q, R and S part of the ECG. The ventricles then contract.

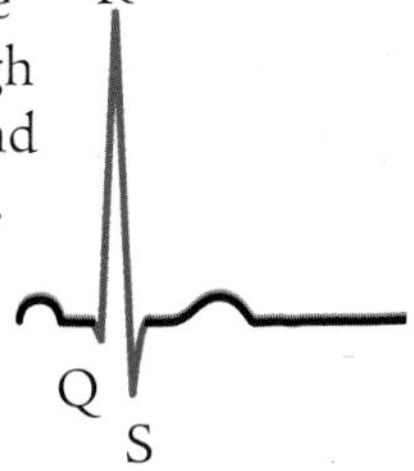

Fig 5.4 How electrical impulses move through the heart.

SAQ

5.1a Which part of the ECG represents the delay between the atria contracting and the ventricles contracting?

b Explain why it is important that the ventricles should not start contracting at the same time as the atria.

c How does the AVN help to ensure that the ventricles contract after the atria?

d Suggest why it is useful for the ventricles to contract from the bottom upwards, rather than from the top downwards.

Abnormal ECGs

Ventricular fibrillation

Features The ECG shows no pattern (Fig 5.5a).
Cause The muscle in the ventricle walls just flutters. This could be because the person has suffered myocardial infarction.

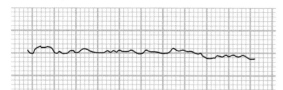

Fig 5.5a Ventricular fibrillation.

Effect The victim has no blood circulation and is usually unconscious. Without immediate treatment, they will almost certainly die.
Treatment Immediate treatment is to use a defibrillator. If the patient survives, then the root cause of the problem will need to be determined before appropriate treatment – such as surgery to provide a heart bypass – can be decided upon.

Bradycardia

Features The heart rate is slower than normal. It is usually defined as a heart rate of less than 60 beats per minute. The ECG looks normal (Fig 5.5b), but with an interval of more than one second between the 'waves'.
Cause A slow heart beat can be a sign of a healthy heart in a fit person. However, bradycardia may indicate that the sino-atrial node is not functioning properly.

Effect In most cases, bradycardia has no effect. But if it is severe, the person may feel very tired, as insufficient blood is reaching the organs.
Treatment If there is a problem with the SAN, then an artificial pacemaker may be fitted.

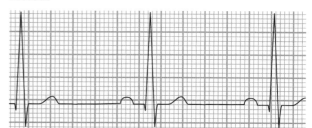

Fig 5.5b Bradycardia.

Heart block

Features There are many different types of heart block. The ECG in Fig 5.5c has a much longer than normal time interval between the P and R sections.
Cause Electrical impulses are not passing normally through the heart. In this example, they are taking much longer than usual to pass from the atria to the ventricles. This could be because the Purkyne fibres are damaged.

Effect The person with this ECG probably has no symptoms. Other types of heart block may be more serious. In 'complete heart block' the atria contract at a faster rhythm than the ventricles, greatly reducing the flow of blood around the body.
Treatment This person probably requires no treatment. Other types of heart block could require a pacemaker to provide stimulation to both the atria and the ventricles.

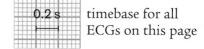

0.2 s   timebase for all ECGs on this page

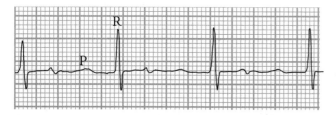

Fig 5.5c Heart block.

Drugs to help the heart

Although no nervous impulses are needed to make the SAN beat, the actual *rate* at which it beats is affected by impulses from the nervous system.

Two nerves carry impulses from the brain to the SAN. One of these is called the vagus, or parasympathetic, nerve. It releases a chemical called acetylcholine next to the cells in the SAN, which makes them beat more slowly. The other, called the sympathetic nerve, releases a different chemical called noradrenalin, which makes the SAN beat faster. The hormone adrenalin, released from the adrenal gland just above the kidneys when a person is nervous or excited, has the same effect.

Everyone's heart normally beats faster when they take exercise or are excited or nervous about something. However, an erratic or over-fast heart beat which continues over a long period of time, or happens inappropriately, needs treatment. The aim of a medical team treating such a patient will be to get to the root of the problem and try to solve it. However, before this is achieved, it is often helpful to give drugs which make the heart beat at a more appropriate rate. There are

many different drugs which can be used, but two of the most widely used are propranolol and digoxin.

Digoxin inhibits a sodium-potassium ATPase pump in the cell surface membrane of heart muscle cells. The pump normally keeps sodium ion concentration low inside the cells. Rising sodium ion concentration reduces the excretion of calcium ions from the cells, so calcium concentration rises inside the cells. This increases the force of muscle contractions.

Propranolol belongs to a class of drugs called beta-blockers. They work by decreasing the effect of noradrenalin on the SAN. Noradrenalin, as we have seen, is secreted by the sympathetic nerve, and this happens when a person is excited, angry or frightened. Beta-blockers therefore help to stop the heart rate from becoming as high as it might otherwise do, and they are therefore often given to people with angina. They reduce the chance that the oxygen demand of the heart muscle will exceed its supply, and so reduce the risk of myocardial infarction. Beta-blockers are sometimes used by sportspeople whose sport requires steadiness and concentration, such as archers and snooker players.

SAQ

5.2a Using Fig 5.2 (a normal ECG) on page 88, calculate the time intervals between each R section. Calculate the mean of these values and determine the pulse rate in beats per minute.

b Repeat this procedure for Fig 5.5b.

c Using Fig 5.2, calculate each of the PR interval times and then determine the mean PR interval.

d Repeat this procedure with Fig 5.5c.

e Use your findings to help you to construct a table summarising the differences between these ECGs (normal, bradycardia and heart block).

Monitoring the heart with a stethoscope

In the cardiac cycle the closure of the heart valves is so violent that they make distinct sounds, which are easily heard with a simple instrument – a stethoscope. Despite its simplicity, it is still used by doctors because it is such a quick way to get important information. For example, defects in the working of heart valves can often be heard.

The heart sounds – 'lub' followed by 'dup' – can be precisely linked to the ECG as shown below. Both AV valves shut at the same time producing 'lub'. The aortic valve and pulmonary valve shut at the same time producing 'dup'.

One end of the stethoscope has a diaphragm at the end of a cone. This end is placed on the surface of the body. It acts like an old-fashioned ear trumpet. Sound is collected from the vibrating diaphragm at the wide end and is amplified by being forced into a narrower space. The sound is then carried by the tube to the ears.

Being able to interpret the sounds takes considerable training and experience. This particularly applies to detecting defects of the heart valves.

> **! Care !** You will probably hear strange sounds, but this does not mean that there is anything wrong with the heart. Only a medical practitioner can interpret the sounds correctly.

This exercise can be carried out with the person wearing a normal shirt or top, and you can carry it out on yourself.

1 Locate the fourth and sixth ribs (counting from the top).

2 Keeping to within the fourth and sixth ribs, place the diaphragm on the left side of the chest directly under the breast.

3 Listen to the sounds. Then move the diaphragm slightly to one side and listen again. Repeat the procedure and compare the sounds.

4 Concentrate on the sounds and try to pick out the main heart sounds, 'lub' and 'dup', from all the other noises.

5 When you can recognise the sounds, count the number of heart beats in a 10 second interval. Repeat this several times. Calculate the mean heart rate.

6 Now concentrate on the sounds other than 'lub-dup'. A quieter sound may be heard very soon after the 'dup'. This is a bit like a 'whoosh'. It is the sound caused by blood rushing into the ventricles through the open AV valves, which vibrate a little when the blood rushes past. This is also referred to as a 'murmur'. The strength of the murmur varies from one person to another. Having a louder murmur is quite normal and the heart is perfectly healthy. If a member of the class has a louder murmur, ask if you can listen to it.

left ventricle

aortic valve shuts

aorta

left atrium

AV valve shuts

atrial systole

ventricular systole

diastole

R

P

T

Q

S

| 0 | 0.1 | 0.2 | 0.3 | 0.4 | 0.5 | 0.6 | 0.7 | 0.8 |

time / s

'lub' 'dup'

5.3 This ECG was made from a person who had been brought to A and E as an emergency case.

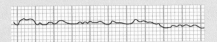

a What term is used to describe this behaviour of the heart?

b Which of these symptoms would you expect to see in this patient?
• high blood pressure • low blood pressure
• hyperactivity • loss of consciousness

c Suggest what may have happened in this person's body to cause this behaviour of the heart.

Summary

1. An electrocardiogram, or ECG, measures the electrical activity of the heart.

2. Each heartbeat is initiated in the sinoatrial node, often known as the SAN or pacemaker.

3. The SAN and the rest of the heart muscle contracts and relaxes of its own accord, with no need for impulses from the nervous system. It is therefore said to be myogenic.

4. The contraction of the muscle in the SAN sends electrical impulses over the rest of the muscle in the atria. This activity produces the P wave on an ECG.

5. The electrical impulse can only pass down to the ventricles through the atrio-ventricular node (AVN) and the Purkyne tissue in the septum. It is delayed slightly at the AVN, thus ensuring that the ventricles contract after the atria. The signals causing the contraction of the ventricles produce the QRS section of the ECG.

6. Because the electrical impulse has to pass down through the septum before it enters the muscle of the ventricle walls, these walls contract from the bottom up. This helps to push blood upwards into the arteries.

7. The electrical effect resulting in relaxation of the ventricles produces the T wave in the ECG.

8. In a heart block, there is some kind of interference with the transmission of impulses that control the stages of the cardiac cycle. For example, in a block in the right bundle of Purkyne fibres there is a delay in stimulation of the right ventricle to contract, making QRS longer.

9. In ventricular fibrillation there are disorganised ECGs with no identifiable QRS waves and no coordinated cardiac cycle. There is no circulation and the victim is unconscious.

10. Bradycardia is an unusually slow heart rate (less than 60 beats per minute). It is often normal in athletes and any person asleep.

11. The first of the two main heart sounds is produced by the AV valves shutting. The second sound is produced by the closure of the aortic and pulmonary (semilunar) valves.

12. A stethoscope amplifies heart sounds. It enables some abnormalities of heart valves to be detected.

Blood circulation

Your blood flows round the body inside tubes called **blood vessels**. The heart and blood vessels make up the **circulatory system**.

The human circulatory system

The human circulatory system is said to be a **closed blood system**, because the blood moves around the body inside blood vessels. This is something we take for granted, but there are animals which have adopted a different solution to getting blood around their bodies – insects, for example.

In fact, many small animals, such as flatworms and jellyfish, don't have a circulatory system at all. Because they are small, no cell in their bodies is very far away from their gas exchange surface. Each cell can get enough oxygen by diffusion. Insects, too, rely on diffusion to supply oxygen to their cells. But if we relied on diffusion to get oxygen from our lungs to our feet, it would take days.

In large animals such as ourselves, oxygen is transported around the body in blood which is pumped around the circulatory system. The blood moves by **mass flow**. Mass flow is the way that water moves as it comes out of a tap, or as a river flows along. In mass flow, everything – water molecules, dissolved substances and cells – all move together in one direction. This is in contrast to diffusion where molecules move around individually and can move in different directions. Mass flow is a much, much faster way of getting materials from one place to another, for distances greater than a few millimetres. The driving force in mass flow is pressure.

Fig 5.6 shows the basic design of the human circulatory system. It is said to be a **double circulatory system**. This means that, for one complete trip around the body, the blood passes through the heart twice. As we have seen, oxygenated blood from the lungs flows into the left hand side of the heart and is pumped out through the aorta to all other parts of the body.

It returns to the heart as deoxygenated blood, this time entering the right hand side of the heart before being pumped to the lungs once more. The pathway from heart to body and back to the heart is called the **systemic circulation**. The pathway from heart to lungs and back to the heart is called the **pulmonary circulation**.

As we will see (see page 100), the pressure of the blood drops as it passes through capillaries. By making the blood go back to the heart after it has picked up oxygen in the capillaries in the lungs, its pressure is raised again when the heart pumps it out into the aorta. So the blood moves into the aorta at high pressure, ensuring that it moves quickly through the arteries and into the capillaries in respiring tissues.

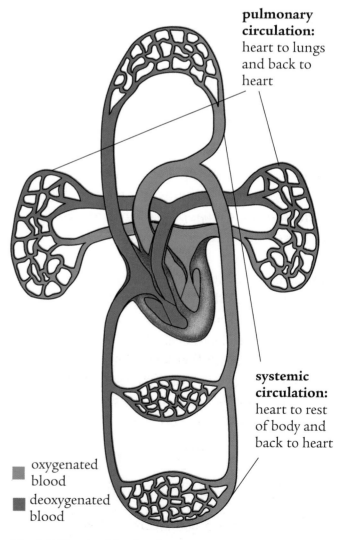

pulmonary circulation: heart to lungs and back to heart

systemic circulation: heart to rest of body and back to heart

- oxygenated blood
- deoxygenated blood

Fig 5.6 The double circulatory system.

94

Types of blood vessels

When the blood first leaves the heart, it does so inside vessels called **arteries**. Arteries always carry blood away from the heart. The largest arteries divide into smaller ones, and these continue to divide to form much smaller vessels called **arterioles**. These in turn divide into even smaller vessels called **capillaries**. Capillaries then join up with each other to form **venules** and these finally merge to form **veins** which carry the blood back to the heart.

These different types of blood vessels therefore have different functions (Fig 5.7).

Arteries carry blood away from the heart. Blood has a high pressure as it is pushed out of the heart, so arteries carry blood at high pressure. They are like motorways – they get fast-moving traffic as quickly as possible from where you are to the general area to which you are going.

Arterioles carry blood, still at a relatively high pressure, to the tissues. They are like A and B roads – smaller routes which take you close to the particular place you want to be.

Capillaries carry blood as close as possible to the individual cells within tissues and organs. They are like unclassified roads – they take you right to the door of your house.

Venules carry blood, now at a very low pressure, away from the tissues. They, like arterioles, can be likened to A and B roads.

Veins carry blood, still at a very low pressure, back to the heart. Like arteries, they can be compared to motorways – but ones on which traffic is moving relatively smoothly and slowly.

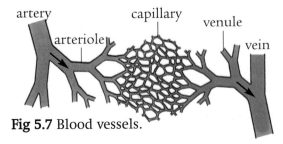

Fig 5.7 Blood vessels.

The structure of blood vessels

As different types of blood vessels have different functions, they have different structures which are related to these functions.

Arteries and arterioles

Arteries carry blood at high pressure. This blood is not flowing smoothly, but is **pulsing**. Each time the muscles of the ventricles contract, a surge of high-pressure blood is forced out of the heart into the arteries. Then the heart muscle relaxes, and the pressure of blood in the arteries falls. You can feel this pulse in your arteries if you place your fingers lightly on your neck, or on the inside of the wrist.

Fig 5.8 shows the structure of an artery. The elastic tissue in the wall allows the artery to expand outwards as a pulse of blood is forced into it. As the pressure of the blood falls, the elastic walls recoil inwards again. This property of the artery walls helps to smooth out the blood flow, because the recoil of the elastic tissue raises the pressure of the blood in the arteries in the 'heart relaxing' stage of the heart beat. We have seen (see page 74) that damage to the artery walls can cause them to lose their elasticity, increasing the risk that an artery might burst or be damaged causing an infarction as high-pressure blood is forced into it.

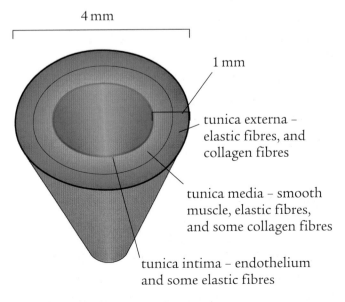

Fig 5.8 A medium-sized artery.

As arteries get further and further from the heart, the amount of elastic tissue in their walls decreases. It is no longer required, because by now the blood pressure inside these arteries is considerably less than in the arteries close to the heart. These arteries therefore have less elastic tissue in them than in the larger arteries.

Further still from the heart, the blood flows into arterioles. These have very little elastic tissue in their walls, but they do contain relatively more smooth muscle than the large arteries (Fig 5.9). When this muscle contracts, it makes the lumen of the arteriole smaller. This ability can be used to divert blood from one area to another and has an impact on blood pressure (see page 100). For example, when you are cold, the smooth muscle in the walls of arterioles carrying blood towards the surface of the skin contracts, narrowing these blood vessels and reducing the amount of blood which flows near the skin surface.

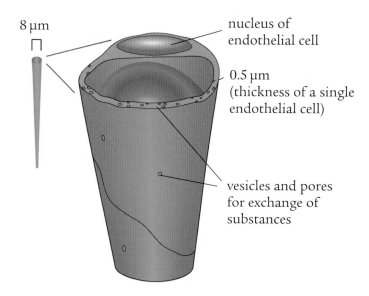

Fig 5.10 A capillary.

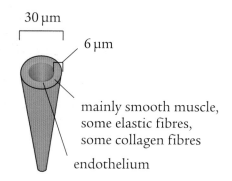

Fig 5.9 An arteriole.

Capillaries

The function of capillaries is very different from that of arteries and arterioles. While these deliver blood quickly to the tissues, the role of the capillaries is to allow substances from the blood to pass to the cells which require them, and to take up substances which need to be removed from these cells.

Fig 5.10 shows the structure of a capillary. Several features can be picked out which help it to perform its function. Capillaries are really tiny, often no more than 8 μm in diameter. This is about the same size as red blood cells, which

can therefore only pass along the capillary in single file. So every single one of them gets as close as it is possible to get to the cells in the surrounding tissues. This speeds up the delivery of oxygen to the cells, and the removal of carbon dioxide from them.

The thinness of the capillary wall is another feature which helps to speed up exchange with the tissues. Most substances pass across the endothelial cells in vesicles. Moreover, the vesicles can fuse to form tiny holes through the cell. So most of the substances in the blood plasma can pass through. Water and many of the substances dissolved in it move out of capillaries and into the spaces between the cells, forming **tissue fluid**. As we have seen, most large protein molecules such as fibrinogen are left behind in the plasma (see pages 37 and 100).

Venules and veins

The blood which enters veins is at a much lower pressure than the blood which enters arteries. Veins therefore have no need of thick, elastic walls, as you can see in Fig 5.11. The walls are so thin that veins tend to collapse when a section of tissue is cut to make a microscope slide. This explains the difference in shape of the vein and the artery in Fig 5.12.

Veins also tend to have relatively larger lumens than arteries. This provides less resistance to the blood, easing its flow back towards the heart. Even this, though, is not enough to get blood back from your feet up to your heart. Help is required from the leg muscles next to the veins. When you move your feet or legs, the contracting muscles press against the veins, squeezing on the blood inside them and making it move. Valves in the veins ensure that the blood can go only one way – towards the heart and not back down into your feet (Fig 5.13).

Venules are small veins that collect blood from capillaries, which then drains into veins.

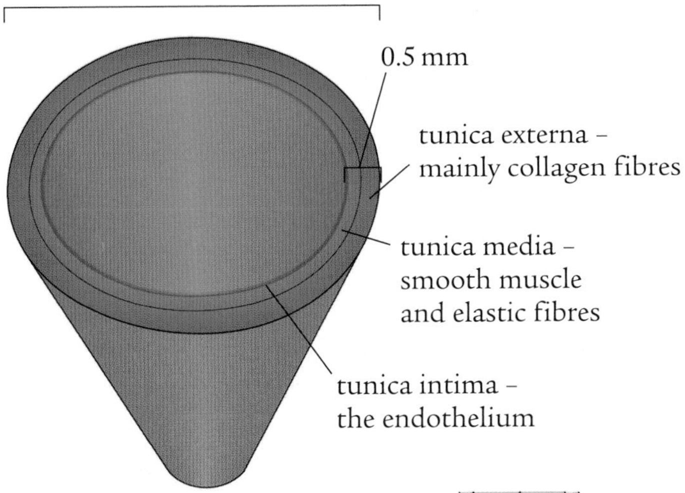

Fig 5.11 A medium-sized vein.

5 mm

0.5 mm

tunica externa – mainly collagen fibres

tunica media – smooth muscle and elastic fibres

tunica intima – the endothelium

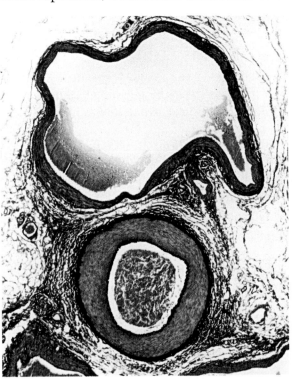

Fig 5.12 Photomicrograph of an artery (bottom) and a vein (top) in transverse section (TS).

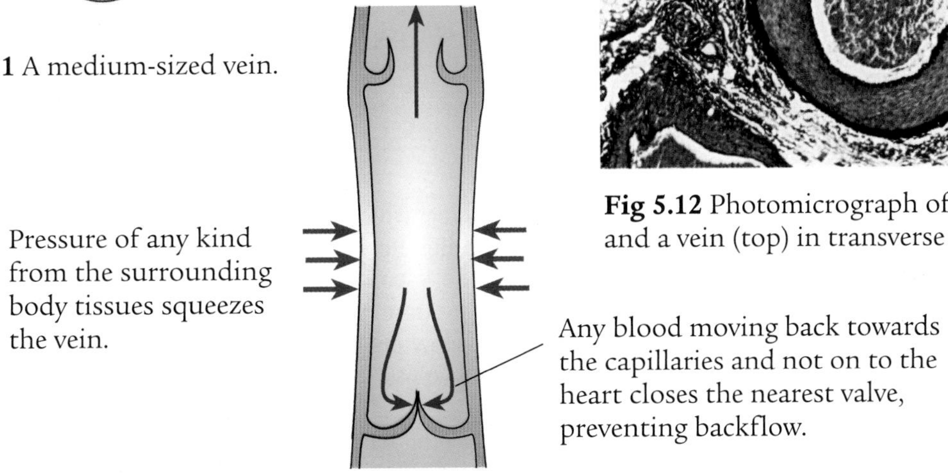

Pressure of any kind from the surrounding body tissues squeezes the vein.

Any blood moving back towards the capillaries and not on to the heart closes the nearest valve, preventing backflow.

Fig 5.13 How valves work in a vein.

SAQ

5.4 The risk of developing deep vein thrombosis (DVT) is increased on long-haul flights.
  a Explain what is meant by the term 'deep vein thrombosis'.
  b Using the information on this page about how blood is made to flow in veins, explain why a long-haul flight may increase the risk of developing DVT.
  c If left untreated, a DVT may lead to pulmonary embolism.
    i Explain what is meant by 'pulmonary embolism'.
    ii Using Fig 5.6 on page 94, explain why DVT in a leg vein is more likely to lead to a pulmonary embolism than to myocardial infarction.

Table 5.1 Summary of blood vessel structure and function.

Feature	Artery	Vein	Capillary
Elastic tissue in wall	Large amount, especially in arteries close to the heart. This allows the wall to stretch and recoil as high-pressure blood pulses through.	Small amount. Blood in veins is at low pressure, so there is no need for the walls to be elastic.	None.
Smooth muscle in wall	Relatively large amount in small arteries and arterioles. Contraction of this muscle reduces the size of the lumen, which can divert blood from one area to another.	Small amount. All blood in veins is travelling back to the heart, so there is no advantage in being able to divert it to different tissues.	None.
Thickness of wall	Relatively thick. Artery walls must be strong enough to withstand the high pressure of the blood flowing inside them.	Relatively thin. The blood in veins is at low pressure, so there is no need for a thick wall.	The wall is only one cell thick. Moreover, these cells are thin and flattened, so the wall is as thin as possible. This allows rapid transfer of substances by diffusion between the blood and tissue fluid.
Endothelium (inner lining)	Thin and smooth. This allows blood to flow freely and quickly. A rough wall would present more resistance to blood flow. Intact endothelium reduces the risk of a thrombus (blood clot) forming.	As arteries.	The wall of a capillary is made of endothelium only, with no other layers of tissue. The thin endothelium and pores speed up exchange of substances with the tissues.
Valves	There are no valves in arteries, except those in the aorta and pulmonary artery as they leave the heart.	Veins have valves, which allow blood to flow towards the heart but not away from it. They are necessary because of the low pressure of blood in the veins.	There are no valves in capillaries.
Diameter of lumen	Relatively small compared with veins. This ensures that large volumes of blood, which is at high pressure, move quickly from the heart to the tissues.	Relatively large. The wide lumen of a vein provides less resistance to blood flow than the narrow lumen of an artery, allowing blood at low pressure to move through easily.	Tiny. Many capillaries are only 8 μm wide. This brings the blood as close as possible to the cells in the tissues with which it is exchanging materials such as oxygen and carbon dioxide.

SAQ

5.5 These statements are common errors made by students in exams. Explain why each statement is incorrect.

a The muscle in the walls of arteries contracts and relaxes to pump the blood through them.

b Arteries are bigger than veins because they carry more blood.

c Arteries need thicker walls than veins because they carry oxygenated blood.

d The cell wall of capillaries is only one cell thick.

Summary

1. Blood is distributed around the human body by mass flow. The body is much too large for diffusion to supply oxygen to all the tissues.

2. The human circulatory system is said to be a closed system, as the blood is contained within vessels.

3. Humans have a double circulatory system, as the blood passes from the heart through the systemic circulation and then back to the heart and through the pulmonary circulation.

4. Arteries carry blood away from the heart. They have relatively small lumens and relatively thick walls. These contain elastic tissue which allows the artery to expand each time the ventricles contract, and then recoil while the ventricles relax. This helps to make the flow of blood smoother.

5. Arterioles are small vessels which carry blood between the arteries and capillaries. In general, they have less elastic tissue and more smooth muscle in their walls than arteries. Contraction of this muscle can divert blood from one part of the body to another.

6. Capillaries are tiny. Their thin walls and the gaps between the cells making up the wall allow easy and rapid exchange of substances with the surrounding tissues.

7. Venules transport blood from the capillaries to the veins.

8. Veins have much larger lumens than arteries, so there is less resistance to the flow of blood. As the blood in them is at a low pressure, their walls can be thinner and have no need for elastic tissue. Veins contain valves to help blood to move constantly towards the heart.

Blood pressure

The term **blood pressure** refers to the force exerted by the blood on the walls of the blood vessels as it passes through them.

Blood pressure changes in the circulatory system

Fig 5.14 (page 100) and Fig 5.16 (page 101) show how the pressure of the blood changes as it makes a complete journey around the circulatory system.

Note
Units of pressure

In science and in the health service all units should be S.I. units. The S.I. unit of pressure is the pascal (Pa). However, to describe blood pressure, an old unit of pressure is still used – millimetres of mercury (mm Hg). Why is this done?

It is because this is the reading on the old style of sphygmomanometer (an instrument that measures blood pressure – see page 102). On this instrument pressure is read as the height in mm of the column of mercury in the manometer tube, which forms a part of it.

Pressure changes in the systemic circulation

2 Each time the muscle in the ventricle wall contracts, a surge of blood at high pressure moves into the aorta. Each time the muscle relaxes, the pressure drops momentarily, before the ventricle contracts again. Each oscillation (up and down) represents one heart beat.

3 The oscillations lessen as the blood passes through the arteries. The elastic artery walls expand when the blood pressure is highest, and spring back again when the blood pressure is lowest. This recoil helps to increase the blood pressure a little in between heart contractions. It gradually smooths out the flow of blood.

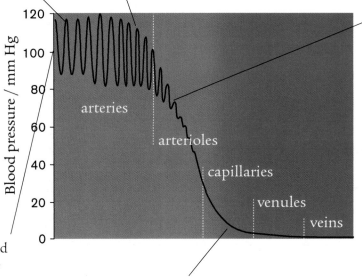

4 The blood moves rapidly through the arteries, which get smaller, then through the arterioles. There is now more contact between the blood inside and the walls of the vessels. The blood is therefore slowed down by friction and this is why the blood pressure falls so quickly as it passes through the arterioles.

1 The blood is at high pressure as it is pumped out of the left ventricle and into the aorta.

5 Many capillaries arise from each arteriole, and their total cross-sectional area is greater than that of the arterioles. The blood has more room to spread out in the capillaries. So its rate of flow decreases, and its pressure. This slow rate of flow in the capillaries is needed to give time for substances such as oxygen and carbon dioxide to diffuse between the blood and the tissues.

Fig 5.14 Pressure changes in the systemic circulation.

If you look at Fig 5.14, you will see that the pressure of the blood drops as it passes through the capillaries. The blood entering a capillary is at a fairly high pressure. This helps substances to move out of the capillary and into the tissue fluid (Fig 5.15). If someone's blood pressure is too low, a condition called **hypotension**, then this does not happen so effectively, and exchange of materials between blood and tissues is poor.

By the time the blood has passed through the capillaries, its pressure is very low. The pressure remains fairly constant as the blood flows through the veins and back to the right atrium of the heart. The pressure is so low that valves are necessary to stop the blood from flowing backwards.

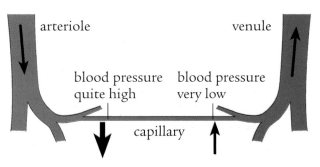

Fluid (water and dissolved substances, except large proteins) leaks out from the blood plasma due to the blood pressure.

Some water diffuses back by osmosis due to the proteins still dissolved in the blood plasma.

Fig 5.15 How blood pressure affects exchange of substances between blood and tissues.

Pressure changes in the pulmonary circulation

1 Blood pressure rises as blood moves from the systemic veins, through the right side of the heart and into the pulmonary arteries. This is caused by the contraction of the right ventricle of the heart. The pressure is much less than that produced by the left ventricle – there is less muscle in the left ventricle wall and less work is needed to take blood to the lungs and back.

2 Pressure in the pulmonary arteries oscillates in time with the heart beat. The pressure drops, and the oscillations smooth out, especially in the arterioles.

3 The blood arriving in the lung capillaries has a much lower pressure than that arriving in capillaries in other parts of the body. Whilst the average blood pressure in capillaries in the systemic circulation is about 17 mm Hg, it is only about 7 mm Hg in the lung capillaries.

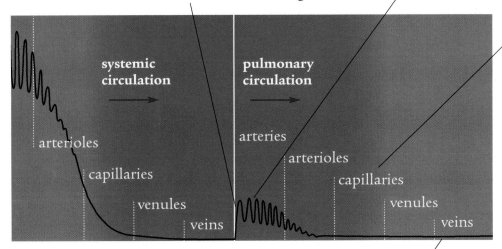

4 The blood then flows through the pulmonary veins and back into the left atrium and ventricle of the heart. As the left ventricle contracts, the blood pressure is raised once more to about 110 mm Hg, and the cycle runs through again.

Fig 5.16 Pressure changes in the pulmonary circulation.

SAQ

5.6 On a flight to the UK from Singapore, the flight attendants were just clearing away people's trays after they had eaten their meal. In a bid to get to the toilets before everyone else got there, a young man stood up quickly. He took two steps forwards and then fell, unconscious, to the floor of the aisle.
A flight attendant rushed to the front of the plane and came back with a colleague and a large box containing a defibrillator. However, before they could even unpack it, the man had opened his eyes and struggled to his feet, looking very sheepish. To their great relief, the flight attendants did not have to put their first-aid skills into action.

a The man had fallen unconscious because of a brief time when his brain was not receiving enough blood.
  i Explain why a lack of blood supply to the brain can result in unconsciousness.
  ii Suggest why standing up quickly, especially after being seated for a considerable time, can result in a temporary lack of blood supply to the brain.
  iii How may the flight have contributed to this young man's fainting incident?
b It was important for the flight attendants to make checks on the man before they used the defibrillator. What checks should they have made, and why was this important?

Measuring pulse

Most sphygmomanometers give a reading for the pulse rate over the period in which the blood pressure readings are being taken, so this activity could be combined with Activity 5.3. However, it is useful to be able to take pulse readings manually, as this is quicker and does not require any equipment other than a clock.

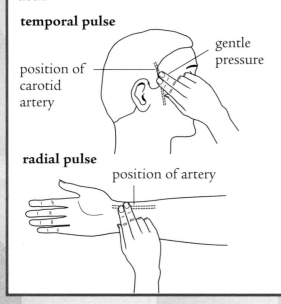

temporal pulse

gentle pressure

position of carotid artery

radial pulse

position of artery

1 Find one of the positions where the pulse can easily be detected. Two examples are shown on the left.

2 Sit down, rest and relax. When fully relaxed measure pulse rate. It is usual to measure the number of pulses in a 10- or 30-second period and multiply by 6 or 2 to give a heart rate in beats per minute. Repeat three times and take an average.

3 Relax some more and repeat the procedure.

4 Perform some gentle activity according to your teacher's instructions, such as rising to a standing position from a seated one, a specified number of times. Sit down and take three readings of pulse.

5 Note the results of the class and present the data in an appropriate manner – that is, a correctly labelled table and an appropriate and fully labelled graph summarising the data. Discuss the results.

Measuring blood pressure

There are two different pressures that are commonly measured, **systolic blood pressure** and **diastolic blood pressure**. The systolic pressure is the maximum pressure produced in the left ventricle during systole. The diastolic pressure is the pressure in the aorta at the end of diastole. Though the diastolic pressure is the lower of the two, this is the one that reveals most about the condition of the circulatory system.

A persistently high diastolic pressure in a person at rest is known as **hypertension** (high blood pressure).

Much attention is paid to long-term hypertension, as there is an increased risk of suffering myocardial infarction and stroke, for example.

A persistently low diastolic pressure is known as **hypotension**.

The instrument that is used to measure blood pressure is the **sphygmomanometer**. Many slightly different models are available but they all work in a similar way.

Note – Normal blood pressure
There is no such thing as a 'normal' blood pressure. All sorts of factors, inherited and environmental, will affect what is normal for one person, and this can change over time. Blood pressure values for the population are just averages.

Using a sphygmomanometer

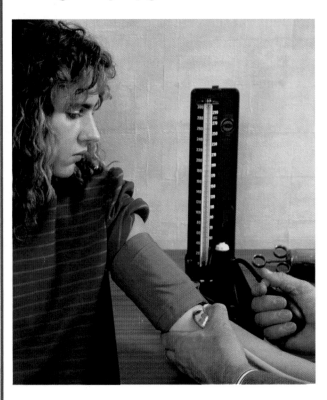

How a sphygmomanometer works

A cuff is inflated around the upper arm. The pressure inside the cuff is raised sufficiently to cut off the blood supply to the lower arm through the brachial artery.

The pressure in the cuff is then allowed to drop slowly. When blood is just beginning to enter the brachial artery again, this indicates that the systolic pressure has been reached. This pressure is noted.

The cuff pressure is allowed to drop again. When it reaches the diastolic pressure, the brachial artery is now wide open. Again, the pressure is noted.

These two pressures are discovered by the distinctive increases in sound that are heard. The sounds are known as Korotkov sounds. When using the older design of sphygmomanometer the sounds were listened to through a stethoscope placed on the arm just below the cuff, but this requires much practice. Sphygmomanometers now use microphones built into the cuff and pressures are recorded automatically.

Procedure

! Care ! Follow carefully the instructions that are supplied with the instrument you are using.
This technique prevents blood entering the lower arm. It is dangerous if the blood flow is stopped for more than a short time.

1 Sit down, rest and relax. When fully relaxed measure blood pressure according to the manufacturer's instructions. Note systolic and diastolic pressures.

2 Relax some more and repeat the procedure. If the values are lower, repeat the period of relaxation and measurement. These values represent your resting systolic and diastolic blood pressures. However, it may not be possible for you to relax sufficiently to obtain your true resting values in a laboratory situation, so do not be surprised if they are higher than average values.

3 Perform some gentle activity according to your teacher's instructions, such as rising to a standing position from a seated one a specified number of times. Record systolic and diastolic pressures.

Table – Average blood pressures in the UK population.

Age / years	Average pressure / mm Hg	
	systolic	diastolic
newborn	80	46
10	103	70
20	120	80
40	126	84
60	135	89

Questions

1 Why is it dangerous to hold the cuff pressure at a value that prevents arterial blood from entering the lower arm?
2 Why would you expect variations in the values obtained when you took repeated readings of the resting pressures?
3 Describe what happens to the pressures as a result of gentle exercise. Compare your own results and use class results as well, if available.

Summary

1. Blood pressure is usually measured in mm Hg.

2. Blood pressure is highest in the arteries, and gradually drops as it passes through the arterioles and capillaries. The blood pressure in the systemic system is much greater than that in the pulmonary system.

3. In arteries, the blood pressure rises each time the ventricles contract and then drops as the ventricles relax. This makes the blood pulse as it passes through the arteries. Thus the heart rate can be measured by measuring the pulse rate.

4. The highest pressure in a systemic artery, relating to the contraction of the left ventricle, is called the systolic pressure.

5. The systemic arterial pressure at the end of diastole is called the diastolic pressure. These pressures can be measured using a sphygmomanometer.

6. Hypertension is having a diastolic pressure which is persistently raised to a much higher value than average for the population.

7. Hypotension is having a persistently low diastolic pressure.

8. Blood pressures are raised by stress and exercise, especially diastolic pressures.

9. Average diastolic and systolic pressures in the population increase with age.

Maintaining a healthy heart

We all know that having a 'healthy' lifestyle is good for us. If we exercise regularly, eat a good diet, don't drink too much and don't smoke, then we expect to stay healthy and avoid coronary heart disease. And a few of us do actually have the will-power to live that kind of lifestyle. So why is it that health-conscious people may still have – and may die from – heart attacks?

There are many well-known people who have taken trouble to get and remain fit, yet have suffered cardiac arrest. They include Douglas Adams (the author of 'The Hitchhiker's Guide to the Galaxy') who died of a heart attack at the age of 49 while working out on his exercise bike; and Ernest Shackleton (leader of a world-famous expedition to the South Pole) who died of a heart attack in 1922 on his last expedition. And what of Jim Fixx, the great American fitness guru who really started the jogging craze? He died of a heart attack when he was 52, while he was out running. Sir Ranulph Fiennes survived his heart attack in 2003, as he had already survived many other life-threatening situations. He was lucky that it occurred while he was boarding a flight and the flight attendants had been trained in how to give first aid. He was only 59 when that happened.

Does this mean it is pointless, or even dangerous, to get super-fit? Probably not, say the experts. There is a whole raft of different factors which influence our risk of suffering from CHD (coronary heart disease) or CVD (cardiovascular disease – disease of the heart or circulatory system). Some of us may just be unlucky and have genes which predispose us to CHD or CVD. Maybe Adams, Shackleton, Fixx and Fiennes would have had heart attacks even earlier in their lives if they hadn't been so fit.

There again, maybe it is not good to be 'too fit'. There is some evidence that people who regularly put excessive strain on their hearts – for example, people who regularly run marathons or who play sports such as football at the highest level – may actually increase their risk of a heart attack. Every year, there are reports of young people, sometimes in their twenties or even teens, who die while playing their favourite sport.

Lipids and heart disease

It seems that every week there is some new twist on what we should and should not be doing to maintain a healthy heart. In the 1950s, we were all told to drink milk and eat eggs to stay healthy. Then the health experts decided that these, and many other 'fatty' foods, were bad for us. And in 2003 the Atkins diet, which entails cutting out practically all carbohydrate-rich foods and eating as much fat-containing food as you like, suddenly became all the rage. So why all the confusion?

It really all boils down to the great difficulty of doing properly controlled experiments into the effect of a particular factor on human health. There are too many variables involved, which we cannot control. In the case of diet, it would be unethical to make some people eat a diet which you are pretty sure is 'unhealthy'. It is just not easy to do experiments of this kind on people.

There *is* a great deal of evidence, however, which shows, without a doubt, that having a high level of cholesterol in your blood does increase your risk of suffering from heart disease. Measuring your blood cholesterol level and taking action to decrease it if it is too high is undeniably 'good for you'.

What is less clear is the extent to which your *diet* affects your blood cholesterol level. There is some evidence that eating a diet high in saturated fats can increase your blood cholesterol level and therefore your risk.

However, other investigations don't support this view. And, overall, there is no really clear link between the amount of cholesterol you eat in your diet and your risk of heart disease.

This is all very confusing. Should we worry about fats in our diet or not?

Fats belong to a group of substances called **lipids**, and cholesterol is closely related to lipids (indeed, some authorities actually classify it as one). Cholesterol is used in the body to make steroids, which are also usually considered a kind of lipid. So a good starting point for trying to unravel some of these tangled threads is to look at how the different types of lipids are used in the body, and how they might affect the blockage of arteries and thus the risk of heart disease.

The structure of triglycerides

Triglycerides are a type of lipid (Fig 6.3). They get their name because their molecules are made of three **fatty acids** (Fig 6.1) attached to a **glycerol** molecule (Fig 6.2).

There is also a simple reason for the name 'fatty acids'. Fatty acids are found as part of fat molecules, and they are acidic. The acidity comes from the —COOH group (a carboxyl group) which they contain. An acid is a substance which releases hydrogen ions, H^+. The —COOH group has a tendency to release a hydrogen ion, like this:

$$-COOH \longrightarrow COO^- + H^+$$

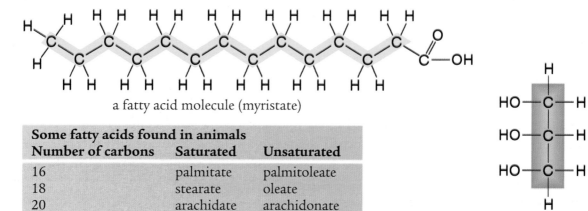

a fatty acid molecule (myristate)

| Some fatty acids found in animals | | |
Number of carbons	Saturated	Unsaturated
16	palmitate	palmitoleate
18	stearate	oleate
20	arachidate	arachidonate

Fig 6.1 Fatty acid molecules.

Fig 6.2 A glycerol molecule.

Each of the —OH groups in glycerol is able to
combine with the —COOH group of a fatty acid.

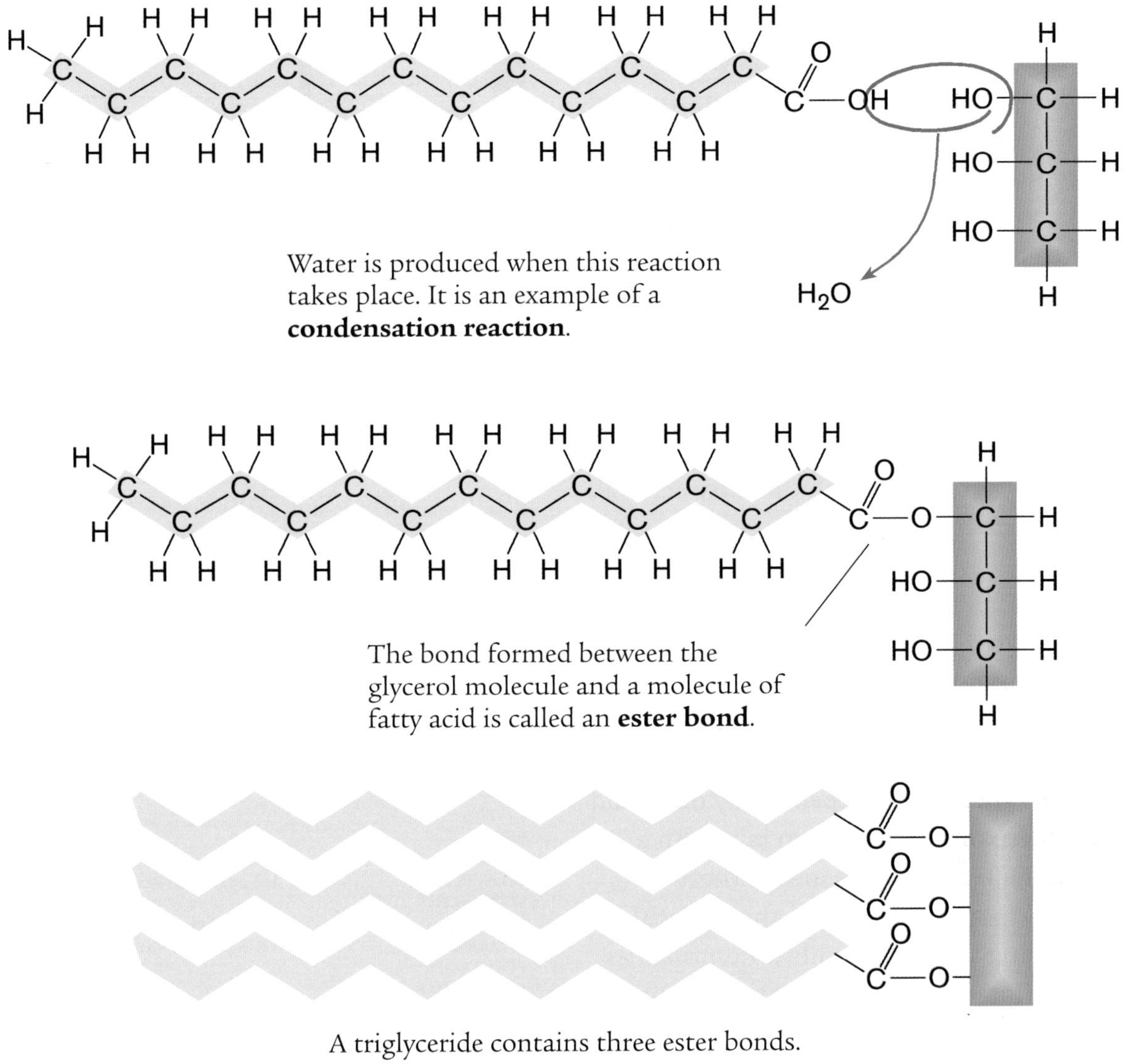

Water is produced when this reaction
takes place. It is an example of a
condensation reaction.

H_2O

The bond formed between the
glycerol molecule and a molecule of
fatty acid is called an **ester bond**.

A triglyceride contains three ester bonds.

Fig 6.3 How a triglyceride lipid is formed from glycerol and three fatty acids.

SAQ

6.1 The formation of a triglyceride from
glycerol and fatty acids is an example of a
condensation reaction.

a What is meant by the term 'condensation
reaction'?

b Give two other examples of condensation
reactions which happen in living
organisms.

6.2 A molecular formula shows which kinds of
atoms are present in a substance, and how
many of each atom there are.

a The molecular formula for glucose, which is a
carbohydrate, is $C_6H_{12}O_6$. What does this tell
you about the atoms in one glucose
molecule?

b Use Fig 6.3 to help you to work out the
molecular formula of a triglyceride. Assume
that all three of the fatty acids are identical
with the one shown in the diagram.

c How do the proportions of carbon, hydrogen
and oxygen in a triglyceride differ from their
proportions in a carbohydrate such as glucose?

107

Saturated and unsaturated triglycerides

You will probably have heard or read about saturated and unsaturated fats. Food manufacturers and retailers often advertise their products as being 'high in polyunsaturated fats'. Many food labels list both the total fat content and the saturated fat content. When the food does contain unsaturated fats, the label usually breaks down the content into mono-unsaturates and polyunsaturates.

In the English language we use the word 'saturated' to describe being thoroughly soaked with water. The meaning when applied to fats is being 'thoroughly soaked' with hydrogen. A **saturated fat** is one in which the fatty acids all contain as much hydrogen as they possibly can. All the carbon–carbon bonds in the fatty acids are single bonds.

An **unsaturated** fat is one in which the fatty acids don't contain as much hydrogen as they can. Two carbons use *two* of their four bonds to join to another carbon atom. This is called a **double bond**. When this happens, only one bond of each of these carbons is free to join with a hydrogen atom (Fig 6.4). This means there is room for *two* more hydrogens in the molecule. A fat containing such fatty acids is described as mono-unsaturated. Unsaturated fats are more easily used by the body.

STEM GINGER COOKIES NUTRITIONAL INFORMATION		
TYPICAL COMPOSITION	Each Cookie (25g) contains	100g provide
Energy	529 kJ	2116 kJ
Protein	1.1 g	4.4 g
Carbohydrate	15.6 g	62.2 g
of which sugars	9.8 g	39.3 g
Fat	6.7 g	26.6 g
of which saturates	3.3 g	13.0 g
mono-unsaturates	2.6 g	10.4 g
polyunsaturates	0.7 g	2.9 g
Fibre	0.9 g	3.7 g
Sodium	trace	trace

59% VEGETABLE FAT SPREAD NUTRITION INFORMATION		
	Per 2 x 10 g Servings	Per 100 g
ENERGY	437 kJ	2183kJ
PROTEIN	Trace	Trace
CARBOHYDRATE	Trace	Trace
OF WHICH SUGARS	Trace	Trace
FAT	11.8 g	59.0 g
OF WHICH SATURATES	2.6 g	13.0 g
MONOUNSATURATES	3.5 g	17.5 g
POLYUNSATURATES	5.6 g	28.0 g
OMEGA 6 FATTY ACIDS	4.9 g	24.5 g
OMEGA 3 FATTY ACIDS	0.7 g	3.5 g
TRANS	0.1 g	0.5 g
FIBRE	0 g	0 g
SODIUM	0.1 g	0.6 g
VITAMIN A	180 μg (23% of RDA)	900 μg (113% of RDA)
VITAMIN D	1.5 μg (30% of RDA)	7.5 g (150% of RDA)
VITAMIN E	7.5 g (75% of RDA)	37.5 g (375% of RDA)
VITAMIN B6	1.0 mg (50% of RDA)	5.0 g (250% of RDA)
FOLIC ACID	200 μg (100% of RDA)	1000 μg (500% of RDA)
VITAMIN B12	1.0 μg (100% of RDA)	5.0 μg (500% of RDA)
		RDA = Recommended Daily Allowance

Fig 6.5 Two food labels.

If there are some fatty acids with more than one double bond in the same fatty acid, then the fat containing it is described as **polyunsaturated**.

Foods from animal sources tend to be high in saturated fats, while those from plant sources tend to be high in unsaturated fats.

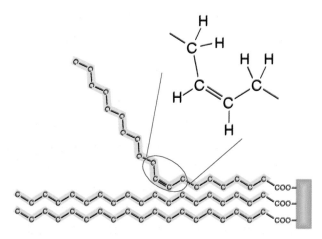

Fig 6.4 An unsaturated fat. Quite often in a plant oil all three fatty acids in one triglyceride molecule will be unsaturated.

SAQ

6.3 One of the food labels in Fig 6.5 lists 'omega fatty acids'. Find out what they are, and why they are listed in some foods.

Statins

In July 2002, the results of the largest ever study into the effects of cholesterol-lowering drugs on the risk of heart attack or stroke were published.

For some years, drugs called **statins** had been available but not widely used, being prescribed only for people who were thought to be at high risk of a heart attack or stroke and who already had high blood cholesterol levels.

The study (1994–1997) involved 20 356 people. They were aged between 40 and 80, and all had some form of cardiovascular disease or diabetes – which is known to increase the risk of CHD. Unusually, women were also included in the trial and also people over the age of 70, as up to then there had been little research on them. 10 269 of the participants were given 40 mg of statin each day, while 10 267 were given placebo tablets. (A placebo looks like a treatment but, unknown to the recipient, contains no active agent.)

The results of the study showed that taking statins reduced the risk of heart attacks and strokes for practically everyone – for older as well as younger people, for women as well as men, for people with fairly low blood cholesterol levels as well as those with high levels and there were no serious side effects. This study, in fact, is unusual in giving such apparently conclusive results in this area.

There are problems when trying to find out what makes a healthy heart. It is impossible to do controlled experiments on people, in the way you would do for laboratory investigations. For example, imagine you wanted to find out the effects of a diet low in saturated fats on the

Table – Results of the statin trial.

Events during study period	Given statin	Given placebo
total number of people dying	1328	1507
number dying from CHD	587	707
number dying from other circulatory diseases	194	230
number suffering a first, non-fatal heart attack	898	1212

incidence of heart disease in mice. You would obtain a group of mice which were as genetically similar as possible, keep them in identical conditions and give them identical quantities of food at identical times. You would make their experiences (such as amount of handling) identical. The only factor you would vary would be the quantity of saturated fats in the diet. But it would be almost impossible to find a large group of humans who are genetically very similar. Even if you did, you cannot successfully impose dietary restrictions on a group of people over a long period of time. So, we cannot control enough variables to be sure that any differences we find amongst people are genuinely due to the differing amounts of saturated fats in their diets and not to some other factors that are not constant.

However, if we use huge numbers of people, we can hope that within each of the two groups the spread of all the uncontrolled variables is about the same, and that any difference we find between the two groups is due to the factor we are studying. The larger the study group, the more likely this will work. Studies on this scale are very expensive. No wonder there is still so much conflicting advice about diet.

Uses of triglycerides in the body

As an energy reserve

Triglycerides are the main form in which energy is stored in the human body. They make good storage substances because their molecules do not dissolve in water. They are **hydrophobic**. This means that the triglyceride molecules tend to clump together inside cells, making as little contact with the watery cytoplasm as possible. They keep out of the way, and take up little space, because they don't absorb water.

Triglycerides also pack in much more energy than carbohydrates do. Each gram of triglyceride can be broken down in respiration to yield 38 kJ. In contrast, one gram of carbohydrate yields only 17 kJ. Fat deposits allow organisms to survive periods of starvation.

As heat insulation

Triglycerides are stored inside the cells which make up **adipose tissue**. The triglycerides are in liquid form, and they may take up as much as 95% of the space inside the cell (Fig 6.6).

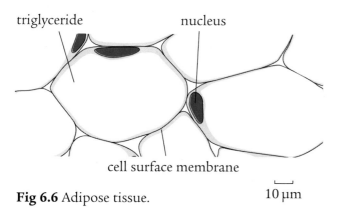

Fig 6.6 Adipose tissue.

10 μm

Much of our adipose tissue lies under the skin. It is a poor conductor of heat, so it reduces heat loss from the skin. When our surroundings are particularly cold, the arterioles supplying blood to the skin capillaries close off, diverting the blood to flow in capillaries beneath the adipose tissue. Animals such as seals and whales, that are adapted to live in very cold environments, often have an especially thick layer of adipose tissue. Substantial fat deposits in humans are probably an adaptation to cope with periods of starvation rather than coping with cold, however.

As a storage site for fat-soluble vitamins

Lipid globules containing triglycerides in the cytoplasm of cells in the liver contain dissolved fat-soluble vitamins, such as vitamins D and A. They act as a store for these vitamins.

Other lipids

Phospholipids

A **phospholipid** molecule is like a triglyceride in which one of the fatty acids is replaced by a phosphate group (Fig 6.7).

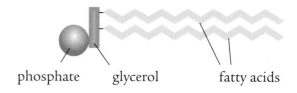

phosphate   glycerol   fatty acids

Fig 6.7 A phospholipid molecule.

Whereas the fatty acids in the phospholipid molecule are hydrophobic, the phosphate group is **hydrophilic**. This is because the phosphate group has a negative electrical charge on it, which is attracted to the tiny positive electrical charge on the hydrogen atoms in a water molecule. This is written as δ+ (delta plus) on the hydrogen atoms (Fig 6.8).

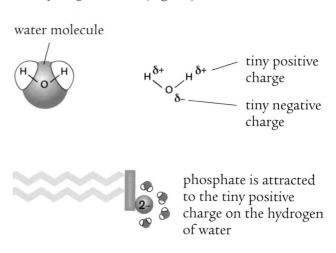

water molecule

tiny positive charge

tiny negative charge

phosphate is attracted to the tiny positive charge on the hydrogen of water

Fig 6.8 Phospholipids and water.

So, when it is in water, the two ends of a phospholipid molecule do different things. The phosphate associates with the water molecules and dissolves in them. The fatty acids are repelled by the water molecules and avoid them. In water they can arrange themselves in a sheet (Fig 6.9). This is called a **bilayer**. You should recognise it as the basic structure of a cell membrane. Phospholipids are therefore one of the most important types of molecules in a cell. Without them, there could be no cell surface membrane and the cell would simply cease to exist.

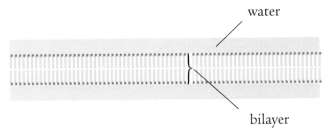

Fig 6.9 Phospholipid bilayer.

Cholesterol and steroids

The structure of a molecule of cholesterol is shown in Fig 6.10. Some people classify cholesterol as a lipid, whereas others do not. Here, we will follow the line that cholesterol is not a lipid itself, but that many lipids are synthesised from it. These lipids, and cholesterol itself, are called **steroids**.

There is a huge number of different kinds of steroids in the body. Many of them are hormones – for example, testosterone and oestrogen. Cholesterol itself is a major component of cell membranes (see page 28), where it helps to regulate the fluidity of the membrane.

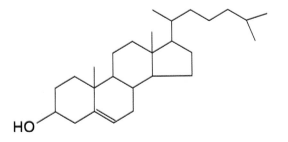

Fig 6.10 A cholesterol molecule.

Transport of lipids in the body

We have seen that lipids are not soluble in water, because their molecules are hydrophobic. This creates a problem in transporting them around the body. Most molecules which need to be transported – for example, glucose, amino acids and oxygen – are soluble in water and can simply dissolve in the blood plasma. But lipids won't do this.

Triglycerides in adipose tissue can be broken down to fatty acids and glycerol for transport. Glycerol is water soluble, so it can just be carried as it is in the blood plasma. The fatty acids tend to combine with plasma proteins such as albumin and are carried like that.

However, most lipids are transported in the blood in **lipoproteins** (Fig 6.11). These are minute balls made up of various lipid molecules and protein molecules. Triglycerides, phospholipids and cholesterol are all transported in these structures.

Lipoproteins come in several varieties, with different proportions of protein molecules, lipid molecules and cholesterol molecules. Proteins tend to be denser than lipids and cholesterol, so the more protein there is the greater the density. The lipoproteins are named according to their densities and where they are formed.

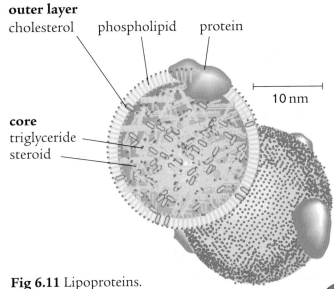

Fig 6.11 Lipoproteins.

Table 6.1 Lipoproteins.

High density lipoproteins (HDLs)	a lot of protein and relatively small amounts of triglyceride and cholesterol
Low density lipoproteins (LDLs)	more triglyceride and cholesterol but less protein than HDLs
Chylomicrons	formed by the ileum wall, contain a lot of triglyceride, some cholesterol and very little protein

HDLs usually pick up cholesterol from body cells that are dying, or whose membranes are being restructured, and transport it to the liver.

LDLs usually carry lipids and cholesterol from the liver to other tissues in the body.

Chylomicrons are formed in the wall of the ileum from fats which have been digested and absorbed. They transport lipids from the small intestine to the liver.

Cholesterol and CHD

Low density lipoproteins have a tendency to deposit the cholesterol which they carry in the damaged walls of arteries. This cholesterol makes up a large proportion of an atheromatous plaque (see page 74). There is a positive link between the amount of LDLs in your blood and the risk of suffering from CHD and possibly a heart attack.

HDLs, on the other hand, seem actually to protect against CHD. They remove cholesterol from tissues, including the tissues in blood vessel walls.

In the past, health professionals were simply concerned about the quantity of cholesterol in the blood. Now attention has shifted to the relative proportions of 'good' HDLs and 'bad' LDLs. The higher this proportion, the lower the risk of heart disease.

So how can we increase our HDL : LDL ratio? Diet does have some effect in some people. A diet that is very rich in saturated fats may result in a high LDL concentration. If you eat that sort of diet you may reduce your LDL levels by switching to a diet that is low in saturated fats. This would probably involve reducing the amount of meat and dairy products that you eat, and increasing the amount of plant-derived foods and marine fish. Whereas the results of many studies into the effect of diet on the risk of CHD seem to contradict each other, almost all studies show a definite beneficial link between eating fish and protection against CHD.

Although an atheromatous plaque contains a lot of cholesterol, in most people the amount of cholesterol in the diet is not directly linked to the development of atherosclerosis. This is because the cholesterol in our blood is not only derived directly from what we eat, but also from the liver itself. The liver actually makes cholesterol, because we need it to make cell membranes and steroids. So, if we eat less cholesterol, the liver tends to increase its cholesterol production. And, if we eat more cholesterol, then the liver reduces its production. Various studies suggest that the greatest effect a 'better' diet can have on LDLs is to reduce them on average by around 10%.

A much more effective way of reducing LDLs is to use drugs called **statins**. These have been around for some years now, mainly prescribed to people with high blood cholesterol levels and other high risk factors for developing heart disease. Statins inhibit an enzyme in liver cells which catalyses one of the reactions involved in the synthesis of cholesterol.

SAQ

6.4 Explain why taking statins can have a greater effect on blood cholesterol levels than changing your diet.

6.5a Explain why lipids cannot be transported dissolved in blood plasma.

b Using Fig 6.11, explain how the structure of lipoproteins enables them to be transported in blood plasma.

Summary

1 Fats belong to a class of substances known as lipids.

2 Triglycerides are a type of lipid. A triglyceride molecule is made up of a glycerol molecule to which three fatty acids are attached. The bonds holding the glycerol and fatty acids together are called ester bonds.

3 A fat is said to be saturated if all of its fatty acids contain as much hydrogen as is possible. A triglyceride is unsaturated if there is room for more hydrogen in the fatty acids. If this is due to one double bond in a fatty acid, then the fat made from it is said to be mono-unsaturated. If there are more double bonds in the fatty acids, the fat is said to be polyunsaturated.

4 Triglycerides are the main form of energy storage in the body. They contain 38 kJ per gram, whereas carbohydrates contain only 17 kJ per gram.

5 Triglycerides are stored in liquid form inside vacuoles in cells which make up adipose tissue. Adipose tissue also helps to provide heat insulation, greatly reducing the rate at which heat is lost from the skin.

6 Phospholipids, like triglycerides, have a backbone of glycerol. However, they contain only two fatty acids, the remaining −OH group being used to bind to a phosphate group. The phosphate group is hydrophilic and the fatty acids hydrophobic, which explains the way in which phospholipids orientate themselves into a bilayer to form membranes.

7 Cholesterol is a lipid-like substance which can be converted into lipids, including steroids such as oestrogen and testosterone, in the body. Cholesterol is also an important component of cell membranes.

8 Because lipids are insoluble in water, they are transported in the blood as lipoproteins. Lipoproteins with a large proportion of protein are relatively dense and are known as HDLs. Lipoproteins with a large proportion of lipid are relatively less dense and are known as LDLs. Chylomicrons, containing a very high proportion of lipid, are formed in the intestine from the fats we have eaten, from where they are carried to the liver.

9 There is a tendency for cholesterol to be deposited in damaged artery walls, where it makes a large contribution to the formation of atheromatous plaques.

10 LDLs tend to increase the deposition of cholesterol, whilst HDLs decrease it. Thus having a high HDL : LDL ratio reduces the risk of developing CHD.

11 Reducing the intake of saturated fats in the diet can help to increase the HDL : LDL ratio. However, it is difficult for diet to have much effect on the overall concentration of cholesterol, because the liver responds to a drop in cholesterol concentration by making more of it. Drugs called statins, on the other hand, can bring about large reductions in LDLs, and a greatly reduced risk of CHD.

Other risk factors for coronary heart disease

Is there a health timebomb ticking away for many young people? Will the lifestyles of this generation increase the risk of heart disease and other illnesses in later life? It is being predicted that, after more than a century during which life expectancy has been steadily rising, it may begin to fall in the next generation due to poor diet and the low level of exercise being taken by many.

In the past, young people tended to play outside, walk to school and take part in sports, but now much more time is spent indoors watching television or using computers. Twenty years ago, 80% cycled or walked to school. Now only 5% do.

There has been a huge rise in the consumption of fast foods. If they form the main part of a diet they can be damaging to health. Such foods – for example, beefburgers, pizzas and soups – often contain large quantities of salt. They contribute about 75% of the salt in people's diets. The Food Standards Agency and the Department of Health are targeting a reduction in people's salt intake by about 1 g per day by 2006. More than one third of adults suffer from high blood pressure, which is linked to a high salt intake and contributes to about 100 000 deaths per year. A high salt intake when you are young may increase the risk of high blood pressure developing later in life.

High levels of sugar and fats in food are another problem. Fast foods 'trick' the body into eating too much of them. They tend to be very high in energy content, but our bodies don't 'know' this – so we eat as much of them as we would eat of a low-energy food. A beefburger has an amazing energy content of 1200 kJ per 100 g, whereas the average energy content of the British diet is about 650 kJ per 100 g. We probably evolved to cope with a diet containing about 450 kJ per 100 g.

In 2003, 8.5% of six-year-olds and 18% of 15-year-olds were obese. Type 2 diabetes, which has a strong link with obesity, is being increasingly diagnosed in teenagers. Government health agencies say that watching television for two hours a day increases the likelihood of obesity by 25%, and that a third of all cases of obesity could be prevented by taking a 30 minute brisk walk each day.

So far in this chapter, we have concentrated very much on how lipids and cholesterol can affect the risk of suffering from CHD. But these are by no means the only factors involved. They are focused on at least partly because, unlike most risk factors, they are under our control – we can actually do something about them by changing our lifestyle. There are other lifestyle factors which we can also control, as well as many factors which we cannot, such as our age, sex and genes.

Salt intake, hypertension and CHD

In Chapter 5, we saw that a young person's blood pressure should normally be about 120 mm Hg during systole (when the heart is contracting) and 80 mm Hg during diastole. If a person's resting blood pressure is persistently high, they are said to have **hypertension**. (A value above 140/90 for an adult is commonly quoted, but opinions vary. See page 102.)

Hypertension increases the risk of CHD. It results in a thickening and hardening of the walls of larger arteries. This increases the risk of damage to the inner lining of the wall, followed by the development of atheromatous plaques in the wall and eventually the possibility of a heart attack (see page 74). It also means that the heart is having to cope with more blood flowing through it at higher pressures, increasing the workload on the heart, and making heart failure more likely.

In most cases, the cause of high blood pressure cannot be pinned down. A diet high in salt can sometimes be part of the problem (Fig 6.12). A high salt concentration in the blood draws water into it by osmosis, thus increasing the blood volume and therefore the blood pressure. The kidneys should react to this situation by excreting more liquid with more salt in it, but they do not always do this.

People with chronic (long-term) hypertension will often be told to eat a low-salt diet. They may also be given **diuretics** ('water pills') which make the kidneys excrete large amounts of fluid. This reduces the volume of fluid in the body, and so reduces blood pressure.

Age

The risk of CHD increases with age. This is largely because of wear and tear on the arteries over time and their gradual hardening. Moreover, a person's blood pressure tends to increase as they get older.

Smoking

Smoking increases the development of atherosclerosis, and also increases the risk of a

Fig 6.12 Many processed foods, like the ones shown here, contain added salt. You may have more salt in your diet than you need if you eat large amounts of such foods.

thrombus or embolus (blood clot) forming. For a smoker, stopping smoking is the lifestyle change which will have the single biggest effect on his or her risk of CHD. People with hypertension (high blood pressure) who smoke have a 3–5 times greater risk of dying from a heart attack than non-smokers.

Diabetes

Diabetes is a condition in which the body is unable to regulate the concentration of glucose in the blood. Normally, when blood glucose levels rise too high, the pancreas secretes **insulin**. The insulin is carried in the blood to liver and muscle cells, where it slots into insulin receptors on the cell surface membranes and brings about a chain of events resulting in glucose being taken up by the cells and therefore removed from the blood.

In diabetes, either the pancreas stops secreting insulin when it should, or the liver and muscle cells stop responding to it. Either way, it means that blood glucose levels may soar

> **SAQ**
>
> 6.6 Use the internet to find the recommended daily salt intake for a person of your age and gender. Use the internet and food labels to find the total salt content of the food you eat in a typical day. How do they compare?

out of control or drop well below normal. For reasons which are still not completely understood, this has a significant effect on the risk of developing CHD.

One type of diabetes, often known as insulin-dependent diabetes, normally begins very early in life. In this form of the disease, the body's own immune system attacks the insulin-secreting cells in the pancreas and stops them from working. At present, there is nothing that a person can do to stop this disease from occurring.

The second type of diabetes, however – sometimes known as type 2 diabetes – does seem to be very dependent on lifestyle. It tends to occur in obese people who take little exercise and eat high-sugar diets. With the increase in sedentary lifestyles in the UK, this disease is becoming more and more common. In the past, it normally only developed in people approaching or past middle age, but it is now beginning to appear in worryingly large numbers of school children. Thus, unless this trend can be reversed, we may expect to see increasing numbers of people suffering from CHD which is linked to diabetes as we move forward through the twenty-first century.

Familial hypercholesterolemia

A small number of people have genes which have such a strong effect on their cholesterol levels that, without treatment, they are likely to die before the age of 20. This genetic disease is known as familial hypercholesterolemia.

The problem is a faulty gene which codes for a cell membrane receptor to which LDLs dock before unloading their cargo of cholesterol.

LDLs' role is to transport cholesterol to body cells, such as those in adipose tissue and cells using it to make steroids or new membrane. LDLs can bind to a receptor glycoprotein that is found in the cell surface membranes of the cells. Only then can their content of cholesterol be taken up by the cell, so cholesterol goes only where it is wanted. If a cell has enough cholesterol, it does not make the LDL receptors and won't take any more.

In familial hypercholesterolemia, body cells do not have the right DNA code for this glycoprotein, so they don't have any LDL receptors. The LDLs are still made as usual, but they just accumulate in the blood, producing exceptionally low HDL : LDL ratios and very high blood cholesterol levels. Because the LDLs cannot bind with the cell surface membranes of liver cells, the liver cells do not 'know' that they are there. So the liver goes on and on making cholesterol.

People who have two copies of the faulty allele of the gene (that is, they are homozygous for it) may have enormous cholesterol levels of as much as 800 mg cm^{-3} – around 4 to 6 times normal. Heterozygotes (that is, people with one normal allele and one faulty one) are less badly affected, and usually have blood cholesterol levels within the range of 300 to 400 mg cm^{-3}. Until quite recently, almost all homozygotes died of myocardial infarction or some other kind of disease of the cardiovascular system before the age of 20. Today, however, statins can greatly reduce this risk.

6.7 The chart below is used to work out how likely a person is to have a cardiovascular event (heart attack or a stroke).

a Use the chart to find the predicted risk for:
- a 56-year-old woman who smokes, whose blood pressure reading is 160/95 and whose total cholesterol : HDL-cholesterol ratio is 5;
- a 45-year-old man who does not smoke, whose blood pressure reading is 160/95 and whose total cholesterol : HDL-cholesterol ratio is 8.

b What could each of these people do to reduce their risk of having a cardiovascular event?

c Suggest how a risk calculator like this could be produced. If possible, use the internet to find out if you are correct. (You may find it helpful to include the word 'Framingham' in your search.)

d In late 2002, it was reported in the press that the risk calculator used in the UK significantly over-estimated risk. For example, out of a sample of 270 men whom the calculator predicted would die within ten years, only 183 had died. And whereas the calculator predicted that 1062 would suffer from a cardiovascular event, only 677 did so. Moreover, of these 677 events, only 106 occurred to men who were in the highest risk group.

What might explain this discrepancy? What effects do you think it might have on people's health?

Table for calculating risk of cardiovascular event, as used in some countries

Notes:

1 'ratio total chol:HDL-chol' is the ratio of the total amount of cholesterol in the blood to the total amount of cholesterol transported in high density lipoprotein in the blood.

2 A 'cardiovascular event' in this table is referring to newly diagnosed angina, myocardial infarction, death from CHD, stroke.

Risk – 5 yr cardiovascular fatal + non-fatal events			Events prevented per 100 treated for 5 yrs
very high		>30%	>10
		25–30%	9
		20–25%	7.5
high/moderate		15–20%	6
		10–15%	4
mild		5–10%	2.5
		2.5–5%	1.25
		<2.5%	<0.8

Gender

On average, women have less risk of developing CHD than men. This is because the hormone oestrogen somehow protects against this disease. After the menopause, when oestrogen is no longer secreted within the menstrual cycle, this protective effect is lost.

It is thought that women's lower risk of CHD may also be linked to their different lifestyles. Up until the 1940s, relatively few women went out to work. During the Second World War, many women took up work to help to keep the country going while the men were fighting. Since then, increasing numbers of women are working full-time. At the same time, there appears to be an increase in the numbers of women with CHD, and these numbers are gradually becoming more similar to those for men. There is speculation that, as women's lifestyles become more like men's lifestyles, with similar stress levels, perhaps women's risk of CHD will also gradually come to be similar to that for men.

Stress

CHD is more common in people who lead stressful lives, especially when the stress is of a kind that cannot be resolved by activity. However, this risk factor is extremely difficult to study.

Protective foods

Apart from lipids from fish mentioned earlier, there are other foods that appear to protect the body against CHD. Many of these contain antioxidants, such as carotene, vitamin C and vitamin E. Fresh fruit and vegetables are good sources of many antioxidants (Fig 6.13).

Fig 6.13 Some foods rich in antioxidants. All fruit, vegetables and salad leaves are rich in antioxidants, but also some processed foods made from them, such as the tinned tomatoes shown here. Also pictured is a packet of green tea (tea which has not been allowed to ferment when it was manufactured) is also rich in antioxidants.

Summary

1. A person's genes can affect their risk of developing CHD.

2. The risk of developing CHD increases with age, and is higher for men than for women.

3. Lifestyle factors, such as diet, smoking and stress levels, can have a large influence on the risk of developing CHD.

4. High salt intake increases the risk of hypertension, and therefore of CHD.

5. High sugar and fat intake, particularly if little exercise is taken, may cause obesity. This in turn may cause hypertension, increases the risk of developing type 2 diabetes, and therefore the risk of CHD.

CHAPTER 7

The lungs

The emergency call went through to the police at 1400 hours. A resident of an apartment block reported seeing a man outside running and shouting, swinging something that looked like an iron bar or perhaps a baseball bat. The caller thought he looked 'out of his mind'. Two men who lived in the flats were trying to calm him down.

An ambulance crew who happened to be parked at a supermarket in the same area of the city overheard the radio messages dispatching police to the scene. Without waiting to be officially asked to attend, they moved quickly, arriving there within four minutes of hearing the call, before the police.

The two paramedics had had experiences like this before and were half expecting what they saw. Two men were holding another on the ground. He was lying prone (on his stomach) with his hands held behind his back, and did not seem to be moving. One of the men had a knee in his back to hold him down.

The paramedics leapt from their vehicle, shouting 'Get off his back! Get off his back!' as they ran towards the group. 'Roll him on his side!' they yelled. As they reached the prone captive, they pushed the two men away from him, holding his arms tightly in case he struggled and rolling him onto his side. There was no sign or sound of breathing or any other movement. With the help of his two captors, the man was placed on a stretcher, supine (lying on his back), and rushed into the ambulance. By the time it reached the A and E department of the hospital, the paramedics had got the patient breathing again. It had been a near thing – another minute or so and the patient could have become another statistic of death caused by restraint asphyxia.

Ventilating the lungs

Positional asphyxia, sometimes known as restraint asphyxia if it results from a person being forcibly held down, has caused a number of deaths. It happens when a person is forced into a position which stops their chest from moving out, and their diaphragm from moving down, so that they cannot breathe. It was positional asphyxia which killed most of the 96 people who died in April 1989 as they were crushed by the crowd at Hillsborough, the Liverpool football ground.

The risk of dying from positional asphyxia is increased if the person has a 'beer belly', because their internal organs are pressed in against their diaphragm as they are forced to lie on their front. It is especially dangerous when the person has been in an 'out of control' mental state, causing them to behave so wildly that they almost completely exhaust themselves. Police are trained in how to safely restrain someone showing what is known as 'acute behavioural disturbance' without inhibiting their breathing movements.

Death from positional asphyxia occurs because the blood flowing to the body organs does not contain sufficient oxygen. In order for the blood to become well oxygenated in the lungs, it is essential that there is a regular movement of fresh air into them and stale air out. This process is called **ventilation**, and it is caused by **breathing movements**.

Breathing movements

The lungs have no muscles, so cannot move by themselves. Breathing movements are caused by two sets of muscles – the **intercostal muscles** between the ribs, and the **diaphragm muscle** (Fig 7.1).

Contraction of the external intercostal muscles and muscle in the diaphragm increases the volume of the thoracic cavity, lowering its pressure and thus allowing air from outside the body, which is at a higher pressure, to flow down the pressure gradient into the lungs.

As these muscles relax, the contents of the thorax go back to their original volumes. Elastic fibres in the lungs, which were stretched when the thorax expanded, fall back to their usual

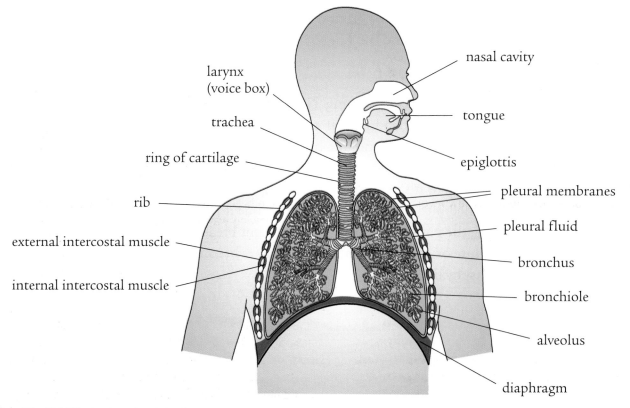

Fig 7.1 The gas exchange system.

length. As the volume of the thorax decreases, the pressure inside the thorax is increased. This causes mass flow of air out of the lungs. Fig 7.2 shows how this happens.

Breathing in

2 Pressure in the thorax falls with the increase in volume caused by rib and diaphragm movements. Air flows in down a pressure gradient.

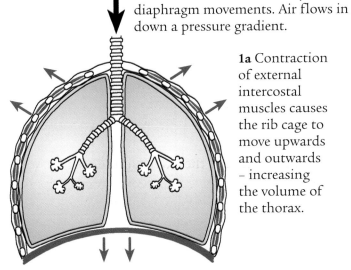

1a Contraction of external intercostal muscles causes the rib cage to move upwards and outwards – increasing the volume of the thorax.

1b Contraction of muscle in the diaphragm pulls the diaphragm lower – increasing the volume of the thorax.

Fig 7.2 Breathing movements.

Relaxed breathing out

Elastic fibres in the spaces between alveoli are stretched when breathing in. When the diaphragm and intercostal muscles relax, the elastic fibres recoil causing the pressure in the thorax to rise. Air flows out of the lungs.

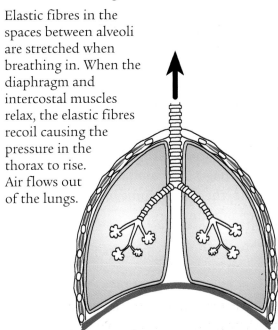

Forced breathing out

Contraction of the internal intercostal muscles causes the rib cage to move downwards and inwards. These decrease the volume of the thorax and increase the pressure of air inside so that it now flows out of the lungs. Diaphragm muscle relaxes. Contraction of the abdominal wall raises pressure in the abdomen and raises the diaphragm.

PROCEDURE 7.1

Expired air resuscitation

Expired air resuscitation is also known as 'rescue breathing' in first aid terminology – see page 77. It can be used to help a person survive **respiratory arrest**. Respiratory arrest is when a person's breathing has stopped or reduced to a very low level. If this is a consequence of cardiac arrest, procedures for cardio-pulmonary resuscitation (CPR) must be applied.

If respiratory arrest is not a consequence of cardiac arrest, it may be due to mechanical obstruction of the airways or puncture of the alveolar cavities as a result of injury.

Respiratory arrest requires specialist help, which must be called as quickly as possible by dialing 999.

Procedure

1 Check if the person can communicate with you.

2 If there is no response, tilt the head back and open the mouth. Remove anything that is obstructing the airway and check for breathing.

3 With the head tilted back give two rescue breaths in the following way. Pinch the soft part of the nose. Take a deep breath and place your lips around the victim's mouth to seal it. Blow steadily to inflate the lungs. Take your mouth off and let the air come out. Repeat as necessary.

Note: For a baby it is difficult to detect breathing movements. To detect breathing movements, put your cheek on the baby's chest and your ear near the baby's mouth. If there is no breathing movement give two rescue breaths and check again. If this is not successful in five attempts, CPR is immediately required.

Lung volumes

The volumes of air which are moved into and out of the lungs during breathing can provide useful information about the health of a person's lungs. These volumes can be measured using a **spirometer** or a **peak flow meter**.

During relaxed breathing, you probably move about 0.5 dm³ of air into and out of your lungs with each breath. This is known as your **tidal volume** (Fig 7.3). If you take 12 breaths per minute, the total volume of air you breathe out in one minute is

$$0.5 \times 12 \ = \ 6 \text{ dm}^3 \text{ per minute.}$$

This is your **ventilation rate**.

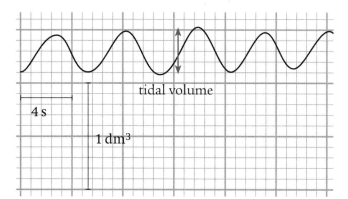

Fig 7.3 Tidal air movements.

However, you should be able to move much more air than this into and out of your lungs when you breathe really hard. If you take the biggest breath out which you can, moving as much air out of your lungs as possible, then the extra air you breathe out is your **expiratory reserve volume** (Fig 7.4). There is always some air left in your lungs, because they never collapse completely, and this air is your **residual volume**.

Similarly, if you follow up your huge breath out with a huge breath in, you should be able to breathe in quite a bit more air than usual. The extra air breathed in is your **inspiratory reserve volume**.

Added together, your expiratory reserve volume, inspiratory reserve volume and tidal volume represent the very greatest volume of air you can move into and out of your lungs in one breath. This is known as your **vital capacity**.

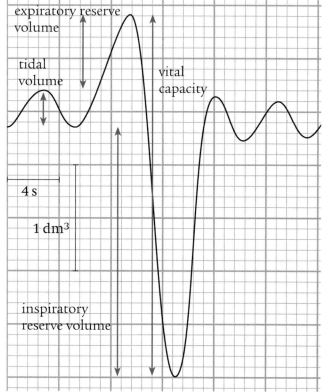

Fig 7.4 Lung volumes.

SAQ

7.1 Calculate the mean tidal volume shown in the graph in Fig 7.3. Then calculate the mean breathing rate and finally use both values to determine the ventilation rate.

122

Using a spirometer

How a spirometer works

In the type of spirometer shown below, a person breathes into and out of an enclosed air chamber. This chamber is formed between the spirometer float and water. A pen records the up and down movement of the float on a kymograph as air in the chamber is rebreathed.

The chamber can be filled with atmospheric air or it can be filled with medical grade oxygen. The spirometer can be used without soda lime for this activity. Alternatively, soda lime can be used to absorb carbon dioxide from expired air. However, the soda lime is only really required if a person rebreathes the air for an extended period or the apparatus is being used to measure the volume of oxgyen being consumed.

> ! Care ! When a spirometer is used without medical oxygen and soda lime, carbon dioxide builds up in the rebreathed air. This will affect the breathing rate and could cause dizziness. Do not rebreath the air for more than a very few breaths.

Procedure for measuring lung volumes

1 Check the water level in the spirometer. Push the float to roughly its middle position and adjust the counter-balance so that the float stays in this position when not in use. Select a slow chart speed. Check that the pen is writing.

2 Take a mouthpiece that has been sterilised and rinsed and attach to the two-way valve.

3 Relax and allow a relaxed breathing pattern to become established.

4 Grip the mouthpiece, open the two-way valve and breath normally into the mouthpiece, then start the kymograph. Check the pen is writing.

   It is best not to look at the kymograph trace whilst recording, as it may affect your pattern of breathing.

5 After a few minutes of relaxed breathing, force all the air out of your lungs, then take a maximum inspiration. This will record your expiratory reserve, inspiratory reserve and vital capacity. Close the two-way valve and release the mouthpiece.

6 Calibrate the chart by introducing a known volume of air into the spirometer and note this on the chart. Repeat this several times on the same chart.

Question

When recording tidal air movements over a period of time, what would be the effect on the appearance of the trace of having soda lime in the apparatus?

A spirometer

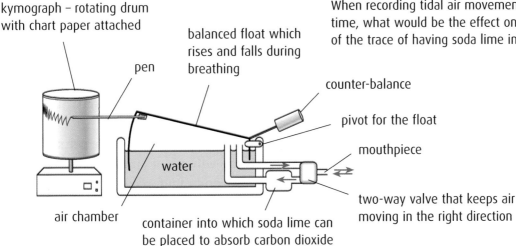

kymograph – rotating drum with chart paper attached

pen

balanced float which rises and falls during breathing

counter-balance

pivot for the float

mouthpiece

water

two-way valve that keeps air moving in the right direction

air chamber

container into which soda lime can be placed to absorb carbon dioxide

7.2a Using the trace in Fig 7.4, what is the expiratory reserve volume, inspiratory reserve volume and vital capacity?

 b Explain why a spirometer cannot help you measure residual volume.

7.3 Using the trace in Fig 7.5, construct a table of time interval between each breath and the tidal volume of each breath. Calculate 'instant' breathing rates* and tidal volumes for each entry. What do these values indicate about the regularity of breathing at rest?

* To calculate instant breathing rate:

Time interval between first two peaks = 3 small squares
                                     = 3 s

So there is 1 breath in 3 s.
This is an instant breathing rate of

$$\frac{1 \times 60}{3} \text{ breaths per minute}$$

= 20 breaths per minute

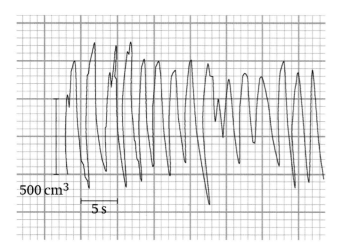

Fig 7.5 Spirometer trace for a student at rest in a standing position. It shows two common features for such a trace – a slow change between deeper and shallower tidal volumes and the occasional and random deep inspiration.

Flow rates

The rate at which air can be expelled during a forced expiration is an effective way of checking for any restriction or resistance in the airways leading from the lungs to the mouth. This can be detected by relatively simple equipment and it is used to diagnose and monitor conditions such as asthma (see pages 135–136).

Two measurements are commonly made. Both give information about airway resistance.

Peak expiratory flow rate (PEFR) is the maximum rate at which air can be forceably expelled from the mouth. It is measured in dm^3 per minute.

The **forced expiratory volume per second (FEV$_1$)** is the volume of air that can be expired in the first second of a forced expiration.

Using a peak flow meter

There are several types of peak flow meter. They can all measure peak expiratory flow rate (PEFR). Some also measure the forced expiratory volume per second (FEV$_1$).

Exercise is a common trigger for asthma. This activity will be able to detect increased airway resistance, which occurs in exercise-induced asthma. However, people suffering severe asthma should not try this activity.

Procedure for measuring PEFR

Note: Instructions will vary, depending on the manufacturer of the meter.

1 Select a clean and sterile mouthpiece and attach it to the peak flow meter. The mouthpiece must be absolutely dry.

2 Stand or sit upright and hold the peak flow meter level, taking care not to obstruct air exit holes.

3 Take as deep a breath in as possible and then close your lips firmly around the mouthpiece.

4 Blow as hard and as fast as you can into the mouthpiece. Think of it as a hard 'huff'.

5 Note the PEFR value. Push the marker back to the lower end of the scale.

6 Repeat the procedure and note the highest value reading amongst the repeats.

7 Take a short period of mild exercise as instructed by your teacher. Take readings at 1-minute intervals after the exercise has stopped. Compare these with your readings before exercise. Asthma-induced airway resistance is noticeable a few minutes after exercise is stopped.

The graphs below show the normal range of values for peak expiratory flow rate (PEFR) for males and females at different ages.

Males of 175 cm height

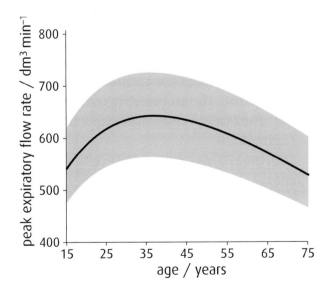

Females of 160 cm height

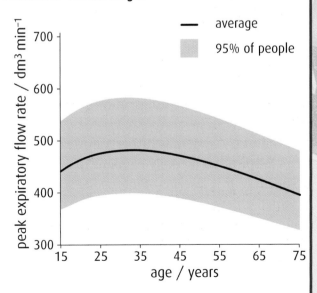

Summary

1. The lungs are ventilated by breathing movements. These are caused by the contraction and relaxation of the muscles between the ribs (intercostal muscles) and in the diaphragm.

2. A spirometer can be used to measure lung volumes. The subject breathes in and out using air contained within the spirometer. As the subject breathes out, the float of the spirometer rises, and it falls as the subject breathes in. A pen connected to the float moves over a rotating chart, recording movements against time.

3. The volume of air breathed in or out with one breath is the tidal volume. The volumes of the extra air which can be breathed in or out with one breath are the inspiratory reserve volume and the expiratory reserve volume. The maximum possible volume of air which can be breathed in or out with one breath is the vital capacity.

4. A peak flow meter can be used to measure peak expiratory flow rate (PEFR). PEFR is the maximum rate at which air can be forceably expelled, in dm^3 per minute.

5. The forced expiratory volume per second (FEV_1) is the volume of air, in dm^3, that can be expired in the first second of a forced expiration.

Structure and function of the respiratory system

The **respiratory system** includes all of the organs which enable oxygen to enter the blood and carbon dioxide to leave it. These organs are the airways leading to the lungs, and the lungs themselves.

'Respiratory' system is rather a misleading term. **Respiration** actually happens in every cell in the body. It is a series of metabolic reactions in which glucose or other substrates are oxidised, releasing energy which can be used by the cells. What happens in the lungs is **gas exchange**, in which gases move between the blood and the air outside the body. So 'gas exchange system' would be a better term to use. However, the term respiratory system is very widely used, as is the term 'artificial respiration' – which should perhaps be called 'artificial breathing'.

Epithelial tissue in the airways

Air flows down towards the lungs through the **trachea** and **bronchi** (Fig 7.1). These tubes are lined by cells which are adapted to remove particles from the air before it reaches the lungs. The layer of cells makes up a **tissue** called an **epithelium**.

A tissue is a group of similar cells with a common origin, which work together to perform a particular function. An epithelium is a tissue which covers the surface of an organ. (Another example of an epithelium is the layer of cells which covers the inside of the stomach and other parts of the alimentary canal.) An **organ**, such as the trachea, a bronchus or a lung, is made up of several different tissues grouped together.

The production of specialised cells from unspecialised ones is dealt with on page 142.

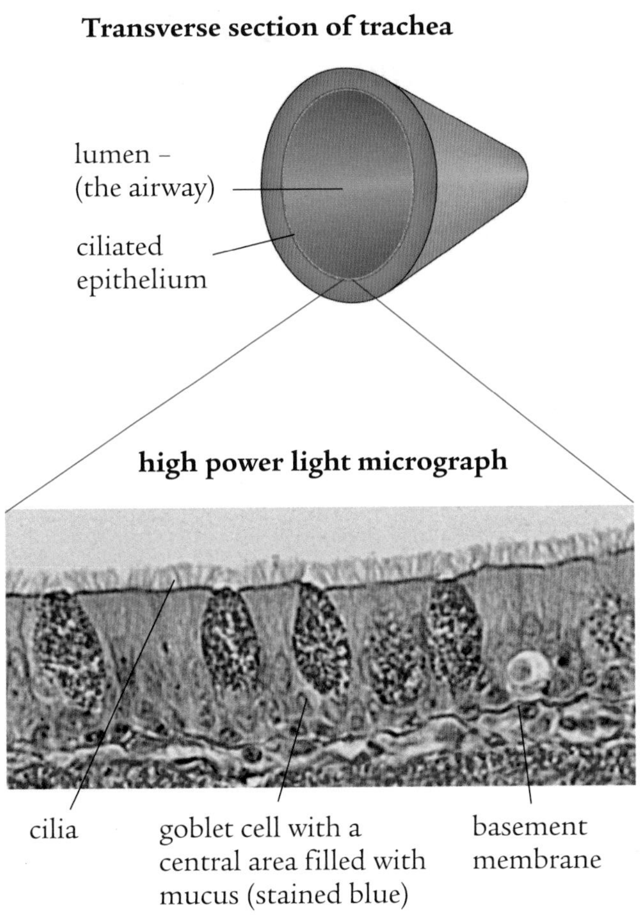

Transverse section of trachea

lumen –
(the airway)

ciliated
epithelium

high power light micrograph

cilia

goblet cell with a
central area filled with
mucus (stained blue)

basement
membrane

Fig 7.6 Ciliated epithelium in the trachea.

The cells making up the epithelial tissue lining the airways are of two main types – **ciliated cells** and **goblet cells** (Fig 7.6). All of these cells sit on a **basement membrane** which contains fibres made from proteins they have secreted. Most of the cells are **ciliated cells**, so the epithelium can be called a ciliated epithelium. Cilia are tiny extensions of the cytoplasm that are found on the free surface of the cells (Figs 7.6 and 7.7). Each cilium is about 3–4 μm long, and there are many of them on each cell. Each cilium contains microtubules which can slide past each other, causing the cilium to bend.

In between the ciliated cells there are numerous **goblet cells**. These get their name from their shape. Their function is to make and secrete **mucus**. Mucus contains glycoproteins, whose molecules contain very long chains of sugar molecules, which makes mucus so slimy and sticky. Mucus forms a complete protective covering over the epithelium.

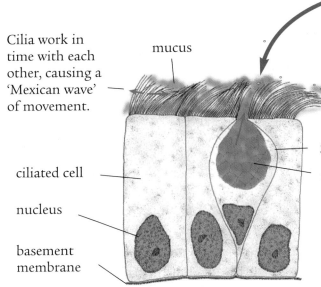

Cilia work in time with each other, causing a 'Mexican wave' of movement.

mucus

Particles in the air being breathed in – sand, dust, bacteria or pollen grains – are trapped in the sheet of mucus, so they don't reach the lungs.

The cilia sweep the mucus upwards to the back of the throat at about 1 cm per minute. Here the mucus is swallowed.

goblet cell

mucus

ciliated cell

nucleus

basement
membrane

Fig 7.7 How the ciliated epithelium in the trachea and bronchi helps to keep the lungs clean.

SAQ

7.4 Ciliated cells have more mitochondria than most human cells, while goblet cells contain a lot of rough endoplasmic reticulum and Golgi apparatus.
Explain how these features relate to the functions of each of these types of cells.

127

The structure of the epithelia in the airways

1 Place a slide of a transverse section through a trachea or bronchus onto the stage of a microscope, and focus on it using the low power objective lens. Move the slide around until you find a part where the inner lining – the epithelium – looks clear. Leave the slide in a position where the epithelium is over the hole in the centre of the microscope stage.

2 Change to the ×40 high power objective lens, and focus on the epithelium once more (then oil immersion objective if available). Look for goblet cells and ciliated cells. The epithelium may look like the micrograph in Fig 7.6, though it could be stained using different colours.

3 Using the micrograph in Fig 7.6 and the diagram in Fig 7.7 to help you to identify what you can see, make your own diagram of part of the epithelium. Do not copy the micrograph, or draw what you think you *ought* to be able to see. Do not include any cells other than those that form the epithelium. Draw each cell larger than it appears in the image and do not draw more than about eight cells at the most.

4 Label your diagram as fully as possible, and include annotations explaining how the structures you have drawn help the epithelium to carry out its functions.

The gas exchange surface

If you were able to crawl down into one of the lungs through a bronchus, you would find that the passageway kept dividing, each tunnel becoming smaller than the previous one. You would wriggle through the ever-narrowing **bronchioles**, and eventually end up inside a roughly spherical space at which you could go no further. These spaces are called **alveoli**, and this is where gas exchange takes place. Each alveolus is only about 100 μm in diameter. There are millions of them in your lungs. It has been estimated that the total surface area of all the alveoli in a person's lungs is around 70 m².

Table 7.1 Characteristics of gas exchange membranes.

Thin
Large surface area
Permeable to the substances diffusing across
Movement of fluids on one or both sides, which maintains the concentration gradient across the membrane

The wall of an alveolus is made up of very thin, flat cells which form a **squamous epithelium**. The cells are arranged tightly together forming a continuous surface. Each cell is no more than 5 μm thick.

Wrapped around the outer surface of each alveolus are numerous blood capillaries. They make close contact with the alveoli. As we have already seen (see page 96), the wall of a capillary is made up of a single layer of thin cells. So in the depths of the lungs there are millions of thin-walled, air-filled alveoli separated from blood-filled capillaries by two layers of exceptionally thin cells.

These thin walls allow gases to diffuse through very rapidly. The blood brought to the lungs has come from the right side of the heart, and is deoxygenated. The air inside the alveoli has a higher concentration of oxygen than there is in the blood. Oxygen molecules therefore move by diffusion, down a concentration gradient, through the two layers of thin cells which separate them from the blood. Carbon dioxide molecules diffuse in the other direction.

The structure of lung tissue

1 Place a slide of a section through lung tissue onto the microscope stage, and focus using low power.

2 Still on low power, identify: air spaces; thin walls of alveoli; blood vessels. Try to find an artery and a vein. (Look back to pages 95–98 if you have forgotten how to tell the difference between them.)

3 Make a drawing of a small part of the lung tissue that you can see. Label and annotate it.

4 Move the slide around until you can see an area where the walls of the alveoli look clear. Change the objective lens first to medium power, then – when you are sure you have found a good area – to high power (and oil immersion, if available). Try to find and identify: air space; squamous epithelial cells lining the alveolus; blood capillary containing blood cells; connective tissue between the alveoli, containing elastic fibres. You may also be able to see white blood cells (macrophages), which patrol the air spaces in the lungs.

5 Make a drawing of what you can see. Label it, and annotate it to describe the functions of each part.

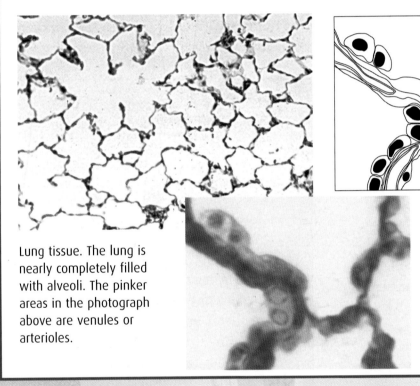

Lung tissue. The lung is nearly completely filled with alveoli. The pinker areas in the photograph above are venules or arterioles.

alveolar air space

macrophage

epithelial cell forming alveolar wall

blood capillary

Using the highest power objective for the light microscope it is still not possible to clearly see the two thin alveolar cells and blood capillaries between them. This is because they are all so thin and we are at the limit of resolution of the microscope. However, an interpretation is shown in the drawing above.

7.5a How many cell surface membranes does an oxygen molecule pass through as it moves from the air space inside an alveolus and into a red blood cell?

 b Explain how the oxygen molecule moves through one of these membranes.

 c Describe what happens to the oxygen molecule inside a red blood cell.

7.6a Breathing movements ventilate the lungs. Explain how this helps to maintain a concentration gradient for oxygen between the alveolus and the blood.

 b What other process helps to maintain this diffusion gradient?

Surface-area-to-volume ratio

Cells and organisms have problems of scale to solve if they get bigger. As an object gets bigger, both its surface and its volume increase. However, its surface area does not increase as much as the volume. This can cause problems with the exchange of substances with the surroundings.

Imagine a very small body cell only 3 μm across. Assume it is in the shape of a cube to make the calculation easier.

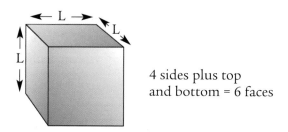

4 sides plus top
and bottom = 6 faces

Surface area of a cube	=	L × L × 6
SA of a 3 μm cell	=	3 × 3 × 6
	=	54 μm²
Volume of a cube	=	L × L × L
Vol of a 3 μm cell	=	3 × 3 × 3
	=	27 μm³

Now imagine a typical liver cell 20 μm across, which is about average for a body cell.

SA of a 'cubic' liver cell	=	20 × 20 × 6
	=	2400 μm²
Vol of a 'cubic' liver cell	=	20 × 20 × 20
	=	8000 μm³

If you divide the surface area by the volume, the difference between the two cells becomes obvious.

SA of a 3 μm cell	=	54 μm²
Vol of a 3 μm cell	=	27 μm³
SA divided by Vol	=	2
Ratio	=	2 : 1

SA of a 20 μm cell	=	2400 μm²
Vol of a 20 μm cell	=	8000 μm³
SA divided by Vol	=	0.3
Ratio	=	0.3 : 1

Surface area divided by volume is the **surface-area-to-volume ratio**. This is much smaller for the larger cell. The bigger cell has far less surface area to serve each unit of volume inside.

Surface-area-to-volume ratio partly explains why humans have to have lungs. Try working through SAQ 7.8 below.

SAQ

7.7 Calculate the surface-area-to-volume ratio for a large body cell, such as an egg cell, which is 100 μm across. Assume it has the shape of a cube.

7.8a The volume of an earthworm is about 0.005 dm³. The surface area of its skin is about 0.0004 m². Calculate the surface-area-to-volume ratio of an earthworm.

 b The volume of a person's body is about 68 dm³. The surface area of the skin is about 1.8 m². Calculate the surface-area-to-volume ratio of a person.

 c The surface area of the alveoli in the lungs is about 70 m². What is the ratio of the area of gas exchange surface to the volume of the human body?

 d Use your answers to a, b and c to explain why earthworms can use their skin for gas exchange, whereas humans cannot.

Surfactant in the lungs

The inner surface of the alveoli is kept moist. This prevents the squamous cells from drying out. The moisture is secreted by the cells themselves.

When you breathe out, the volume of the lungs, and therefore of the alveoli, decreases. As the alveoli deflate, their inner surfaces may actually touch each other. The surface tension of the liquid on their wet surfaces could easily make them stick together, making it almost impossible to inflate them again. To avoid this, the fluid which the cells secrete contains a **surfactant**. Surfactants are like detergents. They reduce the surface tension, stopping the alveoli from sticking together and allowing the lungs to deflate and reinflate with ease.

Respiratory distress syndrome

While a baby is still in the uterus, it does not use its lungs for breathing. Oxygen is supplied to its body through the umbilical cord, which contains two veins bringing oxygen from the placenta, where oxygen from the mother's blood diffuses into the baby's blood.

As the baby's lungs are not yet being used, there is no need for surfactant to be secreted, so this does not happen until fairly late in the pregnancy. If a baby is born very prematurely, then its lungs may not be producing enough surfactant to stop the alveoli from sticking together. In this situation, the newborn baby may be unable to inflate its lungs when it tries to breathe. This condition is called respiratory distress syndrome of the newborn, often shortened to RDS. The more premature the baby, the greater the chance of RDS.

In a special care baby unit at a hospital, a baby with RDS will quickly be provided with extra oxygen, usually by placing a hood over the head and feeding oxygen-rich air into the hood. Alternatively, oxygen can be fed through tubes leading down towards the lungs. This allows the oxygen to be delivered under pressure, which may help to force the alveoli open.

The baby's breathing muscles need to work very hard to make the lungs inflate, and they may not be able to do so without help. If this is the case, the baby will be placed inside a machine which helps it to breathe. The machine rhythmically increases and decreases the air pressure around the baby's thorax, creating pressure gradients between the external air and the air inside the lungs, which causes air to move into and out of the lungs. The baby may also be given surfactant through a tube leading down into its lungs.

All of this is very frightening for new parents to see happening to their baby. What is more, the RDS is likely to get worse before it gets better. A relatively mild case may mean that the baby can breathe on its own after less than a week, but sometimes it takes weeks before it can be taken off oxygen and out of the breathing machine. However, unless there are other problems or complications, there is a very good chance that the baby will recover fully.

Summary

1. Humans, being relatively large organisms, have a low surface-area-to-volume ratio. They therefore need a specialised gas exchange surface to provide enough surface area to obtain sufficient oxygen.

2. The airways leading down into the lungs are lined with a ciliated epithelium. This is a tissue made up of ciliated cells and goblet cells.

3. Goblet cells secrete mucus, which traps dust, bacteria and other particles present in air as it is breathed in. Cilia sweep the mucus up and away from the lungs.

4. The gas exchange surface is the alveoli. Their walls are made of squamous epithelium, a tissue made of very flattened cells which fit closely together. The total surface area of the alveoli is very large, and only two layers of very thin cells separate the air inside them from the blood in the capillaries which wrap around them.

5. The thin film of fluid on the inner surface of the alveoli contains surfactant. This acts like a detergent, reducing the surface tension of the fluid and therefore preventing the surfaces from sticking together.

6. Elastic fibres in the tissue between the alveoli enable the lungs to inflate and deflate. When the breathing muscles are relaxed, the stretched elastic fibres recoil to their usual length, helping the lungs to deflate so that air is expired.

Preventing lung disease

Lung diseases are a major cause of illness and death in modern society. Lung diseases include:

chronic obstructive pulmonary disease (COPD), which includes many related diseases, such as emphysema, which prevent the normal flow of air through the respiratory system;

asthma, which is thought to be caused by problems with the way the immune system develops early in life;

lung cancer, where cells in the lungs divide uncontrollably and form a malignant tumour;

illnesses caused by infectious organisms (pathogens) such as influenza, SARS (sudden acute respiratory syndrome) and tuberculosis.

Some of these diseases, such as SARS, happen quickly and last a relatively short time. These are known as **acute** illnesses. Others, such as COPD, last over a long period of time – the sufferer has to learn to live with them. These are known as **chronic** illnesses.

As we will see, there is a great deal that a person can do to lessen their risk of suffering from at least some of these diseases, because they are very much affected by lifestyle.

Chronic obstructive pulmonary disease

Chronic obstructive pulmonary disease, usually shortened to **COPD**, is an illness in which the airflow into and out of the lungs gradually and progressively becomes more and more obstructed. COPD happens in everyone to a certain extent as they get older, but it is hugely accelerated and worsened by smoking. It is thought that around 600 million people suffer from COPD world-wide, and that 300 million die from it each year. Somewhere between 80% and 90% of these cases are caused by smoking cigarettes.

How smoking causes COPD

Cigarette smoke contains a wide range of different chemicals, many of which stimulate neutrophils – a type of white blood cell (see page 6) that normally attacks bacteria – to come to the scene. So neutrophils collect in larger numbers than normal in the lungs and the airways. And it is actually these neutrophils, normally such an important part of the body's defence against disease, which are responsible for causing the symptoms of COPD.

How do they do this? The neutrophils secrete an enzyme called **neutrophil elastase**. This enzyme is a protease – a protein-digesting enzyme – which breaks down several different kinds of protein, including the elastin which forms the elastic fibres in the tissues of the lungs and airways. Usually, there are inhibitors present which stop this enzyme from doing too much harm. But, in a smoker, the balance between the concentrations of protease enzymes and inhibitors tips too far in favour of the enzymes. The proteases gradually break down the tissues, causing irreversible damage.

The symptoms of COPD

One of the effects of this tissue damage is that the walls of many of the alveoli are broken down. Instead of millions of tiny alveoli, separated from blood capillaries by exceptionally thin walls, the lungs become a mass of larger spaces, much more widely separated from the blood capillaries. What's more, many of these capillaries also disappear. The total surface available for gas exchange is therefore greatly reduced. This condition is called **emphysema** (Fig 7.8). Not surprisingly, someone with emphysema has great difficulty in getting enough oxygen into their blood.

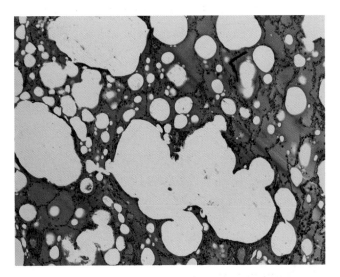

Fig 7.8 Light micrograph of lung tissue from a person with chronic emphysema showing large spaces where there should be thousands of tiny alveoli.

The progressive damage to the lungs causes them to lose their elasticity, whilst damage to the airways causes their walls to thicken. This happens because the attempts by the tissue to repair itself cause it to become fibrous. Both of these changes make it more difficult for air to move into and out of the lungs.

The damage to the airways also includes the ciliated cells and the goblet cells which normally help to keep the lungs clear of dust, bacteria and other foreign particles in the air that is breathed in. In smokers, the ciliated cells stop working while the goblet cells often work even harder. More mucus is produced, but there is nothing to carry it up and out of the bronchi and trachea. Instead, mucus accumulates in the airways, where it provides a breeding ground for bacteria. People with this condition therefore tend to suffer from bacterial infections of the bronchi, or **bronchitis**. They may have a chronic cough, as they attempt to clear the mucus from their lungs.

7.9   The graph shows how FEV$_1$ changes with age, in smokers who have continued

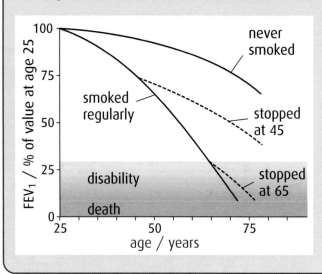

smoking all their lives, smokers who have given up, and in non-smokers.

a   Explain what is meant by FEV$_1$, and describe how it is measured.

b   Describe the changes in FEV$_1$ which occur in a non-smoking person, as they get older.

c   Compare the changes you have described in (b) with the changes in FEV$_1$ which occur in a lifelong smoker as they get older.

d   Explain the reasons for these differences in FEV$_1$ between smokers and non-smokers.

e   Is it worth a smoker giving up? Explain your answer.

Treating COPD

There is not really a great deal that can be done to help a person with COPD. Once the tissues have been damaged, they stay that way. Usually, the best that can be hoped for is to stop it getting any worse.

The first thing that anyone with COPD will be told to do is to stop smoking. This will almost immediately produce an improvement in the frequency and severity of infections, and may also reduce the cough. Ciliated cells and goblet cells can recover to a certain extent. But it is very unlikely that any great improvements will be made in the breathlessness which is caused by emphysema. Emphysema is irreversible.

Many patients may be helped a little by drugs called beta agonists, which may help to dilate the airways. This is described on page 136.

As the patient ages, and the symptoms get worse, they may need to breathe oxygen on a regular basis. This can be done at home, where the patient has an oxygen cylinder and breathing mask which they can use whenever they need to. In the advanced stages of the disease, even walking a few steps becomes impossible without getting out of breath.

Lung cancer

Whilst COPD causes about 15% of smoking-related deaths, lung cancer causes almost double that number. Lung cancer causes around 35 000 deaths per year in England and Wales. Smokers are almost 20 times as likely to die from lung cancer as are non-smokers.

Cigarette smoke contains several chemicals which are **carcinogenic**. Carcinogens are substances which affect the control of cell division. The cells may begin to divide much more than they should, forming a lump of disorganised cells known as a **tumour**. The tumour can be almost anywhere in the respiratory system, but most frequently occurs where the trachea branches into the two bronchi, or at other branching points.

As the tumour grows, it displaces other tissues. Eventually, this can lead to the blockage of the airways or other parts of the lungs. Cancerous cells may break away from the primary (original) tumour and begin to form tumours in other parts of the body. If this happens, survival rates are low.

The treatment of lung cancer is described on page 172.

Asthma

David hadn't felt too well all day. All the same, he played football with the other Year 5 boys at lunch time. But after only about 15 minutes he was having real difficulty getting his breath. He was making quite loud wheezing noises as he breathed, and having to work hard to get enough air into his lungs. It was frightening, and the more frightened he got the worse the breathing problems became.

Hannah, who was on playground duty, thought it could be an asthma attack, because she had seen children like this before. There were several children in the school who had asthma, and Hannah knew who they were and knew that she should make sure they used their inhalers if they had a wheezing attack. But David hadn't ever had an attack before, and he didn't have an inhaler. So Hannah took him inside and asked the school secretary to find someone to drive him to A and E.

Hannah was right – David was diagnosed as having asthma. Like many people with asthma, his attack had been brought on by exercise. Over the next few weeks, he had tests to find out what else might trigger attacks, and he was given an inhaler to use if another attack happened. David now has his asthma under control, and he can still play football most of the time.

Symptoms and causes of asthma

Asthma is a condition in which the airways become inflamed. The muscle in the bronchi and bronchioles contracts, narrowing the passageways along which air flows into and out of the lungs. Extra mucus is secreted, and this can block the airways, making it even more difficult to breathe in and out. A really acute, severe attack can be life-threatening if no treatment is given.

This all happens because the white blood cells are over-reacting to something in the environment. This could be such things as debris from house dust mites, nitrogen dioxide in exhaust fumes or cat hair. Many people find that pollen makes their asthma worse. The body launches an all-out attack on these substances, going way over the top in its immune response (see page 233). Substances which have this effect are called **allergens.**

Asthma can first appear at any age, though this happens most often in children or in middle-aged people. About half of those who will develop asthma do so before they are ten years old.

We still don't know exactly what causes some people to get asthma while others don't. There does seem to be some genetic component – people with a history of asthma in the family are more likely to get it than those who don't. But the environment is also important. People who are regularly exposed to irritants such as cigarette smoke or waste products of house dust mites have an increased risk of developing asthma. Many children with asthma also have other conditions which are caused by allergies, such as eczema. Sometimes asthma first develops after a person has had a severe viral infection in the bronchi or the lungs.

7.10 The graph shows how the PEFR of a person with asthma varies over a 6-day period.

a What is PEFR, and how is it measured?
b Describe the relationship between time of day and PEFR in this patient.
c This person often wakes up at about 3 am, coughing and wheezing. Describe what is happening in their body to cause these symptoms.

Controlling asthma

There are quite a few drugs which a person can use to control their asthma. They mostly fall into two categories – steroids and beta agonists.

Steroids such as beclomethasone are the major part of many people's therapy for asthma. These are substances whose molecules are very similar to some kinds of hormones. They are normally taken by breathing them in using an inhaler. They act quite slowly, but have a long-term effect. They act by reducing the inflammatory response in the airways. Steroids are taken regularly if a person needs to control their asthma. They are used to stop an attack that is underway.

Beta agonists such as salbutamol work much more quickly than steroids. They are breathed in from an inhaler if a person has an asthma attack, because they give immediate relief. Beta agonists relax the smooth muscles, which helps the airways to stay open. They are **bronchodilators**.

If an attack is really bad, the patient may need hospital treatment. They will be given oxygen to breathe. Steroids will be injected into the blood. Beta agonists will be given, probably inhaled along with the oxygen.

It is also important that a person with asthma learns what environmental factors can trigger an attack, so that they can avoid them. If they are smokers, they should stop immediately. If they live in a house where someone else smokes, they must do whatever they can to avoid breathing in cigarette smoke. Pets may have to go. The household may have to replace bedding, to reduce problems caused by dust mites.

7.11a Which of these drugs, steroids and beta agonists, could be classified as 'preventers', and which as 'relievers' of asthma?
b Suggest why it is better for these drugs to be inhaled, rather than injected into the blood.

Tuberculosis

Ben has been injecting cocaine since he was 19 years old. Now 35, he has lived on the streets for years. Some nights, he sleeps in a shelter, but as often as not he sleeps rough.

A year ago, the people running the shelter persuaded him to have a blood test. He was found to be HIV positive.

Ben resisted any attempts to counsel him or give him treatment. He just wanted to be left alone. However, now he is feeling so ill that he cannot resist people's help any longer. He coughs constantly and wakes in the night soaked with sweat. Weight has dropped off him alarmingly. He is admitted to hospital for tests which show that he has tuberculosis. The prognosis is not good for him, because his general health is poor and because he has HIV, but nevertheless the doctors insist that he undergoes treatment not only for his own sake, but also to reduce the risk of other people catching the disease from him.

Tuberculosis, often abbreviated to TB, is caused by a bacterium called *Mycobacterium tuberculosis*. Up until the middle of the nineteenth century, it was a common, chronic illness amongst people from all walks of life, many of whom died after gradually being worn down by it for many years. Then improvements in sanitation and housing caused a decline in the number of people suffering from TB and this decline continued steadily in all the industrialised countries of the world until about 1985. This was partly due to continued improvements in living conditions and also to the use of antibiotics to treat the disease and prevent infected people from passing it on.

Then, in the late 1980s, a dramatic change occurred. The number of people with TB began to increase, even in countries such as the USA and Britain. One of the main reasons for this has been HIV. The human immunodeficiency virus, which first appeared in the late 1970s, destroys one type of lymphocyte and so reduces the body's ability to fight off bacteria and other viruses. As the number of people with HIV has increased, so has the number of people with TB. It is estimated that around one third of the world's population is infected with TB. Every year, 3 million people die from it. A disease which we thought we had beaten is beginning to get out of control.

Symptoms of tuberculosis

The bacterium which causes TB usually enters the body in droplets of liquid in the air. People who have TB cough a great deal, and each cough sends millions of tiny droplets, each full of the bacterium, into the air around them, ready for other people to breathe them in. So the first point of entry to someone's body is usually the lungs.

Only about 10% of people who have *M. tuberculosis* in their body develop TB. No-one fully understands what determines whether an infected person will get the disease or not, but certainly general health does play a role.

Where the bacterium does take a hold and TB

develops, the first symptoms generally include problems with the lungs and airways. The patient often has a persistent cough which may bring up blood-stained mucus. There may be chest pain and breathlessness. Fever may develop, and there are often night sweats. As the bacterium spreads to other parts of the body, appetite is lost and weight decreases.

Treating tuberculosis

Once TB is diagnosed, the patient will be treated using **chemotherapy**. This means giving chemicals – drugs – to kill the bacteria inside the body. The drugs used are **antibiotics**. An antibiotic is a drug which kills bacteria without harming human cells. Some of the antibiotics which are used against TB are isoniazid and rifampicin.

These drugs must be taken regularly for a long time in order for the bacterium to be completely cleared from the body. A full six months of treatment must be followed to be sure that relapse will not occur. It is very unlikely that someone like Ben, in the case study (page 137), could be trusted to take his drugs at the right times and over such a long period, especially once he begins to feel better. To try to get around this, the World Health Organization advises that the patient is asked to attend an outpatient clinic twice a week, where they take their drugs while someone watches them. This is called directly observed therapy, or DOT.

Unfortunately, some strains of *M. tuberculosis* have now become resistant to some of the antibiotics that used to kill them (see page 238). If a patient does not respond to chemotherapy with one antibiotic, then others can be tried. Usually, two different antibiotics will be given together, to increase the chances of destroying the population of bacteria.

JUST FOR INTEREST

How TB bacteria hide

Part of the body's defence system against bacteria is the army of macrophages. These cells take in bacteria by phagocytosis (page 6). The bacterium is imprisoned in a vacuole, called a phagosome, surrounded by a membrane (see page 225).

Also inside the cell are small, membrane-bound structures known as lysosomes. These contain hydrolytic (digestive) enzymes. Once a bacterium has been captured, the cell lays down a 'railway track' made of a protein called actin, along which lysosomes travel through the cytoplasm to get to the phagosome. On arrival, the lysosome fuses with the phagosome, emptying its contents into it. The enzymes attack the bacterium and destroy it.

But this doesn't happen with *Mycobacterium tuberculosis*. Although macrophages take in the TB bacteria in the usual way, the process stops there. No railway tracks are laid down, so the lysosomes don't travel to the phagosomes. Not only does the bacterium survive, but it actually breeds, using the macrophage as a hiding place where it is protected from the other cells which might destroy it. This is why TB is so hard to treat.

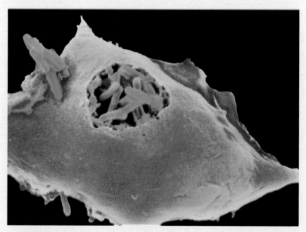

A macrophage containing *M. tuberculosis*.

Summary

1. Chronic obstructive pulmonary disease, COPD, is a condition in which the airways become progressively narrowed and damaged. Most cases of COPD are caused by smoking.

2. In COPD, the walls of the alveoli break down. This reduces the surface area for gas exchange. This condition is called emphysema. It is irreversible.

3. In COPD, the walls of the airways are damaged by irritants in cigarette smoke, often becoming thicker and more fibrous as the body attempts to repair the damage. Excess mucus is produced, which increases the risk of bacteria breeding in the airways. The bronchus and bronchioles therefore become inflamed, causing bronchitis.

4. Lung cancer is also strongly associated with smoking. Carcinogens in cigarette smoke can cause the normal control mechanisms in cells to break down, so that the cells divide repeatedly and uncontrollably, forming a tumour.

5. Asthma is a condition in which the airways become narrowed and inflamed. This is often caused by an allergen such as nitrogen dioxide or house mite dust. The immune system over-reacts to the allergen. This results in the muscle in the walls of the bronchi and bronchioles contracting, which makes the airways narrower.

6. An asthma attack can be helped by breathing in beta agonists, which make the muscle relax. Steroids reduce inflammation if taken regularly. A person with asthma may take steroids on a regular basis to reduce the risk of an attack.

7. Tuberculosis, TB, is an infectious disease caused by the bacterium *Mycobacterium tuberculosis*. A person becomes infected when they breathe in droplets containing the bacterium. Only about 10% of infected people go on to develop TB.

8. The bacterium enters cells and breeds there. This damages the lung tissues, and the person coughs a great deal, sometimes bringing up blood. As the bacterium spreads through the body, fever and weight loss can eventually lead to death. This takes many years to happen.

9. TB can be treated using antibiotics. Usually two antibiotics are given at once, to lessen the chance that the bacterium will be resistant to both of them. They need to be taken regularly for at least six months.

CHAPTER 8

Stem cells and DNA

Aroona Sharma lived an active life. She had successfully juggled a career as a university academic with bringing up her three children. Now her children had left home and, at the age of 49, she was looking forward to being able to think about herself a little more.

For a few months she had noticed that her hands trembled slightly when she was relaxing and reading. She hadn't really thought too much of it at first, but as it was obviously getting a little worse rather than better she decided to ask her doctor to check it out. By the time she got round to making an appointment, her husband was beginning to notice changes in her. He thought that she was becoming a little clumsy, and that her face did not seem as expressive as it always had been.

Aroona was shocked when her doctor diagnosed Parkinson's disease. She knew only too well that there was no cure. He explained that the illness was caused by the gradual death of a group of neurones – nerve cells – in her brain which secreted a chemical called dopamine. Without dopamine, other nerve cells do not transmit appropriate impulses to muscles.

She learned that there was a drug called levodopa which could help her. Her brain would be able to convert levodopa into dopamine. It would be very important to get the dose just right. Too little and her symptoms would get worse; too much and she would suffer from jerky, unintentional movements and perhaps mental disturbance. The drug could be expected to work for her for several years, but eventually it could prove impossible to keep her illness under control.

Since being diagnosed, Aroona has read everything she can find about her disease, hoping against hope that a cure may be found before she is too old to benefit from it. And, indeed, there is a glimmer of hope. Articles in newspapers and in scientific and medical magazines describe experiments being done with 'embryonic stem cells' which look as though they could lead to a real cure. Aroona desperately hopes that embryonic stem cell transplantation will become reality in the next few years, and that she can be one of the first to receive this revolutionary new treatment.

Stem cells

Parkinson's disease affects more than 2% of people over the age of 65. It happens when a group of neurones dies, for reasons that no-one yet understands. Without the dopamine that these neurones secrete, the control of body movements is gradually lost. Tremor, rigidity and decreased mobility are usually the first symptoms.

The best hope of a cure is to transplant new dopamine-secreting neurones into the brain. And the best hope of obtaining these neurones is by growing them from human stem cells.

Sources of stem cells

When an egg is fertilised in a human oviduct, a zygote is produced. This single cell divides repeatedly, forming a little ball of cells called a **blastocyst**. By about 3 to 5 days old, the ball contains a group of about 30 cells – these will eventually give rise to the hundreds of different kinds of cells which will make up a person.

Well before a baby is born, most of the cells in its body will have become specialised for a particular purpose. They are said to have **differentiated**. There will be specialised muscle cells, skin cells, liver cells, nerve cells and many, many more types. Once a human cell has become specialised, it usually does not change into any other kind of cell. A heart muscle cell cannot change into a bone cell; neither can a bone cell change into a skin cell.

This is very different from the abilities of the cells in the blastocyst. These cells have the potential to become any of the many different kinds of cells within a human. They are said to be **pluripotent**. Cells which can do this are called **stem cells**. Stem cells differ from most human cells because:

- they are unspecialised;
- they can divide repeatedly (proliferate) to make large numbers of new cells;
- they can differentiate into several kinds of specialised cells;
- they have a large nuclear to cytoplasmic ratio.

> A **stem cell** is a cell that can divide and produce new cells that can differentiate into many kinds of specialised cells.

Embryos at the blastocyst stage are the best source of stem cells. These are called **embryonic stem cells**. However, stem cells can also be obtained from the umbilical cord after a child has been born. And there are also some kinds of stem cells in adult humans, but – unlike embryonic stem cells – all the ones so far discovered in adults are not pluripotent. For example, bone marrow contains stem cells which divide repeatedly to form cells which differentiate into erythrocytes (red blood cells) and also all the different kinds of leucocytes (white blood cells) (Fig 8.1). But they cannot differentiate into neurones, muscle cells or any other kind of cell.

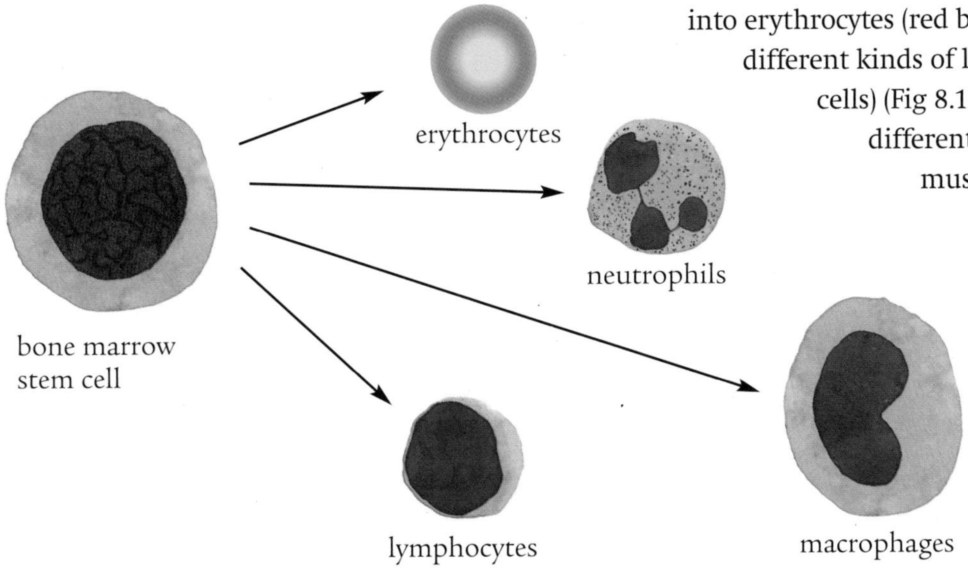

erythrocytes

neutrophils

bone marrow stem cell

lymphocytes

macrophages

Fig 8.1 Bone marrow stem cells differentiate into the different types of blood cells.

How stem cells are cultured

Growing stem cells in a laboratory is not easy. The aim is to keep a group of embryonic stem cells in conditions that encourage them to divide repeatedly, always forming new pluripotent stem cells. If you can do this, then you can produce millions of stem cells per year.

Human embryonic stem cells are grown in shallow culture dishes. A special solution, called a **culture medium**, is placed in the dish and a few stem cells are added. If you get the ingredients of the culture medium just right, the stem cells will divide repeatedly until they practically fill the dish. You can then take some of them and introduce them into new dishes with fresh culture medium. In this way, millions of stem cells can be grown in the course of just a few months (Figs 8.2 and 8.3).

Making stem cells differentiate

If you want to use stem cells to produce a particular kind of specialised cell, you need to provide them with exactly the right stimulation to produce specialised tissues (see page 126).

Stem cells, like all body cells, contain a full set of genes. These genes, which are made of DNA, provide a full set of instructions for making every kind of cell in the body. Each gene provides instructions for making a particular kind of protein. In a differentiated cell, only a particular set of these genes is switched on, so only one particular mixture of proteins will be made. The trick is to switch on the set of genes that the cell needs to use if it is to become the kind of cell you want.

This is sometimes done by growing the cells in a certain kind of culture solution. It has taken many years to find the right 'recipe' for culture solutions to make the stem cells differentiate into a particular kind of cell. No-one fully understands why a particular mixture of chemicals, or **growth factors**, makes stem cells change into nerve cells rather than muscle cells, or muscle cells rather than skin cells. It has taken many years of trial and error to find recipes that work.

Another way is to add genes to the stem cells. For example, mouse embryonic stem cells can be persuaded to differentiate into dopamine-secreting neurones by introducing a gene called Nurr1 into their nuclei.

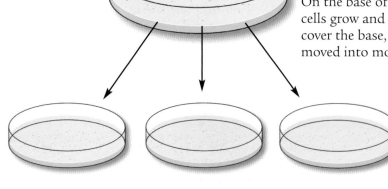

cells from inside an early embryo

culture medium in dish

On the base of the dish the stem cells grow and divide. When they cover the base, they need to be moved into more dishes.

Growth factors are added and the cells clump into groups of cells which differentiate, forming specialised tissue.

Fig 8.2 Stem cell culture and differentiation.

Ethical issues

Stem cells were first isolated from human embryos and then grown in the laboratory in 1998. As their potential was realised, people began to ask questions about the ethics of this research. The embryos from which the stem cells are taken are destroyed. They usually come from surplus embryos which were not placed into a woman's uterus during fertility treatment. Some people consider that it is unacceptable to use embryos for this purpose, even if there was never any chance of the embryo becoming a baby. Others feel that the potential benefits outweigh the ethical concerns.

Because of the ethical problems surrounding the use of embryonic stem cells, researchers are trying to find other sources of pluripotent stem cells in adults, and also ways of harvesting stem cells from very early embryos without destroying them.

This is a very new and exciting area of biology, and by the time you read this there will undoubtedly be many new techniques being tried out. Human stem cells could be used to treat not only Parkinson's disease, but also heart disease, diabetes, liver diseases, Alzheimer's disease, multiple sclerosis and some cancers.

Fig 8.3 Stem cells are being grown in this vessel in a laboratory. The cells grow on the base and are covered by a solution containing nutrients.

ACTIVITY 8.1

Ethics of using stem cells

These points of view have been put forward by various people engaged in the ethical debate about the use of human stem cells. Choose one or two of them, with which you either agree strongly or disagree strongly, and write a succinct explanation and justification of your point of view. Introduce other points of view if you wish. Support your argument by using biological facts wherever you can.

• A blastocyst is a human being, and should not be destroyed.

• We should feel no qualms about using blastocysts 'left over' from fertility treatments as a source of embryonic stem cells, because they were never going to become human beings in any case.

• If we can use human embryonic stem cells to cure common, life-destroying illnesses such as Parkinson's disease and multiple sclerosis, we should not hesitate to do so.

• Researchers should stop all work using embryonic stem cells immediately.

• Researchers should concentrate on finding sources of pluripotent stem cells from adults, but be allowed to continue using embryonic stem cells in the meantime.

• The repeated division of stem cells is an example of cloning; we should not be cloning human cells.

• You cannot stop science advancing; even if British scientists don't work with human stem cells, someone else will do it anyway.

Summary

1. A stem cell is an undifferentiated cell which is able to divide and give rise to cells which can develop into different kinds of specialised cells.

2. Stem cells in a blastocyst (very early embryo) are able to give rise to all of the different specialised cells in the human body.

3. The stem cells so far discovered in adult humans are able to give rise to only a small range of different specialised cells. For example, stem cells in bone marrow can give rise to blood cells but not to nerve cells.

4. The development of a young cell into a cell specialised for a particular function is known as differentiation. For example, cells derived from stem cells in bone marrow can differentiate into red blood cells and all the different types of white blood cells.

5. Stem cells can be cultured by growing them in a solution known as a culture medium. Different kinds and concentrations of chemicals called growth factors can stimulate the stem cells to differentiate into different kinds of specialised cells.

6. Stem cells could potentially be transplanted into people to replace cells which are not working properly. Possible diseases which could be treated in this way include Parkinson's disease, Alzheimer's disease, diabetes, multiple sclerosis and some cancers.

7. The rapid development of stem cell technology has brought many ethical issues into question. In particular, the use of stem cells from embryos needs to be considered, as it involves destroying human embryos. This needs to be balanced against the potential benefits it could bring to people suffering serious illnesses.

DNA and RNA

On February 28th 1953, Francis Crick walked into The Eagle, in Cambridge, and announced to everyone that he had found the secret of life.

Only nine years earlier it had been finally proved beyond doubt that a chemical called DNA was the substance which carried hereditary information from one cell to the new cells which formed from it. Since then, there had been much interest in finding out exactly what DNA was. And how did it work? How did it store and transmit this information? What exactly was the information that it transmitted?

Early in 1951, the physicist Rosalind Franklin began work in a laboratory at King's College in London, trying to find out the structure of DNA. Her speciality was using X-rays to work out the structures of large molecules – a technique known as X-ray crystallography. The head of the department she worked in was Maurice Wilkins. It soon became apparent that there was a personality clash between them, so that they did not share information and ideas as they should.

Rosalind was a brilliant experimenter. She set up, modified and used the X-ray apparatus to produce some superb photographs. She was beginning to feel that she had nearly enough evidence to suggest that a DNA molecule was made of two helical molecules side by side. But she wanted to collect more data before she was prepared to make her conclusions public.

Meanwhile, in Cambridge, the researchers James Watson and Francis Crick were also thinking about the structure of DNA. On January 30th 1951, James visited King's and spoke to Maurice Wilkins about DNA. Maurice, without asking Rosalind, showed him some of Rosalind's photos. James immediately understood what they meant, especially one really superb one. At dinner that night in London, on the train back to Cambridge and while cycling home he gradually sorted things out in his mind until he was absolutely certain that a DNA molecule was a double helix. He started building his model on February 4th. With the help of a few more facts which came their way via friends and colleagues, James Watson and Francis Crick cracked the structure of this amazing molecule.

Rosalind Franklin had all the evidence in front of her to be able to work out this structure. But it was her nature to be very careful and very sure before committing to anything. She wanted to collect more evidence before she could be really sure about the structure of DNA. This, and the lack of communication between her and other researchers, led her to miss out on achieving recognition for the discovery. James Watson, Francis Crick and Maurice Wilkins were awarded a Nobel Prize in 1962. Rosalind Franklin died of cancer in April 1958.

Looking at where we are now, with the ability to use genetic engineering to alter the structures and functions of living organisms, it is amazing to realise that until the middle of the twentieth century no-one even knew that DNA was the genetic material. After the discovery of its structure in 1953, understanding of the way in which DNA contains information inherited from our parents quickly followed.

In a human cell there are 46 **chromosomes**. Each one contains a very, very long molecule of DNA. The DNA molecules contain particular sequences of four **bases**. These sequences are instructions, written in a code known as the **genetic code**, telling the cell which proteins to make. Slight variations in the sequences of bases in our DNA make our cells construct slightly different proteins. Some of these proteins will be enzymes – proteins which act as catalysts and control the metabolic reactions which take place in our bodies. Slight differences in the structure of an enzyme may result in slight differences in the metabolic reactions in our cells. As a result, we are all slightly different from one another.

The structure of DNA

DNA stands for **deoxyribonucleic acid**. When it was first discovered, it was given the name 'nucleic acid' because it was found in the nuclei of cells.

A nucleic acid molecule is a very long chain of smaller molecules called **nucleotides**. So a nucleic acid is a **polynucleotide**.

A nucleotide contains:

• a phosphate group;
• a five-carbon sugar (a pentose);
• an organic base.

Fig 8.4 shows the components of a nucleotide in DNA. Here, the pentose sugar is **deoxyribose**. The base can be any one of four. These are **adenine**, **guanine**, **thymine** and **cytosine**. They are usually abbreviated to A, G, T and C.

Adenine and guanine molecules each contain two rings in their structure. They are known as **purine** bases. Thymine and cytosine have only one ring. They are known as **pyrimidine** bases.

Fig 8.5 shows how these components link to make nucleotides.

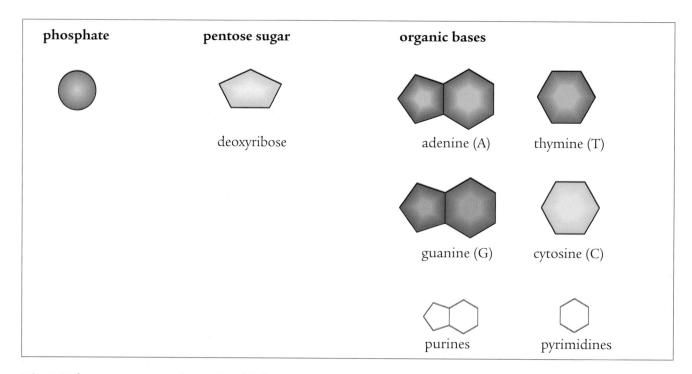

Fig 8.4 The components of a nucleotide in DNA.

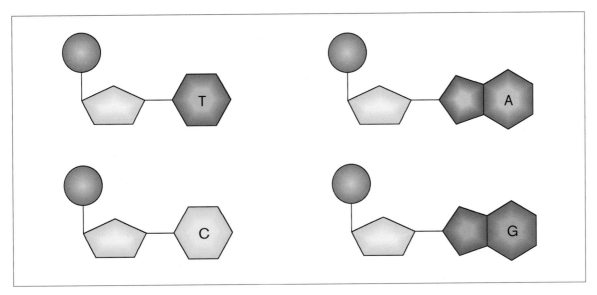

Fig 8.5 The structure of the four nucleotides in DNA.

Fig 8.6 shows how the nucleotides link together to form a polynucleotide. The deoxyribose of one nucleotide links up with the phosphate group of another. The reaction by which this takes place is – as you might begin to expect by now – a condensation reaction, in which a molecule of water is released. The chain can grow to almost any length by adding more and more nucleotides on to it.

condensation reaction between the phosphate of the polynucleotide and the pentose of a free nucleotide

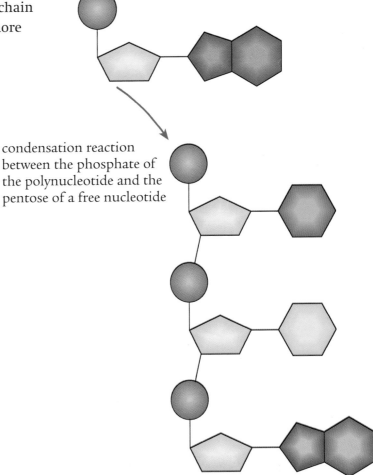

Fig 8.6 How nucleotides join to form a polynucleotide.

You can see that the base of each nucleotide sticks out sideways from the chain. In DNA, two chains of nucleotides lie side by side, one chain running one way and the other in the opposite direction (Fig 8.7). They are said to be **anti-parallel**. The bases of one chain link up to the bases of the other by means of **hydrogen bonds**.

The key to the ability of DNA to hold and pass on the code for making proteins in the cell is the way in which these bases link up. There is just the right amount of space for one large base – a purine – to link with one smaller base – a pyrimidine. And the linking is even more particular than that. A can only link with T, while C can only link with G. This is called **complementary base pairing**.

As you will see, complementary base pairing ensures that the code carried on one molecule of DNA can be copied perfectly over and over again so that it is passed down from generation to generation. It is also what enables the code on the DNA to be used to instruct the protein-making machinery in a cell to construct exactly the right proteins.

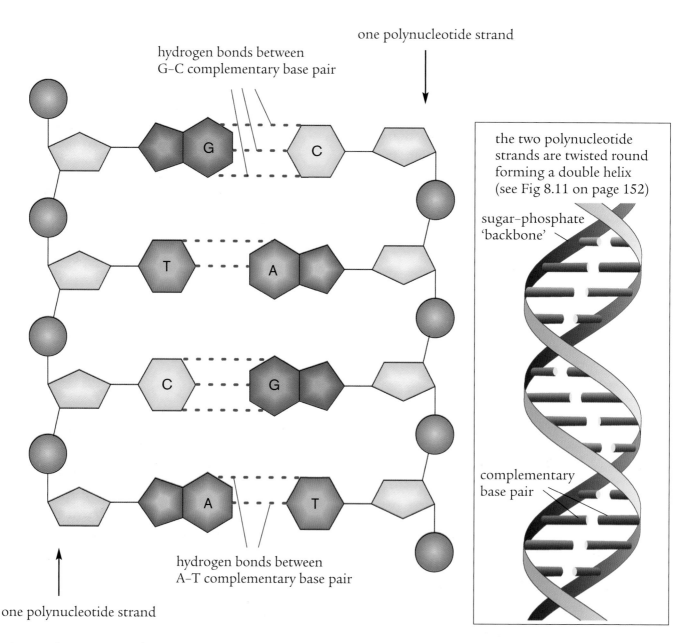

one polynucleotide strand

hydrogen bonds between G–C complementary base pair

hydrogen bonds between A–T complementary base pair

one polynucleotide strand

the two polynucleotide strands are twisted round forming a double helix (see Fig 8.11 on page 152)

sugar–phosphate 'backbone'

complementary base pair

Fig 8.7 The structure of DNA.

Nucleotides for life ... and taste

Nucleotides are fundamental to life, because they carry the genetic code in nucleic acids, which describes how we are and how we work. They also have many other jobs to do on their own.

These are the ingredients of a nucleotide:

a **pentose** sugar (this one is deoxyribose)

an **organic base** – either a purine, like adenine shown here

or a pyrimidine, like thymine shown here

a **phosphate**

You have already met one special property of these bases – complementary base pairing.

thymine   adenine

In a polynucleotide, the phosphate in one nucleotide links to the pentose in the next nucleotide. But the phosphate can have another role in nucleotides that have work

cytosine   guanine

to do on their own, such as adenosine triphosphate (ATP). In ATP several phosphates can join in a line.

adenine–deoxyribose–(P)–(P)–(P)

ATP can release its phosphates and, in the process, transfer some energy. This is the energy transfer we use for nearly every energy-requiring process in our bodies. Aerobic respiration, which makes the ATP, takes place inside mitochondria.

Often only one phosphate is released, producing adenosine diphosphate (ADP). If two phosphates are released, adenosine monophosphate (AMP) is produced. Modified AMP has a very different role, as a regulator of many processes that take place in cells.

Recently, it has been found that a tiny amount of AMP blocks the bitter taste of foods such as black coffee and grapefruit juice. Normally, sugars, salt or fats are used to mask bitterness in foods, so perhaps AMP may have a role in the future as a food additive. Or perhaps it could be used to block the extreme bitterness of cough remedies or anti-ulcer drugs.

149

The structure of RNA

DNA is not the only polynucleotide in a cell. There are also polynucleotides which contain the sugar **ribose** rather than deoxyribose. They are therefore called **ribonucleic acids**, or RNA for short. RNA is single stranded and DNA is double stranded. Another difference between RNA and DNA is that RNA always contains the base **uracil** (U) instead of thymine. Fig 8.8 shows the structure of RNA.

Cells contain three different kinds of RNA. These are messenger or **mRNA**, transfer or **tRNA**, and ribosomal or **rRNA**. Ribosomal RNA makes up part of the structure of ribosomes, whilst the other two types play extremely important roles in protein synthesis. This is described on pages 153 to 156.

How DNA replicates

The information carried in a DNA molecule – that is, the sequence of nucleotides – is passed down from one generation to the next. The DNA in your cells came from both your mother and your father. You began as a zygote, a single cell. This cell divided repeatedly to produce all the cells in your body. Each time a cell divided, it first made perfect duplicates of all the DNA that it contained. The DNA was then shared out

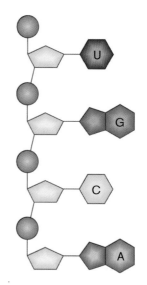

Fig 8.8 The structure of RNA.

between the two new cells. Each of your body cells therefore has an exact copy of the DNA in that original single cell.

DNA can be copied perfectly over and over again. This is called **replication**. Fig 8.9 shows how this happens. It is done by a method called **semi-conservative replication**, because each of the new DNA molecules is made up of one old strand and one new strand of DNA.

3 base pairing between the bases on opposite strands, and condensation reactions between pentose and phosphate in the new strand make new polynucleotide strands – one strand acting as a **template** for the other

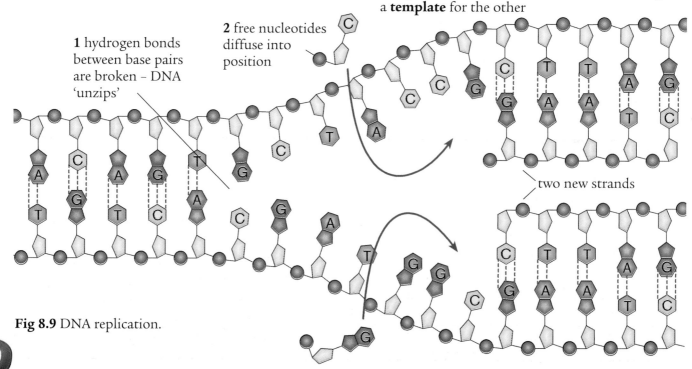

1 hydrogen bonds between base pairs are broken – DNA 'unzips'

2 free nucleotides diffuse into position

two new strands

Fig 8.9 DNA replication.

The genetic code

To understand how the genetic code works, you first need to think back to the structure of proteins. Proteins are made of polypeptides, which are long chains of amino acids. There are about 20 different amino acids, and the sequence in which they are strung together determines the structure, and therefore the function, of the protein molecule which is made. What DNA does is determine this sequence. The sequence of bases in a DNA molecule determines the sequences of amino acids in the proteins that the cell makes.

A length of DNA that codes for one polypeptide is called a **gene**.

There are four bases in a DNA molecule – A, T, C and G. They can be put together in any order along one of the polynucleotide chains which make up the DNA.

The code is a three-letter one. Only one of the two strands in a DNA molecule is copied, and it is referred to here as the reference strand. A sequence of three bases on the reference strand in a DNA molecule codes for one amino acid, as shown in Fig 8.10.

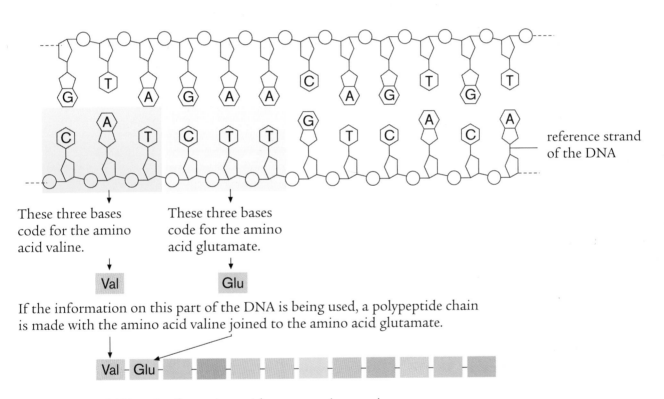

These three bases code for the amino acid valine.

These three bases code for the amino acid glutamate.

Val

Glu

If the information on this part of the DNA is being used, a polypeptide chain is made with the amino acid valine joined to the amino acid glutamate.

Val – Glu –

Fig 8.10 How DNA codes for amino acid sequences in proteins.

SAQ

8.1 Copy and complete this table to compare the structures of DNA and RNA.

	DNA	RNA
Type of sugar in nucleotides		
Bases in nucleotides		
Number of strands in molecule		
Where found in a cell		

8.2a The genetic code is a three-letter code. How many different three-letter sequences can there be? (You may know the mathematical formula used to calculate the actual number of sequences.)

b Can you think of any possible advantage of having more three-letter code sequences than the number of different amino acids to be coded for?

151

8.3 Explain the difference between each of these pairs of terms.
- nucleotide and polynucleotide;
- ribose and deoxyribose;
- purine and pyrimidine.

8.4a Explain how complementary base pairing enables a DNA molecule to be copied perfectly.

b Why is DNA replication said to be 'semi-conservative'?

c Purines and pyrimidines are of different sizes. How does this relate to the fact that in a base pair one purine is linked to one pyrimidine?

Fig 8.11 A DNA molecule magnified ×2 000 000 by a scanning tunnelling microscope.

Summary

1. DNA, deoxyribonucleic acid, is made up of many smaller molecules called nucleotides. DNA is a polynucleotide.

2. A DNA nucleotide contains a phosphate group, the pentose sugar deoxyribose, and one of four bases – adenine, thymine, cytosine or guanine. A and G are purines. C and T are pyrimidines.

3. Nucleotides join together by condensation reactions to make a polynucleotide chain. These reactions form bonds between the phosphate group of one nucleotide and the pentose sugar of the next.

4. A DNA molecule is made of two polynucleotide chains running in opposite directions. They are held together by hydrogen bonds between the bases. The molecule twists into a double helix shape.

5. The base A always bonds with T, whilst C always bonds with G. This is known as complementary base pairing.

6. DNA molecules can be copied perfectly. This is done in a process called semi-conservative replication. The double-stranded molecule separates, allowing new DNA nucleotides to join with each of the exposed strands by complementary base pairing. This results in two new DNA molecules, each containing one old strand and one new strand.

7. The sequence of bases in a DNA molecule determines the sequence of amino acids to be used when building proteins. A length of DNA which carries the information required for building one kind of polypeptide or protein is known as a gene.

8. Each group of three bases in a DNA molecule codes for one amino acid.

Protein synthesis

The DNA molecules are in the nucleus. It is good to keep the DNA shut away from the rest of the cell like this. In this way, the molecules are less affected by chemicals in the cytoplasm.

But proteins are made in the cytoplasm, on the ribosomes. So there needs to be a messenger to take the instructions from the DNA to the ribosomes. The messenger is called **messenger RNA**, or **mRNA**.

The process of using the DNA code to make a polypeptide or protein molecule takes place in two stages. The first, in which the instructions on the DNA are transferred to a mRNA molecule, is called **transcription**. The second, in which the instructions are followed and a polypeptide or protein is made, is **translation**.

Transcription

Usually, only a small part of a DNA molecule is transcribed at one time, just a part which holds the instructions for making a particular polypeptide. That part of the DNA is a **gene**.

First, this part of the DNA 'unzips'. The hydrogen bonds between the bases break, and the helix unwinds (Fig 8.12).

Next, free RNA nucleotides slot into place against one of the exposed DNA strands. The nucleotides pair exactly. C and G always pair together, just as in DNA itself. The base T on the DNA molecule will link up with an A base on a RNA nucleotide, but an A base on the DNA molecule will link up with a U base (uracil) on the RNA (see page 146).

As the RNA nucleotides slot into place and form hydrogen bonds with their complementary bases on the DNA strand, condensation reactions happen between adjacent RNA nucleotides. Step by step, a mRNA molecule is built containing the genetic code (Fig 8.12).

When the end of the gene is reached, the complete mRNA molecule breaks away. The DNA molecule may stay unzipped so that more mRNA molecules can be made, or it may zip back up again.

The mRNA molecule is now guided out of the nucleus through a pore in the nuclear envelope. It passes into the cytoplasm and arrives at a ribosome.

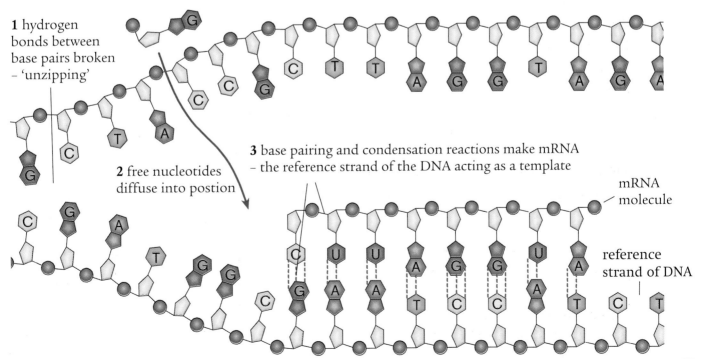

1 hydrogen bonds between base pairs broken – 'unzipping'

2 free nucleotides diffuse into postion

3 base pairing and condensation reactions make mRNA – the reference strand of the DNA acting as a template

mRNA molecule

reference strand of DNA

Fig 8.12 Transcription.

153

The genetic code in this mRNA is read in this direction ⟶

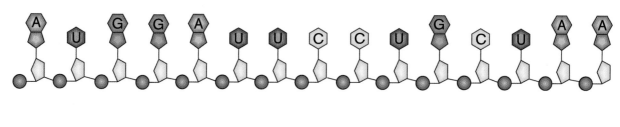

Simplified representation

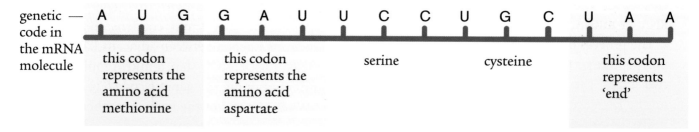

| genetic code in the mRNA molecule | A | U | G | G | A | U | U | C | C | U | G | C | U | A | A |

| this codon represents the amino acid methionine | this codon represents the amino acid aspartate | serine | cysteine | this codon represents 'end' |

Fig 8.13 The genetic code in an mRNA molecule.

Translation

Translation is the process in which the code for making the protein – now carried by the mRNA molecule – is used to line up amino acids in a particular sequence, linking them together to make a polypeptide (or protein) molecule. Each group of three consecutive bases in the mRNA is called a **codon**. Each codon codes for one amino acid (Fig 8.13).

Transfer RNA

In translation, yet another type of nucleotide comes into play. This is a different kind of RNA, known as **transfer RNA** or **tRNA**.

There are at least 20 different kinds of tRNA. Each one has a group of three exposed bases called an **anticodon**. An anticodon can undergo complementary base pairing with a codon.

At the other end of the tRNA molecule there is a site where an amino acid can bind (Fig 8.14). The crucial property of tRNA is that a tRNA molecule with a particular anticodon can only become bound to a particular amino acid. This is what allows the sequence of bases on the mRNA to determine the sequence of amino acids in the polypeptide which is made.

In the cytoplasm, specific enzymes link specific amino acids to specific tRNA molecules. For example, a tRNA molecule with the anticodon UAC will have the amino acid methionine loaded onto its amino acid binding site. You can imagine thousands of tRNA molecules in the cytoplasm, each loaded with their particular amino acid and waiting for the opportunity to offload it at the polypeptide-making production line.

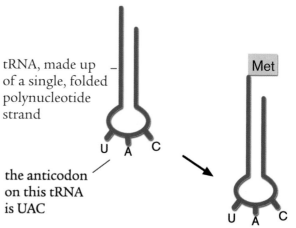

tRNA, made up of a single, folded polynucleotide strand

the anticodon on this tRNA is UAC

Met

this tRNA is linked to methionine – the 'correct' amino acid for the anticodon UAC

Fig 8.14 tRNA.

Building the polypeptide

The mRNA molecule, carrying the code copied from part of a DNA molecule, is held in a cleft in the ribosome so that six bases are exposed. Each group of three bases, which carries the code for one amino acid, is known as a **codon**.

A tRNA with an anticodon which exactly complements the first mRNA codon then binds with it (Fig 8.15). Complementary base pairing ensures that only the 'correct' tRNA can bind. For example, if the mRNA codon is AUG, then a tRNA molecule with the anticodon UAC will bind with it. As we have seen, this tRNA molecule will be carrying the amino acid methionine.

Another tRNA then binds with the next codon on the mRNA. Once again, the tRNA – and therefore the amino acid – is determined by the mRNA codon. If the mRNA codon is GAU, the anticodon on the tRNA will be CUA, and the amino acid will be aspartate.

Now the two amino acids are held in a particular position next to each other on the ribosome. A condensation reaction takes place, and a peptide bond is formed between the two amino acids.

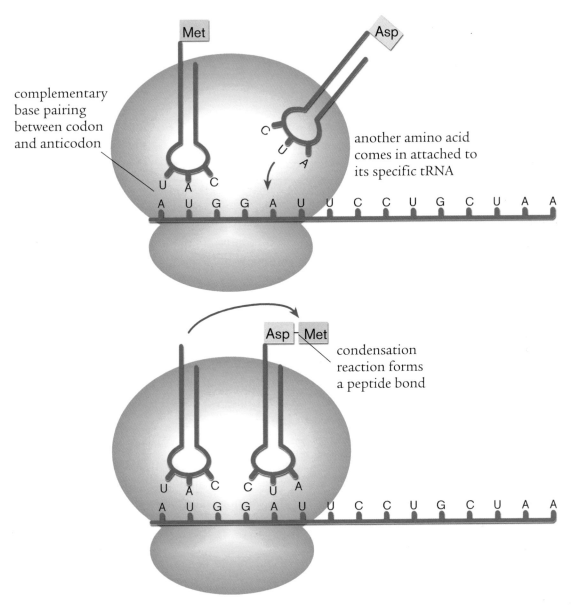

complementary base pairing between codon and anticodon

another amino acid comes in attached to its specific tRNA

condensation reaction forms a peptide bond

Fig 8.15 Translation (continued on next page).

The mRNA moves on through the cleft in the ribosome, bringing a third codon into place. A third tRNA binds with it, and a third amino acid is added to the chain. Meanwhile, the first tRNA (the one which brought methionine) has completed its role. It breaks away, leaving the methionine behind. This released tRNA is now available to be reloaded with another methionine molecule. In this way, the whole polypeptide chain is gradually built up.

A polypeptide is released when a 'stop' codon is reached, such as UAA shown below.

The start of a polypeptide is indicated by the codon AUG – the codon for methionine.

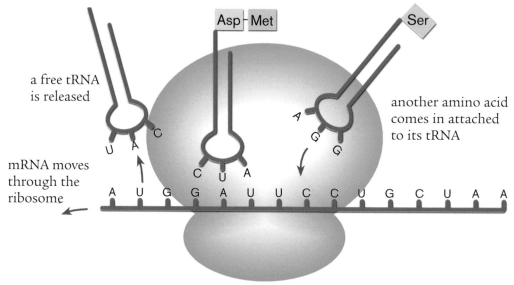

a free tRNA is released

another amino acid comes in attached to its tRNA

mRNA moves through the ribosome

A U G G A U U C C U G C U A A

Fig 8.15 Translation (continued from previous page).

SAQ

8.5 A length of DNA has the base sequence ATA AGA TTG CCC.

a How many amino acids does this length of DNA code for?

b Below are listed some of the DNA codes for amino acids.

AAA	Phenylalanine
AAT	Leucine
AGA	Serine
ATA	Tyrosine
CCC	Glycine
TTG	Asparagine

Write down the sequence of amino acids which the length of DNA codes for.

c What will be the base sequence on the mRNA molecule which is made during transcription of this length of DNA?

d Using the information above, work out the anticodons of the tRNA molecules which carry these amino acids:
i leucine ii asparagine

8.6 These statements contain some very common errors made by AS and A level students in examinations. For each statement, explain why it is wrong and write a correct version.

a "The sequence of bases in a DNA molecule determines which amino acids will be made during protein synthesis."

b "The amino acids in a DNA molecule determine what kind of proteins will be formed in the cell."

c "The four bases in DNA are adenosine, cysteine, thiamine and guanine."

d "During transcription, a complementary mRNA molecule comes and lies against part of a DNA molecule."

8.7 Using all the diagrams in Fig 8.15 as a guide, make annotated drawings of the next stages in the synthesis of the polypeptide shown in the figure. (UGC codes for cysteine.)

Properties of DNA

Now that you know how DNA is used in a cell, we can think about how this molecule is able to carry out its hugely important functions.

DNA is a very stable molecule.

The sugar–phosphate backbone is strongly linked by covalent bonds, and the bases of one strand are linked to the other by hydrogen bonds.

DNA is able to carry a huge amount of information.

Although there are 20 different amino acids to code for, a sequence of only three bases codes for each amino acid. A polypeptide chain made up of 15 amino acids can be specified by a length of polynucleotide in DNA made up of 45 nucleotides.

DNA is able to replicate perfectly.

Complementary base pairing ensures that new DNA molecules carry exactly the same sequence of bases as the original molecule.

DNA can pass on its information to mRNA, using complementary base pairing.

This allows the information to be used in the cytoplasm for protein synthesis, while the DNA remains safely in the nucleus.

If one strand of a DNA molecule is damaged, the information that it contained is not lost.

This is because the sequence of bases on the other strand can be used to rebuild the damaged one using complementary base pairing.

JUST FOR INTEREST

The human genome

The term 'genome' can mean all the genes possessed by an organism or by a population of organisms. Alternatively, it can mean the whole sequence of bases on the DNA of an organism.

In 1988, an enormous, international project set out to discover the sequences of bases in each of the 23 different types of chromosomes which are found in human cells. The project achieved its objectives of producing a working draft sequence in 2000. 'Maps' have now been drawn showing the DNA sequences and known genes in each human chromosome.

There are some strange facts about the human genome. For example, 99.9% of the DNA sequence is identical in all humans, though the remaining 0.1% is very variable. And it is thought that only 2% of the human genome actually codes for the

manufacture of proteins – around 30 000 different proteins. As a gene can be thought of as the code for one protein, this means there are around 30 000 genes in the human genome. There is uncertainty because researchers are still trying to sort out which bits of the code belong to each gene. It was not expected that the number of genes would be as low as 30 000, as even mice have around 21 000 genes.

The non-coding DNA is sometimes called 'junk' DNA, although it is almost certain that some of it does have functions that we don't yet know about. Some of these regions are very variable in their base sequences and they are the ones which are used in DNA fingerprinting. Each person has a different base sequence which is highly unlikely to be exactly matched by anyone else that has ever lived – other than an identical twin.

Summary

1. DNA remains in the nucleus, but protein synthesis takes place on ribosomes in the cytoplasm. Messenger RNA carries the information from the nucleus to the ribosomes.

2. RNA, like DNA, is a polynucleotide. But RNA nucleotides contain ribose instead of deoxyribose and the base uracil, U, instead of thymine, T. The molecules are single stranded rather than double stranded.

3. In transcription, a length of DNA coding for a polypeptide (a gene) unwinds and the strands separate. New mRNA nucleotides line up against one of the strands, using complementary base pairing. A mRNA molecule is therefore formed carrying the same coded information as on the DNA.

4. A codon is three consecutive bases in mRNA, which codes for one amino acid.

5. The mRNA molecule passes through a nuclear pore and attaches in a cleft on a ribosome. Two groups of three bases (codons) are active in the ribosome at any one time.

6. The cytoplasm contains many different kinds of transfer RNA (tRNA) molecules. Each has a particular anticodon and can be loaded with a particular amino acid.

7. In translation, the anticodons of tRNA molecules bind to the codons of the mRNA, using complementary base pairing. The amino acid molecules they are carrying are brought close together, and condensation reactions form peptide bonds between them. In this way, the sequence of bases on the mRNA molecule determines the sequence of amino acids in the polypeptide molecule which is formed.

CHAPTER 9

Cell division

Alison had been helping her father burn some of the old cabbage stalks and other rubbish on his allotment. She stayed behind for a while after he went home. Trying to throw a large bundle of old tree prunings onto the fire, she lost her balance and fell forward into it. Alison panicked. Instead of rolling on the ground to try to put out her burning clothing, she ran, screaming for help. By the time help arrived, she had extensive, deep burns.

The treatment of such deep burns is not easy. Normally, when the skin is wounded, stem cells in the epidermis divide repeatedly to form new skin cells that advance from all sides to cover the wound. If the burns are deep and extensive, it is difficult for the skin to regenerate and heal the wound. The deep burns covering large areas of Alison's body put her in danger of suffering fluid loss, infection and shock.

If the burns are not too extensive, surgeons may take skin from other parts of the body and graft it onto the wound. But when very large areas of the body are burned, there may not be enough undamaged skin to do this.

The hospital where Alison was treated had been having success with a new technique. This involved taking a few cells, called keratinocytes, from Alison's own skin and culturing them in the laboratory. The stem cells amongst them divided repeatedly and formed a layer of skin. This was grafted over the areas of Alison's skin which would otherwise not have been able to repair themselves. As all of the cells in the grafts were derived from Alison's own cells, her immune system did not reject them. Her wounds are now all healed, though the new skin is paler than usual and she has many scars. "But," she says, "I still have my life".

The cell cycle

The technique of growing new cells in a laboratory, as was done with the stem cells from Alison's skin in the case study, is called **tissue culture**. The cells divide repeatedly, forming a tissue of cells all containing identical genes to the parent cell or cells. For example, a 2 cm × 2 cm piece of skin taken from a patient can produce enough skin to cover their whole body in the space of 3 weeks.

We have seen that, as a zygote becomes an adult human being, cells divide repeatedly to produce an entire human body made up of cells which each contain identical genetic information. Some cells retain their ability to divide even in an adult. They are needed for numerous reasons, such as to produce new cells to heal wounds, to replace skin cells that have worn away, to produce new blood cells to replace worn-out ones and to produce new cells in the digestive system to replace those which are constantly being worn away. Most cells, however, differentiate into cells which have specific functions, such as nerve cells or blood cells, and most of these specialised cells do not normally divide again.

Cells which do divide go through a process known as the **cell cycle**. In a cell in a human embryo, the cell cycle lasts about 24 hours. In this chapter, we will first look at how the cell cycle normally takes place and then consider some examples of how out-of-control cell cycles can lead to cancer.

The stages of the cell cycle

Fig 9.1 shows the stages of the cell cycle.

The longest stage of the cell cycle is **interphase**, during which the cell carries out normal metabolic activities such as respiration and protein synthesis. It is during this stage that DNA replication takes place. This is necessary so that, when the cell divides, each daughter (newly-produced) cell can receive a complete set of genes.

In a human cell, there are 46 chromosomes. In a cell which is not about to divide, each chromosome contains a very long molecule of DNA. But when the cell gets ready for division, the DNA in a chromosome replicates, forming two identical DNA molecules which lie side by side. The chromosome is therefore now made up of two threads called **chromatids**. They remain firmly attached to each other at a point known as the **centromere** (Fig 9.2).

interphase

mitosis

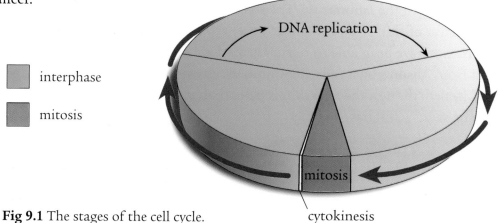

Fig 9.1 The stages of the cell cycle.

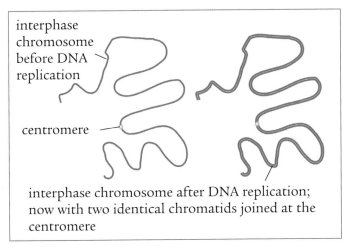

interphase chromosome before DNA replication

centromere

interphase chromosome after DNA replication; now with two identical chromatids joined at the centromere

Fig 9.2 Chromosomes during the cell cycle.

The cell then moves into the next stage of the cell cycle, called **mitosis**. This is the stage at which the nucleus of the cell divides into two nuclei. During mitosis, the two chromatids which make up each chromosome break apart. One of them goes into one new nucleus and one into the other. In this way, the new cells will be genetically identical to each other and to the original parent cell.

The cell itself usually divides next, in a process called **cytokinesis**. After this, each of the daughter (newly-produced) cells goes back into interphase again.

SAQ

9.1 Make a copy of the pie chart below, which represents the cell cycle. Use label lines and annotations to summarise what is taking place during each stage.

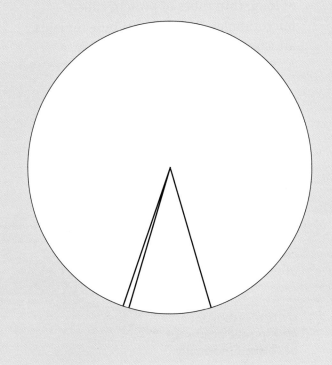

9.2 The graph below shows how the quantity of DNA and the mass of a cell changed during two cell cycles. Make a copy of the graph and mark on it:
   a when DNA replication occurs;
   b the name of the part of the cell cycle in which DNA replication occurs;
   c the time periods in which mitosis occurs;
   d when cytokinesis occurs.
      In each case explain how you arrived at your conclusion.

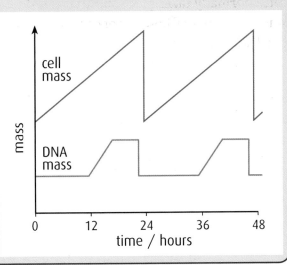

Mitosis and cytokinesis

In mitosis, the chromatids of each of the 46 chromosomes are split apart and shared out into two new nuclei. The chromatids are moved around inside the cell by means of **microtubules** made of a protein called **actin**. Each chromosome is first made to lie in the middle of the cell, and then pulled apart into its two chromatids. These are then pulled to the two ends of the cell, so that there are two identical groups of 46 chromatids. Usually, new nuclear envelopes form around each group. Mitosis is now complete.

Usually, the cytoplasm also divides, so that there are now two cells each containing a nucleus. The division of the cytoplasm happens during cytokinesis.

Mitosis is made up four stages: **prophase**, **metaphase**, **anaphase** and **telophase**. The four stages run into each other.

late interphase

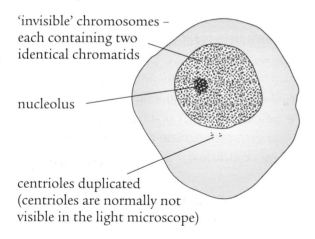

'invisible' chromosomes –
each containing two
identical chromatids

nucleolus

centrioles duplicated
(centrioles are normally not
visible in the light microscope)

Note
In Figs 9.3–9.7, the cells are shown with 4 chromosomes instead of the actual number of 46.

Fig 9.3 Late interphase and prophase.

Prophase

During prophase (Fig 9.3), the chromosomes become visible. Up to now, they have been lying in the nucleus as extremely long and thin threads, so thin that they cannot be seen at all with a light microscope. As prophase begins to get under way, the DNA molecules coil and supercoil, shortening and getting thicker until they eventually form threads that are thick enough to be visible if they are stained. This process is called **condensation** (but has nothing to do with 'condensation reactions').

When the chromosomes appear, they can sometimes be seen to be made of two threads – chromatids. The chromatids are held together at the centromere. The two chromatids of each chromosome contain identical molecules of DNA, formed in DNA replication during interphase.

As prophase proceeds, the nucleolus disappears. It is also at this stage that the **spindle** begins to form. Earlier, the **centriole** will have divided to form two centrioles. These now move away from each other to opposite ends of the cell. The centrioles organise the formation of long, thin tubes of protein called microtubules. Each microtubule remains attached to a centriole at one end.

prophase

chromosomes
condense and are
visible as threads,
but individual
chromatids not
often visible

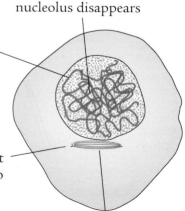

nucleolus disappears

centrioles move apart
and spindle begins to
be formed (normally
not visible)

microtubules forming part of
the developing spindle

Metaphase

The nuclear envelope disappears. The loss of the nuclear envelope means that the whole of the cell is available for manoeuvring the chromosomes. By the time the nuclear envelope has completely broken down, the microtubules have attached themselves to the centromeres of the chromosomes. Each centromere is grabbed by one microtubule on either side. The microtubules pull in opposite directions on the centromeres, bringing the chromosomes to lie at the centre, or **equator**, of the cell (Fig 9.4).

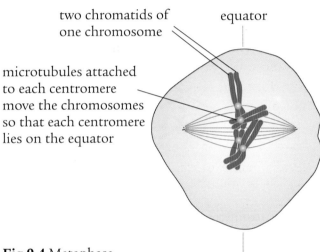

two chromatids of one chromosome

equator

microtubules attached to each centromere move the chromosomes so that each centromere lies on the equator

Fig 9.4 Metaphase.

Anaphase

Now the centromeres split. The microtubules are still pulling on them, so the centromeres and the chromatids are pulled apart and moved to either end, or **pole**, of the cell (Fig 9.5).

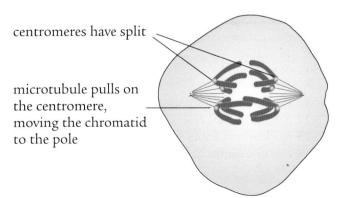

centromeres have split

microtubule pulls on the centromere, moving the chromatid to the pole

Fig 9.5 Anaphase.

Telophase

The two groups of chromatids have now arrived at the poles. Each group contains a complete set of chromatids (46 in reality), which we can now call chromosomes again. The microtubules making up the spindle fibres break down, so the spindle disappears. New nuclear envelopes form around each group of chromosomes. The chromosomes slowly decondense (get thinner again) and 'disappear' (Fig 9.6).

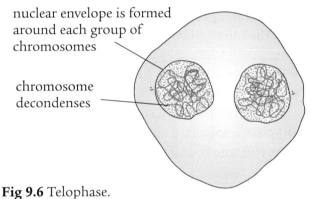

nuclear envelope is formed around each group of chromosomes

chromosome decondenses

Fig 9.6 Telophase.

Cytokinesis

Usually, the cytoplasm now divides (Fig 9.7). This forms two new cells, each with a nucleus containing a complete set of 46 chromosomes, and each with a centriole. The new cells are genetically identical to each other and to the original, parent cell.

The cell then moves into interphase once more.

A summary of mitosis and cytokinesis is shown in Fig 9.10.

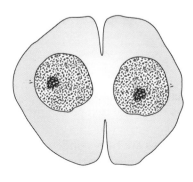

Fig 9.7 Cytokinesis.

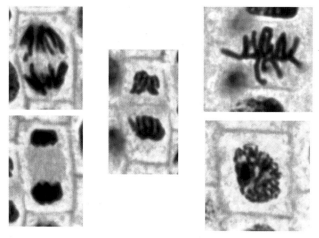
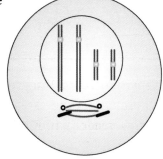
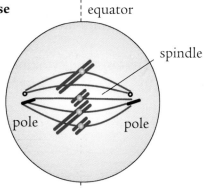

Fig 9.8 Stages of mitosis and cytokinesis in an onion root tip, as seen in a light microscope, but not in the correct order.

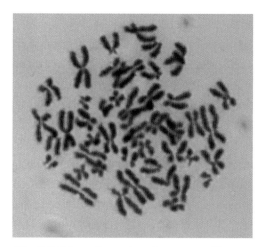

Fig 9.9 Metaphase in a human cell.

prophase

1 chromosomes condense and become visible
2 each chromosome is made up of two chromatids
3 centrioles move and spindle starts to form

anaphase

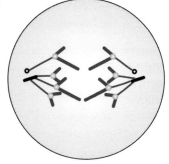

8 centromeres split
9 microtubules pull chromatids apart
10 chromatids of each chromosome pulled to opposite poles

metaphase   equator   spindle   pole   pole

4 nuclear envelope disappears
5 centrioles reach the two poles and spindle is completed
6 chromosomes are fully condensed
7 microtubules move centromeres to equator

telophase

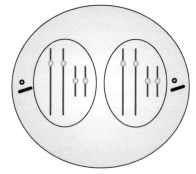

11 chromatids now called chromosomes
12 chromosomes reach poles
13 nuclear envelopes form
14 chromosomes decondense

cytokinesis

15 cytoplasm divides into two

Fig 9.10 Summary of mitosis and cytokinesis.

SAQ

9.3a Compare the photographs in Fig 9.8 with the diagrams in Figs 9.3–9.7. Identify the stages in the photographs and give your reasons.

b The metaphase shown in Fig 9.9 looks very different from the metaphase in Fig 9.8 (ignoring colour, number and shape of chromosomes). Suggest why it looks different.

9.4 A student looked at a prepared slide of a group of cells in various stages of cell division. He identified the stage in 100 cells and counted up how many cells he could see in each stage. These are his results.

Stage	Number of cells
interphase	71
prophase	16
metaphase	8
anaphase	3
telophase	2

a How many cells were in a stage of mitosis?

b Explain what these data tell us about the relative lengths of time taken to complete each stage of the cell cycle.

The significance of mitosis

Mitosis produces new cells which are genetically identical to the parent cell. They have the same number of chromosomes and identical DNA.

This is how cells divide when the body just needs more of the same. Mitosis is the type of division which occurs in a developing embryo, and throughout the growth of a human being.

Mitosis continues to occur in some parts of the body even when we are fully grown. For example, keratinocytes in the epidermis of the skin divide by mitosis to produce new cells which gradually work their way up to the surface before becoming filled up with keratin to form a dead, protective layer. These dead cells are constantly being rubbed off, and are replaced with new ones.

Mitosis also comes into play when part of the body is damaged and needs repair. For example, if you cut yourself, keratinocytes will produce new cells which spread across the wound to form a new, protective layer of skin.

Mitosis and meiosis

Mitosis is not the only kind of nuclear division. There is another one, known as **meiosis**.

(Do take great care over the spellings of mitosis and meiosis, because unless they are spelt absolutely correctly a reader will not be sure which you mean.)

Fig 9.11 shows why meiosis is needed. At fertilisation, the nucleus of an egg cell fuses with the nucleus of a sperm cell. If the egg and the sperm each had 46 chromosomes, then the

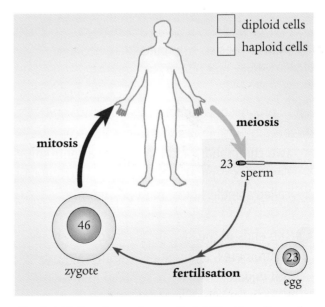

Fig 9.11 Mitosis produces diploid body cells and meiosis produces the haploid gametes – egg and sperm.

zygote would have 92. As the zygote divides by mitosis and becomes first an embryo and then an adult human, each cell would have 92 chromosomes. The eggs and sperms which this person made would also have 92 chromosomes. So, there would be a doubling of chromosomes in each generation.

Obviously this is not what happens. There needs to be a stage at which the number of chromosomes is halved so that the normal number is restored when fertilisation takes place. This is done by means of meiosis.

Meiosis is often known as a **reduction division**, because it reduces the number of chromosomes. In the testes and the ovaries, cells divide by meiosis to produce eggs and sperm. Each egg and each sperm therefore has only 23 chromosomes instead of 46. When the egg and sperm fuse, the zygote has the full number of 46 once more.

You may remember that our cells contain 23 different kinds of chromosomes. Eggs and sperm each have one complete set. They are said to be **haploid** cells. Our body cells, however, have two complete sets. They are said to be **diploid** cells. Meiosis produces haploid cells from diploid cells. Two haploid cells can then fuse together at fertilisation to form a diploid zygote.

Summary

1. The cell cycle is a repeated sequence of interphase, mitosis and cytokinesis.

2. During interphase, cells carry out their normal activities such as protein synthesis. DNA is replicated.

3. In mitosis, chromosomes are shared out equally between two daughter nuclei.

4. Mitosis consists of prophase, metaphase, anaphase and telophase.

5. In prophase, chromosomes condense and become visible, using a light microscope, as two chromatids held together at a centromere. Centrioles separate and lay down microtubules, called spindle fibres, between them.

6. The ends of the spindle fibres connect to the centromeres, and pull the chromosomes to the cell equator. This stage is called metaphase.

7. In anaphase, the centromeres split. The spindle fibres pull the chromatids apart and towards the poles of the cell.

8. In telophase, the chromosomes decondense. A nuclear membrane forms around each new nucleus.

9. Usually, cytokinesis follows, in which the cytoplasm divides so that two new daughter cells are formed.

10. The two daughter cells are genetically identical to each other and to the parent cell. Mitosis is the type of cell division which is used for growth and repair.

11. In the production of gametes, a different type of cell division called meiosis is used. The division of a cell by meiosis results in daughter cells which each have half the number of chromosomes of the parent cell.

12. A cell with one set of chromosomes, such as an egg or a sperm, is said to be haploid. A cell with two sets of chromosomes, like all other body cells, is said to be diploid.

Detecting and treating cancer

It was Pete's wife, Emma, who saw it first. He'd always had a couple of moles on his back, but this one seemed to have got bigger, spreading out sideways and looking dark, uneven and reddish around the edges. Pete couldn't see it himself even when he tried using a mirror, but Emma nagged him so hard that eventually he went to see his GP.

His doctor was very concerned when he saw the spreading mole. He asked Pete whether he spent much time out of doors, and Pete said, yes, he did because he worked as a roofer. The doctor drew out the information that Pete often worked without a shirt in the summer, and that he had to be a bit careful because his skin didn't tan easily.

"Well," said the doctor, "I think we have to consider the possibility that this is a melanoma. That's a kind of skin cancer, and we need to get that mole out of your skin as soon as we can."

Pete first had a biopsy, in which his skin was anaesthetised and a small sample of the mole taken away so that the cells in it could be examined microscopically. Without waiting for the results of the test, he had an operation in which the entire mole, and a large area of tissue around it, was removed. Tests on the biopsy material and on the removed mole itself showed that it was definitely a melanoma. Three years afterwards, Pete is fine, but he goes back for tests every few months to make sure that the cancerous cells have not got a foothold anywhere else in his body. So far, so good.

Pete has been told that he has 'skin type 1' which doesn't tan easily and is readily damaged by ultraviolet (UV) rays from the Sun. He's careful now to keep his skin covered as much as he can. So are the other men who work with him – it has given them all a scare.

Pete was lucky. Without quick action, his type of melanoma becomes untreatable and deadly. Melanomas have been getting more common in the UK population, possibly because more of us now go on holidays abroad where we expose our unaccustomed skin to bright sunlight and its damaging UV rays.

Sometimes cells divide too much and form a lump or **tumour**. This may not be harmful if the tumour stays in one place and as long as it does not grow too much. A tumour like this is said to be **benign**. But if the tumour invades tissues around it or spreads around the body, this is dangerous and is a cancer. The most dangerous behaviour is when cells break away and start producing more tumours elsewhere in the body, which is known as **metastasis**. Then the tumour is said to be **malignant**.

Many cancers can be cured, and the percentage of people who are successfully treated for cancer is going steadily upwards. The earlier the cancer is detected, the better the chance of a cure. This is because, in its early stages, a tumour may be benign, only later becoming malignant. But, as with most diseases, prevention is much better than cure.

In this chapter, we will concentrate on two very common cancers – breast cancer and lung cancer. We will consider what triggers them, how they can be treated and how they can be prevented.

What causes cancer?

Fig 9.12 shows that the older you get the more likely you are to suffer from several forms of cancer. Cancers often only appear after a number of separate events have each damaged a cell. The older you are, the more likely that this has happened in one cell, which then may become a cancer. In the case study, the original damage to

Pete's skin which caused the melanoma to develop might have occurred while he was in his teens.

A person's risk of getting cancer is affected both by their genes and by their lifestyle. In Pete's case, he had skin type 1, as a result of his genes. He had then exposed his susceptible skin cells to an environmental factor – ultraviolet rays from the Sun – which damaged the DNA in some of his vulnerable skin cells. In other cases, either genes or environmental factors may be enough to trigger the cancer on their own. Even people with other skin types can still get melanomas, if they expose their skin to too much sunlight.

Our cells contain many different genes which regulate cell division. They are responsible for making sure that cells do divide when needed, but also that they do not divide when they shouldn't.

Some of these regulatory genes, called **proto-oncogenes**, can mutate to form slightly different ones called **oncogenes**. Oncogenes can cause cancer. They allow the cell to divide uncontrollably, over and over again.

Cells also contain **repressor genes**. These genes normally inhibit cell division. They can mutate so that they lose their function, which once again allows uncontrollable division to take place (Fig 9.13).

Cells contain a number of different proto-oncogenes and repressor genes, and usually more than one mutation is needed to start off a cancer. Our cells contain many more different proto-oncogenes than repressor genes, and often several of these must mutate before cancer develops. But there are different versions of these genes, and some of them are more likely to mutate than others. Some people may therefore have ones which make them more susceptible to certain types of cancer than others.

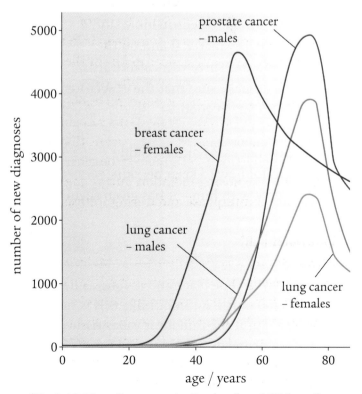

Fig 9.12 New diagnoses in England and Wales of selected cancers in 2000.

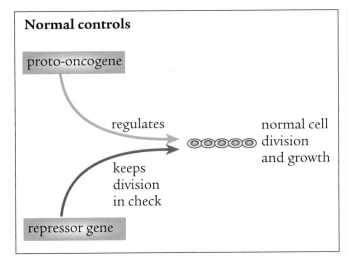

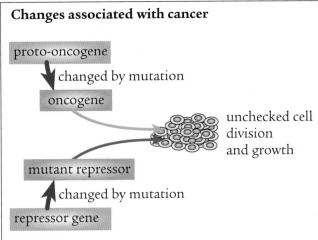

Fig 9.13 Oncogenes and repressor genes in cancer.

This helps to explain why cancers become more common as people get older. The longer you live, the more chance there is that several regulatory genes in a cell may become altered.

So, if we want to know what causes cancer, we must look for what makes proto-oncogenes and repressor genes mutate. This can happen absolutely randomly, because mistakes do occasionally get made when DNA replication occurs. But the risk of mutations happening can also be increased by many different environmental factors, known as **carcinogens**. They include:

- ionising radiation, such as X-rays and cosmic rays;
- ultraviolet light;
- some chemicals, such as mustard gas, aflatoxin and chromium;
- infection by certain kinds of viruses.

All of these damage DNA, changing base sequences and therefore changing the primary structure of the proteins for which they code. These proteins are often enzymes, and they affect metabolic reactions in the cell.

Ionising radiation

Ionising radiation includes X-rays, alpha rays and beta radiation. We are all exposed to some of it all the time, and this is known as **background radiation**. Exposure increases when we are given X-rays or if we are exposed to radon gas (which can leak out of some kinds of rocks and build up inside houses) or to nuclear fall-out from a nuclear bomb. Some forms of ionising radiation can penetrate deep into the body, and so can cause cancer in any of the organs. Ionising radiation contains great quantities of energy, and is powerful enough to break bonds in DNA molecules. This can change the base sequences in DNA. For reasons that are not fully understood, cells seem to be most vulnerable to ionising radiation during the latter part of interphase and during mitosis.

Ultraviolet light

Ultraviolet light is electromagnetic radiation with wavelengths just a little shorter than our eyes can detect. Many insect eyes do 'see' ultraviolet light. Ultraviolet light has less energy than ionising radiation, so it cannot penetrate beneath our skin and the cancers it causes are skin cancers. Cells are most sensitive to ultraviolet light when they are in early interphase.

Slip, slop, slap

The whole world got to know about the Australian 'slip, slop, slap' campaign in the 1990s. It was introduced to try to reduce the frightening rates of melanoma and other skin cancers in the population. Much of Australia receives a lot of sunshine, and people's lifestyles include many outdoor activities, especially on the beach and in the water. With their mostly fair skins, Australians don't have much inbuilt protection against the Sun's ultraviolet rays.

So Australians were encouraged to slip on a shirt, slop on sun protection cream and slap on a hat, to reduce the exposure of skin to sunlight. The campaign was very successful, and there has been a major change of attitude in people's behaviour. As skin cancers can take many years to appear, it will be a while before the full benefits are seen.

Sun creams, intended to block ultraviolet rays from penetrating the skin, contain ultraviolet-absorbing substances such as cinnamates, zinc oxides and titanium oxides. The higher the factor, the more protection they give. However, there are now concerns that the creams do not help as much as people have imagined. One reason for this is that people believe that, if they have put on a sun cream, they can stay out in the sun as long as they like, which is simply not true.

Ultraviolet radiation is classified as UVA, with wavelengths longer than 320 nm; UVB, with wavelengths between 290 to 320 nm; and UVC, with wavelengths shorter than 290 nm. UVB is the most important of these in terms of skin cancer. Most UVB is blocked high up in the atmosphere by the ozone layer. The hole in the ozone layer which has developed over the South Pole, and is even affecting some parts of Australia, has increased the exposure of people in that part of the world to damaging UVB radiation. The UK is also affected by high altitude ozone loss, and this, too, is contributing to an increase in skin cancers.

Consult your doctor if a freckle or mole changes shape, colour, size, itches or bleeds...

Most melanomas can be cured.

CANCER SOCIETY'S MELANOMA AWARENESS CAMPAIGN

GUARD AGAINST SKIN CANCER!

Slip on a shirt
Slop on a sunscreen
Slap on a hat

SLIP SLOP SLAP

CANCER SOCIETY OF NEW ZEALAND (INC.)

Chemicals

An ever-increasing number of chemicals are being found to act as carcinogens. Mustard gas, used in the First World War, has been known for a long time to increase the rate of cancers of the nose, bronchus and larynx. Like most other chemical carcinogens, it has its effect by directly reacting with DNA molecules and altering their structure. Tobacco smoke contains several different kinds of carcinogens, including nitrosamines and oxides of nitrogen. Nitric oxide is a type of **free radical**; that is, a chemical which can oxidise other chemicals – including DNA – in our cells. The action of free radicals can be counter-balanced by **antioxidants**, such as vitamins A, C and E. Eating foods with plenty of these in our diet gives some protection against free radicals and helps to reduce the risk of getting cancer. You will already have seen that antioxidants also appear to provide some protection against coronary heart disease (see page 118).

Viruses

Viruses are tiny bags of protein surrounding a nucleic acid, which can be either RNA or DNA (see page 219). They can do nothing on their own, needing to take over a cell and hijack its machinery in order to reproduce. They inject their nucleic acid into a cell, and the cell then follows the instructions on this nucleic acid to make more virus particles.

Some viruses can cause cancer. Perhaps the best known is the human papilloma virus, HPV. Some types of this virus only cause us the slightest of problems – for example, a wart on a hand. Warts are not dangerous because they are not invasive; they are benign tumours. But some kinds of HPV carry a code for a protein which interacts with a region of our DNA coding for a protein called p53. Alteration of the p53 gene is involved in the cause of very many human cancers, and a woman infected with some types of the HPV virus has an increased risk of getting cervical cancer. The virus is passed on during sexual intercourse.

Weakened immune system

It is thought that many cells in all of us become potentially cancerous. Normally, however, our own immune system spots them as being different and destroys them well before they develop into noticeable tumours.

If someone's immune system is badly impaired, then this protective device breaks down. For example, many patients with HIV/AIDS, in which T lymphocytes are destroyed, develop an otherwise rare skin cancer called Kaposi's sarcoma.

Identifying the causes of cancer

Finding clear evidence about exactly what causes particular types of cancer is very difficult, for the same reasons as were described for CHD on page 106. Researchers cannot do an experiment in which they expose one group of people to something that they think might be carcinogenic, and compare the incidence of cancer in that group with a control group.

That kind of experiment is done on animals, and has yielded a very large amount of useful information, saving many human lives. But there are problems with this approach. Firstly, there can be a strong public reaction against these experiments, as for example when dogs were made to smoke cigarettes in the 1960s. Secondly, it is not always safe to assume that the effects of a potential carcinogen in humans will be the same as its effects in other animals.

When looking for the cause of a type of cancer, researchers often use epidemiological studies. **Epidemiology** is the study of the patterns of the occurrence of disease in populations. It involves collecting large amounts of information about how many people in different categories have the disease – for example, in different age groups, of different sexes, of different income groups and so on. Statistical analysis of these figures can provide clues to the factors which are most closely linked to an increased incidence of the disease.

Evidence linking smoking and lung cancer

Fig 9.14 shows how increases in smoking and lung cancer have occurred since 1911. This pattern could be explained if smoking was actually causing lung cancer. The time lag between the rise and then fall in cigarette smoking and the rise and fall in lung cancer deaths is what we would expect, because we know that it can take many years for cancer to appear.

When two things like lung cancer death rate and number of cigarettes smoked seem to be linked in this way, the two are said to be **correlated**. However, this correlation does not prove that smoking *causes* lung cancer. It could also be explained if some other factor was causing both an increase in smoking and an increase in lung cancer.

Much research has been done since the 1950s on the effects of smoking on health. We now have a great deal of evidence that there is a causal link between smoking and lung cancer. Fig 9.15 shows another piece of epidemiological evidence for this.

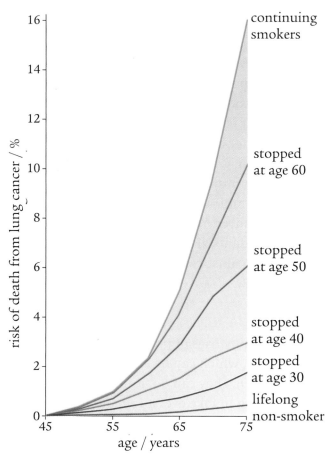

Fig 9.15 The effect on risk of lung cancer of stopping smoking at different ages.

It becomes very difficult to propose a hypothesis, other than that smoking causes lung cancer, to explain why stopping smoking at any age results in the reduced risk of lung cancer shown in Fig 9.15.

Further support comes from our knowledge of how carcinogens in cigarette smoke can affect the DNA in cells, so that they lose their normal control mechanisms and begin to divide uncontrollably.

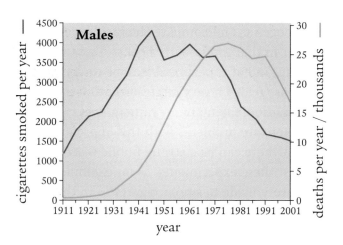

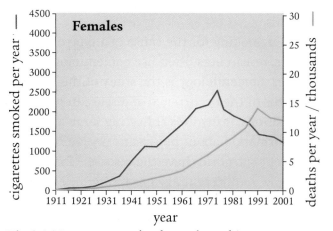

Fig 9.14 Lung cancer deaths and smoking rates from 1911.

9.5 Explain why each of these factors can increase the risk of developing cancer:
a getting older;
b having parents or grandparents who have had cancer;
c being exposed to X-rays.

9.6 In 1951, a study of 40 000 British doctors was started which ended in 1991. As a result of this study the effect of smoking on life expectancy can be shown in the graph below.

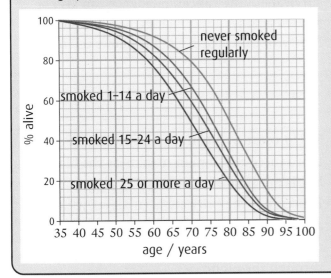

a Which diseases, linked to smoking, could help to explain the data in the graph?
b Using the data in the graph create a table of survivorship (% alive) at ages 45, 65, 85 and 95, for the categories of 'never smoked' and 'smoked more than 25 a day'.

	Survivorship / % alive	
Age	Smoked >25 a day	Never smoked
45		
65		

c This type of study is known as a cohort study. What is the advantage of the data from this kind of study?

9.7 Discuss whether the reduction of lung cancer risk following stopping smoking (Fig 9.15) is more convincing than the data in Fig 9.14 in suggesting that smoking causes lung cancer.

Evidence for the causes of breast cancer

Epidemiology has not given quite such clear-cut information about what causes breast cancer. This is at least partly because there are many different factors which affect a person's risk of getting this disease – which is probably true of most cancers. Fig 9.16 shows how the incidence of breast cancer increases with age. 80% of cases occur in women who have passed the menopause. This is the stage in life when the menstrual cycle stops and the woman no longer ovulates or has periods. It usually happens around the age of 50. After the menopause, the woman's ovaries stop secreting the hormone oestrogen. Oestrogen is known to have a protective effect against breast cancer.

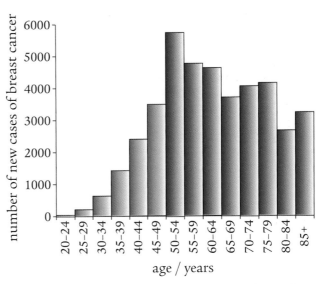

Fig 9.16 Incidence of breast cancer – numbers of new cases in UK in 1998.

173

So, being female and being over 50 are two risk factors for breast cancer. Breast cancer does also affect men, but to a much lesser extent. In 2001, 11 574 women died from breast cancer in the UK, but there were only 80 male deaths from this disease.

Epidemiology has also shown that having a family history of breast cancer, beginning puberty early, having a late menopause, drinking large amounts of alcohol or being obese are all associated with an increased risk of getting breast cancer.

Incidence and prevalence

Governments, and organisations such as those responsible for health care, collect and use epidemiological data in several different ways.

The **incidence** of a disease can be defined as the number of new cases occurring in a population in a given period of time. If these data are collected each year, then we can plot incidence against time, as in Fig 9.17. This can show whether fewer people are now getting the disease, or whether the incidence is increasing. In this graph, **mortality** from lung cancer is also shown. This gives some information about survival of lung cancer. Incidence can also be plotted against other factors, to see if there is a link with that factor. Fig 9.16 shows us the

Prostate cancer worry

Lung cancer deaths in men have been dropping year on year for some time now. This is not surprising as it is essentially avoidable – by not smoking. But the second most common cause of cancer death in men is not showing a drop. This is prostate cancer.

The graph below shows data for England and Wales.

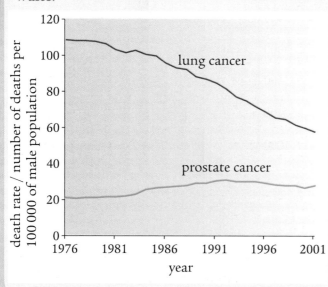

The prostate is a gland forming part of the reproductive system in men, near the bladder, but is not part of the urinary system. However, if the prostate is enlarged, it causes a pressure that interferes with urination. This means that urination has to be frequent, even through the night.

Many men are not aware of the risks or symptoms of prostate cancer. Like breast cancer, it is most prevalent in the over-50s but can occur in younger men.

Another problem is that the prostate enlarges as men age anyway and benign tumours in the prostate are common. So how do you tell the difference?

This can only be done by medical experts. But many men are reluctant to report a worry about the prostate to their GPs. Here is a case for health promotion specialists, if there ever was one (see page 181).

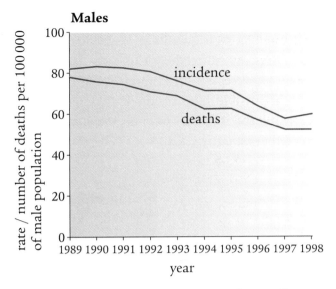

Males

Fig 9.17 Incidence of lung cancer and mortality rate from lung cancer in males from 1989 to 1998 in four central English counties (Berks, Bucks, Northants, Oxon).

incidence of breast cancer plotted against age. We can immediately see that the older you are, the more likely you are to get this cancer.

The **prevalence** of a disease can be defined as the number of existing cases in a population in a given period of time. Governments and health organisations may want to know this because it tells them how much burden is being put on their health care facilities by this disease. The prevalence of a disease is affected by its incidence, but it is also affected by how long people who have the disease survive. If incidence starts to go down while prevalence is going up, that's a good sign. It means that fewer new cases are happening, and that people with the disease are living longer. However, we would soon expect prevalence to go down as well, because fewer new cases are being added.

9.8 A government has introduced better screening programmes for breast cancer. Diagnosis is now happening earlier. They are also running an education campaign alerting people about risk factors and how to avoid them. Treatment for breast cancer is improving, so that more people are surviving for longer.

When figures are published, they show that the incidence of breast cancer does seem to be going down, as hoped. However, the prevalence of the disease is going up.

Explain how each of these factors might be contributing to the changes in incidence and/or prevalence:
• better screening programmes;
• earlier diagnosis;
• education campaign;
• better treatment.

9.9 The prevalence of cigarette smoking among young people aged 11–15 in England is shown below.

Year	Percentage males	Percentage females
1984	13	13
1986	7	12
1990	9	10
1996	11	15
1999	8	10
2000	9	12
2002	9	11

The percentage of people aged 11–15 who were regular smokers in 2002 is shown below.

Age	Percentage of males smoking regularly	Percentage of females smoking regularly
11	1	1
12	4	3
13	5	8
14	13	18
15	20	26

Plot graphs of these data and discuss their implications.

Detecting cancer

It is important to detect cancer as early as possible, as this has a huge effect on the likelihood of it being cured. In the UK, **screening** programmes for breast cancer and cervical cancer have greatly reduced the number of deaths which these diseases cause each year (Fig 9.24). Frequently, however, cancer is not detected until a person feels unwell or is worried about a lump they have noticed. By this time, it could be too late for successful treatment. Making people aware of possible signs of cancer can help in increasing the numbers of cancers which are detected at an early stage.

Mammography is offered on the NHS to all women over 50. It is a very quick and easy process which involves taking an **X-ray** of the breasts to look for small tumours (Fig 9.18). If something unusual or suspicious is seen, the woman will be called to go for further tests. **Chest X-rays** can also be used to look for lung cancer.

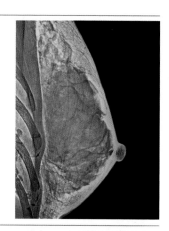

Fig 9.18 Mammography. This mammogram is of a healthy breast and is in false colour. The grey areas in the breast are fibrous tissue and blood vessels are coloured red. The ribs are shown to the left.

Thermography is another method which can detect breast cancer at an early stage. It works on the principle that the development of cancer in a breast is linked to an increase of metabolic activity in it. So, if breast tissue is found to be warmer than other tissues in the body, this can be an early indication of cancer.

The temperature of the breast tissue is detected using cameras sensitive to infrared radiation. The data collected are then used to construct a thermogram – a 'heat map' – of the body. Fig 9.19 shows a thermogram showing increased skin temperature over a cancer in the left breast (yellow = highest temperature).

Fig 9.19 Thermography.

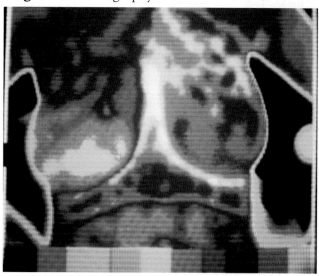

Ultrasound scanning uses sound waves to build up a picture of parts of the body which are suspected of containing cancerous tissues. It is cheaper and easier than CT, PET or MRI scans (see opposite), and it also has the advantage of not exposing the patient to X-rays. Ultrasound scans are often used to help to decide if a lump shown up by mammography is a cancer or not. It is also used to check for cancers in the liver and other parts of the abdomen (Fig 9.20).

Fig 9.20 Ultrasound scan through the abdomen showing an enlarged spleen (pink).

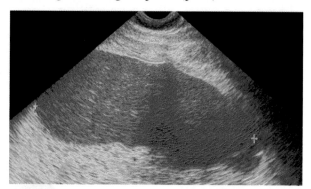

CT scans, often known as CAT scans, also involve using X-rays, which are sent through the body from different angles. CAT stands for **computer assisted tomography**. X-rays are absorbed by different amounts in different structures, so a computer can build up a three-dimensional picture (Fig 9.21), in which a tumour can be picked out.

An injection of a dye that absorbs X-rays makes the blood vessels stand out. CT scans are normally only carried out if a person is suspected of having a cancer. Another reason for keeping the number of CT scans down is the potential harm done by X-rays, which themselves increase the risk of cancer.

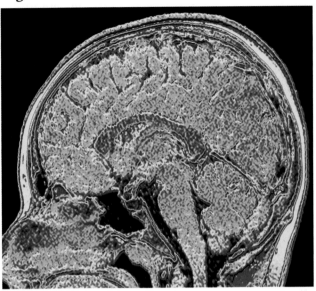

Fig 9.21 CAT scan of a normal brain.

MRI scans involve the patient lying very still inside a huge magnet. The magnetic fields in different parts of the body are measured. MRI stands for **magnetic resonance imaging**. A computer uses the data to build up images (Fig 9.22). MRI scans can provide more information than CT scans. Like all the other tests, MRI scans are completely painless, but some people feel uncomfortably 'closed in' while lying inside the magnet.

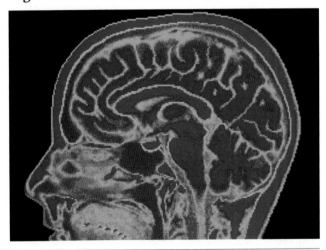

Fig 9.22 MRI scan of a normal brain.

PET scans involve injecting a substance which is very similar to glucose into the blood. The substance is called **2-deoxyglucose**, and it is 'labelled' because it gives off positrons. Cells take up the 2-deoxyglucose and try to use it for respiration, though in fact they cannot do so. The more metabolically active cells are, the more 2-deoxyglucose they take up, and therefore the more positrons they emit. The PET – **positron emission tomography** – scanner detects this, and uses it to build up a picture of the body showing different rates of metabolic activity (Fig 9.23). An area with unexpectedly high activity can indicate that a tumour is growing there.

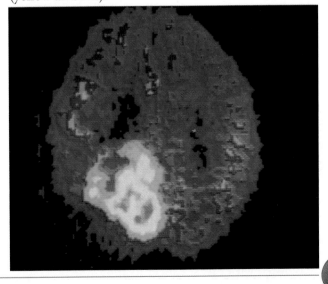

Fig 9.23 PET scan of a brain showing a tumour (yellow and red).

177

Treating breast cancer

When breast cancer has been detected, the patient and her doctors have a number of choices about how to treat it. They will both need to think carefully about this. Their choices will be influenced by knowing whether the cancer is likely to have spread to other parts of the body, or if it is confined to the breast, how early it has been diagnosed (Fig 9.25) and whether breast cancer runs in the woman's family.

In general, breast cancer that occurs in younger women is more 'aggressive' than cancer that does not begin until middle age – that is, it grows and spreads more rapidly.

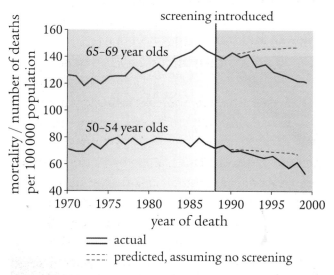

Fig 9.24 Mortality from breast cancer in England and Wales before and after screening was introduced. Screening can detect cancers at an early stage.

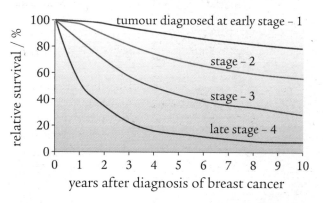

Fig 9.25 Survival after diagnosis of breast cancer by stage of development of the cancer at diagnosis. Data from women in the English West Midlands, diagnosed with breast cancer in 1985–1989.

If **surgery** is decided upon, there are still a number of options to be considered. If the cancer is small, has been caught early and is judged very unlikely to have spread, the patient may only need a **lumpectomy**. This means just cutting out and removing the lump and the tissues immediately around it. If the cancer is more advanced or looks to have spread, then she may have a **mastectomy**, in which the whole breast is removed. Usually, some of the lymph nodes under the arm are removed at the same time, as cancer frequently spreads to there from the breast.

Following surgery, the patient is often given a course of **radiation therapy**. This involves using ionising radiation to kill any remaining cancer cells. It can also be used before surgery, when it may help to shrink a large tumour, making it easier to remove. Modern equipment used for radiation therapy is very good at focussing the radiation precisely on the tumour, minimising damage to other tissues. All the same, many people undergoing radiation therapy feel ill and tired.

Chemotherapy is another option. This involves giving drugs which are designed to destroy the cancer cells while not having too great an effect on other cells in the body. However, most of these drugs work by acting on cells which are dividing. This means that they affect any dividing cells, not only cancer cells. This is why people having chemotherapy usually lose their hair, because the drugs stop the cells at the base of the hair from dividing. Chemotherapy affects the whole body, whereas radiotherapy can be targeted quite precisely on the cancerous cells.

SAQ

9.10 Summarise in words the main conclusions from the data presented in Figs 9.24 and 9.25.

Treatment with **tamoxifen**, first introduced in 1973, has had a very great impact on the survival rate of women with breast cancer. It works by interfering with the effects of the hormone oestrogen. Oestrogen is secreted naturally in the body, by the ovaries. Some tumours, called oestrogen-sensitive tumours, have oestrogen receptors on the cell surface membranes of their cells. Oestrogen binds with these receptors and sets off processes in the cells which encourage them to divide. Tamoxifen works by binding to these oestrogen receptors and so stopping oestrogen encouraging the tumour to grow. Tamoxifen is now the most widely-used treatment for breast cancer.

In a study which was reported in 2003, involving nearly 5200 women and hospitals throughout the world, the advantages of using tamoxifen were demonstrated. It was shown that, in post-menopausal women, there was a 43% reduction in the risk of breast cancer recurrence and a 46% reduction in disease spreading from one breast to the other after surgery for breast cancer with drug treatment. The treatment involved using tamoxifen for five years, followed by 2.4 years of another drug, letrozole. Letrozole reduces the amount of oestrogen circulating around the body.

Treating lung cancer

Lung cancer is more difficult to treat than breast cancer, and the survival rate is lower. Nevertheless, some lung cancers *are* cured, and often their progress can be slowed.

As for breast cancer, there are choices to be made about the best treatment. This will partly depend on the type of lung cancer. **Small cell lung cancer** tumours, as the name suggests, are made up of small, grain-shaped cells. **Non-small cell lung cancer** has tumours with larger cells. These two types of cancer behave in different ways and respond better to different treatments.

Surgery is one option. The operation may involve removing an entire lung, or just part of it. Surgery is normally only used when the cancer has not yet spread to other parts of the body. By the time small cell lung cancer has first been detected, it has almost always spread elsewhere, so surgery is not often used for this.

Radiation therapy and **chemotherapy** may also be used (Fig 9.26). However, in some cases lung cancer patients can be given 'internal' radiation therapy. This is done by passing a tube down one of the bronchi, and then sliding a very narrow catheter containing a radioactive source down inside the tube. In this way, the radiation can be brought really close to the tumour, and there is less chance of other tissues being damaged.

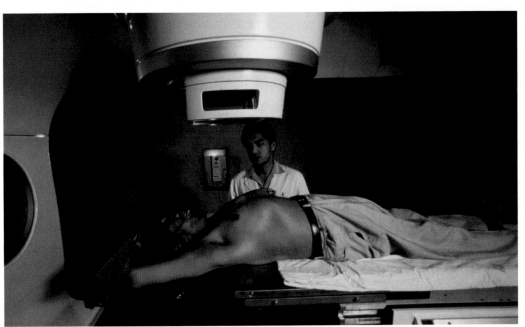

Fig 9.26 This machine is being set up to direct X-rays at a lung cancer tumour. When the operator has left the room, the instrument rotates in a full circle around the patient to give the tumour a lethal dose of X-rays, but not other body tissues.

179

Other treatments for breast and lung cancer

The treatments described above are the main ones currently used against cancer, and they are the most effective. However, there is some success with the development of a different kind of treatment called immunotherapy (Immunology is dealt with in Chapter 12, pages 224–232). People undergoing treatment for cancer may also find that complementary therapies offer them some relief.

Immunotherapy

There are several kinds of immunotherapy, but only a few which have been used with any success against lung cancer or breast cancer.

The most successful use of immunotherapy to date has been against bladder cancer. Patients are given the BCG vaccine, which is normally used to prevent TB. This vaccine stimulates the body's immune system in an unexpected way and it causes the body to attack the cancer cells in the bladder, which the leucocytes now recognise as being 'foreign'.

Melanomas and kidney cancers sometimes respond well to a chemical called **interferon**. This substance is secreted by cells of the immune system when the body is attacked by viruses. Interferon is a **cytokine** – a substance secreted by one type of lymphocyte which affects the behaviour of other cells in the immune system.

There is also some limited success with the use of **cancer vaccines**. The idea here is to prime the immune system to attack cancer cells by injecting a small dose of chemicals (antigens) found only on the cancer cells, but not on other body cells. The leucocytes may 'learn' that this chemical is foreign, and attack the cancer cells. This treatment is in its early days of research, and at the moment it is not widely used as there is only a very small record of any success.

Yet another way of using immunotherapy is to produce **monoclonal antibodies**. First, an antigen found only on the cancer cells is identified. It is then injected into a mouse. The mouse's immune system reacts to it by producing antibodies, which can be injected into the person with cancer. The antibodies can be 'labelled' in some way, so that they show up on scans, allowing the precise position of the cancer to be detected. Or they can have an anti-cancer drug attached to them. As the antibodies bind only to cells with the antigen on them – that is, the cancer cells – the drug is delivered directly to these cells and nowhere else. There has been progress, but there is a long way to go before this technique can be widely used as treatment.

Complementary therapies

Although many cancers are successfully treated, there are still many which are not. People with cancer, whether it is being successfully treated or not, often find that complementary therapies, even if they cannot cure the cancer, can help them to cope with the symptoms and feel better. It is known that mood can influence the effectiveness of the immune system, although this is still not well understood.

There are many different kinds of complementary therapy. Some, including acupuncture and reflexology, involve the practitioner's hands making contact with the body which some people find very reassuring and comforting. Aromatherapy is widely used to help to give the patient a positive outlook and feel better about themselves and their life. Some people try following different diets. There is argument that these therapies on their own cannot cure cancer, but their effect on a person's feeling of well-being can be immense.

Complementary therapies

Collect information about one of the following complementary therapies. Use your results to make a display or presentation to the class.

Possible therapies:

- Nutritional – macrobiotics, diet, nutritional supplements
- Physical approaches – exercise, massage, chiropractic and therapeutic touch
- Traditional Chinese medicine – acupuncture, acupressure, herbal medicine, energy medicine, Qi Gong, homeopathy, Feng Shui
- Unconventional pharmacological therapies – antineoplastins, hydrazine sulfate, chelation therapy
- Spiritual approaches – prayer, meditation
- Psychosocial approaches – stress management, support groups, peer support, individual and family counselling
- Biofeedback, aromatherapy, hyperthermia, magnetic field therapy.

1 Consider:
  a the claims of the therapy, including the mechanism by which it is claimed to work;
  b the evidence presented by supporters of the therapy.

2 Assess the evidence, paying attention to:
  • how much is anecdotal
  • how large the data sets are
  • whether there are controls
  • whether the controls are sound
  • whether there has been any statistical analysis.

3 Are there alternative hypotheses to explain the results other than the ones being claimed, including hypotheses that derive from 'conventional' biological knowledge?

Health promotion specialists

Health promotion specialists are mainly employed by the NHS through Primary Care Trusts and work in a variety of situations, such as schools. Their roles will depend on the context in which they are working. Their work could include such activities as supporting an organisation in its delivery of health promotion and that may involve the provision of specialist advice and resources. It could also include the management and evaluation of health education programmes.

Some of the ways that health promotion specialists may help to reduce the incidence of cancer and increase the chance of successful treatment include:

- advice and support from counsellors to help people give up smoking;
- advice from dieticians – for example, about eating foods containing anti-oxidants and combatting obesity;
- producing leaflets to encourage self-awareness – for example, checking for lumps in the breasts or scrotal sacs, difficulty in passing urine or changes in bowel habits;
- encouraging people to take part in screening programmes – for example, cervical smear tests;
- running menopausal clinics to watch for possible problems.

Health promotion programme

Devise a health promotion programme and outline what it may be expected to achieve, for one of the following:

- reducing smoking rates in either young people or adults;
- promoting participation in breast cancer screening for either pre-menopausal or post-menopausal women.

Summary

1. Cancer is an illness caused by uncontrolled cell division, forming an invasive tumour which grows into surrounding tissues, or a malignant tumour – that is, one containing cells which can break away and form tumours in other parts of the body.

2. Cancer happens when the genes which normally regulate cell division are damaged. Some of these regulatory genes, called proto-oncogenes, can mutate to form oncogenes which cause the cell to divide when it should not.

3. The chance of getting cancer is increased by many different factors, including exposure to ionising radiation, carcinogens such as mustard gas, viruses, genes and ageing.

4. Scans, including ultrasound, CT, MRI and PET scans, can help to detect cancers. Thermography, X-rays and mammography are also used for this purpose.

5. Epidemiological evidence can help to pick out links between the incidence and prevalence of a disease and other factors, to help to identify what factors seem to be associated with it. Incidence is defined as the the number of new cases occurring in a population in unit time, whilst prevalence is the number of existing cases in the population at a certain point in time.

6. There is a great deal of epidemiological evidence to show that smoking increases the risk of many types of cancer, including lung cancer.

7. Breast cancer and lung cancer can be treated with surgery, radiation therapy, chemotherapy, immunotherapy and complementary therapies. There is a high chance of treatment for breast cancer being successful, especially if it is diagnosed at an early stage. Lung cancer is much more difficult to treat.

8. Various types of immunotherapy are being researched and trialled, and many show considerable promise, but as yet there has been only limited success.

9. Many people find that complementary therapies make them feel better during treatment for cancer, helping them to enjoy their lives.

10. Health promotion specialists have a role in designing, managing or participating in programmes designed to increase people's health.

Foetal development

Fauzia had been a heavy smoker since she started smoking in her early teens. Like more than 65% of young, female smokers in Britain, she would really have liked to give up. She had tried several times, but had never managed to stay away from cigarettes for more than about three or four weeks. It wasn't until she knew that she was pregnant that she found the motivation and determination to do it.

It was hard. She couldn't use nicotine patches to supply the nicotine that she craved. Getting a steady supply of nicotine from a patch on its mother might do even more harm to her unborn baby than a burst of nicotine each time she smoked a cigarette.

The thing that really helped her to struggle on without cigarettes was that her partner decided to try to give up too. With no cigarettes around the house – and with a wonderful excuse to eat a bit more than usual – the temptation seemed less than on all the occasions she had tried before.

She's not sure whether she will let herself go back to smoking after the baby is born. She'd like to think that she might be able to become a permanent non-smoker and would like to breastfeed. If she smokes, some of the chemicals will go into her milk. She is also aware of the link between a baby dying from SIDS (sudden infant death syndrome) and smoking by the parents. And there is plenty of evidence that the general health of a baby can be affected by cigarette smoke.

Growth before birth

When a woman becomes pregnant, taking care of her health usually becomes a priority for her. As the foetus grows in her body, whatever she eats, drinks or smokes will effectively be eaten, drunk or smoked by her foetus as well. However careless they have been of their health in the past, most pregnant women want to do whatever they can to ensure the health of their baby.

Before we look at foetal growth, however, you may like to skim through a quick summary of human reproduction.

A review of human reproduction

Fig 10.1 shows the structures of the human male and female reproductive systems.

male – front view of reproductive organs and associated organs

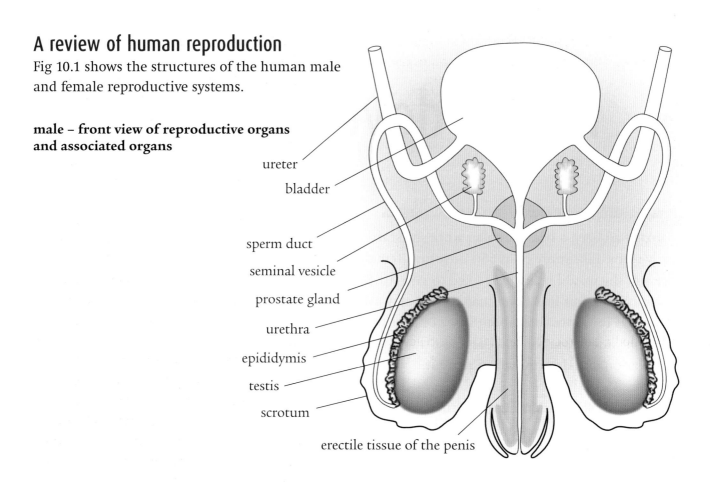

ureter
bladder

sperm duct
seminal vesicle
prostate gland
urethra
epididymis
testis
scrotum

erectile tissue of the penis

female – side view of reproductive organs and associated organs

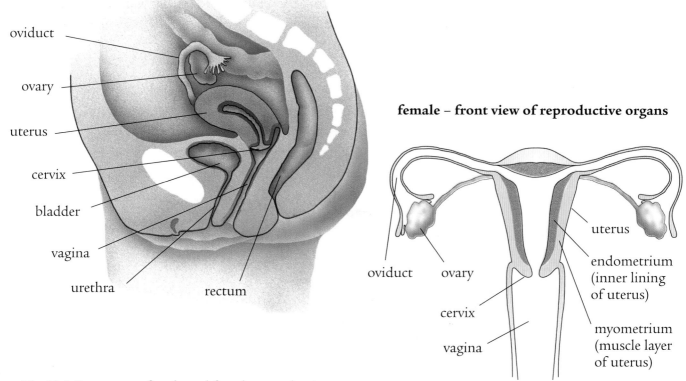

oviduct

ovary

uterus

cervix

bladder

vagina

urethra

rectum

female – front view of reproductive organs

oviduct   ovary

uterus

endometrium (inner lining of uterus)

cervix

myometrium (muscle layer of uterus)

vagina

Fig 10.1 Structures of male and female reproductive organs.

The female gametes (eggs or ova) are made in the ovaries. One egg is released from an ovary approximately each month throughout a woman's fertile years – from puberty at around 12 years old to the menopause at around 50. Millions of sperm are produced in a man's testes from the age of about 13 or 14.

An egg is fertilised by a sperm in the **oviduct**. The new cell formed is a diploid **zygote**. As we have seen, it contains one set of chromosomes from the father and one set from the mother (see page 150).

The zygote slowly moves down the oviduct towards the uterus. As it travels, it divides repeatedly, forming a little ball of about 100 cells called a **blastocyst**. The blastocyst reaches the uterus after three or four days. It sinks into the soft lining – the endometrium – in a process called **implantation**. The cells in the blastocyst continue dividing by mitosis. Some of them form the **embryo**. Others help to form the **placenta**. Cells in the mother's endometrium also contribute to this. The placenta is a quite unique organ, because it is made up of tissues from two different organisms – the embryo and its mother (Fig 10.2).

At ten weeks the embryo is now known as a **foetus**. The foetus depends on the placenta for all of its requirements while it grows in the uterus. Oxygen, water and nutrients (such as glucose, amino acids and minerals) move from the mother's blood into the foetus's blood in the placenta. Waste substances, such as carbon dioxide and urea, move the other way. The foetus is protected inside a sac known as the **amnion**, which secretes **amniotic fluid**.

Pregnancy lasts for about nine months (40 weeks). Birth takes a number of hours, as the outer, muscular wall of the uterus contracts rhythmically. The muscles around the cervix are also involved in the process; they gradually widen the cervix, allowing the baby's head to move through and into the outside world. Still attached to the placenta by its **umbilical cord**, the baby takes its first breath. Shortly after, the placenta falls away from the wall of the uterus and passes out as the afterbirth.

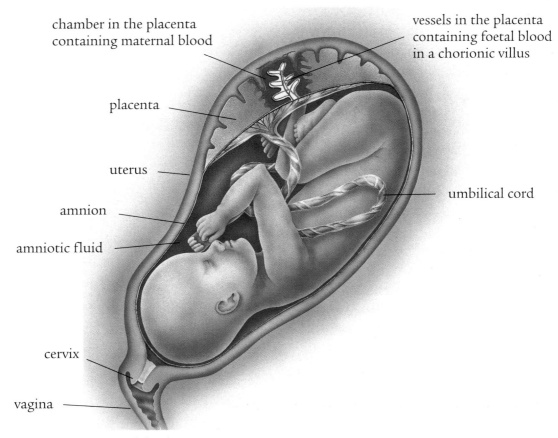

chamber in the placenta containing maternal blood

vessels in the placenta containing foetal blood in a chorionic villus

placenta

uterus

amnion

amniotic fluid

cervix

vagina

umbilical cord

Fig 10.2 A foetus at a late stage of development.

Preconceptual care

Most women will register with an **antenatal** clinic when they know that they are pregnant. 'Antenatal' means 'before birth'. The care that a prospective mother should take of herself, and the care that an antenatal clinic gives to her and her growing foetus, is known as **antenatal care**.

The time for the prospective mother to begin thinking about antenatal care is even before the baby is conceived. This is known as **preconceptual** care. The baby will be conceived inside her body, and will grow and develop there for nine months. So the health of her body can have a direct effect on the health of the baby.

Two particular steps are especially important. They involve the woman's immunity to rubella, and making sure she has plenty of folic acid in her diet.

Rubella

Rubella, sometimes known as German measles, is an illness caused by a virus. It is not usually a dangerous disease for children or adults; they suffer a raised temperature, tiredness and red spots all over the skin, but normally recover within ten days or so. But for a developing foetus it is a very different story. If the mother has rubella, the virus can cross the placenta and get into the foetus's blood. If this happens in the early stages of pregnancy, within the first three months, the baby's heart, brain, ears and eyes may fail to develop properly. Babies which have been exposed to the rubella virus may be born with heart and brain defects, deafness and perhaps cataracts.

So a woman who is trying to become pregnant needs to find out if she is immune to rubella. A simple blood test, to check for antibodies to rubella, will give the answer. If she is immune, she doesn't need to do anything else. If she is not, then she can have a rubella vaccination. But it is really important to do this at least three months *before* getting pregnant, because the vaccine itself could harm the developing foetus.

Folic acid

Another very important thing that the woman should do is begin to take supplements of **folic acid**. This is a B vitamin which is found in foods such as dark green vegetables, some breakfast cereals, milk products, oranges and bananas. A link has been found between lack of folic acid and the birth of a baby with neural tube defects. The neural tube is the part of the embryo which develops into the spinal cord and brain. It forms and grows during the very early stages of pregnancy – probably even before the woman knows that she is pregnant. If the neural tube does not develop properly, the baby may be born with spina bifida or other serious defects of the central nervous system. So, even if she eats a good diet, she should think about taking folic acid supplements. Taking folic acid pills each day before getting pregnant reduces the risk of having a baby with spina bifida by about 70%.

Postconceptual care

Once a woman knows that she is pregnant, she will be showered with advice about what she should and should not do. Friends, neighbours, relatives and magazines will all have their particular tips to give her. Some of it will be nonsense but a lot of it could be very helpful. The advice that she should be most ready to take will come from her antenatal clinic.

The antenatal care programme

The aims of the antenatal care programme are to assess a pregnant woman's health needs, to keep her and her baby healthy throughout pregnancy, and to prepare her for the birth.

- On her first visit, the mother's general health is assessed. A record will be made of whether this is her first baby, or if she already has other children. If she or her partner smoke, they will be given strong advice to give up, and given help with this if needed. She will be provided with advice on her diet, and encouraged to exercise regularly (Fig 10.3).
- An assessment is made of the probability of the baby being born with any kind of genetic disorder. The parents will be asked whether any genetic diseases run in the family. For example, if any members of the family are deaf, or have been born with a cleft palate, then the parents and health care team will be made aware that the baby could be born with this condition. If there is reason to suspect problems, the mother will be offered an amniocentesis or chorionic villus sampling, to check for the presence of a genetic disorder in her baby. These tests are described on pages 203–205.
- Blood tests will be done. A great deal of information can be collected from these. The mother's haemoglobin level will be measured, to check for anaemia. As we have seen, her blood will be checked for the presence of antibodies to rubella. Her blood group will be determined, in case something goes wrong and she needs a transfusion at any time. She and her partner will be tested for the presence of the Rhesus factor – the reason for this is explained below. She will also be tested for any sexually transmitted diseases, including HIV/AIDS. The results of this test are reported anonymously, and used to gather statistics about the prevalence of these diseases.

Fig 10.3 Antenatal exercises, often involving stretching of the spine and pelvis, help to strengthen muscles in the back and hips.

This woman is eight months (32 weeks) pregnant, and unusually flexible; not many women can do this comfortably even when not pregnant!

- Each time that she attends the antenatal clinic, the mother will be weighed and her blood pressure will be measured. She should expect to gain about 400 – 500 g per week. Her blood pressure may increase a little even in a healthy pregnancy, but sometimes it soars very high, a condition known as pre-eclampsia. A sudden weight gain is another sign of this condition, because the high blood pressure causes tissue fluid to accumulate, which can cause swelling of the legs and hands. Pre-eclampsia puts both the mother and baby in danger.

- The position of the baby in the uterus, and its size, will be checked at each visit by an external examination. The baby's heartbeat will be measured.

- The mother will be booked in for an ultrasound scan at 12 weeks and again at 20 weeks.

- A urine sample will be collected from the mother, and tested for the presence of glucose, which indicates that she may have diabetes; and for protein, which is an indication of kidney problems.

- She will be advised on how to spot any problems that may be developing, for example a swelling of the fingers which could be an early sign of pre-eclampsia. She will be given a contact number to ring if she is worried that all may not be well at any stage. She will be given help to choose how and where she wants the birth to take place.

- If this is a first baby, the mother and her partner will be encouraged to attend a series of antenatal and parenting classes (Fig 10.4). Here, there is the chance to learn about and discuss a whole range of things – for example, what to expect before and during the birth, advice on breastfeeding and so on.

- The programme provides many chances for the mother to get to know her midwife and develop a relationship with her.

Fig 10.4 A midwife conducts an antenatal class for pregnant women and their partners. It is a valuable opportunity to cover all aspects of health during pregnancy, childbirth and coping with a young baby.

The Rhesus factor

We have seen that red blood cells can carry A or B antigens in their cell surface membranes (page 18). These are not the only antigens they carry. Another important one is the Rhesus antigen.

People who have this antigen are said to be Rhesus positive, while those who don't are Rhesus negative. Problems can arise when the mother is Rhesus negative and her partner is Rhesus positive. If this is the case, there is a chance that the baby might be Rhesus positive. Then, if during pregnancy or childbirth Rhesus positive baby's blood contacts the mother's blood, the mother becomes sensitised and makes anti-Rhesus antibodies. Should this occur during pregnancy the antibodies will attack the baby. If it occurs at childbirth, it affects the next Rhesus positive foetus in her uterus.

Since 1969 these problems have been reduced a hundred fold. Rhesus negative women are injected with anti-Rhesus antibodies after any potentially sensitising incidents in pregnancy, and routinely after childbirth. This stops the mother becoming sensitised. However, there are still about 50 cases a year mainly arising from small, unrecognised bleeds in the placenta in the last 12 weeks of pregnancy.

Diet during pregnancy

Growing a complete, new human being from a starting point of just one cell is quite an achievement. The developing foetus needs a very wide range of different nutrients in order for all the organs to form and develop as they should. All of these nutrients come from the mother's blood. During pregnancy, it is important for her to eat a diet which not only supplies her foetus with these nutrients, but also supplies her own body with what it needs.

In the early stages of pregnancy, some women feel so ill with morning sickness that they don't really want to eat anything. But many women don't suffer in this way, and even those that do usually feel much better after some weeks.

However careless she normally is about what she eats, a pregnant woman needs to begin to think very carefully about what she is feeding to her unborn baby. Table 10.1 on page 191 lists some important nutrients that she should ensure she has in her diet. Overall, she should try to make sure that the food she eats each day contains:

- fresh fruit and vegetables, including ones which contain folic acid;
- complex carbohydrates (starch), found in bread, rice, pasta, potatoes;
- proteins, found in dairy products, fish and meat and pulses;
- vitamins and minerals, especially iron and calcium.

There is some evidence that increasing dietary intake of certain fatty acids, known as omega 3 fatty acids (one group of the essential fatty acids) may benefit the development of the nervous system of the foetus. Oily fish, such as herring, mackerel, salmon and sardine are rich sources of these fatty acids.

Pregnant women are usually recommended to avoid soft cheeses, smoked fish, precooked meat (such as chicken) and foods made with unpasteurised milk. These foods may contain a bacterium called *Listeria*. This bacterium doesn't usually cause people much harm, but even a mild infection in a pregnant woman may cause miscarriage.

Women often worry about how much they should eat once they are pregnant, and how much weight they are putting on. A pregnant woman certainly does need to eat a little more, as the food she eats must supply her growing foetus as well as herself. In general, a woman will put on around 10 to 13 kg during pregnancy.

Vegetarian diets during pregnancy

Vegetarian diets are generally very healthy diets, but a little care has to be taken to make sure no nutrients are in short supply, because a few are not present in any quantity in plants. Vitamin B12 is one of these.

Vitamin B12 is needed for rapidly dividing cells, such as those in bone marrow producing new erythrocytes. Lacto-ovo-vegetarians (those who will eat dairy products and eggs) and vegans (who eat no animal products at all) need to supplement their intake of this vitamin. There is disagreement over the amount required, but about 10 μg daily is often considered to be about right.

Eating foods fortified with the vitamin can provide this, or supplement tablets can be taken.

Vitamin D is another vitamin that may be deficient in lacto-ovo-vegetarians and vegans, but only if the skin is not exposed to sunlight, because the vitamin is made in skin when sunlight falls on it. Exposure of the hands and face to sunlight for about 20 minutes a day is probably sufficient, but this may not be achieved if a person rarely goes outside or has the skin covered. Again, eating foods fortified with the vitamin or taking tablet supplements will avoid a deficiency in the mother or her foetus.

Alcohol during pregnancy

Should a woman give up alcohol once she is pregnant?

Moderate drinking is thought to pose some risk of having a low-birthweight baby. One study has shown that women drinking four alcoholic drinks a week in the early stages of pregnancy had babies which were on average 155 g lighter than babies born to non-drinking mothers. This is a small difference, but it does need to be borne in mind.

However, regular heavy drinking most certainly can cause major problems for the unborn child. Alcohol easily crosses the placenta. When a pregnant woman drinks alcohol, it goes into her blood and can then diffuse from her blood into her baby's blood. A child born to a mother who is a heavy drinker, and who often has blood alcohol levels of more than 80 mg 100 cm^{-3} of blood, may be born with **foetal alcohol syndrome**. The alcohol affects the development of its nervous system, so its brain does not grow as it should. There is reduced growth both before and after birth. Other symptoms of this syndrome include poor muscle tone, abnormal limbs and heart defects. There is an increased risk of the child having a cleft palate. A baby born with foetal alcohol syndrome may have learning difficulties throughout life.

The NHS recommends that a pregnant woman should limit her drinking to no more than two units a week. A unit is a small glass of wine or half a pint of beer.

Table 10.1 Nutrients important for maintaining foetal growth.

Nutrient	Function	Good food sources	Notes
Carbohydrates	Providing energy, which is released from them by respiration inside body cells.	Bread, potatoes, rice, pasta, breakfast cereals, pulses.	Complex carbohydrates (starches) are better than sugars, because the energy in them is released steadily.
Proteins	Forming new cells and tissues. Also for formation of haemoglobin, plasma proteins, collagen (in skin and bones), enzymes.	Meat, eggs, fish, dairy products, pulses.	Proteins contain 20 different amino acids, of which 8 are essential in the diet as the body cannot make them from other amino acids.
Lipids	Making cell membranes. Formation of nerve cells. Provide energy when they are broken down in respiration.	Dairy products, red meat, oily fish.	Lipids contain several different fatty acids, of which two are essential.
Vitamin A	Making the pigment rhodopsin, needed for vision in dim light.	Meat, egg yolks, carrots.	Daily doses at around 100 times the recommended daily intake are toxic. Pregnant women should not eat too much of this vitamin.
Vitamin D	Formation of bones and teeth.	Dairy foods, oily fish, egg yolks.	This vitamin is made in the skin when exposed to sunlight.
Folic acid	Formation of the neural tube.	Dark green vegetables, some breakfast cereals, milk products, oranges and bananas.	Folic acid supplements are often recommended before pregnancy and up to about the 12th week, after which the neural tube will have formed.
Iron	Formation of haemoglobin.	Meat, beans, chocolate, shellfish, eggs.	Shortage of iron can cause anaemia in the mother.
Phosphorus and calcium	Bone formation.	Dairy products, fish (especially with bones, e.g. sardines).	

Smoking and pregnancy

Everyone who smokes knows that it is bad for their health. They know they should give up, but many don't have the willpower or motivation to do it. However, smoking during pregnancy is a different matter. It isn't only the mother's health that is affected, but also her unborn baby's. Moreover, the number of miscarriages is higher in women who smoke.

Every time a pregnant woman smokes, harmful chemicals from the cigarette smoke enter her blood. They readily pass through the placenta and enter the foetus's blood. It is as though the foetus is smoking cigarettes, too.

There are many different harmful chemicals in tobacco smoke. Of these, perhaps carbon monoxide and nicotine are the most dangerous for the foetus.

Carbon monoxide combines with haemoglobin (Hb) in the foetus's red blood cells. If the Hb is combined with carbon monoxide then it cannot combine with oxygen. So when a mother smokes, she reduces the amount of oxygen being carried in her own blood and also the baby's blood.

Nicotine reduces the diameter of the foetus's blood vessels. This reduces the volume of blood that can flow through them. This, too, reduces the amount of oxygen reaching the foetus's developing tissues. Nicotine also appears to affect the development of the nervous system. In addition, it has been found that the combination of carbon monoxide and nicotine can reduce the size of the baby's lungs by as much as 30%.

These effects of carbon monoxide and nicotine result in a retardation of the foetus's growth in the uterus. They increase the chance of the baby being born prematurely, of respiratory problems in the newborn child, and also of perinatal mortality – that is, death of the child before, during or shortly after birth.

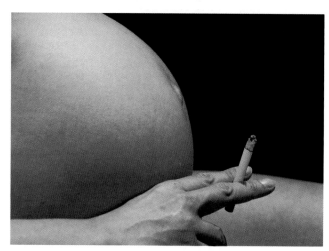

Fig 10.5 Smoking during pregnancy can do considerable harm to the unborn child.

Smoking and fertility

"Men who smoke are twice as likely to be infertile and to have damaged DNA in their sperm. And with women, we found higher incidences of miscarriages," says Dr. Sinead Jones, the author of a British Medical Association report published in 2004, *Smoking and Reproductive Life*, based on 20 years of published research studies.

The report says that between 3000 and 5000 miscarriages per year in the United Kingdom can be directly linked to smoking.

The report also concludes that 120 000 men in England between the ages of 30 and 50 are impotent due to smoking. And both men and women may have less response to fertility treatments if they smoke.

10.1 The table shows some statistics about smoking by women before and during pregnancy in England in 2000.

Age of mother	Percentage who smoked in the year before or during pregnancy	Percentage who smoked throughout pregnancy	Percentage of smokers who gave up smoking in the year before or during pregnancy
under 20	64	39	38
20–24	52	29	44
25–29	36	19	45
30–34	25	12	50
35 and over	23	12	48

a i Describe the relationship between smoking in the year before or during pregnancy and age.

ii Suggest reasons for this relationship.

iii Do the data about the percentages of women who smoked throughout pregnancy support your answer to (ii)? Explain your answer.

b The number of women between 25 and 29 who took part in this survey was 1397. Calculate the number of smokers in this age category who:

i smoked in the year before or during pregnancy;

ii gave up in the year before or during pregnancy.

c Explain why health professionals always strongly advise a woman smoker to give up while she is pregnant.

Measuring foetal growth

Health professionals will keep an eye on the mother throughout her pregnancy. She may have the growth of her embryo or foetus measured using ultrasound (see Procedure 10.1).

Ultrasound to measure growth of the embryo or foetus

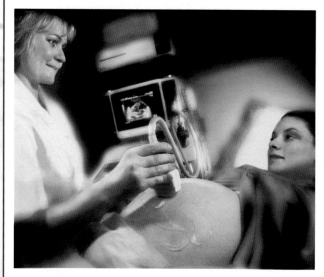

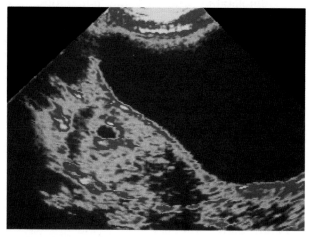

An ultrasound scan can be used to view the foetus in the uterus. The skin on the mother's abdomen is covered with a slippery gel, which allows an ultrasound scanning probe to be slid gently over its surface. The probe emits ultrasound, which is reflected back from the structures inside her body. The patterns of these reflections are detected and converted into a picture on a screen.

The scan can show whether the mother is carrying a single baby or twins; whether it is a girl or boy; and whether everything is normal or if there is a problem such as spina bifida (see page 186) or a malformed heart. However, the main reason for the scan is to measure the growth of the embryo or foetus.

Data about the size of many foetuses have been collected, and then used to construct standard tables or graphs showing the size expected at different ages. These tables can be used in two ways.

- If the woman knows when she had her last period, then the measurements taken can be used to check if the foetus is the right size for its age. If it is not, then her antenatal care team can try to find out what is going wrong, and provide treatment that may help.
- If the woman does not know when she became pregnant, then the measurements can be used to work out how old the foetus probably is. This is useful because it means that the probable date at which the baby will be born can be predicted.

The ultrasound scan above shows the amnion. It is the small dark circle left of the centre of the photo, half circled in pink. This is an early stage of pregnancy (4–5 weeks). The smooth blue region on the right is a full bladder; the pear-shaped outline of the uterus is visible below the bladder at the bottom left. The cervix is towards the bottom right.

Measurement of the size of the amnion is the first of the ultrasound measurements that can be made in early pregnancy. Later, **crown–rump length** and **biparietal diameter** may be measured by electronic caliper.

Crown–rump length is the length of the embryo or foetus along the longest axis.

Biparietal diameter is the width of the head at its widest. The size of the head is related to brain growth. If brain growth is slow it is likely there is a genetic problem, infection or toxin affecting the foetus. Biparietal diameter is normally only measured after 12 weeks.

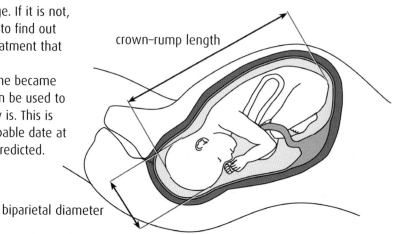

crown–rump length

biparietal diameter

10.2 The graph shows mean crown–rump length plotted against the age of a foetus in weeks, timed from when the mother had her last period.

a Describe how the data shown on this graph would have been collected.

b Ros was not planning to get pregnant, and was not keeping track of her periods. She cannot remember when her last one happened. Her foetus's crown–rump length is 53 mm. What does this tell her? Why is this useful to know?

c Fauzia knows that she had her last period 10 weeks ago. Her foetus's crown–rump length is 30 mm. What does this tell her? Why is this useful to know?

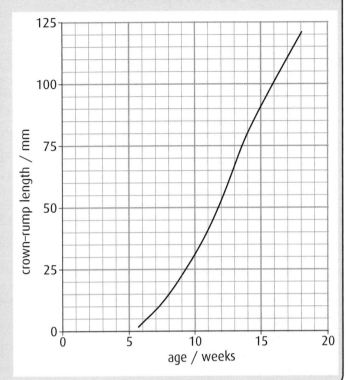

Summary

❶ The UK has an antenatal care programme, aiming to keep the mother and her developing foetus healthy.

❷ Preconceptual care includes checking for immunity to rubella, and ensuring there is plenty of folic acid in the diet. If a pregnant woman is infected with rubella, the virus can cross the placenta and may cause heart, brain, eye and ear defects in the foetus. Lack of folic acid increases the risk that the baby will be born with spina bifida or other defects of the nervous system.

❸ Postconceptual care includes ensuring that the diet is balanced and sufficient for the mother and foetus. A pregnant woman needs especially large amounts of iron (to form red blood cells in the foetus) and calcium (for bone formation).

❹ Alcohol should be avoided in pregnancy. Two or three glasses of wine a week might do no harm, but moderate drinking increases the chance of a low birthweight baby, and heavy drinking can cause foetal alcohol syndrome.

❺ Smoking should be given up even before pregnancy begins. Smoking by the mother greatly reduces the supply of oxygen to the foetus's developing tissues. The nervous system, the lungs and the blood system may not grow as they should.

❻ Foetal growth can be measured using ultrasound scans. Crown–rump length and bi-parietal diameter are two measurements that are used. These can be compared against charts showing the normal range of measurements expected at each week.

DNA and development

One small part of the DNA that Queen Victoria inherited from one of her parents has had great consequences for history. Queen Victoria was not affected herself, but passed a faulty gene onto some of her offspring. Boys with this gene suffered the disease of haemophilia. For someone with haemophilia, even the smallest bruise becomes serious, as blood does not clot and continues to flow out of the damaged vessels. Nowadays, treatment is available for haemophilia, but in the nineteenth and early twentieth century this was not so.

A great grandson of Queen Victoria, Alexis, was born as the only male heir to the Russian throne. The Russian Tsar and his wife had produced only daughters in the years up to 1901. Then in 1904 they had Alexis, who was a haemophiliac. The Tsar and his wife Alexandra were desperate to keep Alexis healthy, for the sake of the future of Russia. A failure to produce a male successor to the Tsar would result in political instability.

Alexis, as with all haemophiliacs, suffered agonies of pain following just the mildest of knocks, and sometimes life-threatening internal bleeding. The Tsar's brother-in-law once said that Alexandra "refused to surrender to fate ... she talked incessantly of the ignorance of the physicians. She turned toward religion ... but her prayers were tainted with a certain hysteria. The stage was set for the appearance of a miracle-worker."

The miracle-worker appeared – Rasputin the mystic with his hypnotic eyes and a great interest in women. He was allowed to see Alexis in one of his haemophiliac crises. Alexis recovered, and after that Rasputin became a frequent visitor and confidant of Alexandra.

During the First World War the Russian army suffered badly while fighting the Germans and in 1915 the Tsar went to the front to direct the war. Alexandra was left in charge of the government, but it was Rasputin who was making important decisions. This was deeply resented by the Russian people. Some historians feel that this helped to trigger the Russian revolution. The Tsar and all his family, Alexis included, were shot and the government became a communist one, with consequences still being felt in today's world politics.

The change that affected one of Queen Victoria's genes is an example of a **mutation**. A mutation is a random, unpredictable change in the genetic material in a cell. Mutations may affect just one small part of a DNA molecule, or they may affect large pieces of chromosomes or even the number of chromosomes present. Mutations can be classified as gene (point) mutations or chromosome mutations.

Gene (point) mutations

A gene mutation is a change in a single base pair in a DNA molecule. Point mutations can happen at any time, but most of them seem to occur while the DNA is replicating (Fig 10.6).

Substitution of one base for another sometimes has no effect. One reason for this is that the genetic code is **degenerate**, meaning that each amino acid has more than one triplet of bases which encode it. For example, GAU and GAC both code for the amino acid aspartate.

So a substition of the base U for C in the third position will make absolutely no difference to the polypeptide or protein which is produced.

Deletion, however, is almost certain to make a big difference. Deletion involves the loss of one base pair from the DNA molecule. You will remember that the bases are read as triplets from one strand of the DNA (see page 151). If one pair goes missing, then the whole sequence is read differently. This is called a **frame shift**.

Insertion, in which an extra pair is inserted, also results in a frame shift.

A point mutation can produce a different primary structure of protein. This may result in the secondary and tertiary structures being different. If so, the protein's function is likely to be disrupted.

Point mutations are generally only revealed if they produce a noticeable effect on the body. They are difficult or impossible to detect directly.

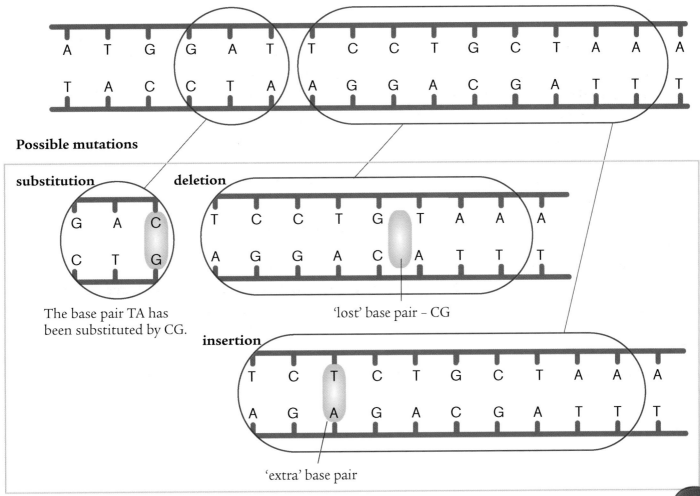

Fig 10.6 Point mutations.

10.3 The base sequence on the mRNA strand transcribed from the bottom strand of the 'normal' DNA shown in Fig 10.6 is:

AUG GAU UCC UGC UAA A

a Write down the mRNA base sequence that is transcribed from the DNA after each of the three mutations shown in Fig 10.6.

b What are the amino acid sequences coded by the 'normal' DNA and by the DNA affected by each of the three mutations? You will need to use the following information for mRNA codons:

AUG – methionine	AAA – lysine
CUA/CUG – leucine	GUA/GUC – valine
GAU/GAC – aspartate	UAA – 'end'
UCC/UCU – serine	UGC/UGU – cysteine

Sickle cell anaemia

Sickle cell anaemia is a disease which is caused by a point mutation. You may remember John Taylor (see page 1), who had this genetic disease.

Haemoglobin, the red pigment found in erythrocytes which transports oxygen, is a protein whose molecules are made up of four polypeptide chains. Two are α-chains, and two are β-chains (see Fig 2.7). Sickle cell anaemia is caused by a mutation of the gene encoding the β-chains.

Normally, part of this gene has a base sequence which codes for:

– valine – histidine – leucine – threonine – proline – glutamate – glutamate – lysine –

The base sequence which codes for the first of the glutamate amino acids is usually CTT. But in the faulty gene a base substitution has occurred. The base sequence of this triplet is CTA. And CTA does not encode glutamate. It encodes valine. So now the amino acid sequence in this part of the β-chain is:

– valine – histidine – leucine – threonine – proline – valine – glutamate – lysine –

You might think that this won't make much difference. But it does.

When the four polypeptide chains of the haemoglobin molecule curl up and join to form a haemoglobin molecule, they form a very

precise three-dimensional shape. One factor which influences this shape is that some amino acids have side chains which are hydrophilic while others are hydrophobic. They tend to curl up so that most of the hydrophobic amino acids are in the middle of the molecule, well away from the watery cytoplasm inside the erythrocyte, while most of the hydrophilic ones are on the outside.

Glutamate has an R group (see Fig 2.1) which is hydrophilic. It lies on the outside of the molecule, where it interacts with water. Valine, however, has an R group which is hydrophobic. But it finds itself on the outside of the molecule, even though it cannot interact with water.

Instead, the R groups of the valines on the outside of different haemoglobin molecules can interact with each other. Most of the time they don't. But if the oxygen level in the blood falls, it can happen. Then the hydrophobic valines form bonds which stick haemoglobin molecules together, especially when they are not carrying oxygen. Long fibres of stuck-together haemoglobin molecules are formed. As the fibres form inside the erythrocytes, they pull the cell out of its usual biconcave shape. Some cells become sickle-shaped (Fig 10.7).

In this state, the erythrocytes are not only useless but also dangerous. The fibres of

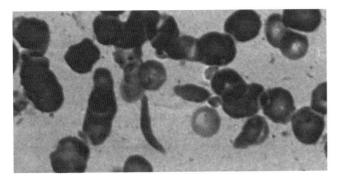

Fig 10.7 Blood film from a person who has sickle cell anaemia and is having a sickle cell crisis. Some erythrocytes have abnormal shapes.

haemoglobin cannot carry oxygen – hence the name 'anaemia'. Moreover, these cells cannot pass through blood capillaries. They form blockages, which are very painful and can do serious damage to tissues.

When this happens, a person is said to be having a 'sickle cell crisis'. This usually occurs when the oxygen demand from their tissues is increased – such as when John Taylor ran to catch a bus (see page 1). The extra exertion reduced the oxygen levels in his blood just sufficiently for the sickling to take place.

Chromosome mutations

So far, we have looked at mutations that affect a single gene in a chromosome. But sometimes errors occur in the number or form of the chromosomes in a cell.

Chromosome mutations happen when a cell is dividing, either by mitosis or meiosis. For example, one of the daughter cells might get two copies of a chromosome, while the other daughter cell gets none. This is known as **non-disjunction**. Or part of one chromosome might break off and re-attach to a different one (Fig 10.8). This is known as **translocation**.

If this happens during one of the cell divisions in a testis or ovary, then sperm or eggs may be produced with the 'wrong' number of chromosomes. If one of these faulty gametes is fertilised, then the zygote will also have the wrong number. And so will all the cells in the body of the person who eventually develops from this zygote.

Some chromosome mutations involve the two sex chromosomes, X and Y. A woman usually has two X chromosomes, XX. All of her eggs contain an X chromosome. A man usually has one X chromosome and one Y chromosome, XY. Half of his sperm contain an X chromosome, and half contain a Y chromosome. If something goes wrong with the way these are shared out into the gametes, then eggs or sperms may end up with either no sex chromosome at all, or with two of them. Two conditions which may occur as a result of this are **Klinefelter's syndrome** and **Turner's syndrome**.

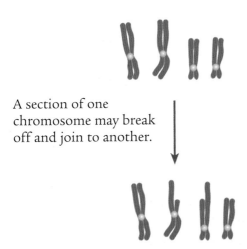

A section of one chromosome may break off and join to another.

Fig 10.8 Chromosomal mutations.

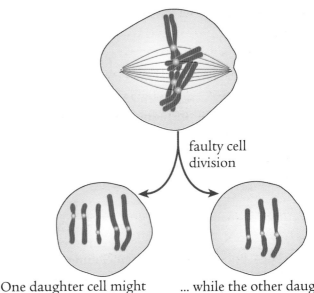

faulty cell division

One daughter cell might get one more chromosome than it should have …

… while the other daughter cell has one less chromosome than it should have.

Klinefelter's syndrome

If an error occurs during a cell division in a woman's ovaries, then one of her eggs may end up with two X chromosomes. If this egg is fertilised by a normal Y-carrying sperm, then the baby will be XXY. The baby is a boy, with Klinefelter's syndrome and his cells contain 47 chromosomes instead of the usual 46 (Fig 10.9).

About one in every 700 boys born are XXY. The extra X chromosome affects the development of the testes. These normally start to grow quickly at puberty, and to secrete testosterone, but in Klinefelter's this does not happen. Very few sperm are made at all, so an XXY man has a high chance of being infertile.

Boys with Klinefelter's syndrome are more likely than other boys to have slow development of speech and also of their muscles. They are less likely than other boys to have an IQ above 110.

When Klinefelter's has been diagnosed, a boy may be given the hormone testosterone when he reaches puberty, to replace that which his testes should be making. This can help to ensure that the boy's muscles grow reasonably normally at this stage in his life.

Turner's syndrome

About one in every 2500 girls is born with Turner's syndrome. This results when one of the gametes did not carry a sex chromosome, producing a zygote with only one X chromosome instead of the usual two (X0). The girl's cells contain only 45 chromosomes instead of the usual 46 (Fig 10.9).

Many of her body systems will be affected because of the 'missing' X chromosome. Most girls with Turner's syndrome do not develop functioning ovaries, so they are infertile. They tend to be shorter than usual, and there may be abnormalities in the blood system.

It is often helpful for the girl to be given some kind of hormonal treatment as she grows up. For example, giving growth hormone can make her grow taller, while giving thyroid hormones can help with growth and general health. Oestrogen can help her body to develop normally at puberty, although her ovaries will never develop and produce eggs. It is, though, possible for a woman with Turner's syndrome to have a baby using an egg donated by another woman and *in vitro* fertilisation – the 'test-tube baby' technique.

Normal

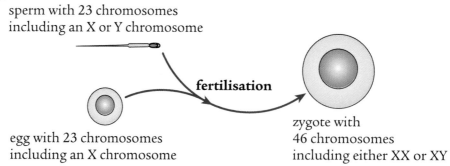

sperm with 23 chromosomes including an X or Y chromosome

fertilisation

egg with 23 chromosomes including an X chromosome

zygote with 46 chromosomes including either XX or XY

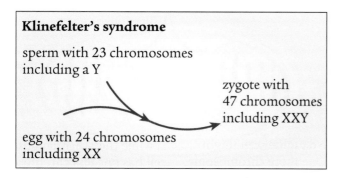

Klinefelter's syndrome

sperm with 23 chromosomes including a Y

zygote with 47 chromosomes including XXY

egg with 24 chromosomes including XX

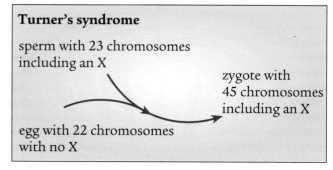

Turner's syndrome

sperm with 23 chromosomes including an X

zygote with 45 chromosomes including an X

egg with 22 chromosomes with no X

Fig 10.9 Klinefelter's and Turner's syndromes.

Summary

1. A random, unpredictable change in the DNA in a cell is known as a mutation.

2. A point (gene) mutation is a change in one base pair in a DNA molecule. Point mutations include substitution, deletion and insertion.

3. Substitution may not make any difference to the amino acids which are encoded. One reason for this is that the genetic code is degenerate – that is, there is more than one base triplet which encodes one amino acid.

4. Deletion and insertion are almost certain to make a significant change in the amino acids which are encoded. This is because they bring about a frame shift, in which the triplets of bases all become different beyond the affected area of the DNA.

5. Sickle cell anaemia is caused by a point (gene) mutation (a substitution) in the gene coding for the β-chains of the haemoglobin molecule. This changes one amino acid from glutamate to valine, which causes the haemoglobin molecules to link together and form fibres in conditions of low oxygen concentration. This reduces oxygen carriage to the tissues. Some erythocytes become misshapen, for example, sickle-shaped and may get stuck in capillaries.

6. A chromosome mutation is a change in the number or form of the chromosomes.

7. If errors occur during cell division in the testis or ovary, gametes may be produced with the wrong number of chromosomes.

8. The fertilisation of an egg with two X chromosomes by a sperm with one Y chromosome produces a zygote which is XXY. This results in a male with Klinefelter's syndrome.

9. The fertilisation of an egg with no X chromosome by a sperm with one X chromosome produces a zygote which is X0. This results in a female with Turner's syndrome.

Detecting genetic disorders

CASE STUDY

Beth became pregnant for the first time just after her 35th birthday. She and her husband David had been concentrating on their careers up until then, although they had always known that they wanted children. Beth still felt very young and fit, so she was surprised when her GP suggested to her that she should have an amniocentesis test to check that her baby did not have Down's syndrome.

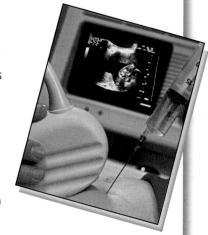

"The older you are, the greater the chance that the baby may have Down's," she told Beth and David. "At 35, there is a 1 in 360 chance that this will happen. Would you like to have the test?"

The doctor explained that the test, which could be carried out around 15 weeks into the pregnancy, involved guiding a fine needle into the uterus, under local anaesthetic. Ultrasound scanning would be used to help the doctor to place the needle exactly in the right place, avoiding any damage to the foetus. A tiny amount of the amniotic fluid around the baby would be removed, which would give the information they needed. As this could be done so early, there would be plenty of time for Beth to have an abortion if she chose to do so. There would be a small risk that the procedure might cause Beth to have a miscarriage.

Beth cringed at the thought of a needle sticking into her stomach, especially knowing that her growing baby was there. It was a very difficult decision, but they had to make it quickly. They thought that if the doctor had suggested it, then she must think it would be a good idea to have it done. They decided to go ahead with the test.

Still, they could scarcely believe it when the results came back positive. It was quite likely that the baby Beth was carrying would have Down's syndrome. "We can book you in for an abortion within the next few days," said their doctor.

Beth cried all day. It was bad enough being pregnant, without having such a huge decision to make. Actually, she had not expected to be making a decision now – they had already made up their minds that she would have an abortion if this happened. But, when it came to it, she could not bear the thought of losing her baby. Her GP was rather cross with her. "Why did you have the test, then," she asked, "if you weren't going to act on its results?"

More tests to investigate the health of a foetus are being developed all the time. Fifty years ago, women could not even find out what sex their baby was. Now a number of genetic diseases can be diagnosed during the first few weeks of pregnancy. But, however many such tests are developed, there is still the very difficult decision to be made about what to do if the test proves positive.

Tests to assess foetal well-being

Of the different tests which can be carried out on an unborn foetus, most women will be offered an ultrasound scan at some stage. If there is a risk of the foetus having a genetic disease, then amniocentesis or chorionic villus sampling can be carried out.

Ultrasound scans

The use of an **ultrasound scan** to obtain a 'picture' of structures inside the body is called ultrasonography. Ultrasound scans are very safe and easy to perform (see Procedure 10.1 on page 194). They are non-invasive – that is, they do not enter or harm the body in any way. Ultrasound waves are high frequency sound waves. There are no X-rays or other types of potentially harmful radiation involved.

Most pregnant women are offered an ultrasound scan at around 16 to 20 weeks into their pregnancy.

Amniocentesis

A pregnant woman over the age of 35 will probably be given the choice of having **amniocentesis** (see Procedure 10.2). This is because the frequency of the birth of a child with Down's syndrome increases with the mother's age. Amniocentesis may also be carried out if an ultrasound scan has detected some abnormality which needs further investigation, or if there is reason to suspect other disorders such as sickle cell anaemia or spina bifida.

PROCEDURE 10.2

Amniocentesis

This is used to obtain a sample of amniotic fluid at 15 to 16 weeks of pregnancy. Various tests can be carried out on this sample to check the health of the foetus. Most amniocentesis samples, however, are for karyotyping (see Procedure 10.4, page 201) to look for chromosomal mutations.

Firstly, ultrasound scanning is used to visualise the foetus and locate the position of the placenta, foetus and umbilical cord. A suitable point for the insertion of the hypodermic syringe needle is chosen and this is marked on the abdominal skin surface. Generally, this position is away from the foetus, umbilical cord and placenta.

The ultrasound probe is placed so that the needle, when inserted, will show up on the scan as a bright spot.

At the insertion point, the skin surface is swabbed with a disinfectant. Then about 20 cm³ of amniotic fluid is withdrawn using a sterile hypodermic syringe with a narrow needle. The insertion site is protected from infection with a dressing.

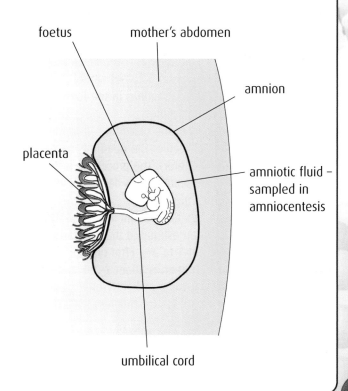

foetus   mother's abdomen

amnion

placenta

amniotic fluid – sampled in amniocentesis

umbilical cord

The test can be done by about 15 weeks or later into the pregnancy. It is possible to do the test earlier, but there is a higher risk of causing a miscarriage if this is done. The test involves using a needle to take a small sample of amniotic fluid. This will contain some of the foetus's cells.

The DNA in cells from the amniotic fluid can be tested for genetic diseases by cytogeneticists.

Karyotyping (see Procedure 10.4) will show how many chromosomes the foetus has, and whether their shapes and sizes look normal. It can detect Down's syndrome, in which there are three chromosome 21s instead of two. It can also detect Klinefelter's syndrome (XXY) and Turner's syndrome (X0). The results take around four weeks to come through.

Having amniocentesis done slightly increases the risk of miscarriage, by about 0.7 to 1%. It is therefore not a test which is done routinely – only when there is a good reason for it.

Chorionic villus sampling

Chorionic villus sampling (CVS) is an alternative test to amniocentesis, and it is used for the same reasons (see Procedure 10.3). It involves taking a sample of cells from the chorionic villi – tiny finger-like projections – in the placenta. These cells belong to the foetus. Their DNA can be analysed in the same way as for the cells obtained by amniocentesis.

The results of CVS usually come through faster than those for amniocentesis. This is because relatively few cells are collected from amniocentesis, and they may need to be given time to divide into more cells before they can be analysed. The larger number of cells obtained by CVS avoids this delay, so results are often obtained within 10 to 14 days.

Having results coming through quickly gives more time for the mother, father and medical team to decide what to do if something is found to be wrong. If the mother decides to have a

---

PROCEDURE 10.3

Chorionic villus sampling

This test can be carried out between 10 and 13 weeks of pregnancy, so it allows parents to get earlier warning of any genetic abnormalities in the foetus than is possible with amniocentesis.

A small sample of part of the placenta called the chorion is removed by a needle. The needle is narrow (less than 0.8 mm in diameter). The procedure is monitored by ultrasound scanning, as described in Procedure 10.2 *Amniocentesis.*

Like amniocentesis, CVS has a small increased risk of miscarriage. It has been estimated that miscarriage rate is increased by about 1 to 2%. (The typical miscarriage rate for all women is about 2–3% at 10 to 12 weeks of pregnancy.) This is a slightly greater risk than for amniocentesis, but is probably less risky than amniocentesis before 15 weeks.

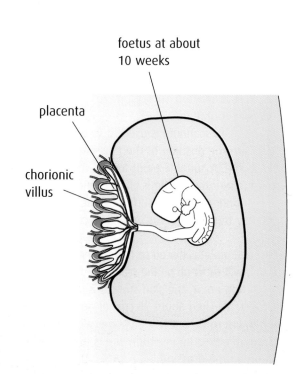

termination, it is best if this is done early in the pregnancy. If she does not want to do this, at least it gives everyone advance warning of possible problems that the child may have after it is born, so that treatment can be given as early as possible.

Karyotyping

A karyotype is a picture of all the chromosomes in a cell, organised into their pairs so that they can easily be counted.

A karyotype is made by photographing the chromosomes during metaphase of mitosis. At this stage, they are at their shortest and fattest, and so are relatively easy to see.

To make a karyotype of a foetus's chromosomes, you first need to collect some cells. This can be done by amniocentesis (Procedure 10.2) or chorionic villus sampling (Procedure 10.3). The cells are then treated with a chemical from kidney beans, called phytohemagglutin. This stimulates the cells to divide by mitosis. Next a chemical from the autumn crocus, called colchicine, is added to the cells. This stops the spindle being formed, so they cannot get any further through the process of mitosis. They are all stuck in metaphase.

The cells are then placed in a dilute salt solution. They absorb water by osmosis, and swell up, which helps to spread the chromosomes out. Next, the cells are stained so that the chromosomes show up clearly. They are viewed through a microscope, and many photographs are taken of them. Cytologists can identify each chromosome by its relative size, the bands on it, and the position of its centromere. Each chromosome is identified, and its image placed in an appropriate position within the karyotype (see photograph below). In the past, this had to be done manually by cutting and pasting the images. Now it is done by digitally manipulating the images.

Karyotyping is used to search for any chromosome mutations in the foetus. It can show, for example, if the foetus has an extra chromosome 21, which leads to Down's syndrome. It can detect Klinefelter's or Turner's syndrome.

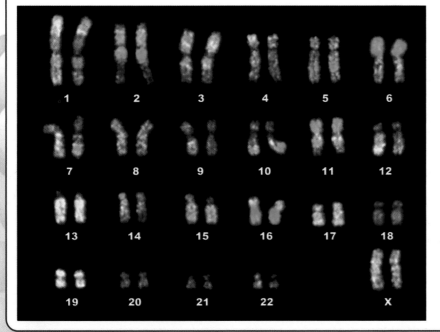

Fluorescence light micrograph of a normal female karyotype. Individual chromosomes are 'cut and pasted' into this pattern.

10.4a Is the karyotype below of a male or a female?
Explain your answer.

b The karyotype below is from a different individual.

i What condition does the person with this karyotype have?

ii By means of annotated diagrams show how this mutation could have arisen.

c Explain why chromosomal mutations are easier to detect in the foetus than gene mutations.

The human genome project

The idea of making a complete analysis of the genetic make-up of humans was inspired by the thought that it would lead to improved health. The project was launched in 1990. Now, with much of the human genome sequenced (DNA code read), people are busy on the next steps, which attempt to put the information to good use. These uses are very diverse and can be divided into three areas: increasing biological knowledge, improving health and the impact of genomics on society.

In terms of biological knowledge, we still know little about the way genes make us the way we are – for example, our susceptibilities to disease and how diseases affect us. The genetic conditions of Turner's syndrome and Klinefelter's syndrome show there are implications to having XXY or X0 chromosomes, but we don't know how the features we see in these syndromes arise from the different genes inherited. The project will help us understand this.

Improving health should follow from our improved biological knowledge. For example, when we know exactly what the genes on the X and Y chromosomes do that gives rise to the effects we see, new treatment possibilities open up.

Your genetic make-up affects your susceptibility to most, possibly all, diseases, even things like the common cold. So improvements should be seen in all areas of disease treatment, and not just genetic diseases such as Klinefelter's and Turner's syndromes, sickle cell anaemia or haemophilia.

Much of the excitement in the earlier stages of the human genome project came from the idea that we might be able to give 'normal' genes to people whose genes did not work correctly. This has proved to be far more difficult than had been predicted. However, there have been some advances. For example, a harmless virus has been used to introduce a 'normal' gene involved in muscle growth into mice. Their muscles grew in size and it halted muscle wastage typical of old age. This suggests it may be possible to introduce this gene into humans who are suffering muscle wasting in disease or old age.

It was realised from the earliest stages of the project that there were serious social and ethical implications. These issues can be considered at different levels: at an individual level, religious level, ethnic level, multiracial level, law makers' level or governmental level. Here are some specific issues.

- **Privacy**
  Decisions need to be made about who gets access to information about the genes in a person that predict what diseases they will get and when they get them. If life insurance companies get the information, it might be impossible for some people to buy life insurance.
- **Patenting genes**
  Who owns your genes? Some genes have been patented, though it is not certain what the legal impact of this will be in different countries. Scientists generally believe that no genes should be patented, so as to allow full access to information for future research.
- **Genetic diagnosis**
  People may need to learn to cope with the results of the many genetic tests that will become available in the future.
- **Social implications**
  We need to think about the sort of society we want to have in the future. This includes deciding whether it is right or wrong to modify our genetic make-up to improve our general health.

Increased knowledge of our genome will change society, but these changes could be modified either by our actions or by our laws. It may be best to discuss these things now, before the events we may wish to prevent actually take place.

10.5 Using a range of resources discuss the role of one of the following people in monitoring foetal health:

doctor, midwife, radiographer, cytogeneticist

10.6 Prepare a presentation on one of the following issues related to the human genome project:

privacy, patenting genes, genetic diagnosis, future society

Concentrate on discussing this from one of the following perspectives and include both positive and negative arguments:

individual, religious, ethnic, multiracial society, law makers, government

Summary

① Foetal well-being can be assessed by ultrasound scanning. This can detect problems such as spina bifida or a malformed heart.

② If a problem with the foetus is suspected, a mother may be offered tests on tissue samples obtained by amniocentesis or chorionic villus sampling.

③ Amniocentesis samples a small volume of amniotic fluid by syringe and hypodermic needle. Tests can be carried out on foetal cells in the sample.

④ Chorionic villus sampling takes a small amount of tissue from the placenta by syringe and hypodermic needle. Tests can be carried out on the sample. This can be carried out earlier in pregnancy than amniocentesis.

⑤ Foetal tissue can be karyotyped to give early detection of a chromosomal mutation, such as those that give rise to Klinefelter's and Turner's syndromes.

⑥ Karyotyping involves preparing an image of the chromosomes of a cell to show their number, shape, size and banding. It shows if any chromosomal mutation has affected the cell.

⑦ The human genome project provides information that has the potential for increasing the number of diagnoses of genetic disorders, developing treatments for genetic disorders or correcting genetic disorders.

⑧ The human genome project and the uses made of its findings have social and ethical implications with regard to privacy, patenting genes, genetic diagnosis and the future of society.

CHAPTER 11

Infant development

In March 2003, a mother and father from New York, USA, were sentenced to six years and five years imprisonment on charges of assault, reckless endangerment and endangering the welfare of a child.

The mother gave birth to her first child, Amy, in July 2000. Both parents followed an extreme diet. They ate no foods of animal origin, except cod liver oil. They fed a similar diet to their baby girl.

Amy was fed on herbal tea, fruit juice, flax seed oil, cod liver oil and a home-made soya drink. At 16 months old, when her condition first came to the notice of the childcare authorities, she weighed 10 pounds (4.54 kg), had spindly arms and legs showing signs of rickets, no teeth and a distended belly. She could not walk, sit or roll over. Her parents insisted she was a healthy child.

One doctor, providing evidence for the prosecution, stated that the parents fed their child "like a gerbil". Another said that she looked like "someone you'd see coming out of a famine". For the defence, it was pointed out that Amy's mother had had problems with obesity and had found that this diet helped her own health. She loved Amy, and her motives for giving her this diet were to help her to be healthy.

After four months in hospital and a rehabilitation centre, Amy was placed with foster parents. Her condition has improved immensely. She is still fed on a vegetarian diet, but one providing the full range of nutrients that a growing child needs.

Measuring infant growth

Amy's case was not the first, and will certainly not be the last, of loving parents feeding their child on an unsuitable diet. It is perfectly possible for a child to be brought up on a vegetarian diet, but it is important that parents realise that the needs of a baby are not the same as their own needs.

In the UK, parents are encouraged to have their child weighed and measured regularly, so that any problems can be picked up early and addressed.

Measuring infant weight

A naked baby is placed on scales that are specially designed for weighing babies. An important design point is that the baby is safe and cannot fall out. They are also more accurate than scales designed to weigh adults.

Experience is needed in handling babies, as they can become distressed by being handled by someone other than a parent.

The weight of the baby is recorded in writing. The baby is then repositioned and another weight reading is taken. Repositioning and reweighing are done again, so there are three readings altogether. There should not be a difference greater than 0.1 kg between these readings. If there is, it is probable that infant movements have made one or other of the readings inaccurate.

The mean of two readings that are closest together is calculated. This is recorded as the infant's weight.

If the infant is so active that it is not possible to obtain three close readings, an alternative approach can be tried. The mother is asked to stand on adult scales. The weight is then set to zero (using the tare function on the scales). The infant is then held by the mother to allow the infant's weight to be recorded. This too should be repeated twice more. Though the weight reading is less likely to be affected by the infant's movements, it can be affected by the mother's. It is also less accurate and weights are taken to the nearest 0.1 kg.

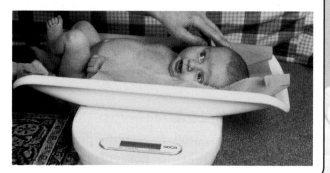

Measuring infant height (length)

The height of the infant is measured with the baby lying on specially designed equipment. The infant's head rests against a fixed headpiece and a moveable footpiece can be slid to touch the feet. A ruler in the device is used to take a reading. The infant must not be wearing shoes or have any ornaments on its head. It should be dressed in light underclothing.

Measuring infant head circumference

A tape is used that is flexible but cannot stretch. Plastic tapes are often used, designed so that one end of the tape can be inserted into the other end to take a reading. The tape is placed over the most protruding part at the back of the head, above the ears and just above the eyes, where there is a bony ridge.

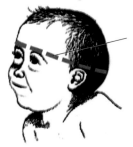

position of the tape for measuring head circumference

Patterns of infant growth

You only have to look around you to realise how very different we are from each other. We are all different shapes and sizes. Both our genes and our environment contribute to this variation.

In the twenty-first century it is estimated that we are, on average, about 4 cm taller than people living in Britain in the Middle Ages. This is thought to be almost entirely because of improvements in diet and general health. But it is also clear that we inherit genes which help to influence our height. Tall parents tend to have tall children. Our genes give us the potential to grow to a certain height, and our environment determines whether or not we reach that potential.

Despite this variation, it is still important to keep track of a young child's growth. Over many years, thousands of readings have been made of the height, weight and head circumference of babies of different ages. These figures have been used to calculate the mean (average) values for each age. Fig 11.1 shows graphs for the mean weights of boys and girls at different ages.

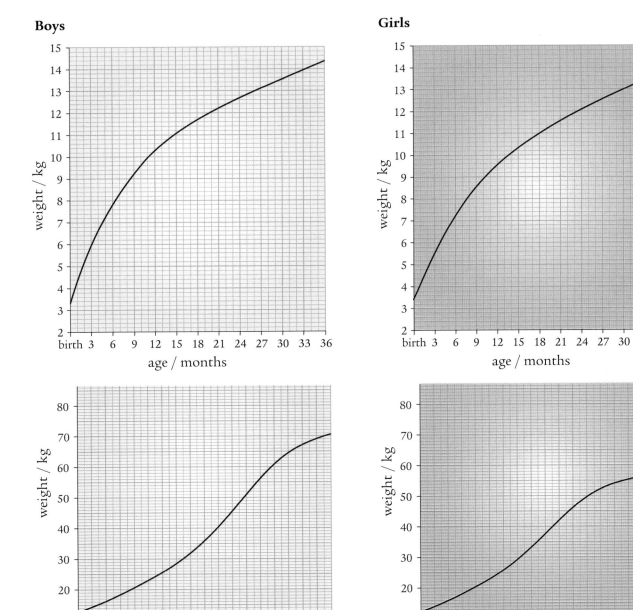

Fig 11.1 Mean weights for boys and girls at different ages.

11.1 Use the data in the growth charts shown in Fig 11.1 to answer this question.
   a Describe the relationship between mean weight and age for:
      i boys from birth to 2 years;
      ii boys from 2 years to 20 years;
      iii girls from birth to 2 years;
      iv girls from 2 years to 20 years.
   b Discuss the differences between the mean growth of boys and of girls shown in these graphs.

ACTIVITY 11.1

Absolute growth curves and absolute growth rate curves

The graphs in Fig 11.1 are **absolute growth** curves. They simply show how the value which is measured (in this case, weight) changes with time.

An absolute growth curve

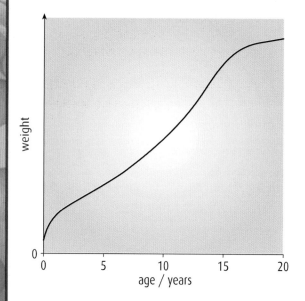

We may also want to know about how fast a child grows at different ages. To do this, we can calculate the **absolute growth rate**. This is the change in size (for example, weight) in a particular period of time.

For example, in Fig 11.1, you can see that the mean weight of a 24-month-old boy is 12.6 kg. The mean weight of a 36-month-old boy is 14.4 kg. So, in a period of one year, he has grown by 1.8 kg. His absolute growth rate is 1.8 kg yr^{-1}.

You can get an idea of absolute growth rate by looking at the steepness of the lines in these graphs. The steeper the line, the faster the absolute growth rate.

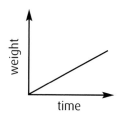
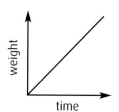

The rate of growth in the second graph is higher than in the first one.

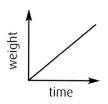
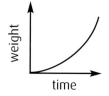

Here, growth rate is constant.

Here, the growth rate is increasing over time.

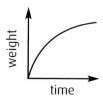

Here, growth rate is decreasing over time.

continued ...

You can also draw an **absolute growth rate curve**. First, you calculate how much the child grows each year. Then you plot this rate of growth per year against time. The graph below is an absolute growth rate curve calculated from the same data used for the absolute growth curve on the previous page.

An absolute growth rate curve

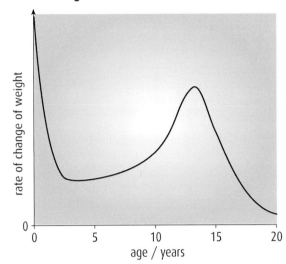

Questions

1 Use the graphs in Fig 11.1 (page 211) showing the mean weights of girls between 0 and 20 years old to calculate the increase in weight during each year of their lives. For example, in the second year, the mean weight increased from 9.6 kg to 12.1 kg. This increase took place over one year, so the absolute growth rate for that year is 2.5 kg yr⁻¹.

Use your results to complete this table. The first values have been recorded for you. (Year 1 means the first year of life – that is from the age of 0 to 1 year old.)

Girls 0 – 20 yrs	
Year	Growth rate/kg yr⁻¹
1	6.2
2	2.5
3 …	

2 Now plot a graph of absolute growth rate against year. You will need to draw a 'line of best fit' in order to get a smooth line like the one shown on the graph to the left.

3 Describe the shape of your curve.

4 Use your curve to identify the time when the growth rate is at its greatest.

5 During adolescence, growth rate rises to a relatively high level. Identify this period on the graph.

6 In any one person, the increased rate of growth during adolescence generally lasts no longer than two years. Why is the period you have identified in 5 different than this?

7 A student wrote:
"The absolute growth rate curve drops between 16 and 18 years. This means that the person was getting smaller then."
What is wrong with this statement? Explain what a falling absolute growth rate curve indicates.

8 Explain the differences between a graph showing absolute growth, and a graph showing absolute growth rate.

Relative growth rates

Imagine a 3-year-old girl. On her third birthday, she weighs 14 kg. On her fourth birthday, she weighs 16 kg. She has grown by 2 kg.

Now imagine a 15-year-old girl. On her 15th birthday, she weighs 52 kg. On her 16th birthday, she weighs 54 kg. She has grown by 2 kg.

So these two girls both have the same absolute growth rate. They have both grown by 2 kg yr^{-1}. But the younger girl has grown much more in proportion to her size. She was only 14 kg to start with, and she has grown by 2 kg – that is, by 1 kg for every 7 kg of her initial body weight. The older girl was 52 kg to start with. She has grown 1 kg for every 26 kg of her initial body weight.

These values, showing the weight increase in relation to the initial weight, are the relative growth rates. You calculate them like this:

$$\text{relative growth rate} = \frac{\text{change in weight in one year}}{\text{weight at the beginning of that year}}$$

The following graph is a relative growth rate curve calculated from the same data as that used for the graphs shown in Activity 11.1.

Relative growth rate curve

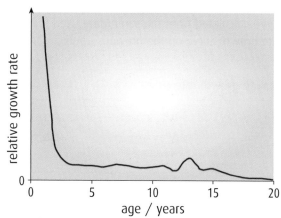

Questions

1 Look back to the table that you completed showing absolute growth rates for girls between 2 and 20 years old. Use these figures to calculate relative growth rate in each year. Record your results in a table. (You could do this by adding columns to your first table.)

2 Use your results to draw a graph of relative growth rate against time.

3 Use your graph to describe how relative growth rate changes with a child's age.

4 What are the advantages of a relative growth rate curve, compared to an absolute growth rate curve?

SAQ

11.2 Explain what is meant by:
 a an absolute growth curve;
 b an absolute growth rate curve;
 c a relative growth rate curve.

Weight and mass

Although we talk about 'weighing' children, what we actually record is their **mass**. Mass is the amount of matter there is, and it is measured in kilograms, kg. Weight is the force that gravity exerts on this mass, and it is measured in newtons, N.

On Earth, at sea level, gravity pulls each kg downwards with a force of about 10 N. So a child with a mass of 10 kg has a weight of 100 N. But if this child was in a spacecraft he would weigh nothing, even though he still had a mass. As scales generally read in kg this is the unit that is used to describe the weight of children in the tables and graphs in this chapter.

How normal is 'normal' growth?

Few children will have weights that sit exactly on the lines shown in Fig 11.1. Most will have weights which are above or below this line. To see how normal a child's growth is, you need to know the percentage of children which, on average, have weights at different distances from this mean value. This will help parents and health workers decide if a child falls within the normal range of growth or if it is so high or low that they should be concerned about it.

On average, 50% of girls fall between the red lines (that is, between the 75th and 25th percentiles). On average, 90% fall between the 95th and 5th percentiles (green lines). Percentiles are sometimes known as 'centiles'.

Girls – 2 to 20 yrs – weight percentiles

Data from the USA

Diet for a growing child

A growing child needs a good diet to help all the organs of the body to grow and develop fully. In general, all the nutrients listed in Table 10.1 on page 191 are still required as a child grows up.

Carbohydrates and lipids are needed for energy. Lipids also supply the raw materials for making cell membranes, and the protective sheaths which form around many nerve cells. There is considerable evidence that the presence of certain kinds of fatty acids in the diet can have a significant effect on brain development. It would therefore not be appropriate to feed a growing child a diet which is extremely low in fats.

Growth occurs as cells divide to form new cells. A large component of these cells is protein, so a growing child needs plenty of protein in the diet. Calcium is needed for growing bones and teeth, while iron is needed for the formation of haemoglobin in the millions of new red blood cells which are being formed.

Differential growth

As a child grows, some parts of its body grow faster than others. Different organs show patterns of growth that are not the same as the overall pattern. This is known as **differential growth** (Fig 11.2).

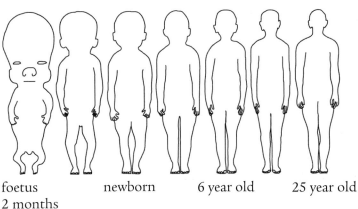

Fig 11.2 Differential growth. Drawing the stages of development to the same size shows that parts of the body make up different proportions of the whole body at different ages.

foetus 2 months   newborn   6 year old   25 year old

One of the most noticeable things about an infant is that the head is much larger in proportion to the rest of the body than in an adult. In an embryo and foetus, the head grows more rapidly than other parts of the body. This is related to the growth of the nervous tissue inside it, forming the brain.

In contrast, a foetus's lymphatic system grows more slowly than other parts of the body (Fig 11.3). This system is involved in the immune response. The foetus does not need it while it is in the uterus, because its mother's antibodies cross the placenta and protect the foetus from pathogens. After birth, the child's antibody levels fall – although it will still receive some from its mother if she breastfeeds. About one month after birth, the infant begins to make its own antibodies. It is not until it is 12 to 20 months old that the lymphatic system is fully formed and the child's body can mount a full immune response.

The reproductive organs complete their development even later in life. They do begin to develop while the foetus is in the uterus and indeed, by the time a girl baby is born, she will

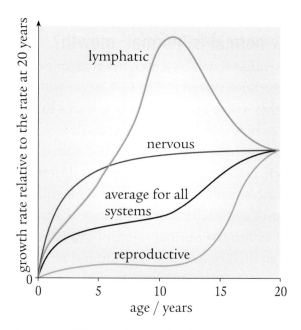

Fig 11.3 Differential growth of some organ systems.

already have large numbers of eggs in her ovaries. But the main growth of the reproductive organs does not take place until puberty. In boys, this is somewhere between the ages of 8 and 16 years, while in girls it normally happens between 7 and 15.

Summary

1 Parents are encouraged to have their child weighed and measured regularly, so that any growth problems can be picked up early.

2 Infant weight needs to be measured with care to make it accurate.

3 Infant length is measured using a device designed for this purpose.

4 Head circumference is measured around the widest portion of the head.

5 The normal patterns of infant growth can be shown in growth curves obtained from many measurements. The growth of an individual infant can then be compared with them.

6 In an absolute growth curve the recorded growth data, such as weight or height, are plotted against time.

7 Growth rate is the steepness of the line in an absolute growth curve.

8 In an absolute growth rate curve, the rate of growth is plotted against time.

9 In a relative growth rate curve, the rate of growth per kg is plotted against time.

10 At birth, growth rate is high. It then falls but rises again during adolescence, falling once more after that.

continued ...

Fish oil in the mind

In your grandparents' generation, it was common for children to be given regular doses of cod liver oil. "Fish is good for your brain", they might have been told. New evidence shows this may be absolutely correct.

Two of the many kinds of fatty acids that are found in lipids are necessary in our diets, because we cannot make them from other kinds. Of these essential fatty acids one kind, called omega 3 fatty acids (sometimes known as linolenate), are found in quantity in oily fish such as tuna, salmon and mackerel, and in linseed and rapeseed oils.

Studies have suggested that a deficiency of omega 3 fatty acids in the diet may be linked with some kinds of behavioural problems. For example, Durham County Council has carried out a trial to see if dietary supplements containing omega 3 fatty acids have any effect on children with learning difficulties, such as attention deficit hyperactivity disorder (ADHD). Early results suggest that they do result in improvements in behaviour.

It may be that many of us have diets that are deficient in these essential fatty acids. Perhaps the most enjoyable way to ensure that we eat enough of them is to eat fish on a regular basis. Cod liver oil is rather an acquired taste.

These fatty acids are used to make the phospholipids of which cell membranes are formed. Omega 3 fatty acids have double carbon-carbon bonds in their 'tails', making the tails kink. A membrane with a lot of these fatty acids in it tends to be more flexible and fluid than one without. Somehow, they seem to reduce your risk of developing coronary heart disease, and help to keep blood cholesterol levels and blood pressure low. Some people with autoimmune diseases, such as rheumatoid arthritis, report improvements in their symptoms when they take omega 3s. It has also been suggested that they may help patients with depression, reduce the risk of breast cancer, and generally assist brain function. As yet, however, relatively few large-scale trials have been carried out, and it may be some time before we really know how important they are.

Summary continued

11 Organs of the body can show differential growth. This means that they develop at rates which are different to the rates of development of other organs.

12 At first the nervous system develops at a greater rate than other organ systems and is highly developed by birth. This is why the head of a newborn takes up such a large proportion of the whole body.

13 The lymphatic system of a foetus and newborn baby up to one month old is not fully developed. During this period antibodies from the mother defend the foetus or infant against disease.

14 The reproductive systems of boys and girls do not develop any more after birth until a brief period of final development, known as puberty, occurs.

CHAPTER 12

Infectious disease

On the evening of March 24th 1882, a middle-aged German scientist called Robert Koch stood in a lecture room in Berlin and told his audience that he had discovered the cause of the disease which was killing one in seven human beings.
The disease was tuberculosis, and Koch had discovered the bacterium *Mycobacterium tuberculosis*. He had brought along much of his laboratory, and at the end of the lecture people were able to look through his microscopes and actually see the bacteria for themselves.

Koch continued his studies on tuberculosis, trying to find a cure.
Even though it was now known that it was caused by a bacterium, people had no way of killing the bacterium without harming the infected person as well. The pressure on Koch was great, and in 1890 he announced that he had found a cure, which he called tuberculin. People rushed to Berlin from all over Europe, bringing their sick loved ones with them, desperate to try this cure. They would be suffering fevers, chest pains and constantly coughing, bringing up mucus mixed with blood. It was a false hope; within a short time it became clear that tuberculin did not cure tuberculosis. Treatment continued as it had before – lots of rest, preferably in a climate with clean air such as the Alps for those with money, and no treatment at all for those who had none.

It was not until 1943 that a cure was found. Then, during the Second World War, a substance called streptomycin was discovered in America. It was made by a fungus, and stopped *M. tuberculosis* from growing. Crucially, it did not harm humans. In 1944 the first patient was treated with streptomycin, and was completely cured of her disease.

But the story is not yet finished. Streptomycin cannot cure all cases of tuberculosis. We still do not have complete control of this infectious disease. Even today, more than 120 years after Robert Koch made the breakthrough in our understanding its cause, it is estimated that up to 10 million people get tuberculosis each year, and 3 million of them die from it. These numbers are increasing. TB is one of the most serious of the global health problems for the twenty-first century.

Pathogens

Tuberculosis is an **infectious disease**. An infectious disease is one that can be passed from person to person – or, in some cases, from another animal to a person. We now know that infectious diseases are caused by microorganisms. A microorganism that causes disease is known as a **pathogen**.

There are several different kinds of microorganisms which act as pathogens. Tuberculosis, like many other infectious diseases, is caused by **bacteria** (see Fig 12.1). Influenza is caused by **viruses**, while malaria is caused by **protoctists**. There are also a few infectious diseases, such as ringworm, which are caused by fungi. In this chapter, we will concentrate on bacteria and viruses, and look at how the body defends itself against attack from these pathogens.

Tuberculosis

The structure of *Mycobacterium tuberculosis*

Fig 12.2 shows the simplified structure of the bacterium which causes tuberculosis, **Mycobacterium tuberculosis** *(M. tuberculosis)*. Like all bacteria, it is a single cell (although some other kinds of bacteria group together). Its shape is that of a rod or **bacillus**, but it is somewhat variable in shape.

The cells of bacteria have many differences in their structure compared with the cells of humans. We have cells which contain a nucleus surrounded by a nuclear membrane. These are **eukaryotic** cells. Bacterial cells do not have a membrane-bound nucleus, and they are known as **prokaryotic** cells. Prokaryotic cells are much smaller than eukaryotic cells. Table 12.1, overleaf, compares the structure of a prokaryotic cell with that of a eukaryotic cell.

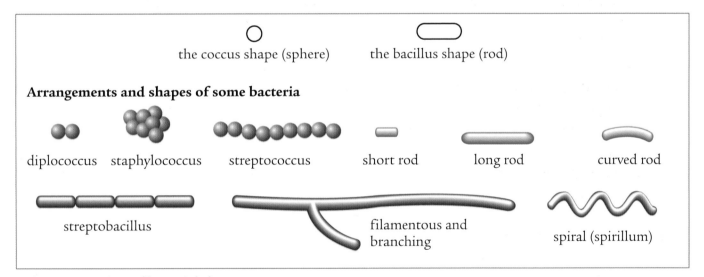

Arrangements and shapes of some bacteria

diplococcus	staphylococcus	streptococcus	short rod	long rod	curved rod

the coccus shape (sphere)   the bacillus shape (rod)

streptobacillus   filamentous and branching   spiral (spirillum)

Fig 12.1 A variety of bacterial shapes.

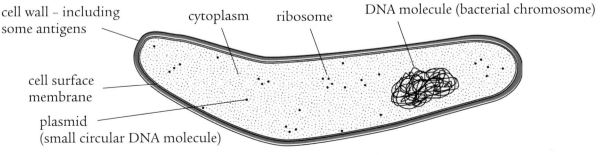

cell wall – including some antigens

cytoplasm   ribosome   DNA molecule (bacterial chromosome)

cell surface membrane

plasmid (small circular DNA molecule)

Fig 12.2 Structure of a bacterial cell as shown by *Mycobacterium tuberculosis*.

Table 12.1 Comparison of prokaryotic and eukaryotic cells.

Feature	Prokaryotic cell	Eukaryotic cell
Cell surface membrane	always present	always present
Cell wall	always present; has a very complex structure, containing peptidoglycans	present in plants and fungi, but not in animals; in plants it contains cellulose, and in fungi it may contain various substances such as chitin
Nucleus	no membrane-bound nucleus present	nucleus usually present, surrounded by a nuclear envelope
Other membrane-bound organelles	none present	some membrane-bound organelles always present – for example, mitochondria, chloroplasts, Golgi body, lysosomes
Endoplasmic reticulum	none present	always present
Ribosomes	relatively small ribosomes present, about 20 nm in diameter	relatively large ribosomes present, about 30 nm in diameter
DNA	present as one or more circular molecules, not associated with histones; many bacteria also have one or more smaller circular DNA molecules called plasmids	present as linear molecules, associated with proteins called histones to form chromosomes
Cilia and flagella	some have flagella, but these have a completely different structure from those found in eukaryotic cells and are outside the cell surface membrane	some have cilia or flagella which are surrounded by the cell surface membrane

The transmission of tuberculosis

If a large number of *M. tuberculosis* bacteria get into your body, you run the risk of getting tuberculosis. These bacteria will have come from someone else in whose body the bacterium is breeding.

Tuberculosis, usually known as TB, is not actually a very infectious disease. It is not that easy to catch it from someone. It seems that you need to be in close association with an infected person for some time before you run a high risk of getting TB. People who sleep in crowded conditions seem to be most at risk. This is partly why homeless people, or those living in substandard housing, are more likely than most to get this disease. Malnutrition, being infected with the human immunodeficiency virus (HIV) or having a weakened immune system also increases the risk.

The most usual way for the bacterium to enter the body is when a person breathes in droplets of moisture that have been exhaled by an infected person.

TB can affect almost any organ of the body, but the most commonly affected part is the lungs. If the bacteria reach the alveoli of the lungs, macrophages (phagocytic white blood cells) engulf them. But, instead of being digested and destroyed, the bacteria remain undamaged inside the cells. They divide, releasing new bacteria which are in turn engulfed by other white cells. Slowly, more and more cells become infected with the bacterium (see pages 137–138).

In perhaps 85 to 90% of people, the disease does not get beyond this stage, because their immune system is able to contain the growth of the bacteria. But in others, the bacterium continues to spread, causing severe tissue damage in the lungs and perhaps also in other parts of the body. As the disease progresses, symptoms gradually appear – weight loss, a general feeling of being unwell, night sweats and a cough which eventually brings up blood-stained mucus and pus. Untreated, people with the disease are likely to die.

HIV/AIDS

The structure of the HIV virus

The devastating disease AIDS, acquired immune deficiency syndrome, is caused by a virus known as the **human immunodeficiency virus**, or HIV. Fig 12.3 shows the structure of this virus. It is a **retrovirus**, one containing RNA rather than DNA.

Like all viruses, HIV is much, much smaller than even the very smallest bacterium. Viruses range in size from about 10 nm to 300 nm in diameter (Fig 12.5). For this reason, viruses were not seen until the 1940s, when the electron microscope was first invented.

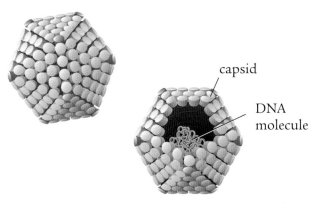

Fig 12.4 Some viruses do not have an envelope, such as this, the wart virus.

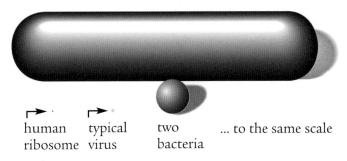

human ribosome   typical virus   two bacteria   ... to the same scale

Fig 12.5 The sizes of bacteria and viruses compared to a human ribosome.

Viruses are not made of cells. At their centre lies a strand of either DNA or RNA. In HIV, this is RNA. Enzymes may also be present in the core. In HIV, there is an enzyme called **reverse transcriptase**. This enzyme is responsible for making a 'DNA version' of the virus's RNA when it gets inside a human cell. The human cell then follows the code on this DNA to make new viruses. The virus essentially hijacks the human cell's protein-making machinery.

Surrounding the core of the virus is a protein coat called a **capsid**. This is made up of many identical protein molecules arranged in a geometric pattern. HIV also has an **envelope** made of phospholipids and glycoproteins.

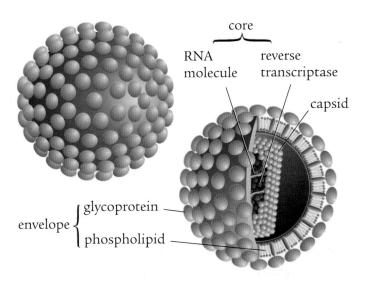

Fig 12.3 The structure of the HIV virus.

Viruses can only reproduce once they are inside a host cell (Fig 12.6). They are incapable of any metabolic activity on their own. For this reason, some biologists would argue that they are not living organisms at all. Others think that the possession of RNA or DNA, which allows them to replicate themselves, is enough to justify their being said to be alive.

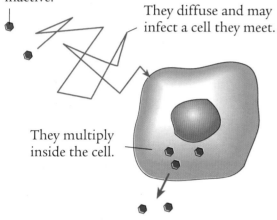

Virus particles outside a cell are metabolically inactive.

They diffuse and may infect a cell they meet.

They multiply inside the cell.

New virus particles are released.

Fig 12.6 Viruses reproduce inside cells.

The transmission of HIV

HIV is passed from person to person when body fluids come into direct contact. The contact must be direct because the virus cannot survive outside the human body (unlike the TB bacterium, which survives in exhaled droplets of moisture for some time). The main ways in which HIV is passed on are:

- transfusions of blood from a person infected with HIV into another person;

- sharing hypodermic needles – a needle used by someone with HIV may contain a small amount of fluid with the virus in it, which can enter the body of an uninfected person if they reuse the needle;

- during sexual intercourse – especially (but not only) if this involves damage to the linings of the vagina or anus, because the virus is most easily spread from blood to blood;

- from a mother to her unborn child – the virus is able to cross the placenta and enter the blood of the foetus.

Fig 12.7 shows the life cycle of the virus.

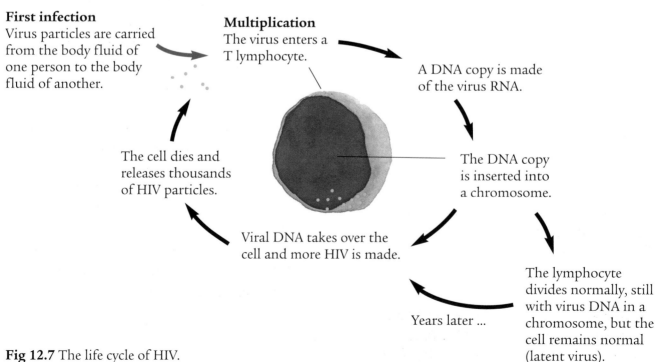

First infection
Virus particles are carried from the body fluid of one person to the body fluid of another.

Multiplication
The virus enters a T lymphocyte.

A DNA copy is made of the virus RNA.

The cell dies and releases thousands of HIV particles.

The DNA copy is inserted into a chromosome.

Viral DNA takes over the cell and more HIV is made.

Years later ...

The lymphocyte divides normally, still with virus DNA in a chromosome, but the cell remains normal (latent virus).

Fig 12.7 The life cycle of HIV.

So far as we know, almost everyone who is infected with HIV goes on to develop AIDS. The virus enters a particular group of white blood cells called **T lymphocytes** (see Fig 12.7) – in particular, a group of them called CD4+ T cells. Here it makes a DNA copy from its RNA, and the viral DNA is incorporated into the chromosomes of the lymphocyte. It may lie low for many years, giving no symptoms and the infected person has no idea they have HIV. However, HIV antibodies can be detected in a blood test, and the person is said to be HIV positive.

T lymphocytes are a very important group of cells because they help to protect us against infectious diseases, especially viral diseases. In a person infected by HIV, more and more T lymphocytes become infected and destroyed, until their number is so low that they can no longer protect against other diseases. Diseases that 'take advantage' of the weakened immune system are called **opportunistic diseases**. They include pneumonia and otherwise rare forms of cancer such as Kaposi's sarcoma (a form of skin cancer). The body becomes weaker, more and more infectious diseases take hold, and the person dies. TB is the main cause of death in AIDS patients.

The statistics for HIV infection are worrying. The country worst affected is Botswana. This is a well-governed, stable, relatively well-off country in southern Africa, with a good record of education and health care. But here, in a population of about 1.6 million, it is estimated that almost 350 000 people are HIV positive, nearly a quarter of the population. Average life expectancy is only 39 years. Already, there are 60 000 children who have been orphaned as a result of AIDS.

SAQ

12.1 Compare the structure of a named virus with that of a named bacterium.

Summary

1 An infectious disease is one which is caused by a pathogen, and can be caught from another person with that disease.

2 Some bacteria and viruses are pathogens. Tuberculosis, TB, is an infectious disease caused by the bacterium *Mycobacterium tuberculosis*. AIDS is an infectious disease caused by the human immunodeficiency virus, HIV.

3 A bacterial cell is a prokaryotic cell. These cells differ from eukaryotic cells as they do not have a nucleus or any membrane-bound organelles.

4 Viruses are not made of cells. They consist of a central core containing either DNA or RNA, surrounded by a protein coat called a capsid.

5 A person may develop TB after breathing in droplets containing *M. tuberculosis*. The disease develops slowly, as the bacteria steadily invade and destroy tissues. This may happen anywhere in the body, but is most common in the lungs.

6 A person may develop AIDS if HIV enters their body. The virus cannot survive outside the body, so HIV is only passed on by direct contact between body fluids. The virus enters T lymphocytes, and may remain there for many years. Eventually it destroys the T lymphocytes, reducing the person's ability to fight other diseases. A combination of several infectious diseases eventually proves fatal.

The immune response

CASE STUDY

Is mother's milk performance-enhancing?

In the first 72 hours after giving birth, the milk produced by a new mother is a watery liquid, yellowish in colour. It is called colostrum. Colostrum is taken as a food supplement by some people who believe it enhances athletic performance.

Colostrum supplements from cows have been shown to help athletes' muscles recover from workouts much more quickly than usual. This enables them to train harder and for longer. In one study, colostrum was estimated to help them to increase their strength and stamina by up to 20%. However, other researchers doubt the validity of these findings. And just how the many different substances which make up colostrum might improve stamina is still unknown.

Recently a study undertaken in Australia found another way in which colostrum supplements may confer an advantage on athletes. It seems to boost their immune systems. The participants in the study took 60 mg of colostrum each day, which was obtained from cows grazing on natural pastures in New Zealand. Those taking the supplements suffered from significantly fewer upper respiratory tract infections (colds, coughs and sore throats). Colostrum is very rich in antibodies, which are known to help to reduce the risk of babies suffering from infectious diseases before their own immune systems are up and running.

The researchers are suggesting that it is worth looking into the possibilities of using colostrum supplements as an extra weapon against illness and possible deaths from 'flu amongst the elderly, alongside the already well-established programme of 'flu vaccinations.

We have numerous defences against invasion of our bodies by pathogens. The way in which certain cells respond when pathogens enter body tissues is called the **immune response**. Cells involved in this response are said to belong to the **immune system**.

Cells of the immune system

The cells which produce the immune response are all **leucocytes**, or white blood cells. All of them are produced in the bone marrow, from stem cells which remain active throughout life.

These cells can be divided into two main groups: phagocytes and lymphocytes.

Phagocytes

Neutrophils and **macrophages** (see page 6) are phagocytes. They engulf and digest foreign particles of almost any type or size (Fig 12.8). These could be particles such as soot or asbestos fibres which have been inhaled into the lungs. They could be bacteria or intact body cells. Phagocytes also act as scavengers, destroying dead cells wherever they occur in the body.

Neutrophils are found in the blood, where they make up about 60% of the white blood cells. They do not live very long, often dying after they have taken in and destroyed bacteria, and so new ones are constantly being made in the bone marrow. They move around actively, and frequently leave the blood and patrol parts of the body where 'invaders' may be found.

Macrophages also leave the blood – indeed, the name 'macrophage' is generally given to them when they are in the tissues. (When they are present in the blood, they are usually known as monocytes.) They are present in especially large numbers in the liver, where they are known as **Kupffer cells**. They also line the passages through which lymph flows inside lymph nodes. They are found on the inside surface of the alveolar wall (see Activity 7.4 on page 129). Unlike neutrophils, they are quite long-lived, tending to survive after taking in foreign particles. They break them up into their component molecules and place some of these molecules in their cell surface membranes. Cells that do this are known as **antigen-presenting cells (APCs)**. They display the molecules to other cells of the immune system, helping these cells to identify the invaders and so destroy them.

1 Phagocytic white blood cell (macrophage / monocyte or neutrophil) moves towards a pathogen.

2 Phagocytosis takes place.

3 Lysosomes join with the vacuole and the pathogen is killed and digested by hydrolytic enzymes.

4 Any chemicals that are not absorbed into the cell are egested.

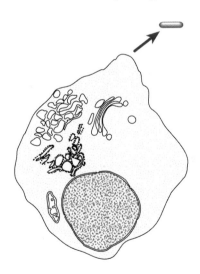
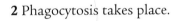
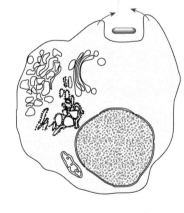
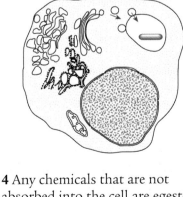

Fig 12.8 Phagocytosis of a pathogen.

225

Lymphocytes

Lymphocytes (see page 6) are relatively small white blood cells. They are of two types, **B lymphocytes** and **T lymphocytes**. They look identical, and differ only in their functions. B lymphocytes are so-called because they develop in the **b**one marrow, while T lymphocytes need to spend time in the **t**hymus gland during a person's childhood to become properly developed. This gland is found in the neck. It disappears by the time a person becomes a teenager.

Invading bacteria or viruses are recognised as foreign because they contain molecules which are different from any of our own molecules. These 'foreign' molecules are known as **antigens**. Antigens may be 'free' or they may be bound to a bigger structure, such as the surface of a bacterium.

We have a huge number of different kinds of lymphocytes in our blood. Each one is capable of recognising and responding to one particular antigen.

As they mature, the lymphocytes produce small quantities of particular glycoproteins called **antibodies** (see page 232). We have perhaps over a million different kinds of lymphocytes, each kind producing an antibody which is slightly different from other antibodies. At this stage, the antibodies are placed into the cell surface membranes of the lymphocytes (Fig 12.9). Here the antibodies act as **receptors**, able to bind with a particular antigen if this should appear in the body. Antigen binding triggers a response (see page 227 opposite).

The binding of an antigen to an antibody is highly specific. Each specific antibody binds to its complementary antigen.

As lymphocytes mature in the thymus gland when we are children, they are exposed to all the different proteins which actually belong in our bodies. This helps to prevent them from mounting an attack against the body's own cells. Sometimes, at a particular point in a person's life, this prevention mechanism can fail. The result is a type of disease known as an **autoimmune** disease (see page 233).

Some antibody is held in the cell surface membrane – acting as a receptor for a specific antigen.

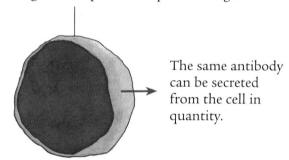

The same antibody can be secreted from the cell in quantity.

Fig 12.9 A lymphocyte can produce one specific type of antibody.

How lymphocytes fight infection

If bacteria enter the body, there is a good chance that some of the lymphocytes will have receptors which bind with antigens on the surface of the bacteria. B lymphocytes and T lymphocytes respond in different ways to this event.

How B lymphocytes respond to antigens

Most B lymphocytes will spend all their lives without anything happening to them at all, because they never meet their particular antigen. But if a B lymphocyte does encounter an antigen which binds to the receptors in its cell surface membrane, it is triggered into action. It could simply meet this antigen in the blood, or it could meet it as it is being displayed in the cell surface membrane of an APC such as a macrophage (Fig 12.10).

You can imagine the macrophages sitting in the lymph channels inside a lymph node, holding out the antigens they have discovered so that the lymphocytes will 'see' them as they pass by.

When it has encountered its specific antigen, the B lymphocyte is stimulated to divide repeatedly by mitosis. A large number of genetically identical cells are formed, a **clone** of the stimulated lymphocyte. As only the B lymphocytes with antibodies complementary to the antigen are selected to divide like this, it is known as **clonal selection**.

Some of these cells differentiate into **plasma cells**. These cells develop extra protein-making and protein-processing machinery – more endoplasmic reticulum, ribosomes and Golgi bodies. They rapidly synthesise more and more molecules of their particular antibody, and release them by exocytosis (see page 12). It has been estimated that a plasma cell can produce and release more than 2000 antibody molecules per second. Perhaps as a direct result of this tremendous rate of activity, plasma cells do not live long, mostly disappearing after only a few weeks.

The antibodies are secreted into the blood and so are carried to all parts of the body. They bind with the antigens on the invading bacteria which, as we will see, results in their destruction.

Other cells in the clone produced by the original B lymphocyte's division do not secrete antibody. Instead, they remain as **memory cells**. These cells live for a long time, and remain circulating in the blood long after the invading bacteria have all been destroyed. These memory cells are capable of responding very quickly if the same type of bacterium enters the body again (see Fig 12.12).

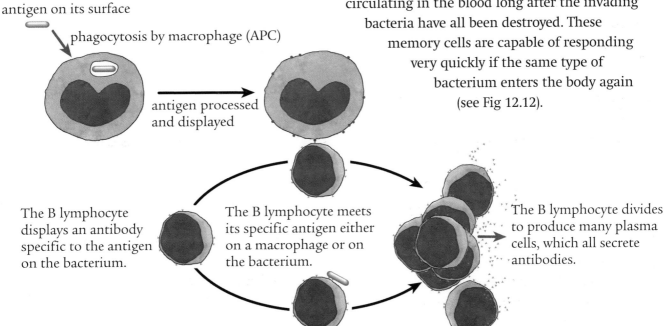

bacterium with an antigen on its surface

phagocytosis by macrophage (APC)

antigen processed and displayed

The B lymphocyte displays an antibody specific to the antigen on the bacterium.

The B lymphocyte meets its specific antigen either on a macrophage or on the bacterium.

The B lymphocyte divides to produce many plasma cells, which all secrete antibodies.

Fig 12.10 B lymphocyte response to antigen.

227

How T lymphocytes respond to antigens

T lymphocytes, like B lymphocytes, are activated if and when their particular antigen binds with the specific glycoproteins that are held in their cell surface membranes. T lymphocytes respond to their antigen only if they find it in the cell surface membrane of another cell. This could be a macrophage (APC) which is displaying some of the molecules from a pathogen that it has taken up. Or it could be molecules on a body cell which has been invaded by a virus, and has placed virus particles in its cell surface membrane as a 'help' signal (Fig 12.11).

T lymphocytes are of two types – **T helper** cells and **T killer** cells. A particular T helper cell with the complementary receptor binds to the antigen that it has found on the surface of an APC. This T helper cell then clones. The APC has effectively 'selected' which T lymphocyte will be cloned, so this is also clonal selection.

The cloned T helper cells then begin to secrete chemicals called **cytokines**. These chemicals stimulate other cells to fight against the invaders. For example, they may stimulate macrophages to carry out phagocytosis, or they may stimulate B lymphocytes specific to this antigen to divide rapidly and become plasma cells. They also help to stimulate appropriate T killer cells.

T killer cells actually destroy the cell to which they have bound. A body cell displaying virus particles will be destroyed by T killer cells. This is the only way of destroying the viruses – it can't be done without destroying the cell in which they are multiplying. The T killer cells destroy the infected cell by secreting chemicals such as hydrogen peroxide. These T killer cells are our main defence against viral diseases.

We have seen that T lymphocytes, like B lymphocytes, divide to form clones when they meet their own particular antigen. While most of these cells act as helper cells or killer cells, some of them remain in the blood as **memory cells**. These, like the memory cells formed from B lymphocytes, help the body to respond more quickly and effectively if this same antigen ever invades again (see Fig 12.12).

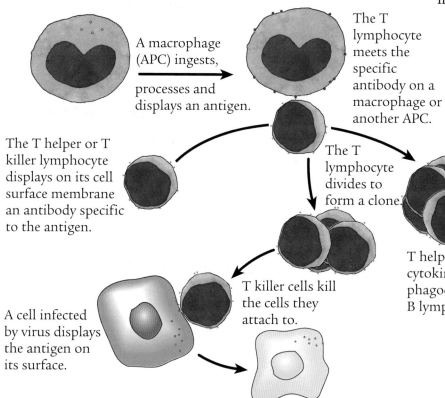

A macrophage (APC) ingests, processes and displays an antigen.

The T lymphocyte meets the specific antibody on a macrophage or another APC.

The T helper or T killer lymphocyte displays on its cell surface membrane an antibody specific to the antigen.

The T lymphocyte divides to form a clone.

T helper cells secrete cytokines to stimulate phagocytic cells and B lymphocytes.

A cell infected by virus displays the antigen on its surface.

T killer cells kill the cells they attach to.

Fig 12.11 T lymphocyte response to antigen.

SAQ

12.3 With reference to the way in which they respond to antigen, suggest why T cells are more effective than B cells in dealing with infection by a virus.

B lymphocytes

Specific binding
B lymphocyte with antibody in its cell surface membrane binds to complementary antigen.

Clonal selection
Stimulated B lymphocyte divides many times.

Memory cells
These survive for a long time.

Plasma cells
These secrete large amounts of antibody.

If the same antigen appears later, the memory cells are stimulated, divide and produce many plasma cells very quickly.

Fig 12.12 Summary of B and T lymphocyte actions.

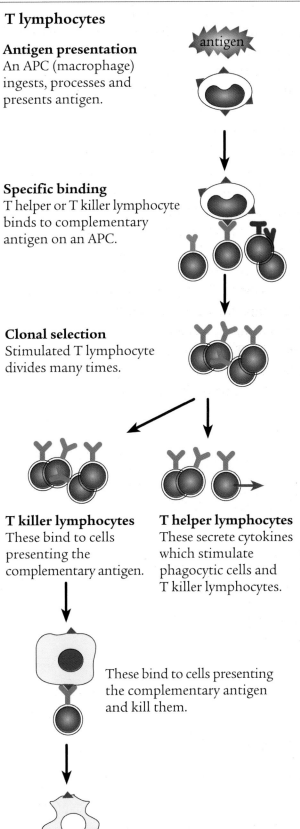

T lymphocytes

Antigen presentation
An APC (macrophage) ingests, processes and presents antigen.

Specific binding
T helper or T killer lymphocyte binds to complementary antigen on an APC.

Clonal selection
Stimulated T lymphocyte divides many times.

T killer lymphocytes
These bind to cells presenting the complementary antigen.

T helper lymphocytes
These secrete cytokines which stimulate phagocytic cells and T killer lymphocytes.

These bind to cells presenting the complementary antigen and kill them.

How immunity develops

When a pathogen first enters the body, there will only be a few lymphocytes with receptors which fit into its antigens. It takes time for these lymphocytes to encounter and bind with these pathogens. It takes more time for them to divide to form clones, and for the B lymphocytes to secrete enough antibody to destroy the pathogens, or for enough T lymphocytes to be produced to be able to destroy all the cells which are infected by them.

During this delay, the pathogens have the opportunity to divide repeatedly, forming large populations in the body tissues. The damage that they cause, and harmful chemicals called **toxins** that they may release, make the person ill. It may be several days, or even weeks, before the lymphocytes get on top of the pathogen population and destroy it.

However, if the body survives this initial attack by the pathogen, memory cells will remain in the blood long after the pathogen has been destroyed. If the same pathogen invades again, these memory cells can mount a much faster and more effective response. More antibody can be produced more quickly, usually destroying the pathogen before it has caused any illness.

SAQ

12.4 Copy and complete the table to summarise the similarities and differences between B lymphocytes and T lymphocytes.

	B lymphocyte	T lymphocyte
appearance		
where in the body they are first formed		
where in the body they mature in childhood		
how they respond to contact with their specific antigen		

The response to the first invasion of the pathogen is called the **primary response** (Fig 12.13). Subsequent invasions of the same pathogen elicit a **secondary response**. You can see that the secondary response happens more quickly after the entry of the pathogen, and produces many more antibodies. This is why we become **immune** to a disease if we have had it once.

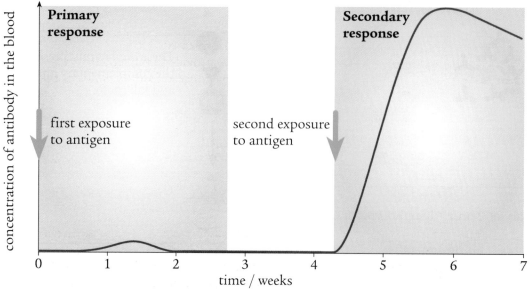

Fig 12.13 Primary and secondary responses to antigen.

Active and passive immunity

Active immunity

The kind of immunity described on page 227 is a type of **active immunity**. The body has been stimulated to make a particular type of antibodies, and can produce these same ones more quickly and in larger quantity if it is exposed to the same pathogen again. The immunity has developed naturally, so it is a type of **natural immunity**.

Another way in which active immunity can develop is by **vaccination**. This involves injecting the antigen into the body. It may be in the form of viruses which have been made harmless, or as an inactivated toxin from a bacterium (see page 244). The body responds in the same way as it would if invaded by the living pathogen, producing memory cells which will make the person immune to the disease if they should ever encounter it. This way of acquiring active immunity is not natural, so it is a form of **artificial immunity** (Fig 12.14).

Passive immunity

We have seen that a young baby's immune system takes time to develop. In the uterus, the foetus obtains antibodies from its mother's blood, across the placenta. After birth, it will continue to receive them in its mother's milk, if she decides to breastfeed. Colostrum, the thin, yellowish milk produced in the first few days after birth, is especially rich in antibodies. These ready-made antibodies help the baby to fight off pathogens. The baby has immunity to the same diseases as its mother. Because it has received ready-made antibodies, rather than making them itself, this is said to be **passive immunity**. It has happened naturally, so it is an example of natural immunity too.

Passive immunity can also be provided by injections. This is not a natural way of gaining immunity, so it is an example of **artificial immunity**. For example, if someone goes to A and E with a cut that may have dirt in it, they need to be protected against the bacterium that causes tetanus, *Clostridium tetani*. It is too late for a vaccination, because by the time their immune system responded, the bacterium would have multiplied and caused the fatal illness tetanus. Instead, the person will be given an injection of **antitoxin**. The antitoxin will bind to the toxin produced by the bacteria, rendering it harmless.

Passive immunity does not last as long as active immunity. No lymphocytes have been stimulated to produce clones of themselves, so no memory cells have been formed. Passive immunity lasts only as long as the antibodies or antitoxins last. The body actually 'sees' them as being foreign, and they will be removed and destroyed quite quickly by cells in the liver and spleen.

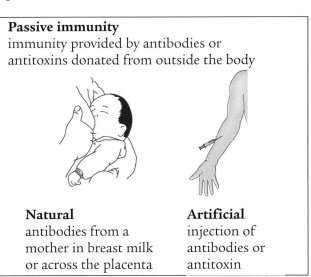

Active immunity
immunity developed after contacting pathogens inside the body

Natural
infection

Artificial
injection of live or attenuated pathogen

Passive immunity
immunity provided by antibodies or antitoxins donated from outside the body

Natural
antibodies from a mother in breast milk or across the placenta

Artificial
injection of antibodies or antitoxin

Fig 12.14 Active and passive immunity.

Antibodies

Antibodies are glycoproteins. Their molecules contain chains of amino acids, and also sugar units. Fig 12.15 shows the structure of an antibody molecule.

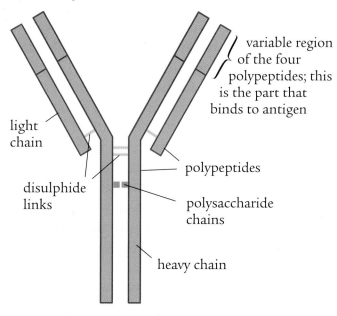

Fig 12.15 The structure of an antibody molecule.

Antibodies are also known as **immunoglobulins**. There are several different kinds of them, given names such as IgG and IgA.

Each antibody contains a variable region that can bind specifically with a particular antigen. We have millions of different antibodies with different variable regions.

When an antibody molecule meets its specific antigen, it binds with it. The effect that this has depends on what the antigen is, and on what type of immunoglobulin has bound to it.

Some antibodies directly neutralise the antigen – for example, by binding with a toxin produced by a bacterium. Others may encourage phagocytes to destroy the pathogen, sometimes by making the pathogens clump together. Yet others may stop the bacteria getting a foothold on body surfaces, by preventing them from attaching to cells or tissues.

SAQ

12.5 An experiment was carried out to follow what happens inside plasma cells as they make and secrete antibodies. Some cells were cultured in a medium containing amino acids which had been 'labelled' with a radioactive marker. The radioactivity in the Golgi body, endoplasmic reticulum and ribosomes was then measured over the next 40 minutes. The results are shown in the graph.

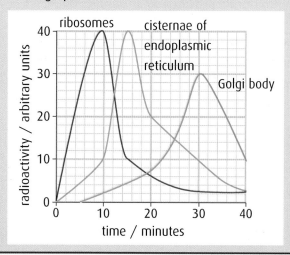

a In which order did the amino acids move through the three organelles? Use the results shown on the graph to justify your answer.

b Using your own knowledge, describe what happened to the amino acids in each organelle.

c Suggest why the peak values for the radioactivity in the ribosomes and the endoplasmic reticulum are the same, whereas the peak value for the Golgi body is lower. (You may be able to think of more than one possibility.)

d Suggest how the amino acids would have been taken up into the cell at the beginning of the experiment.

e Describe how the antibody molecules would be secreted from the cell.

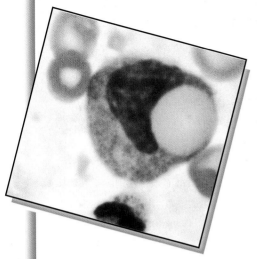

A monocyte which has ingested a red blood cell. This is an autoimmune disease called LE, in which red blood cells are killed.

David, 26 years old and fit, with hardly a day's illness in his life, woke up one sunny June morning unable to move. He could not get out of bed. His wife dressed him and practically carried him to the car. As he slumped on the back seat, the short journey to the hospital was a nightmare for him. His whole body seemed swollen and everything hurt beyond any pain he had ever felt before.

He was wheeled on a stretcher from the car into A and E. After what seemed an eternity, he was given a large dose of NSAIDs (non-steroidal anti-inflammatory drugs).

X-rays and blood tests showed that David had rheumatoid arthritis. It is rare for it to kick in quite this rapidly. For most people, it begins with relatively mild recurrent joint pains and swellings, which gradually get worse over a long period of time.

Rheumatoid arthritis can strike at any age. It is an autoimmune disease – where the immune system attacks the body instead of protecting it. In rheumatoid arthritis a number of tissues are attacked. Joint swelling and pain are usually the first symptoms, but the immune system may also attack the skin, blood vessels, heart, lungs, kidneys, alimentary canal and the nervous system. It affects about 1% of the population in Britain. Women are three times as likely to get it as men.

Treatment for rheumatoid arthritis involves NSAIDs, which reduce the inflammation caused by the attacks by the immune system. Another type of drug, called biologic response modifiers, interfere with the behaviour of cytokines. And if those fail, a third option is to pass the patient's blood through a tube whose walls are coated with a substance that binds to the antibodies that are causing all the trouble. The blood, free of these antibodies, is then returned to the patient.

What causes rheumatoid arthritis? We do not know. You are more likely to get it following a viral illness, or after a very stressful period in your life, or after damage to the body in an accident. Something switches on the immune system to recognise your own cells as 'foreign' and to attack them. There also seems to be a genetic component, and people are more likely to suffer from rheumatoid arthritis if other members of their family have it. As yet, we do not know how to cure this disease, or other autoimmune diseases, such as LE described in the photo above.

David knows that it will get worse, unless someone finds a cure. He knows that he will soon be in a wheelchair. His hands are becoming more and more twisted and useless; he cannot even hold a glass to drink from.

Summary

1. White blood cells, or leucocytes, all help to fight against disease. They include macrophages, neutrophils and lymphocytes. They are formed in the bone marrow.

2. Macrophages and neutrophils are phagocytes. They engulf foreign particles, enclose them in a vacuole, kill them and digest them using hydrolytic enzymes. Macrophages are found in tissues all over the body, while neutrophils are mainly found in the blood.

3. B lymphocytes respond to their specific antigen by dividing repeatedly to form a clone. Some of these cells differentiate into plasma cells and secrete antibodies. Others remain as memory cells.

4. T lymphocytes also respond to their specific antigen by dividing. They do not secrete antibodies, but keep receptor molecules in their cell surface membranes. These allow the cell to bind with their specific antigen. T helper cells respond by secreting cytokines, chemicals which stimulate activity in other cells of the immune system. T killer cells destroy the cell to which they have bound.

5. When a pathogen is first encountered, the response by the lymphocytes is relatively slow, as it takes time for enough plasma cells to be formed to produce large quantities of antibodies. This is known as the primary response. If the same pathogen is encountered a second time, the memory cells help the response to be faster and greater. This is known as the secondary response. The speed of the secondary response usually means that the pathogen does not take hold and cause illness, so the person is now immune to that disease.

6. Immunity is said to be active if the person makes their own antibodies. This type of immunity can result from having had the disease, or from having a vaccination using a weakened form of the antigen.

7. Immunity is said to be passive if the person is given ready-made antibodies. This happens in the uterus, where the foetus gains antibodies from its mother, and also after birth if the mother breastfeeds. Passive immunity can also be given by injecting ready-made antibodies or antitoxins.

8. An antibody molecule is made of four chains of amino acids, together with some sugar chains. It is therefore a glycoprotein molecule. At one end of the molecule are two variable regions, which are the parts which bind with antigen. This makes the antigen more likely to be detected and destroyed by phagocytes, or it may inhibit the pathogen in other ways.

Controlling infectious disease

On Sunday November 17th 1996, Jack Bramley went along with his wife Elaine to a free lunch which was being given for seventy pensioners in the small town where they lived. The food was good – some excellent meat pies bought from the local butcher, who had just been voted Scottish Butcher of the Year.

On Wednesday evening, Jack began to feel a bit ill. He had to get up several times in the night to be sick. Not one to complain, he stayed at home in bed, and didn't bother to call a doctor. His wife didn't feel too well, either, and when their daughter popped in that evening she was very worried about them both. She rang their GP's surgery and asked for a home visit.

The GP arrived within a couple of hours, and was so worried that he got Jack admitted to hospital straight away. Jack was diagnosed with acute food poisoning. On the next day, Friday 22nd, several more elderly people who had attended the lunch became ill. It was now clear that something served at the lunch must be to blame. Environmental Health Officers quickly tracked the problem down to the butcher who had supplied the pies. They visited him at his shop and asked him to clear all cooked meat from his shelves. He did – but neglected to tell them that, earlier that day, a customer had taken two large bags of cooked meat to serve at a birthday party.

By Saturday 23rd, the food poisoning was known to be caused by a bacterium called *Escherichia coli* 157. Most people get over it, but the elderly and very young may not.

Eighty-year-old Jack Bramley was one of the unlucky ones. He died on Tuesday November 26th, 9 days after he had eaten one of the meat pies. He was to be the first of 20 victims, some of whom had eaten cold meat at the birthday party.

Despite investigators tracking down all the outlets that had been supplied by this butcher, in total more than 400 people became ill. It became the world's worst ever outbreak of *E. coli* 157 food poisoning.

The bacterium *Escherichia coli* is found in everyone's intestines, and also in the intestines of most animals. It is normally completely harmless, and is probably beneficial, because it suppresses the growth of harmful bacteria. But some strains can cause harm, and they are a frequent cause of food poisoning. Strain 157 is the most dangerous. It produces a very powerful toxin that causes severe abdominal pain and watery diarrhoea. Most patients recover within about eight days but in some, usually the very young or the elderly, the toxin can break down red blood cells and damage the kidneys so much that they stop working. On average, around 3–5% of victims will die.

It is lucky that *E. coli* 157 is rare because, as yet, we have no effective treatments for it. For many other infectious diseases, however, we are able to prevent people getting them by giving them vaccinations, or can treat them successfully using drugs such as antibiotics.

Antibiotics

Until the middle of the twentieth century, there were very few ways of curing infectious diseases. If you caught one, you had to rely mainly on your own immune system to destroy the pathogens and allow you to recover. Only a few drugs, such as sulphonamides, were available to help you through. But in 1940 the first antibiotic was discovered. This revolutionised our ability to treat infectious diseases caused by bacteria.

An antibiotic can be defined as a substance produced by another organism (usually a microorganism, especially a fungus) which kills or inhibits bacteria, without harming human cells. However, many antibiotics we use now are modified versions of the naturally-occurring substances. Antibiotics are usually taken in the form of tablets, but in an acute or especially dangerous infection a patient may be admitted to hospital and fixed up to a drip which feeds antibiotic continuously into their blood.

The first antibiotic to be discovered was **penicillin**. This and similar ones, such as **methicillin** and **ampicillin**, are still widely used. Penicillin is made by a fungus called *Penicillium*.

Penicillin is an inhibitor of the enzyme glycoprotein peptidase, which links together the peptidoglycan chains that make up much of a bacterial cell wall. (Peptidoglycan is similar to glycoprotein, but contains derivatives of glucose.) When a newly-formed bacterial cell is growing, it secretes enzymes called autolysins, which make little holes in its cell wall. These little holes allow the cell wall to stretch, and new peptidoglycan chains link up across the gaps. Penicillin stops the peptidoglycan chains linking up, but the autolysins keep making new holes. The cell wall therefore becomes progressively weaker.

The bacterium is always in a watery environment, from where it tends to take up water by osmosis. As the wall weakens and the cell takes up water and swells, the cell wall is not able to withstand the pressure exerted on it by the contents of the cell, and the cell bursts (Fig 13.1). As our cells don't have cell walls, penicillin is completely harmless to us.

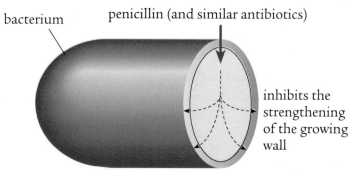

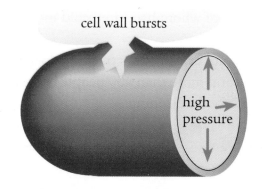

Fig 13.1 How penicillins work.

Not all bacteria are destroyed by any one antibiotic. There are now many different antibiotics in use, such as **streptomycin** and **erythromycin** as well as those derived from penicillin. They may work in different ways (Fig 13.2).

Usually, a doctor faced with a patient who needs immediate antibiotic treatment will make an educated guess at what is causing the infection and what antibiotic is needed, so that treatment can start straight away. But it may be necessary to test which antibiotics the microorganism is sensitive to. This can be done by placing discs soaked in different antibiotics onto agar jelly on which the bacterium is growing. If a clear area of a certain diameter appears around the disc, the antibiotic is known to be effective (Fig 13.3).

Some antibiotics are effective against many different bacteria and they are known as **broad-spectrum** antibiotics. Others, known as **narrow-spectrum** antibiotics, are more specific in the types of bacteria against which they act.

Antibiotics fight bacterial infection by interfering with:

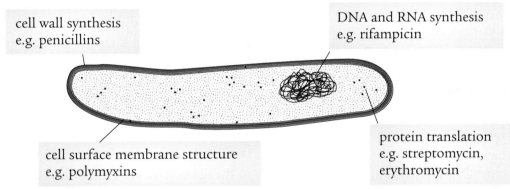

cell wall synthesis e.g. penicillins

DNA and RNA synthesis e.g. rifampicin

cell surface membrane structure e.g. polymyxins

protein translation e.g. streptomycin, erythromycin

Fig 13.2 How antibiotics act.

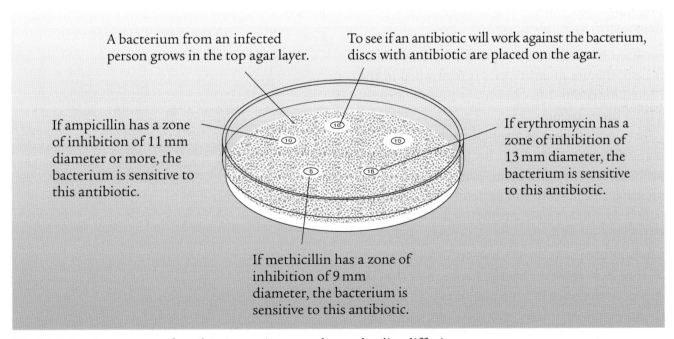

A bacterium from an infected person grows in the top agar layer.

To see if an antibiotic will work against the bacterium, discs with antibiotic are placed on the agar.

If ampicillin has a zone of inhibition of 11 mm diameter or more, the bacterium is sensitive to this antibiotic.

If erythromycin has a zone of inhibition of 13 mm diameter, the bacterium is sensitive to this antibiotic.

If methicillin has a zone of inhibition of 9 mm diameter, the bacterium is sensitive to this antibiotic.

Fig 13.3 Testing a range of antibiotics against a pathogen by disc diffusion.

Antibiotic resistance

A great problem with the use of antibiotics is that bacteria may become **resistant** to them. Imagine a large population – several billion – of a particular species of bacteria that are making you ill. Your doctor prescribes streptomycin. You take the tablets, which destroy almost all of the bacteria.

But amongst all those bacteria there are perhaps one or two which are a little different from the others. They possess a gene which codes for an enzyme that modifies the molecules of streptomycin. These individual bacteria are not killed by streptomycin. They are resistant to it.

The antibiotic acts as a **selective agent** on the bacteria. As most of the other bacteria in the population are killed, these few resistant bacteria now have little competition for resources. In this altered environment, they are the best-adapted. They therefore grow and multiply. They may form a whole population of streptomycin-resistant bacteria, each inheriting that gene. If they now infect someone else, streptomycin will be of no use at all in treating the disease. Some other antibiotic will have to be found, to which resistance has not yet evolved.

You can probably see that, the more we use antibiotics, the more likely it is that antibiotic-resistant strains of bacteria will emerge. For this reason, the use of antibiotics is controlled in the United Kingdom. You can only get antibiotics with a prescription.

The development of antibiotic resistance in many different pathogenic bacteria is a real problem for drug-producing companies, pharmacists, doctors and patients. The rate at which significant new antibiotics are found has fallen to a very low level. It seems that, as fast as a new antibiotic is discovered, yet more strains of antibiotic-resistant bacteria appear. In the UK, it is general policy to keep one or two antibiotics that are only ever used in cases where no other antibiotic is effective. This tactic will, it is hoped, ensure that there will always be one antibiotic to which the bacteria causing a particular disease won't be resistant.

As well as keeping some antibiotics in reserve, there are several things that we can do to reduce the risk of bacteria becoming resistant to antibiotics.

- Doctors should only prescribe antibiotics when really necessary.
- The antibiotic prescribed should be the most appropriate one for the infection.
- If symptoms re-emerge during the patient's course of antibiotics, a different antibiotic should be prescribed.
- The patient should take their antibiotics at regular intervals.
- The patient should finish the course of antibiotics, even if they feel better part way through.

There are numerous ways in which bacteria can resist different antibiotics. For example, some bacteria produce an enzyme called beta-lactamase. This enzyme destroys the penicillins, so these bacteria are resistant to these antibiotics. The resistant bacteria have inherited a gene for the enzyme.

Like many genes for antibiotic resistance, the beta-lactamase gene is found in a plasmid (see page 239), not on the main DNA molecule.

Plasmids and resistance

A plasmid known as R100 carries a gene that confers resistance to streptomycin. Like plasmids in general, this plasmid can transfer from one bacterium to another, even a bacterium of a different kind. So, where many different kinds of bacteria live together, such as in your intestines, a streptomycin-resistant *Escherichia coli* might pass on its resistance to a *Salmonella* bacterium. Sometimes the R100 plasmid carries several different genes which confer resistance to several different antibiotics.

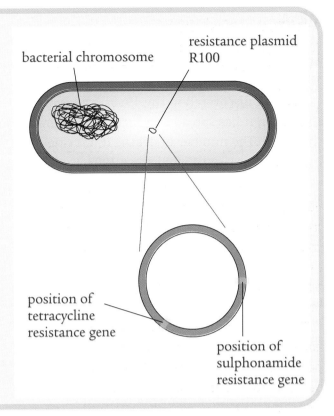

bacterial chromosome

resistance plasmid R100

position of tetracycline resistance gene

position of sulphonamide resistance gene

Antibiotics for treating TB

Mycobacterium tuberculosis, the bacterium which causes TB, can be killed using antibiotics. The ones most frequently prescribed are isoniazid, pyrazinamide, rifampicin and ethambutol. Penicillin is of no use at all against TB. Usually, a patient will be prescribed at least two of these antibiotics, as this reduces the risk of drug-resistant strains of the bacterium evolving.

The antibiotics have to be taken regularly, and over a long period, usually for at least six months. It can be extremely difficult to ensure that all patients do this. In many countries, health workers use a scheme called DOTS, which stands for Directly Observed Treatment Short course. This involves watching the patient each day as they take their drugs (Fig 13.4). The World Health Organisation (WHO) suggests that 95% of patients with TB can be cured using this strategy.

There are, however, several antibiotic-resistant strains of *M. tuberculosis* in existence. Strains which are resistant to two or more antibiotics are called multidrug-resistant TB, or MDR-TB.

Disease caused by these strains is much more difficult to treat, and may involve the use of antibiotics which have been kept 'in reserve' and which may have more unpleasant side effects than the normal ones.

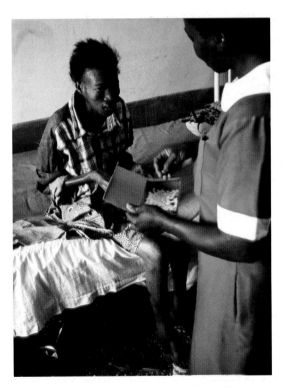

Fig 13.4 An elderly woman with TB being given DOTS drugs.

MRSA

MRSA stands for methicillin-resistant *Staphylococcus aureus*. The media like to call MRSA 'the superbug'. MRSA is on the increase. It was first discovered in the 1960s, and ever since then it has spread and increased, all over the world. The number of deaths it has caused in the UK has risen 15-fold since 1993. It affects about 7000 hospital patients each year. Most of these recover, but many do not, and MRSA causes up to 1000 deaths per year (Fig 13.5).

S. aureus is a common and usually harmless bacterium which lives on the skin or in the noses of around 25% of people. It really isn't a problem at all in normal circumstances. However, if a person has hospital treatment which involves their skin being broken, or if they are especially vulnerable to infection because of their health or the medical treatment they are undergoing, then MRSA may be able to enter their body and grow. The infection it causes may be mild, or it may be so severe that death ensues. The people who die from MRSA infection are usually very ill anyway from another disease. However, it is worrying to find that 53% of infections are of infants under 1 year old.

The MRSA figures have shone a spotlight on hospital hygiene. Hospital patients are being infected with MRSA because it is being transferred from one patient to another. Hospital staff may have MRSA living on their skin but be completely unaware of it. There are government guidelines covering ways to reduce the risk of passing infection between patients and staff and some of these are described in Table 13.1 opposite.

MRSA is more common in hospitals than outside them, probably at least partly because it is in hospitals that most antibiotics are used, creating the circumstances in which a resistant strain is most likely to evolve. It has been shown that everyone working in a hospital, even clerical staff, has more antibiotic-resistant strains of bacteria on their skin than are found in other groups of people (see Fig 13.6).

Some strains of MRSA can be treated using expensive antibiotics which are normally not used, but some strains don't respond to any of the antibiotics that we have at present.

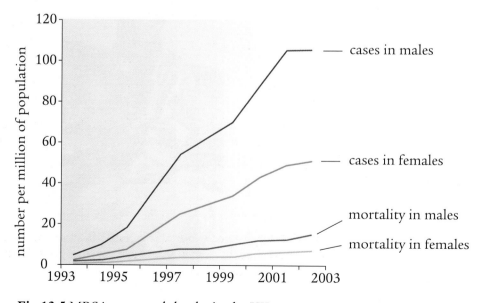

Fig 13.5 MRSA cases and deaths in the UK.

Table 13.1 Some of the ways in which healthcare staff can prevent infections in hospitals.

Hand hygiene	Use of protective equipment
Wash hands with liquid soap and water if visibly soiled.	The appropriate protective equipment for any task is selected and used to reduce the risk of transmission of pathogens to the patient, or to healthcare staff from patients.
Decontaminate hands immediately before every direct patient contact or any activity that might result in hands becoming contaminated.	Gloves must be worn, on a single-use basis, for all activities where there may be exposure to body fluids, secretions, excretions, sharp or contaminated instruments.
Decontaminate hands with an alcohol-based hand rub, making sure all wrist and ideally hand jewellery is removed.	Disposable plastic aprons must be worn where there is a risk of clothing becoming exposed to body fluids.
Cuts and abrasions must be covered with waterproof dressings.	Full-body, fluid-repellent gowns (and possibly face masks and eye protection) must be worn where there is a risk of extensive splashing of body fluids.
Follow the correct procedure for hand washing. Wet the hands under tepid running water before applying liquid soap or an antimicrobial preparation. The handwash solution must come into contact with all of the surfaces of the hand. The hands must be rubbed together vigorously for a minimum of 10 to 15 seconds, paying particular attention to the tips of the fingers, the thumbs and the areas between the fingers. Hands should be rinsed thoroughly before drying with good quality paper towels.	

(Adapted from guidelines published in 2003 by the *National Institute for Clinical Excellence*)

Fig 13.6 *Staphylococcus aureus* can cause infections, such as the one shown on the left, in someone's armpit. But good hospital hygiene can keep infection rates low.

13.1 Explain the difference between each of these pairs of terms:

antibody and antibiotic;
resistance and immunity.

13.2 Explain why:
a antibiotics will not help you to get over influenza;
b doctors should not prescribe antibiotics unnecessarily.

13.3 Explain what is wrong with each of these two statements, and then write a correct version.
a If you take antibiotics too often, you may become resistant to them.
b When exposed to antibiotics, bacteria mutate so that they become resistant to them.

Summary

❶ Antibiotics are substances that kill or inhibit bacteria without harming human cells. Many antibiotics are made by microorganisms, especially fungi.

❷ The widespread use of antibiotics has encouraged the evolution of antibiotic-resistant strains of bacteria. This happens because any bacterium which, by chance, has a gene that confers resistance to the antibiotic will survive and breed while the others are killed.

❸ Antibiotics to cure tuberculosis have to be taken regularly over a long period of time. At least two are used at once, to lessen the risk of antibiotic-resistant strains of *Mycobacterium tuberculosis* evolving.

❹ Methicillin-resistant *Staphylococcus aureus*, MRSA, is an antibiotic-resistant bacterium that is especially common in hospitals. In order to reduce the large number of infections that occur each year, careful hygiene needs to be practised by everyone in hospital wards.

Vaccination

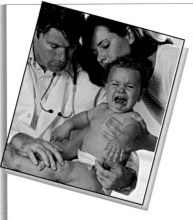

Jennifer and Harry's first child, Jason, has just had his first birthday. He's a healthy and happy child, and he has already had his DTP-Hib jabs and the polio vaccine, as well as the meningitis C jab. But now he is due for his MMR vaccination, and both Jennifer and Harry are worried.

They know MMR stands for measles, mumps and rubella, but have heard talk of a possible link between MMR and autism, a condition where a child finds it difficult to interact with other people in a normal way. The government says the MMR jab is safe, but they would, wouldn't they? They also know that lots of children used to get measles, mumps or rubella and recover from it. So, do they go ahead with the jab or don't they?

Many parents have found themselves in Jennifer and Harry's position, and have found it almost impossible to decide whether to let their baby have the MMR jab. In the end, Jennifer and Harry decide that he should have the jabs, but separately rather than all together. Their own doctor refuses to do this, so they have to find a surgery where it is done. The three jabs cost them £500. And Jason is fine. So perhaps they did make the right decision. There again, perhaps he would have been fine anyway, and they wasted £500, and Jason had the stress of two extra injections.

Table 13.2 The United Kingdom vaccination programme.

Age	Vaccination given	How administered
2, 3 and 4 months	polio	by mouth
	DTP-Hib (diphtheria, tetanus, pertussis, Hib)	injection
	meningitis C	injection
13 months	MMR (measles, mumps and rubella)	injection
before starting school, 3 to 5 years	polio booster	by mouth
	DTP booster	injection
	MMR booster	injection
10 to 14 years	BCG (tuberculosis)	injection, following a skin test
13 to 18 years	tetanus	injection

Vaccination involves giving a person a dose of a preparation that will cause the immune system to react as though an antigen from a pathogenic organism has entered the body. Most vaccinations are given by injection, but the polio (Sabin) vaccine is given by mouth (see Table 13.2). Many vaccines contain an **attenuated** (weakened) form of the bacterium or virus that causes the disease, while others contain a modified toxin produced by them.

When the vaccine enters the body, lymphocytes which 'recognise' the antigen respond to it as if they had encountered live bacteria or viruses (Fig 13.7). The B lymphocytes divide to form a clone of plasma cells which secrete antibody, and also a population of memory cells. T lymphocytes also respond, as described on page 228.

In most cases, a second dose of the vaccine is given later on, as a 'booster'. This raises the antibody level much higher than the first dose, and helps to ensure that protection against the antigen lasts for some time (Fig 13.8).

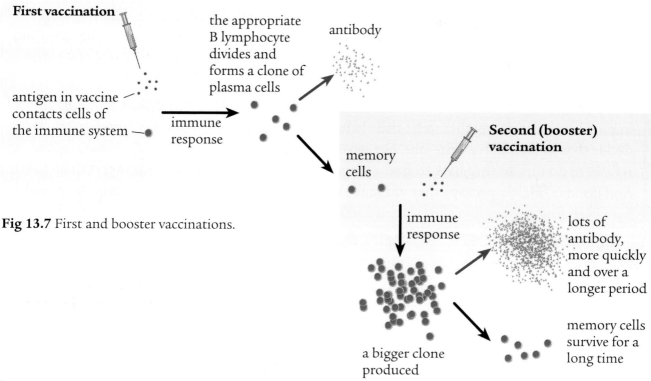

Fig 13.7 First and booster vaccinations.

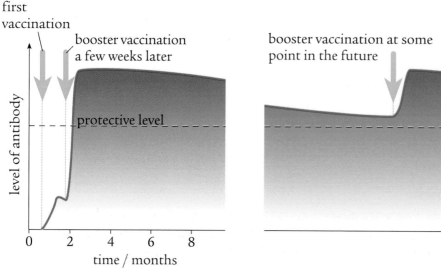

Fig 13.8 Antibody levels after vaccination.

244

Vaccination against TB

Tuberculosis, as we have seen (page 220–221), is an infectious disease which can kill. It has declined in many prosperous countries during the twentieth century (see Figs 13.10 and 13.11). However, despite the use of antibiotics, it is currently on the increase worldwide (see Fig 13.12). But we do have a vaccine which can give fairly good protection against it.

In the UK, the **BCG** (bacille Calmette-Guerin) vaccine is given to most school pupils between the ages of 10 to 14. Before the BCG is administered, each person has a skin test, called the **Heaf test** (see Fig 13.9 and Table 13.3). This test, first introduced in 1951, involves firing a six-pointed array of needles into the skin, usually on the inside of the left wrist. The needles make small, shallow puncture wounds, and introduce a substance called **tuberculin** into the skin. Tuberculin is a harmless extract made from *Mycobacterium tuberculosis*. However, it contains antigens like those from the live bacterium.

The idea of the Heaf test is to check whether the person is already immune to tuberculosis. If they are, then their phagocytes and lymphocytes will respond to the Heaf test injection by congregating at the site of the wound, causing inflammation as they act against the antigen. The site of the Heaf test is checked after about three days. If the six points have joined up to form a circle, or if they are visible as 5–10 mm raised patches, this indicates that the person is already immune to TB and does not need a vaccination. If, however, there is no or very little response to the injection of tuberculin, then the BCG vaccination will be given.

Although most young people in the United Kingdom are now vaccinated against TB, cases of it continue to appear, some associated with immigrants. Worryingly, some of the infections are caused by antibiotic-resistant strains of *M. tuberculosis* (see page 239).

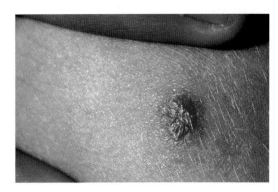

Fig 13.9 One of the results for the Heaf test listed in the table below. Which one do you think it is?

Table 13.3 Responses to the Heaf test.

Grade of reaction	What is seen	What this may mean
1	small puncture scars	the person has had no previous exposure to the TB pathogen, and should be given the BCG vaccination
2	at least 4 puncture points visible as raised bumps	the person has probably been exposed to TB already, and does not need a BCG vaccination
3	the puncture points have joined up to form a complete ring	the person has almost certainly been exposed to TB already, should have an X-ray, and does not need a BCG vaccination
4	the puncture points are considerably raised and hardened and possibly show central blistering	the person has definitely been exposed to TB fairly recently; they may already have TB and should have a chest X-ray (see page 256)

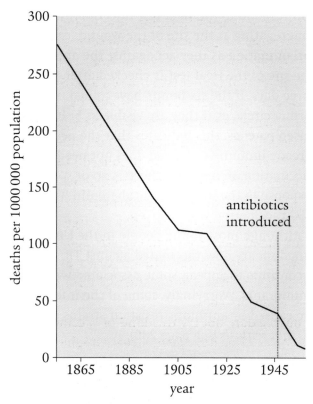

Fig 13.10 Deaths from TB in England from 1855 to 1955.

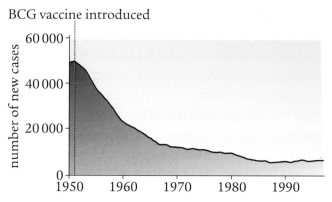

Fig 13.11 Incidence of TB in the UK from 1950 to 1997.

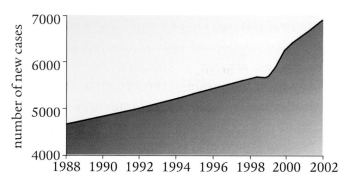

Fig 13.12 Incidence of TB in the UK from 1988 to 2002.

13.4 a Suggest reasons for the trends shown in the graphs in Fig 13.10 and in Fig 13.11.
   b Explain why the numbers on the y axis of the graph in Fig 13.11 are much greater than those in Fig 13.10.
   c Suggest reasons for the trend shown in Fig 13.12.

13.5 a The BCG vaccine contains weakened (attenuated) *Mycobacterium bovis*. This is a bacterium that causes TB in cattle.
   i Suggest why a vaccination with *M. bovis* can protect against infection with *M. tuberculosis*.
   ii Suggest why an attenuated form of *M. tuberculosis* is not used for this vaccination.
   b Explain why the Heaf test is given before the BCG vaccination.
   c Explain why people with a strong reaction to the Heaf test are given a chest X-ray.

Vaccination against HIV/AIDS

AIDS is a very new disease, which first appeared in the late 1970s. By 1983, a team of French scientists had shown that it is caused by a previously unknown retrovirus, the human immunodeficiency virus (HIV). In 1984, their results were confirmed in the USA. Everyone predicted that a vaccine would be developed within two years.

Yet, after more than 20 years of trying, no effective vaccine has been produced. The first really big trial of a potential vaccine, carried out by a biotechnology company based in the USA, ended in February 2003. It had cost US$150 million and showed that the 'vaccine' had no useful effects at all.

Why is it so difficult to develop a vaccine for AIDS, when we have excellent vaccines for so many other diseases caused by viruses? One reason is that the protein coat of the virus frequently changes. So a vaccine that was effective against one type would not be effective against another. But the main difficulty is that the vaccine needs to alert the cells that are of most help against viruses, the T lymphocytes. These cells respond best to the discovery of body cells inside which viruses are breeding. They recognise them because the body cells put pieces of the viruses, which have been made inside them, into their cell surface membranes.

All of the vaccines that are currently in use against other viral diseases – such as measles, mumps, influenza and polio – contain live viruses which have been treated in a way that stops them causing infection (attenuated). The viruses are taken up into the cells and breed there, and this alerts the T lymphocytes that recognise that particular kind of virus. As we have seen (page 229), T cells respond by multiplying and forming clones, some of which become T killer cells that destroy the infected cells. T helper cells are also produced in large numbers, and these secrete cytokines which trigger B lymphocytes to get involved as well. Once things have all settled down, large numbers of memory T lymphocytes and memory B lymphocytes are left, ready to go immediately into action if the real virus should ever enter the body.

But we dare not try this kind of vaccine for HIV/AIDS. Live, attenuated viruses might conceivably cause AIDS in a few people. This is too big a risk to take. Most attempts at producing an HIV/AIDS vaccine have involved injecting proteins from the virus into the blood. But this does not alert the T lymphocytes, because the proteins haven't been made inside the person's own cells.

One way round this problem may be to get some body cells to take up pieces of DNA from the virus. The cells might then make proteins using the instructions on the DNA and post them in their membranes. T lymphocytes might then respond to this just as they would if real viruses were breeding inside the cells.

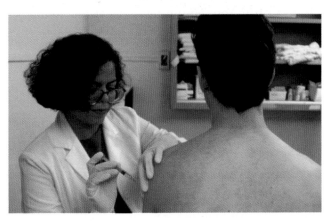

Fig 13.13 This doctor is injecting one of the experimental AIDS vaccines into an HIV-positive patient, as part of the vaccine's clinical trials. This particular one contains a modified protein from the envelope of the virus.

SAQ

13.6 With reference to particular examples, explain the meaning of each of the following terms:
- attenuated;
- retrovirus;
- Heaf test;
- MMR;
- booster vaccination.

Testing possible HIV vaccines

Before any vaccine can be widely used, it must be tested to find out:

- whether it is safe;
- whether it really does make people immune.

Testing HIV vaccines is especially difficult. This is partly because the disease is so feared, and is usually fatal. You could safely test a new 'flu vaccine, for example, on a group of healthy volunteers. You would need to give some of them the vaccine and some of them a 'dummy' vaccine, called a placebo. You could then expose them all to the 'flu virus and compare the number who got 'flu in one group with the number who fell ill in the other group. Or you could take blood samples from each volunteer and check the level of antibodies they have produced against the 'flu virus. If the vaccine didn't work it would not matter too much. Some people would have a miserable few days with 'flu, but they would soon get over it. You can't run that risk with HIV/AIDS.

As well as the seriousness of AIDS, there is also the difficulty of the long **incubation time**. People may not show any symptoms of AIDS for many years after they have been infected with HIV. So any test needs to run over several years.

A third difficulty is that you need thousands of volunteers to take part. This is because it would not be ethical to deliberately expose them to HIV. You would just have to let them live their lives. This means that only a small percentage of them will pick up the virus. To get large enough numbers of infected people to make your results meaningful, you need to start off with an extremely large number in the first place.

This makes it difficult if you want to try out several different vaccines in a particular country. Once you have used your group of volunteers, you cannot use them again when carrying out a new test. This is because some of them may have responded to the first vaccine and have already produced some antibodies.

So you need to find a completely new set of volunteers for each new vaccine that you test. This can become very difficult.

Decisions also need to be made about where to carry out the tests. Pharmaceutical companies have, in the past, tended to look to developing countries for their trialling of new vaccines or drugs. But the people in these countries, very naturally, are distrustful of this practice. They would like to be given vaccines or drugs which have already been tested in a developed country and have already been shown to be effective. They don't want to be used as guinea pigs. Moreover, if the trial involves giving the trialled vaccine to half of the group and a placebo to the other half, moral issues are raised about not giving the best possible treatment to each person.

Several of these problems could be avoided if small-scale testing of a contender for an HIV vaccine is first carried out in a developed country. This preliminary trial would consist of vaccinating a group of volunteers, and then analysing blood samples taken from them to see if they have produced large quantities of antibodies against the vaccine. Only vaccines that look really hopeful would then be taken on to the next trial stage. You could then run a large-scale trial, probably in a developing country with a high infection rate for HIV, in which half of the volunteers were given one trial vaccine and the other half a different trial vaccine. The results would be analysed by comparing the two potential vaccines against each other, rather than against a placebo.

SAQ

13.7 Discuss the moral and ethical issues associated with trialling a vaccine for HIV. What practical problems might you expect to have to face if you wish to find out whether a new vaccine is effective?

The MMR controversy

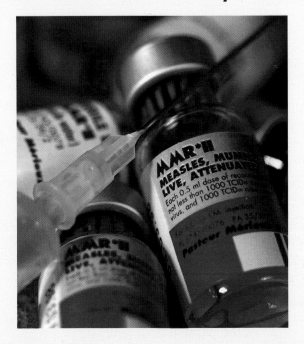

The suggestion that the MMR vaccine might not be safe came from just one group of researchers who wrote a paper that was published in a well-respected medical journal called The Lancet in 1998.

The researchers had been looking to see if there was any link between autism and bowel diseases. They investigated 12 children who had both conditions. One of the researchers thought it might be possible that there was a link between the MMR vaccine and the development of these conditions, and – despite reservations by the other members of the research team, and despite not having any good evidence for it – he mentioned in the published paper that there was a possibility of a link. He suggested that perhaps it would be a good idea for children to be given the three vaccinations separately, instead of all at once – even though there was no convincing evidence to support the suggestion that this would be 'safer'.

His suggestions were given huge publicity. People were already worried about this vaccine, as this research group had suggested in 1993 that the MMR vaccine could cause Crohn's disease. This is a chronic inflammation of the alimentary canal. As a result, take-up of the vaccine had dropped.

But after the 1998 news many more parents reacted by refusing to let their children have the MMR jab. Previously, more than 90% of babies had been having the vaccination, but in some parts of the country this now fell to less than 70%. Many further studies were undertaken by other researchers, overseas as well as in the UK, but none found evidence to support the claims of a link between MMR and autism. But the press were having a field day with the story, and would not let it go.

Meanwhile, the number of children who had not had any vaccinations for measles, mumps and rubella was growing. Unsurprisingly, these illnesses began to show up again. Although most children do recover from them with no problem, all three can have serious side effects and may be fatal. There is also the problem of a child with rubella coming into contact with a pregnant woman; rubella may deform or even kill her unborn child.

In 2004, ten of the thirteen scientists who contributed to the original paper in The Lancet formally withdrew their support for any suggestion that there is a link between MMR and autism. But even that did not immediately put the argument to rest. Many people so distrusted the government's advice on health matters that they simply refused to believe what they said.

13.8 New vaccines for HIV must go through three phases of testing before they can be recommended for use.

Phase 1 Tests conducted on 10–30 healthy volunteers who are not at risk. Main aim is to check for safety of the vaccine. Can also check to see if the volunteers make antibodies. Takes about 8 to 12 months.

Phase 2 Tests conducted on 5–50 volunteers, some of whom are at risk and some who are not. Main aim is to test for safety, and possibly collect some preliminary data about effectiveness as well. Takes about 18 to 24 months.

Phase 3 Tests conducted on thousands of high-risk volunteers in countries where HIV is present. Takes at least three years.

a Suggest what is meant by 'not at risk' (Phase 1).

b Suggest why Phase 1 is conducted on people who are not at risk, while Phase 2 is conducted on some who are at risk and some who are not.

c Suggest why Phase 3 takes much longer than Phases 1 and 2.

d Use the internet to find out about current developments in the search for an HIV/AIDS vaccine. Choose one or two examples and make a short presentation, including information about:
- who is carrying out the trial;
- what the biological principles behind it are;
- where it is being done;
- the phase it is currently in.

Summary

❶ Vaccination involves giving an injection (though a few vaccines may be taken by mouth) containing an antigen which elicits a response from the immune system without causing an infection.

❷ For many diseases, the response to the first vaccination is not great enough to produce enough antibodies or memory cells to confer lasting immunity. Second or third 'booster' injections are given to produce a larger response.

❸ In the UK, most children are vaccinated against polio, diphtheria, tetanus, pertussis (whooping cough), Hib and meningitis C in the first four months after birth. The measles, mumps and rubella vaccination is given at around 13 months, and then boosters for all of these diseases are given before starting school. The BCG vaccination for tuberculosis is given in the early teens, and tetanus a little later.

❹ Before being given the BCG vaccination, a person is given the Heaf test to find out if they already have some immunity to TB.

❺ So far, no effective vaccine has been found for HIV/AIDS. A new type of vaccine will need to be developed, as a traditional vaccine may actually give AIDS to some people.

Controlling the spread of infectious diseases

On February 21st 2003, Professor Liu Jianlun checked into his room at the Metropole Hotel in Kowloon, Hong Kong. A 64-year-old senior doctor, he had been working in Guangzhou in southern China with patients suffering from a respiratory disease which he had never encountered before. It had killed many, and was spreading rapidly amongst other patients in the hospital and the staff.

Did he perhaps suspect that he might have caught this frightening disease when he decided to travel from Guangzhou to Hong Kong? He certainly was not well, and he may have recognised that he had caught the very disease that had been killing his patients. But he took the lift in the hotel to his ninth floor room, coughing and sneezing as he did so.

The next day he walked to Kwong Wah hospital, a short way from the hotel. There he was admitted and, at first, treated as though he had influenza. He had the high fever and aching body typical of this illness. But Liu knew that this was not the illness he had, and he asked to be put into isolation. This was quickly done, but not before the viruses he was carrying were spread to others. Seventy-seven staff at the hospital were already infected, as were six guests at the Metropole Hotel.

The professor's death on March 4th was the first 'official' death from SARS, severe acute respiratory syndrome. By the beginning of May, more than 200 new cases were being reported each day, from over 30 different countries. By late summer in 2003, it is thought that more than 8000 people had caught this new disease. More than 770 of these people had died.

Newly emerging diseases

The emergence of SARS in early 2003 was a wake-up call for the world. Here was a completely new virus which suddenly and without warning seemed to be sweeping through the world population. With so many people now travelling over such large distances, it seemed to take no time for a disease that had erupted in China to spread to countries as far away as Canada and the United Kingdom. Toronto, in Canada, was especially badly affected. And as it was new, no-one had built up immunity to it.

Governments, charities and research organisations all over the world acted quickly once it was realised that Professor Liu Jianlun's illness was caused by a newly-evolved virus. Amazingly, by April 17th, virologists had identifed this virus. Every country, terrified by this completely new and potentially deadly disease, brought in measures to detect anyone suffering from it and keep them away from others. Information was shared between affected countries. The public were informed, so that they could be alert to symptoms of the disease in themselves or others. Airlines screened passengers for any signs of high fever.

We were lucky. This new disease was brought under control by the end of 2003, before it really got a strong foothold.

The big mistake made was that China had not notified the world that a new and fatal disease had emerged in Guangzhou. Hopefully, lessons have now been learned and such information will, in future, be more readily shared. The rapid spread of SARS illustrates just how important it is for us to be able to contain and control the spread of infectious diseases. We still don't know exactly where SARS came from, although it seems probable that it was caused by a virus which had 'jumped' from another animal – possibly one being sold for food in a market – to infect humans.

The World Health Organization (WHO) estimates that at least 30 new diseases have emerged in the last 50 years. As well as SARS, there has been Ebola, HIV/AIDS, Lyme disease and West Nile fever. These examples are all caused by viruses. Many health experts think that it is only a matter of time before the emergence of a new virus that is so dangerous and so easily spread that it could cause an epidemic even greater than that of HIV/AIDS.

Controlling the spread of TB and HIV

As well as being alert to the possibility of new diseases appearing, we need to work hard to get those which are already with us under control. We have not yet succeeded in doing this for TB or HIV/AIDS.

Epidemiology is one of the main tools that can be used to help to control the spread of infectious diseases, whether they are well-established or newly emerged. Epidemiology is the study of patterns of incidence and prevalence of disease (see page 174 and 175). Most national governments collect information within their own countries. For example, our own public health services collect and publish data on many different diseases, which can be used to show whether their incidence is increasing or decreasing, whether they are more prevalent in one part of the country compared with another, or within one social or economic group rather than another. WHO collects epidemiological data from all over the world.

WHO is an agency of the United Nations, and they have a very important role in identifying health needs all over the world, and in controlling the spread of numerous diseases. In cases such as SARS, in the case study, it is easy to see how important it is to have one organisation able to coordinate efforts to fight the illness from every corner of the globe. WHO can give guidelines and advice not only to countries, about how they might halt the spread of a disease for example by a vaccination programme or by quarantining affected people, but also to travellers, so that they know if it is safe to travel to a particular country, whether they should take special care whilst they are there and what vaccinations they should have before they go. WHO's premise is that good health is a fundamental human right.

Epidemiological data can be used to compare the incidence and prevalence of disease in different countries and within different social and economic groups within a country. This can reveal patterns which may help us to understand how social, economic and biological factors affect the distribution of different diseases. This helps international and national organisations to target their resources as effectively as possible, as they try to reduce the incidence of a disease.

Notifiable diseases

In the UK, the collection of epidemiological data is helped by the fact that many infectious diseases, including TB, are **notifiable**. This means that GPs and other medical practitioners must inform their local authority of every patient they see who has, or is thought to have, one of the diseases on the list (Table 13.3). They do this by completing a certificate, on which they have to provide information about the name, age, sex and address of the patient, the date on which they were first seen, and the disease which the patient is suspected to be suffering from. The certificate is sent to a designated person at the local health authority, who then has the duty of sending a copy within 48 hours to the district health authority. If there is reason to think that there is an immediate danger of the disease spreading, then all of this can be done by telephone. The medical practitioner is paid a small fee for the work they have done in completing the form and submitting the information, which helps to ensure that they do so.

The main purpose behind these regulations is to help to limit the spread of these infectious diseases. For example, if a university student is diagnosed with meningitis, this is immediately notified to the health authorities, who can quickly put into place measures to limit the number of other people who might get the

Table 13.3 Notifiable diseases in England and Wales.

Public Health (Control of Disease) Act 1984
cholera, food poisoning, plague, relapsing fever, smallpox, typhus

Public Health (Infectious Diseases) Regulations 1988
acute encephalitis, acute poliomyelitis, anthrax, diphtheria, dysentery (amoebic or bacillary), leprosy, leptospirosis, malaria, measles, meningitis, meningococcal septicaemia (without meningitis), mumps, ophthalmia neonatorum, paratyphoid fever, rabies, rubella, scarlet fever, viral haemorrhagic fever, viral hepatitis, whooping cough, yellow fever

disease. They will trace all close contacts of the infected student so that they can be aware of symptoms should any develop. They can arrange for immediate vaccination of other students on the same campus.

The notifications are also used to show how the incidence of a particular infectious disease changes with time. Fig 13.14 shows how mumps and rubella notifications for under five year olds have changed between 1989 and 1992.

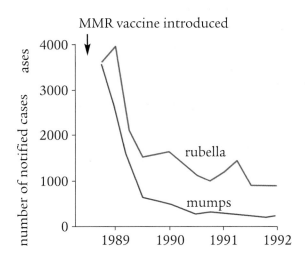

Fig 13.14 Notifications for under five year olds in England and Wales between 1989 and 1992.

13.9 The graph shows notifications of mumps, measles and rubella amongst all age groups in the UK between 1992 and 2002.

a Describe the trends for notifications of mumps, measles and rubella in this graph.

b Suggest the possible impact that the publicity over the suggested links between autism, Crohn's disease and the MMR vaccine (see page 243) might have on mumps, measles and rubella. Is there any evidence for the effect you suggest in the graph?

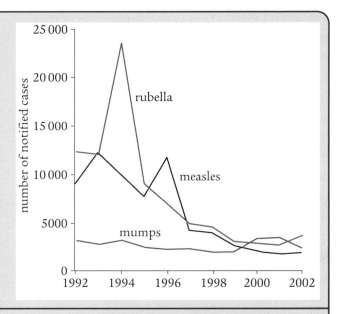

13.10 Whooping cough is a disease caused by the bacterium *Bordetella pertussis*. The graph below shows notifications and deaths from whooping cough between 1940 and 2001. Death rate is the number per 10 000 people under 15 years old in the population. The graph also shows the percentage of children who were given the whooping cough vaccine between 1965 and 1998.

a It is estimated that only 5–25% of cases of whooping cough are notified. Suggest why this is so.

b How might this low rate of notification affect the reliability of the figures shown in the graph?

c Describe the pattern shown by the number of notifications of whooping cough over this period.

d Suggest why the number of deaths from whooping cough fell to zero by 1960.

e Using the information on the graph, suggest reasons for the rise in numbers of notifications in 1977 and 1982.

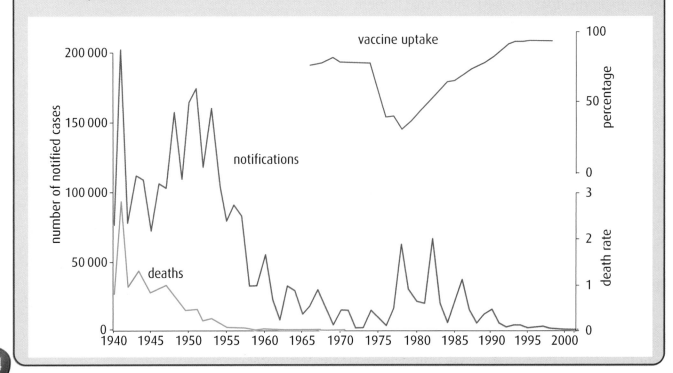

The global distribution of TB and HIV/AIDS

The World Health Organization is very concerned about TB and HIV/AIDS, and they do a huge amount to try to control their spread. Figs 13.15, 13.16 and 13.17 show epidemiological data collected by WHO on the global distribution of HIV/AIDS and TB.

Each year, about eight million people contract TB. 80% of these people live in 22 countries. Two million of these people die from TB. We have already seen that the number of people infected with TB in the UK is actually growing at the moment, despite all the advances we have made in medicine. It is growing in most other countries as well. Resistance to the antibiotics used against it, desperately poor living conditions suffered by many people and crumbling health care services in some countries are all contributing to this problem.

In industrialised countries, the incidence of TB showed a sharp decline since the 1950s as living conditions improved. In some non-industrialised countries, exactly the opposite is happening. War, poverty and drought contribute to poor living conditions and general ill health. As populations increase and impoverished people move into cities, living conditions become even worse. Water supplies contaminated with sewage and other pollutants, poor diet and poor access to health care facilities all weaken the ability of a person's immune system to cope with attacks from pathogens such as *Mycobacterium tuberculosis*.

Another reason for the current increase in TB all over the world is the increase in HIV/AIDS. The TB bacterium quickly takes advantage of an HIV positive person who has a weakened immune system. WHO estimates that one third of new TB infections are in people with HIV/AIDS.

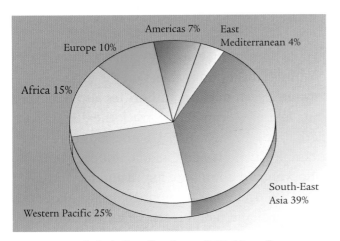

Fig 13.15 Global distribution of TB (data from WHO, 1999).

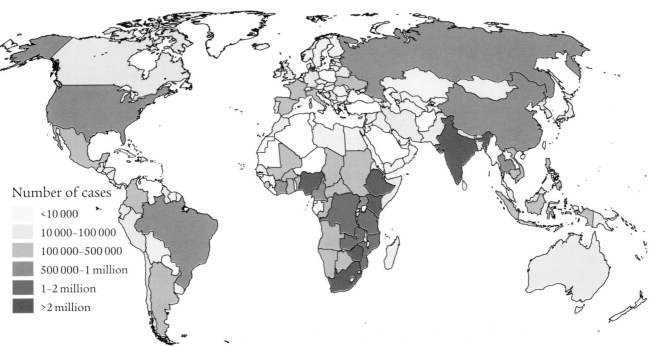

Fig 13.16 Global distribution of HIV infection (data from WHO, 2003).

Screening for TB and HIV infection

The collection of epidemiological data such as those shown in Figs 13.16 and 13.17 relies on being able to test individuals for infection.

For TB, we have seen how the Heaf test (page 245) is routinely used in the UK to check whether a person has antibodies to TB. If their reaction to the Heaf test suggests that they may have TB, then they are given a **chest X-ray** (Fig 13.18). TB in the lungs will show up on this X-ray.

For HIV/AIDS, a blood or saliva sample is taken, and tested for the presence of HIV antibodies. (It is much easier to detect antibodies than the virus itself.) For large-scale testing, the usual method is an ELISA test. This stands for enzyme-linked immunosorbent assay. The ELISA test uses bound antibody which can combine with an antigen in the HIV virus. When it does so, an enzyme reaction produces light which is then detected. However, this kind of test requires skilled staff, special well-maintained equipment and a reliable electrical power supply. For small-scale testing, or testing in less ideal conditions, a number of equally reliable tests are available. Whereas the ELISA test uses serum, obtained from a blood sample, other tests can be carried out on saliva, urine or whole blood. Some of these can give rapid results, in some cases within as little as 10 minutes.

Who should be tested for these diseases? In the UK, all young people are given the Heaf test, so they are all effectively tested for TB. However, we do not test everyone for HIV. People will be given this test if they want to donate blood, if they have had sexual contact with someone else who is known to be HIV+, or if they ask for the test for themselves.

There are arguments both for and against universal screening for HIV/AIDS. At the moment, HIV/AIDS is not even a notifiable disease.

The greatest argument for screening is that, if people know if they are HIV+, then they can ensure that they do not pass on the virus to anyone else. If medical authorities also have this information, it can help to track the disease and perhaps to limit its spread. Some countries, for example Australia and Canada, test everyone who wants to immigrate for TB and for HIV/AIDS. There has been much debate about the ethical and moral issues that this kind of

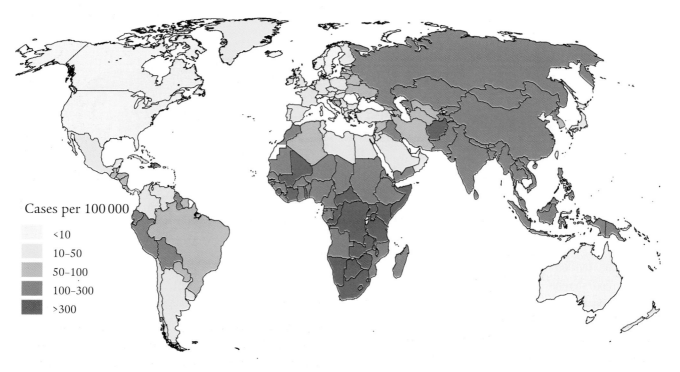

Cases per 100 000

- <10
- 10–50
- 50–100
- 100–300
- >300

Fig 13.17 Incidence of TB (data from WHO, 2001).

compulsory testing raises. The idea behind it is that it would help to control the spread of these diseases. But there are arguments both for and against this kind of screening procedure.

On the other side of the argument, there are concerns about the negative effects that screening might have. People might be asked to state their HIV status when they applied for a job, joined a pension scheme or took out life insurance. If the information was freely available, then perhaps HIV+ people might suffer stigma in the community. Before such a screening programme were to be introduced, very careful thought would have to be given to who should have access to the information and what could be done with it.

In the UK, there has undoubtedly been an increase in the incidence of TB in recent years (Fig 13.12). And epidemiological studies show that this is undeniably associated with immigration. More than 50% of new cases of TB in the United Kingdom are in people who were born abroad.

Screening immigrants for TB could, it is suggested, help to identify cases early. This could mean that the infected person got treatment straight away, and it could also help to stop the infected person passing on the disease to someone else. However, this isn't quite as straightforward as it seems. We have seen that the Heaf test, followed by a chest X-ray, is the way in which TB is diagnosed. Unfortunately, this gives a lot of false positives. Moreover, it is found that most of these cases of TB in immigrants are not active, and even fewer of them are infectious. At present, data collected from Australia and Canada suggest that compulsory screening of immigrants for TB has had little or no effect on the incidence of these diseases in their countries.

As for TB, many of the new cases of HIV in the United Kingdom occur among immigrants, and the incidence of immigrant-related HIV is increasing. Unlike TB, the tests for HIV are much more specific and sensitive, and so the problem of false positives does not arise. But other problems do. If HIV+ people are banned from immigrating into a country, then there is every incentive for them to avoid the test and disappear from official view. And who would be tested? If only asylum seekers are tested, rather than all immigrants, this could be seen as unfair. If only immigrants arriving from certain parts of the world are tested – based on the incidence of HIV in those countries – that, too, would be discriminatory. If all potential immigrants are to be tested, then perhaps everyone already living in the UK should be tested too.

SAQ

13.11a Compare the distribution of HIV/AIDS and tuberculosis, shown in Figs 13.16 and 13.17.

  b Explain why a high level of HIV/AIDS in a country may be related to a high incidence of TB.

  c Research one alternative test for HIV antibodies. How does it work and what are its advantages and disadvantages?

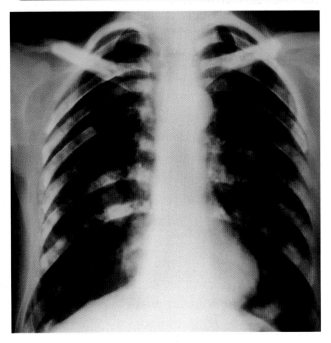

Fig 13.18 Chest X-ray of the chest of a person suffering from TB. Infected areas of the lungs are shown as blue patches. Normal lung tissue is shown black.

13.12 In 2001, the percentage of children in London who had the MMR vaccine had fallen from over 90% to only 73%. In late December 2001, there was a measles outbreak in London. 90 confirmed cases of measles were reported over a period of about 10 weeks. The graph shows the number of suspected cases and the number of confirmed cases during this time period.

a Suggest why a measles outbreak occurred in London at this time.

b Suggest reasons for the steep rise in *suspected* cases during weeks 2 to 6.

c Of these cases, 9% were in infants under 12 months, 46% in pre-school children,

22% in school children and 23% in young adults. Present these data in a suitable graph or diagram.

d Suggest why older people were apparently not affected by this measles outbreak.

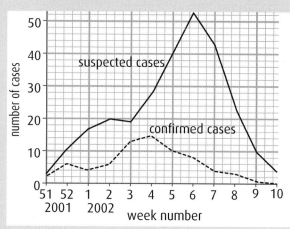

Summary

1 In the recent past, several new infectious diseases have evolved. The control of these diseases requires information to be shared quickly between countries, so that their spread can be limited and so that scientists can cooperate to determine the cause and try to develop vaccines and treatments.

2 Epidemiology is the study of the patterns of incidence and prevalence of disease, related to geographical, social, economic and other factors. It can help to ascertain the root causes of the disease so that resources for prevention and treatment can be efficiently targeted to where they are needed most or can be most effective.

3 In the UK, many infectious diseases are notifiable. This means that each occurrence of the disease which comes to the attention of a medical worker must be reported to the local health authority.

4 Epidemiological studies show that TB and HIV/AIDS have similar global distributions. AIDS makes the body more prone to infectious diseases, including TB. Sub-Saharan Africa has a greater HIV/AIDS incidence and prevalence than anywhere else in the world.

5 The Heaf test and chest X-rays are used to diagnose TB. Blood tests using ELISA or other methods are used to detect the presence of antibodies to HIV, which means that the virus is present in the body.

6 Routine screening for HIV infection could possibly help to reduce the spread of HIV/AIDS, by ensuring that everyone who is HIV+ is aware of it and could modify their sexual behaviour so that they do not pass it on to others. However, if this information did not remain confidential it could put HIV+ people at a disadvantage, perhaps making it more difficult for them to get employment or life insurance.

Drugs from the rainforests

Malaria is a disease caused by a single-celled organism called *Plasmodium*. This pathogen is transmitted from one person to another by a kind of mosquito called *Anopheles*. Today, we have no malaria in the UK, except for a few cases each year of people who have been bitten by a mosquito while abroad and develop malaria when they return. Malaria is now largely confined to the tropics, where it causes around two million deaths each year.

But this was not so in the sixteenth and seventeenth centuries. Then, malaria was a common cause of death in England. It was called 'ague', and treated like all fevers by following the instructions of a physician called Galen, who had written down the 'correct' treatment for every disease 16 centuries earlier. This treatment was blood-letting.

Spain invaded and colonised several countries in South America in the seventeenth century. In 1630, Spanish Jesuit priests living in Peru heard about a kind of bark from a rainforest tree that the native people used to treat fever. They made the locals harvest the bark and plant five trees (in the shape of a cross) for every tree that they cut down. The priests found that drinking an infusion made from the bark had almost miraculous effects in curing malaria. They shipped some of the bark to Europe. It was introduced into England in 1650. The tree was named cinchona.

However, people were still very suspicious of using a treatment that Galen had not written about. Moreover, because it was being used to treat all fevers, not just malaria, cinchona bark often did not work. Oliver Cromwell refused to use it because of it being associated with the Jesuits, which went against his Protestant religion. He died from malaria in 1658.

Powdered cinchona bark was the main treatment for malaria until 1820. Then two French scientists managed to separate the active ingredients from the bark. They called the main one quinine. Quinine was used as a very effective antimalarial drug. It was also used to make tonic water, whose bitter taste is due to quinine. Tonic water was drunk to stave off malaria, often mixed with gin and lemon to mask its taste.

Today, cinchona trees are grown in many tropical parts of the world. Up to 500 metric tonnes of quinine are extracted each year from about 10 000 tonnes of bark. The trees are harvested by coppicing them – cutting them down to a stump from which new trunks and branches will grow. Quinine is no longer used against malaria because other drugs are now manufactured, but it is still used for making tonic water and the bark is still used in herbal medicine.

Finding new drugs

Around 7000 medical drugs that are prescribed by doctors in the United Kingdom and other western countries are derived from plants. Approximately 3000 plant species are used as sources of these drugs, and of these plant species 70% grow in tropical rainforests. This is perhaps not altogether surprising, because the world's tropical rainforests are known to have by far the greatest biodiversity in the world.

Many plants have evolved chemical defences to stop themselves being eaten by animals such as insects or monkeys. Some of these chemicals are very toxic to humans, but even these may be used as drugs. For example, foxgloves contain a poison called digitalin. Taken in large quantities, this can be fatal, but extracts from foxgloves are widely used to treat cardiac arrhythmias.

The story of the discovery of quinine is a classic example of how a new drug from a plant may be discovered. It began by finding out that native people used the bark from the cinchona tree to treat fever. The study of the ways in which native people use plants is now so important that it has a name of its own – **ethnobotany**. Several large companies that produce and market drugs are interested in looking for potential new sources of plant-based drugs (Fig 13.19).

Having found a plant that is used locally as a medical drug, the next step is to try it out to see if it works. Alongside this, the plant extracts will be analysed chemically, so that different components can be extracted and purified. This makes it possible to produce standardised medicines, all known to contain the same concentration of the same drug.

Drug companies may also try to find ways of manufacturing the drug chemically, rather than having to extract it from plants. This is done in some cases – for example, in the manufacture of aspirin. This was initially discovered in willow bark, but now it is much cheaper to make it from scratch in a laboratory. However, in many cases it remains more economic to continue to extract the drugs from plant material.

Fig 13.19 The Madagascan rosy periwinkle is the source of the drug vincristine, which is very effective in the treatment of leukaemia.

The effects of deforestation

Tropical rainforests are under threat. No-one knows exactly what area of rainforest is being lost each year, but there is no doubt that it is being destroyed at a much faster rate than it is regrowing. The loss of forests is known as **deforestation**.

People cut down forests for many reasons. They may want to harvest timber for sale or to make houses and tools; to use the land for other purposes, such as building roads, houses or farming crops; and so that they can use the wood for fuel. Sometimes this is done on a small scale. For example, a family might burn an area of forest so that they can grow maize. It also happens on a very large scale – for example, if a large company wants to establish several thousand hectares of oil palm plantation.

When rainforest is cut down, many harmful effects can occur.

- Soil cover may be lost. The forest trees intercept rain as it falls, stopping raindrops hitting the ground with force. With the trees gone, there is nothing to stop the full force of the raindrops (which are often large in tropical rainstorms) from dislodging particles of soil and washing them away (Fig 13.20). Moreover, if the tree roots have gone, there is

Fig 13.20 The effect of deforestation in the central highlands of Madagascar has produced large areas that are prone to drought and badly eroded. Slopes like these have no protection from rainfall, which easily washes away the thin soil. Few plants can survive here, especially after it has been grazed by farm stock.

little to hold the soil in place. This is especially damaging if the area is on a slope. And the soil on which tropical rainforests grow is usually very thin, making it easy to lose it completely once the trees have gone.

- Species diversity may be reduced. Rainforests are the habitat for a huge number of species of animals and plants, many of which have not yet been identified, let alone studied. Deforestation may cause some of these animals and plants to become extinct, even before we knew they were there. It is very likely that some of these plants might be the source of new drugs, as yet undiscovered. Less than 5% of even the known species of rainforest plants have been properly investigated to see if they contain any potentially useful chemicals.

- Rainfall may be reduced. Trees take up water from the soil and lose it, in the form of water vapour, from their leaves. The water vapour condenses into water droplets in the air to form clouds, which eventually drop their contents as rain. With no trees, less water is returned to the atmosphere, and the climate may become drier.

- Global warming may increase. Growing plants take in carbon dioxide for photosynthesis, and give out oxygen. There are concerns at present that the burning of fossil fuels, such as in vehicles and coal- or oil-fired power stations, is increasing the concentration of carbon dioxide in the atmosphere. This increases the greenhouse effect, which increases the temperature on Earth. So large-scale deforestation could speed global warming.

Conflict and conservation

It is clearly important that efforts should be made to prevent further loss of tropical rainforests. But this is not at all easy to achieve. Very often the wishes or needs of the people who live in or near the forests clash with the wishes of conservationists.

For example, in the large island of Madagascar, tropical forests have been cleared by local people for charcoal production (Fig 13.21) and to use the land for agriculture. They want to grow crops and provide grazing for their cattle. For these people, many living in poverty, this is their livelihood. They have to think about what they will eat today or tomorrow, and the only way they can provide themselves with food is to cut down the forest and grow crops. The thin soil means that each area they use is only fertile for a few years, and its productivity quickly drops. They then move on and cut down and burn a new area, where there are – at first – more nutrients in the soil, giving good productivity once more. Then the nutrients run out, and they move on again. This is called 'slash and burn' agriculture.

Fig 13.21 For people in developing countries charcoal is often the only common domestic fuel, and a lot of woodland has been destroyed to provide fuel for cooking.

You cannot simply expect these people to stop their destruction of the forest just because a conservationist says that they need to. If they are to stop practising slash and burn, they need to be presented with an alternative way of making a living. Numerous such schemes are being tried all over the world, some with more success than others.

Some of the most successful rainforest conservation schemes involve the local people in the decision-making about what should be done, and also offer them other sources of income. This may include making sustainable use of the rainforest. 'Sustainable' means that it can go on happening for a long period of time, without using up the resource.

Using rainforest trees and other plants as sources of therapeutic drugs can be one such income-generating and sustainable use of the rainforest. It needs to be done carefully, giving thought to the potential harm that may be done to the forest, and also to the rights of the people who live there. Harvesting by coppicing, as is done for the bark of cinchona trees, can be relatively undamaging, because the trees are not killed, just cut down and allowed to regrow. But if this is done on a large scale, involving the building of roads and living quarters for workers, the pollution of the area with human sewage and rubbish, or the damage to other plants in the forest by machinery, then it is almost as harmful as deforestation.

Summary

1. Many drugs which are used to cure diseases, or alleviate their symptoms, are originally derived from plants. Tropical rainforests are an especially rich source of plant species, most of which have not been tested to see if they contain potentially useful chemicals.

2. Large areas of tropical rainforests are destroyed each year. This is done by local people to provide wood for building and cooking, and to clear space to grow crops, keep animals or build houses and roads. The timber is often valuable and may be sold abroad. The clearance may be on a large scale if big companies are involved – for example, for selling timber or creating oil palm plantations.

3. The loss of rainforests causes damage to local ecosystems, by increasing soil erosion, decreasing rainfall and destroying the habitats of many different species of animals and plants. On a larger scale, it reduces the quantity of carbon dioxide which is absorbed from the atmosphere by photosynthesising plants, and this may contribute to an increase in the carbon dioxide concentration in the atmosphere. This in turn may lead to global warming.

4. Conflict frequently arises between people who are trying to make a living or big profits by clearing rainforests, and conservationists who want to stop the forests being destroyed. Finding sustainable, profit-making uses for the rainforest is one way in which these conflicts may be resolved. Harvesting native plants for making drugs is one possible way in which this might be done.

Answers to self-assessment questions

Note – answers to open-ended questions are not provided.

Chapter 1

1.1 This kills any bacteria on the skin, so that there is less chance of infection in the puncture wound.

1.2 Veins lie closer to the skin surface than arteries. They have thinner walls. Blood is at a lower pressure in veins, so there is less chance of blood loss.

1.3 real size of object = 5 mm
size in the drawing = 12 mm
real size of object = size in the diagram ÷ magnification
so magnification = size in diagram ÷ real size
= 12 ÷ 5
= ×2.4

1.4a size in photograph = 35 mm (allow 36)
b 35 mm = (35×10^3) μm
c so real size = $35 \times 10^3 ÷ 2200$
= 16 μm

1.5a magnification = size in diagram ÷ real size
b size of diagram = 26 mm
convert to same units as used for real size –
26 mm = 26×10^3 μm
so magnification = 26×10^3 μm ÷ 7 μm
= 3714 (round to 3700)

1.6 If drawn to the same size, then magnification is ×2770 – roughly ×2800.
This means that 1 μm will be drawn as 2.8 mm.
10 μm is drawn as 28 mm.
So it needs a scale bar drawn 28 mm long to represent 10 μm.

1.7 Additional labels should be: cytoplasm, rough endoplasmic reticulum, smooth endoplasmic reticulum, chromatin inside nucleus, nucleolus, pore in nuclear envelope, nuclear envelope, Golgi apparatus, mitochondrion.

1.8a

Leucocyte	Palisade mesophyll cell
no cell wall	has cell wall, made of cellulose
no chloroplasts	has many chloroplasts, containing chlorophyll
no large central vacuole, although there are many small, temporary vacuoles / vesicles	has a large, permanent central vacuole
less regular shape	regular shape (maintained by cell wall)
both have cell surface membrane, cytoplasm, rough endoplasmic reticulum, smooth endoplasmic reticulum, chromatin inside nucleus, nucleolus, pore in nuclear envelope, nuclear envelope, Golgi apparatus, mitochondrion, ribosomes.	

b Neutrophils would have more mitochondria than palisade cells. Aerobic respiration takes place in mitochondria, providing ATP (or energy) for the cells' movement.

c • **cell wall and cell membrane** All cells have a cell membrane. It is made of proteins and lipids. It is partially permeable. Plant cells also have a cell wall. In plant cells, this lies outside the cell membrane, and is made of cellulose. The cellulose fibres lie in a matrix of pectin. The cell wall is fully permeable, and has no role in determining what enters or leaves the cell.

• **chloroplast and chlorophyll** A chloroplast is an organelle found in photosynthetic plant cells. It has a double membrane (envelope) and contains membranes arranged to form stacks called grana. Photosynthesis happens inside chloroplasts. Chlorophyll is a green, light-absorbing pigment found inside chloroplasts. Chlorophyll molecules lie in the membranes of the grana.

1.9

	Name	Function
A	cytoplasm	contains a range of substances; many metabolic reactions take place in the cytoplasm
B	nucleus / chromatin	contains DNA, in the form of chromosomes; this is the hereditary material, which is passed on to offspring during sexual reproduction. DNA is used as a template to make RNA, which controls protein synthesis.
C	nucleolus	ribosomal RNA is being made here, using DNA as a template
D	nuclear membrane / nuclear envelope	a pair of membranes separating the nucleus from the cytoplasm; DNA cannot pass through it; it has pores which enable RNA to pass into the cytoplasm
E	rough endoplasmic reticulum (RER)	carries ribosomes, where protein synthesis takes place; some of these proteins pass into the cisternae enclosed by the RER membranes
F	cell surface membrane	a partially permeable membrane, which controls what enters and leaves the cell; glycoproteins and glycolipids act as receptors or in cell recognition
G	mitochondrion	the site of aerobic respiration, in which ATP is produced
H	Golgi apparatus	vesicles from the RER, containing proteins, fuse together to form the Golgi apparatus; the proteins are then processed and packaged and move off from the Golgi apparatus in small vesicles to be secreted from the cell
I	smooth endoplasmic reticulum (SER)	produces steroid hormones, breaks down toxins
J	vesicle	may contain proteins ready for export; (could also be a lysosome containing digestive enzymes)

1.10a Group O is the universal donor. This blood has no antigens on red cells which will react with the recipient's antibodies.

b Group AB is the universal recipient. This blood has no antibodies in the plasma which will react with the donor's antigens.

Chapter 2

2.1 10

2.2 • primary structure – the sequence of amino acids in a polypeptide or protein
• secondary structure – the regular shapes taken up by parts of a polypeptide chain, e.g. an alpha helix
• tertiary structure – the three-dimensional shape of a complete peptide chain
• quaternary structure – the arrangement of two or more polypeptide chains that associate together to form a protein molecule

2.3a He has confused haemoglobin with a red cell.

b Haemoglobin is a globular protein, so it can dissolve in the watery cytoplasm inside a red cell. This is also helped by it having hydrophilic R groups sticking out of the surface of the molecule, where they can interact with water.

A haemoglobin molecule is made up of four polypeptide chains, each containing a haem group. The haem group contains an iron ion, which can bond with oxygen and then release it.

2.4a difference = 125
You need to work out what this is as a percentage of the starting value, which was 793.
So percentage difference = (125 ÷ 793) × 100
= 15.8
The value has increased, not decreased, so we can give this a positive value. The answer is +15.8.

b The athlete had been given extra red cells, which all contained haemoglobin. So the haemoglobin concentration was 27.5% greater after the transfusion.

c The athlete's blood contained more haemoglobin, so it could supply more oxygen to his muscles in a given length of time. This meant that they could respire aerobically for longer.

d The athlete is given back their own blood cells, so there is no foreign substance present in the body which could be picked up by a test.

2.5 The label 'high concentration of oxygen' should be inside the air sac in the first diagram, and inside the blood vessel in the second. The label 'low concentration of oxygen' should be in the blood vessel in the first diagram, and in the tissue cells in the second diagram. Arrows indicating 'falling oxygen concentration' should point from high to low.

2.6a 2×10^{-5} is the larger value.

b Glucose diffused much more rapidly through the membrane of the erythrocyte than it did through the membrane lacking protein. This suggests that it moves by facilitated diffusion, through transporter proteins. The membrane lacking proteins had no transporter proteins, so glucose could move only slowly through the phospholipid bilayer. It is difficult for glucose to do this because it is quite a large molecule, with a charge, so it is not able to dissolve in lipids.

c Water diffused equally rapidly through both membranes. This indicates that it does not need to pass through proteins, but can simply move through the phospholipid bilayer. Water is a small molecule, so even though it carries a charge, a water molecule can quite easily slip through the lipid bilayer. In both membranes, it passes through more quickly than the much larger glucose molecule.

2.7a Water would enter the blood cell by osmosis, passing down its water potential gradient (that is, from a high water potential outside to a lower water potential in the cytoplasm). The cell would burst.

b Water would still enter the plant cell, for just the same reasons. However, it would not burst because it is surrounded by a strong cell wall.

c Water would move out of the blood cell by osmosis, down its water potential gradient. The volume of the cytoplasm would therefore decrease, and the cell would look shrivelled.

2.8a A solute is a substance that is disssolved in a solvent. (Here, the solvent is water.)

b $8 \, \mu g \, dm^{-3}$, reached at 1 hour 15 minutes.

c $2 \, \mu g \, dm^{-3}$, reached at about 40 minutes.

d $8 \, \mu g \, dm^{-3}$ is a higher concentration than that outside the cells. $2 \, \mu g \, dm^{-3}$ is the same.

e i A must have been entering by active transport, as it moved up its concentration gradient.

ii B would have been entering by diffusion or facilitated diffusion, moving down its concentration gradient until concentrations were equal.

2.9a Potassium ions; their concentration inside the cell is greater than outside.

b Sodium ions, chloride ions and hydrogencarbonate ions. Their concentration outside the cell is greater than inside.

c Glucose inside the cell is being used for respiration, therefore keeping its concentration low.

d Proteins are made on the ribosomes, so the newly-made ones contribute to their concentration inside the cell.

e All of these substances consist of either charged ions (Na^+, K^+, Cl^-, HCO_3^-) or large molecules (glucose and proteins). None of them can pass through the lipids in the membrane. They enter and leave the cell through transporter proteins.

2.10

	Glucose	Glycogen
type of carbohydrate	monosaccharide	polysaccharide
where it is found in the body	dissolved in blood plasma; small amounts in the cytoplasm of most cells	stored in granules in the cytoplasm of liver and muscle cells
functions	a substrate for respiration, supplying energy in the form of ATP for the cell to use	an energy store, that can be broken down to glucose to use as a respiratory substrate

2.11a On ribosomes.
   b Liver and muscles.
   c They are both condensation reactions.
2.12a Orange squash.
   b Glucose is used in respiration to produce ATP.
   c Transport up a concentration gradient, using energy supplied by a cell.
   d Salt.
   e Sodium ions will have been lost in sweat.
   f Water will also have been lost in sweat.
   g The sodium ions and glucose decrease the water potential of the cell. This provides a water potential gradient down which water moves by osmosis.
   h The ions and glucose in the drink are absorbed into the blood in the small intestine. As they lower the water potential, water follows them by osmosis.

Chapter 3

3.1 The shape of the active site, and the R groups of the amino acids around the active site, must be exactly right to fit with, and bind with, the substrate. So fibrinogen fits and binds perfectly in thrombin's active site, whereas starch does not.
3.2 globular, catalysts, substrate, product, unchanged, active, substrate, specific, thrombin, fibrinogen, fibrin.
3.3a Both the number of cases of DVT and of pulmonary embolism vary about a relatively stable mean value. The mean number of cases remains about the same year on year.
     Both the number of cases of DVT and of pulmonary embolism tend to peak in winter (in late December and early January) and fall in summer (July and August).
    {Note that we cannot compare the actual number of cases of the two illnesses, because we don't know how many cases of each there were – only how much they deviated from their mean value.}
   b There are many possible hypotheses you could suggest. For example, cases of DVT and pulmonary embolism are higher in winter than in summer because many old people stay indoors and do not move around much when the weather is colder. This increases their likelihood of getting a deep vein thrombosis.

   c You cannot do a controlled experiment with people to test this hypothesis. You can only do it by collecting more data, or by analysing the figures in a different way. For example, you could record the number of cases in each age group. If you found that a higher percentage of cases during the winter were in old people, that would support the hypothesis. You could then do further analyses to see if this was related to their degree of activity at different times of year.
3.4 Freezing damages cells, because ice crystals can break cell membranes and other structures. Plasma and serum do not contain any cells.
3.5a There is no definite trend, as the numbers fluctuate. There has possibly been an overall increase in the number of people who reported hepatitis B, and possibly an overall decrease in the number of people who acquired the disease through blood transfusion – but you would need to use a statistical test to see if these are significant.
   b To do this calculation, divide the number acquired by blood transfusion by the total number, and multiply by 100. So, for 1991:
    $(5 \div 572) \times 100 = 0.8\%$
    1992   0.6%
    1993   0.8%
    1994   0.5%
    1995   0.8%
    1996   0.3%
    1997   0.2%
   c Perhaps some blood containing the virus had been missed in the screening process.

Chapter 4

4.1

Stage of cardiac cycle	Chambers contracting	Chambers relaxing
atrial systole	atria	ventricles
ventricular systole	ventricles	atria
diastole	none	atria and ventricles

Stage of cardiac cycle	Valves pushed open	Valves pushed closed
atrial systole	atrio-ventricular valves (bicuspid valve and tricuspid valve)	semilunar valves (in aorta and pulmonary artery)
ventricular systole	semilunar valves	atrio-ventricular valves
diastole	atrio-ventricular valves	semilunar valves

4.2 One cycle lasts 0.8 s.
    So there are $1 \div 0.8$ cycles per second.
    There are 60 s in one minute.
    So there are $(1 \div 0.8) \times 60$ cycles per minute
    = 75 cycles per minute (that is, beats per minute).

4.3

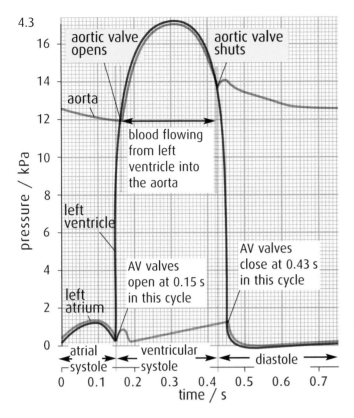

d During the period of blood flow from the left ventricle into the aorta, blood pressure is higher in the ventricle than in the aorta.

4.4a Calculate the cardiac outputs by multiplying the stroke volume by the heart rate.
resting non-athlete 5625 cm^3 min^{-1}
maximum for non-athlete 21 450 cm^3 min^{-1}
resting marathon runner 5250 cm^3 min^{-1}
maximum for marathon runner 29 970 cm^3 min^{-1}

b A higher stroke volume means that more blood is pumped out of the heart at each beat. This means that a greater volume of blood is pushed to the muscles at each beat. The muscles therefore receive more oxygen per second at a particular heart rate. It also means that more blood is pumped to the lungs with each beat, so more oxygen can be collected per second at a particular heart rate.

c Training causes the amount of muscle in the walls of the heart to increase, which increases the force with which it contracts and pushes inwards on the blood. The heart increases in size – this is especially true of the wall of the left ventricle. The number or extent of blood vessels supplying the heart wall – that is the coronary circulation – also increases.

4.5 The definitions refer to the following terms in sequence: atheromatous plaque; coronary heart disease (CHD); coronary thrombosis; cardiac arrest; myocardial infarction; angina; atherosclerosis.

4.6a Reducing body weight means that the heart has less body tissue to supply with blood, so the demands on the heart decrease. It does not need to push as much blood out, with as much force. The reduction

in weight of the body also decreases the amount of energy which is needed for moving around, once again decreasing the demand made on the heart. Being overweight also increases the risk of hypertension (high blood pressure). Hypertension puts more strain on the heart.
Being overweight increases the risk of developing non-insulin dependent diabetes. Diabetes increases the risk of developing atherosclerosis.

b Squash is an 'explosive' sport, where rapid, very energy-demanding movements are made between short periods of lesser activity. These movements can put short-lived but very high demand on the heart. This can be dangerous, especially if the person is not fit. Steady, regular exercise is likely to be less risky, because this increases fitness and increases the ability of the heart to supply the demands of the exercising muscles without excessive strain (see answer to 4.4c above).

4.7a and b

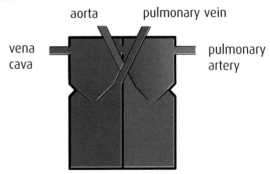

c A blood clot in a leg vein will be carried to the heart through the vena cava, and will enter the right atrium of the heart. In a 'normal' heart, it will then by pushed out of the right ventricle into the pulmonary arteries, and will go to the lungs. The capillaries in the lungs are the first capillaries it will reach, so this is where it is most likely to get stuck.
If the person has a 'hole in the heart', then the blood clot could pass through the hole from the right atrium into the left atrium. From here it will enter the left ventricle, and then be pushed out into the aorta. The first capillaries it will reach could be anywhere in the body except the lungs, and could well be in the capillaries supplying blood to the brain.

4.8a There are many different types of results chart which could be constructed. This is one example (overleaf).

	1996 Before introduction of specialist team	1999 After introduction of specialist team
Total number admitted to hospital	19 317	22 847
Number of unexpected cases of cardiac arrest	73	47
Percentage of patients suffering unexpected cardiac arrest	0.38	0.21
Number of patients dying from unexpected cardiac arrest	56	26
Percentage of patients dying from unexpected cardiac arrest	0.29	0.11

It is important to calculate percentages because the total number of patients admitted to hospital (which has absolutely nothing to do with the introduction of the specialist medical emergency team) is different in the two years.

b The medical emergency team appears to have decreased the percentage of patients who suffered from unexpected cardiac arrest, and, to an even greater extent, the percentage of patients who died from this.

c i Uncontrolled variables include: the state of health of the patients; the ages of the patients; the genders of the patients; the treatment received by the patients (other than from the medical emergency team); any other changes which may have taken place in the hospital between 1996 and 1999 (for example, the food served to patients, the cleanliness of the wards, the daily routine in the wards, the general state of health of the patients and so on).

ii These variables cannot be controlled because it would be unethical to provide patients with anything other than what is considered to be the very best treatment possible. If it is thought that improving the cleanliness of the wards could improve patient health, it would be wrong not to do this for a control group just so that the results of the investigation could be more easily interpreted.

Chapter 5

5.1a PQ

b If both chambers contracted at once, the ventricles would produce greater pressure than the atria. This would force the atrio-ventricular valves shut. So the blood in the atria could not go down into the ventricles when the atria contracted. It has to go somewhere, so it would be pushed back into the veins. This could place excess strain on the heart, and decrease the volume of blood which is moved through the heart with each cycle.

c The AVN delays the impulse which originated in the SAN. By the time the electrical impulse sweeps up the ventricle walls, the atria have already contracted.

d The 'bottom upwards' contraction helps to push the blood upwards, rather than downwards, so it is forced up into the arteries.

5.2a normal ECG – 18.5 small squares between the first and second R

17.5 small squares between the second and third R

So the mean number of small squares is

(18.5 + 17.5) ÷ 2

= 18

5 small squares represent 0.2 s, so 18 small squares represent

(18 ÷ 5) × 0.2 = 0.72 seconds

Therefore the pulse rate is (1 ÷ 0.72) × 60 = 83 beats per minute

b bradycardia – 29 small squares between the first and second R

28 small squares between the first and second R

So the mean number of small squares is 28.5

5 small squares represent 0.2 s, so 28.5 small squares represent

(28.5 ÷ 5) × 0.2 = 1.14 s

Therefore the pulse rate is (1 ÷ 1.14) × 60 = 53 beats per minute

c normal ECG – 3.5 small squares between first P and R followed by 3, 4 and 3 small squares for the next three PR intervals

So the mean number of small squares is

(3.5 + 3 + 4 + 3) ÷ 4

= 2.38

5 small squares represent 0.2 s, so 2.38 small squares represent

(2.38 ÷ 5) × 0.2 = 0.10 seconds

d heart block – 7.5 small squares between first P and R followed by 7.5 and 7 small squares for the next two PR intervals

So the mean number of small squares is

(7.5 + 7.5 + 7) ÷ 2

= 7.33

5 small squares represent 0.2 s,

so 5.25 small squares represent

(7.33 ÷ 5) × 0.2 = 0.29 seconds

e

Normal	Bradycardia	Heart block
Pulse rate about 83 beats per minute PR interval about 0.10 s	Pulse rate slow e.g. 53 beats per minute	PR interval long e.g. 0.29 s

5.3a fibrillation

b low blood pressure, loss of consciousness

c There could have been a myocardial infarction, perhaps because of a blood clot in a coronary artery. Another possibility is electric shock.

5.4a A deep vein thrombosis is a blood clot in a deep-lying vein; they often form in leg veins.

b Blood flowing through the veins back to the heart is at a very low pressure, and relies on surrounding muscles to squeeze the veins and push the blood along. If these muscles are not working, the blood can just pool in the veins in the lower parts of the legs, especially if the legs and feet are below the heart (as they are when sitting). People on a long-haul flight may sleep sitting upright in a cramped position for many hours, during which there is nothing helping to push the blood in the veins back to the heart. When blood is stationary, clotting factors may build up in it, causing a clot to form.

c i A pulmonary embolism is a blood clot that has formed elsewhere in the body and has been carried to the lungs, where it gets stuck in the fine capillaries, causing blockage.

 ii A clot breaking away in a leg vein enters the vena cava, then the right side of the heart and then the pulmonary artery to the lungs. It can only get to the coronary arteries by returning from the lungs, entering the left side of the heart and then passing out via the aorta. If it can get through the lung capillaries without causing any trouble, then it can also get through coronary vessels without trouble and so would not cause a myocardial infarction.

5.5a Large arteries contain relatively small amounts of muscle and its role is to help strengthen the wall. The walls do contain large amounts of elastic tissue, which is stretched as blood pulses through from the heart, and then recoils passively between pulses.

 Smaller arteries and arterioles, however, contain quite a lot of smooth muscle in their walls. This muscle does not contract and relax rhythmically. It is used to decrease blood flow to one area of the body by altering the diameter of the lumen and diverting blood to another area.

 b All the blood which leaves the heart in the arteries must return to it in the veins. So the quantity of blood carried in veins is the same as that carried in arteries. (Leakage from the capillaries does occur, but this should eventually return to the veins via the lymphatics.) Moreover, arteries are not 'bigger' than veins. Arteries do have thicker walls than veins, but their lumens are smaller.

 c There is no difference between oxygenated and deoxygenated blood in terms of volume or pressure. Arteries need thicker walls because they carry blood at higher pressure than the veins. This blood does happen to be oxygenated in the aorta, but in the pulmonary artery it is deoxygenated.

 d The term 'cell wall' applies to the wall around plant cells or bacterial cells, outside the cell surface membrane. There are no cell walls in animal cells. This statement would be correct if the word 'cell' was deleted.

5.6a i Brain cells need a constant supply of oxygen so that they can produce usable energy (in the form of ATP) by respiration. Without it, they rapidly run out of energy and stop working.

 ii The person's blood pressure may have dropped. The heart was beating slowly, as the person was at rest. When he quickly stood up, the blood rapidly drained downwards from his head; it took a few moments for blood pressure to increase – for example, by an increase in heart rate and stroke volume.

 iii Substantial volumes of blood may have pooled in his leg veins (see answer to 5.4b), decreasing the volume available for the head.

 b Using a defibrillator is quite a violent procedure. If the young man's heart was already beating, the defibrillator could have done more harm than good. The flight staff should check for breathing and heart beat. If these are present, then the defibrillator should not be used. They should also check for any obstruction in the airways, in case this is preventing breathing.

Activity 5.3
1 If blood is prevented from flowing into the lower arm, the tissues there will not receive oxygen. They can become damaged within minutes.

2 Heart rate can vary according to changes in the person's body or in their surroundings. They may have moved a little at some stage. Something may have happened around them that made them temporarily more alert. These can affect heart rate and therefore blood pressure.

Chapter 6

6.1a A reaction in which a bond is formed between two molecules, with the release of a water molecule.

 b The formation of a peptide bond between two amino acids. The formation of a glycosidic bond between two sugars.

6.2a There are 6 carbon atoms, 12 hydrogen atoms and 6 oxygen atoms.

 b There are 13 carbon atoms in each fatty acid, which makes 39 altogether. There are also 3 carbon atoms in the ester linkages, and another 3 in the glycerol molecule. This makes 45 carbon atoms in total. There are 27 hydrogen atoms in each fatty acid, which makes 81, plus 5 in the glycerol molecule – 86 altogether. There are 6 oxygen atoms. So the molecular formula is $C_{45}H_{86}O_6$.

 c A glucose molecule has twice as many hydrogens as carbons, and the triglyceride also has very nearly twice as many. But whilst the glucose molecule has the same number of carbon atoms and oxygen atoms, this triglyceride has more than seven times as many carbons as oxygens.

6.3 Omega-3 fats have at least one double bond, three carbon atoms in from the end of the fatty acid molecule, counting from the opposite end from the carboxyl group. Linolenate is an example. Fish oils are a rich source of omega-3 fatty acids. This term can be applied to both mono- and polyunsaturated fatty acids. Some studies have suggested that omega-3 fatty acids help protect against cardiovascular disease. For this reason, a Dietary

Reference Intake (DRI) of 1.1 grams per day for women (1.6 for men) was established in September 2002 in the UK.

6.4 Statins inhibit one of the enzymes which produces cholesterol in the liver. So, no matter how low the level of cholesterol in the blood may be, the liver cannot respond by making more to compensate. If dietary cholesterol is reduced, however, with no use of statins, then the liver will respond by making more cholesterol.

6.5a Lipids are hydrophobic, which means they will not dissolve in water. Lipid molecules would collect together into big globules, not interacting with the water in the blood plasma.

b The outside of each lipoprotein ball is made up of a phospholipid bilayer. The phosphate groups of the outer layer of molecules all face outwards. The phosphate groups are hydrophilic, and can interact with the water molecules around them, enabling the lipoprotein 'balls' to disperse amongst the blood plasma.

6.6 A good web site to try is that of the American Heart Association, http://www.americanheart.org.

6.7a The woman – high to moderate risk, 10–15%
The man – mild risk, 5–10%

b The woman should give up smoking, as this is by far the greatest factor contributing to her risk of having a cardiovascular event. She could also try to reduce her total cholesterol to HDL cholesterol ratio, perhaps by reducing the quantity of saturated fats in her diet, and possibly by taking statins.

The man definitely needs to reduce his total cholesterol to HDL cholesterol ratio. The fact that it is so high suggests that he may be genetically liable to high cholesterol levels, in which case he will need to take statins and not just try to get the level down by changing his diet.

c The risk calculators are built up by studying a large number of people over many years, recording various factors about their life-styles (smoker or not, blood pressure readings, blood cholesterol levels), and all the cardiovascular events they have. These findings are then used to search for relationships between a particular life-style factor and the likelihood of suffering a cardiovascular event.

d The risk calculator is no more than a statistical tool. Even if you are in a very high risk bracket (greater than 30% on this chart) you still stand a 70% chance of not having a cardiovascular event. And if you are in a very low risk bracket, you still have a 2.5% chance of having one.

Moreover, the risk calculator does not take every possible factor into account. And perhaps it was constructed from data from people in one country – so things might be different in another place. And the data were collected from only a sample of people, so they might not be representative of a population as a whole.

This discrepancy could cause people to lose faith in the predictions of risk made by the calculator. Most people do not really understand the concept of risk, and might find it difficult to appreciate that, if you are in a 'high risk' bracket, you still only have a 30+% chance of having a cardiovascular event.

The discrepancy could make people less sure that changing their life-style could improve their health. In the long run, this could possibly mean that health improvement might not be as great as it could otherwise be.

Chapter 7

7.1 Measure the tidal volume for each breath. It is quickest to do this in small squares for each one, then calculate the average before converting to a volume. You will get a slightly different answer depending whether you measure from the low point to the high point each time, or from the high point to the low point – in other words, whether you start measuring at the very left hand edge of the graph, or from the top of the first breath.

If measuring from bottom to top each time, and measuring to the nearest half square, the values are:
3.5 + 5.0 + 5.5 + 5.0 + 4.5 = 23.5
So the mean value is 23.5 ÷ 5 = 4.70
As we could only measure to the nearest half square, we should round this value to the nearest half square as well. So our mean value is 4.5 small squares.
From the scale on the graph, 10 small squares = 1 dm^3.
So 5.0 small squares = 4.5 ÷ 10 = 0.45 dm^3.
The mean tidal volume is thus 0.45 dm^3.
The quickest way to calculate the mean breathing rate is to look at the biggest number of whole breaths on the graph, and see how long they took altogether.
The bottom of the first breath was at time 0, and the bottom of the last complete breath was at 21 s.
In that time, there were 4 complete breaths.
So in 60 seconds there would be (60 ÷ 21) × 4 = 11.4 breaths per minute.
Therefore the mean ventilation rate = 0.45 × 11.4 = 5.13 dm^3 per minute.

Activity 7.1

The soda lime absorbs carbon dioxide. The expired air passes through the soda lime each time the person breathes out.

Each time the person breathes in, they take in air from the chamber. Some of the oxygen contained in this air is taken in, absorbed into the blood and used for respiration in the body cells. These cells produce carbon dioxide as a waste product.

The air that is breathed back out contains less oxygen and more carbon dioxide than the air that is breathed in. The actual volume of air breathed out is the same as the volume of the air that is breathed in.

However, the carbon dioxide in this breathed-out air is absorbed, so the volume of air going back into the chamber is less than the volume that was taken out of it.

So the lid of the chamber gradually drops, and the trace on the kymograph gets lower.

7.2a The scale on this graph is 10 small squares to 1 dm³.
Tidal volume = 5 small squares
= 5 ÷ 10 = 0.5 dm³
Expiratory reserve volume = 10 small squares
= 10 ÷ 5 = 2.0 dm³
Inspiratory reserve volume = 33 small squares
= 33 ÷ 5 = 6.6 dm³
Therefore vital capacity = 0.5 + 2.0 + 6.6 = 9.1 dm³.

b The residual volume is the air which remains in the lungs and cannot be moved out. This volume of air never goes into or out of the spirometer, so you can't measure it.

7.3 The time intervals have been measured from peak to peak. It would be equally valid to measure them from trough to trough.
The tidal volumes have been measured from peak to trough. It would be equally valid to measure them from trough to peak.

Breath	Time interval in small squares	in seconds	Instant breathing rate / breaths per minute	Tidal volume in small squares	in dm³
1	3.0	3.0	20	17.0	0.85
2	3.0	3.0	20	17.0	0.85
3	2.0	2.0	30	19.0	0.95
4	2.0	2.0	30	18.5	0.93
5	2.0	2.0	20	14.0	0.70
6	2.5	2.5	24	15.0	0.75
7	2.0	2.0	30	12.0	0.60
8	2.0	2.0	30	19.0	0.95
9	1.5	1.5	40	8.0	0.40
10	1.0	1.0	60	5.0	0.25
11	2.0	2.0	30	11.0	0.55
12	2.0	2.0	30	9.0	0.45
13	3.0	3.0	20	12.0	0.60
14	2.0	2.0	30	17.0	0.85
15	2.0	2.0	30	14.5	0.73

These data show that both breathing rate and tidal volume vary considerably at rest.
This variation is between extremes of 0.95 dm³ and 0.25 dm³ for tidal volumes and 60 and 20 breaths per minute for instant breathing rate. There is no obvious correlation between breathing rate and tidal volume. Tidal volumes tend to gradually increase and then decrease, though there is an occasional deep breath.

7.4 Ciliated cells require energy to produce the movement of the cilia. Mitochondria are the organelles in which aerobic respiration takes place. They make ATP, the universal energy currency of a cell.

Goblet cells make and secrete glycoproteins. Proteins are synthesised on ribosomes, attached to rough endoplasmic reticulum. The proteins made are packed into vesicles and transferred to the Golgi apparatus. Here, the carbohydrate components are added to them so that they become glycoproteins. Small vesicles containing these then break away from the Golgi apparatus and move to the cell surface membrane, from where they are secreted.

7.5a Two belonging to a cell in the alveolar epithelium, two belonging to a cell in the wall of a capillary, and one belonging to a red blood cell. So five altogether.

b By diffusion. Oxygen molecules are moving randomly, and some hit and pass through the cell surface membrane. Some will also move through the membrane in the other direction, but as there are more oxygen molecules on the alveolar side than on the blood capillary side, more will move from the alveolus than into it. In other words, the oxygen moves down its concentration gradient. Oxygen is able to pass easily through cell membranes because its molecules are small, and because they do not carry a charge, and so are not repelled by the hydrophobic phospholipids.

c The oxygen molecule combines with a haem group in a haemoglobin molecule, forming oxyhaemoglobin.

7.6a Air containing a relatively high concentration of oxygen is brought into the lungs with each breath. Air containing a relatively low concentration of oxygen is moved out with each breath.

b The movement of blood through the capillaries also helps to maintain the concentration gradient. Deoxygenated blood flows into the capillary, and is brought close to the air in the alveolus where it becomes oxygenated. It then flows away. Breathing movements and blood flow therefore maintain a relatively high concentration of oxygen in the alveoli, and a relatively low concentration of oxygen in the blood flowing into the lung capillaries.

7.7 Surface area = 100 × 100 × 6 = 60 000 μm²
Volume = 100 × 100 × 100 = 1 000 000 μm³
So surface area : volume = 60 000 : 1 000 000
= 0.06 : 1
This is better expressed as 6 x 10⁻² : 1
Notice that this is much smaller than for the 20 μm cell.

7.8 Note that here the volumes are given in dm³, whereas the surface areas are given in m². We really need to use the same units for each. We can either convert the dm³ to m³, or the m² to dm². It doesn't matter which you choose, but here we will do the calculation using dm³ and dm².
There are 10 dm in 1 m, so there are 100 dm² in 1 m².

a For earthworm
0.0004 m² = 0.0004 × 100 = 0.04 dm².
So surface area : volume = 0.04 : 0.005
= 8 : 1

b For person
1.8 m² = 1.8 × 100 = 180 dm².
So surface area : volume = 180 : 68
= 2.6 : 1

c For alveoli of a person
70 m² = 7000 dm²
So surface area of alveoli : volume of person
= 7000 : 68
= 103 : 1

d The earthworm has 8 dm² of skin across which gases can diffuse to supply every 1 dm³ of its body. Earthworms are not very fast-moving or active in any other way, so this is sufficient to allow enough oxygen to diffuse into the body each minute to provide its cells with the oxygen they need.

For the human, however, there is only 2.6 dm² of skin for every 1 dm³ of its body. This would not be anywhere near adequate to supply enough oxygen to its cells, especially as humans use energy at a greater rate than earthworms. The large surface area provided by the alveoli is therefore needed in order to allow enough oxygen to diffuse into the blood each minute to supply all the body cells with their needs.

(There is also another very good reason why we don't use our skins for gas exchange. We have a thick, waterproof layer on our skin surface, which stops the living cells beneath from drying out. This layer is much too thick to allow any appreciable diffusion of oxygen to flow through it.)

7.9a FEV_1 is the forced expiratory volume per second. This is the maximum volume of air that can be expired in the first second of a forced expiration. It can be measured using a peak flow meter.

b As a person ages, their FEV_1 decreases. Between the ages of 25 and 75, the FEV_1 drops by 30%. The rate of decrease becomes greater in later years. (That is, the gradient of the curve becomes steeper.)

c The FEV_1 declines much faster in a smoker than in a non-smoker. As for a non-smoker, the rate of decrease becomes greater in later years. By the age of 65, the FEV_1 would, on average, have dropped to a level where some disability occurs, but in a non-smoker it never falls this low. By the age of 50, the FEV_1 of a smoker is already at the level of that of a non-smoker of 75.

d In a smoker, there is damage to the linings of the airways, which become narrowed and inelastic as fibrous tissue is laid down to try to repair the damaged tissues. There may also be quite a bit of mucus in the lungs and airways, as the goblet cells will make more than usual and the cilia will not be functioning to move it out. All of these factors reduce the volume of air which can be rapidly forced out of the lungs.

e Yes. As soon as a smoker gives up, the curve for FEV_1 stops dropping so steeply. This means that breathing will become easier almost immediately. Even though the FEV_1 never comes to match that of a non-smoker, it stays much higher than that of someone who continues to smoke. However old the smoker is, their health will benefit from giving up.

7.10a PEFR is peak expiratory flow rate. It is the maximum volume of air that can be forceably expelled, measured in dm³ per minute. (Remember that anything to do with 'rate' must take time into account.) It is measured using a peak flow meter. You 'huff' as hard as you can into the mouthpiece. Repeat several times. The PEFR is the largest value the meter reads.

b In this person, PEFR is highest at the end of the day, and lowest in the early hours of the morning.

c The muscle in the airways is contracting, narrowing them and making it difficult to get air into and out of the lungs. There may be some environmental trigger which causes this, such as house mite dust in bedding, or it may be related to some internal diurnal (daily) rhythm in the person's body, such as hormonal changes.

7.11a Steroids are preventers. Beta agonists are relievers.

b Inhaling delivers the drugs straight to where they are needed – in the airways. If they were injected into the blood stream they would be taken all over the body, and so would be more likely to cause side effects.

Chapter 8

8.1

	DNA	RNA
Type of sugar in nucleotides	deoxyribose	ribose
Bases in nucleotides	adenine guanine cytosine thymine	adenine guanine cytosine uracil
Number of strands in molecule	two	one
Where found in a cell	nucleus (there is also some DNA inside the mitochondria)	nucleus (where it is produced) in ribosomes and in cytoplasm

8.2a There are 64 different three-letter sequences. There are four bases, so at each position in a three-letter sequence there are four different possibilities. So the total number of different possibilities is 4 × 4 × 4 = 64.

b One advantage is that if one base in the DNA or RNA is accidentally altered, this won't necessarily mean a difference in the amino acid which is coded for.

Also, some of the base sequences are used to signify 'start here' or 'stop'. The first amino acid involved in the formation of a polypeptide is always methionine, whose DNA triplet code is TAC. The triplets ATT, ATC and ACT all mean 'stop'.

8.3 A polynucleotide is a molecule made from many nucleotides linked together. RNA and DNA are polynucleotides.

A nucleotide is a molecule made from a pentose sugar (which is deoxyribose in DNA and ribose in RNA), a phosphate group and a nitrogenous base. In a polynucleotide, the nucleotides are linked together by covalent bonds between the phosphates and sugars.

Ribose and deoxyribose are both pentose (5-carbon) sugars. They differ in that ribose has an –OH group attached to the second carbon atom in the ring whereas deoxyribose has an H in this position. The molecular formula of ribose is $C_5H_8O_6$ while that of deoxyribose is $C_5H_8O_5$. Ribose is found in RNA, and deoxyribose is found in DNA.

Purines and pyrimidines are two types of nitrogenous bases. They both have molecules in which nitrogen and hydrogen atoms form rings. Purines have two such rings, while pyrimidines have one. Purines are therefore larger molecules than pyrimidines. In DNA, the distance between the two helical strands is just enough to allow a pyrimidine on one strand and a purine on the other to fit together. The purine and pyrimidine bases are held together by hydrogen bonds. In DNA, the two purine bases are adenine and guanine, and the two pyrimidine bases are cytosine and thymine. In RNA, the pyrimidine uracil replaces thymine.

8.4a When a DNA molecule is to be replicated, the two strands are unzipped by breaking the hydrogen bonds between the bases. This exposes the bases on both strands.

Each base is only able to form hydrogen bonds with its complementary base. Cytosine always bonds with guanine, whilst thymine always bonds with adenine.

So, if the base pair in the two strands was adenine–thymine, there is now an adenine base exposed on one strand and a thymine base on the other. Free nucleotides can now form hydrogen bonds with these exposed bases. Only a nucleotide with an adenine base can form bonds with the exposed thymine, and only a nucleotide with a thymine base can form bonds with the exposed adenine.

As this happens all along the unzipped DNA molecules, the bases are all lined up in exactly the same sequence as before. The sugar–phosphate backbones are linked together, forming two double-stranded DNA molecules exactly like the original one.

b In each of the new DNA molecules which are formed, one strand is an 'old' one and the other strand is a 'new' one. One of the strands has been conserved (kept) in each new molecule, and has acted as a template while a new strand has been built against it. 'Semi-conservative' means 'half-kept'.

c The two polynucleotide strands in a DNA molecule are twisted into a double helix. There is just enough space between them for one purine and one pyrimidine base. Two purines would take up too much room, while two pyrimidines would be too far away from each other to form hydrogen bonds.

8.5a 4.

b tyrosine, serine, asparagine, glycine

c UAU UCU AAC GGG

d i Leucine is coded for by AAT on a DNA molecule. So the mRNA codon for this will be UUA. The tRNA anticodon will be AAU.

ii Asparagine is coded for by TTG on a DNA molecule. So the mRNA codon for this will be AAC. The tRNA anticodon will be UUG.

8.6a Amino acids are not 'made' during protein synthesis. The amino acids are already there, in the cytoplasm. During protein synthesis, they are lined up on the ribosome and linked together. A better statement would be: 'The sequence of bases in a DNA molecule determines the sequence in which amino acids are linked together during protein synthesis.'

b DNA does not contain amino acids. DNA is a polynucleotide, made of many nucleotides linked together. Amino acids are found in proteins. A better statement would be: 'The sequence of bases in a DNA molecule determines what kind of proteins will be formed in the cell.'

c The names of the bases are spelt incorrectly. The student has confused other names with those of the bases. For example, 'thiamine' is a vitamin, not a base. The correct names are adenine, cytosine, thymine and guanine.

d During transcription, an mRNA molecule is built up. It is not already made, so it cannot 'come and lie' next to the DNA strand. A better statement would be: 'During transcription, a complementary mRNA molecule is built up against part of a DNA molecule.'

8.7 The next step would involve a tRNA molecule with the anticodon ACG, which can link with the codon UGC on the mRNA molecule. This tRNA will be carrying the amino acid cysteine. The cysteine will be held in position so that a peptide bond can be formed between it and the last amino acid to be added to the chain, which was serine.

Chapter 9

9.1 The largest sector of the circle represents interphase. During this stage, the cell carries out its normal activities, including respiration and protein synthesis. DNA replication also occurs during this stage.

The next largest sector represents mitosis. In this stage, the duplicated chromosomes are separated and shared between two nuclei, so that each receives a complete set of the DNA in the original cell.

The smallest sector represents cytokinesis, in which the cytoplasm splits to form two new cells, each with a nucleus containing a complete set of chromosomes.

9.2a DNA replication is occurring where the red line slopes upwards, between 12 and 16 hours and again between 36 and 40 hours.

b This part of the cycle is interphase.

c and d We cannot tell exactly when mitosis begins, but it will be shortly after DNA replication has occurred. It finishes when cytokinesis begins, which is shown by the sudden halving of the DNA content and mass of each cell.

9.3a Top left – anaphase, centre – cytokinesis, top right – metaphase, bottom left – telophase, bottom right – prophase

b In 9.8 the metaphase is viewed with the poles top and bottom and the equator inbetween. In 9.9 the view is onto the equatorial plane with the poles above and below the surface of the paper. The difference is due to the fact that only the centromere of each chromosome aligns at the equator.

9.4a All the cells except those in interphase were in a stage of mitosis – that is 29 cells.

b The longer the stage, the more likely it is that you will catch a cell in that stage. So these data suggest that the longest stage in the cell cycle is interphase, followed by prophase, metaphase, anaphase and telophase. However, this is quite a small sample and it would be best to collect data from many more samples before coming to any firm conclusions.

9.5a Cancer is caused by changes in genes which control when and how often a cell divides. There are numerous genes which do this, and for cancer to develop several of them must be altered. The older a person is, the more time there has been for several such changes to accumulate.

b Some of the genes which control cell division seem to be more likely to mutate than others. If a person has inherited such genes, then they have a greater chance of developing cancer.

c X-rays are high-energy, short-wavelength radiation. They can penetrate right through the body, and have enough energy to alter the structure of biological molecules, including DNA. This can cause mutations in some of the genes involved in the control of cell division.

9.6a The graph shows that smokers have a lower life expectancy than non-smokers. The more you smoke, the greater is this negative effect on life expectancy.

The causes of these earlier deaths could be heart disease, cancer or chronic obstructive pulmonary disease.

b

	Survivorship / % alive	
Age	Smoked more than 25 a day	Never smoked
45	95	98
65	64	87
85	8	32
95	0	4

c A cohort study investigates a sizeable and distinct group of people; in this case, men of one age were chosen and they were studied through their lives. A cohort study will have fewer uncontrolled variables than a random sample of the population.

9.7 In this study it was possible to look for specific links between the life-style of a person and their chance of getting disease. The data were collected over a long period of time, following the group right through until their deaths. The data in Fig 9.13 simply show the total numbers of people who died from lung cancer each year and the numbers of cigarettes which were smoked.

9.8 Better screening programmes will pick up more breast cancers at an early stage. They may therefore increase the apparent incidence of the disease (that is, the number of new cases per year) and also its prevalence (that is, the number of people with the disease at any one time). Earlier diagnosis will have the same effect.

Education campaigns may result in more women being aware of breast cancer, and going to their doctor earlier to have their worries checked out. So this, too, can lead to earlier diagnosis and hence an apparent increase in incidence and prevalence. However, education campaigns may also alert women to life-style factors which could decrease their risk of the disease, such as drinking less alcohol, giving up smoking or eating a better diet. This could reduce the incidence of breast cancer. In this instance, it appears that this aspect of the education campaign is causing such a great reduction in the number of breast cancer cases that it outweighs the effect of the greater effectiveness in diagnosing cancer at an early stage.

Better treatment will enable more people with breast cancer to live for longer. Although many of these people will be pronounced to be completely cured, and so will no longer be part of the prevalence figures, the increase in prevalence suggests that more people who still have breast cancer are living for longer.

9.9 Between 1984 and 2002, there has been a slight drop in the prevalence of smoking in boys between the ages of 11 and 15. However, the numbers fluctuate from year to year, and there is no entirely convincing trend that is indicated by these data. Throughout these years, the percentage of girls who smoke has always been slightly higher than that of boys, apart from 1984 when the percentages were the same. As for boys, the numbers fluctuate, but may indicate a slight downward trend in the numbers of girls smoking.

The figures for regular smoking show that, in both boys and girls, the numbers of regular smokers increase between the ages of 11 and 15 years. They show that, by the age of 15, 20% of boys and 26% of girls are regular smokers. It is likely that these young people will find it very difficult to give up smoking later in their lives.

The high figures for females are a particular concern, because smoking may affect the health of their children as well as themselves. The health implications of smoking are now very well known, yet despite this many young people are becoming regular smokers. Perhaps a new direction is required in health education campaigns, to attempt to reduce this high number. Many of these people will have poor health as a direct result of their smoking, decreasing their ability to enjoy their lives and increasing the burden they cause on the National Health Service.

9.10 The graphs in Fig 9.24 show that, between 1970 and 1988, the number of deaths from cancer in women between 65 and 69 years old was rising, and doing so at a greater rate than in women between 50 and 54 years old. The death rate for 65–69 year olds was about 122 per 100 000 in 1970, whilst that for 50–54 year olds was just under 70 per 100 000. At its peak, in 1987, the death rate for 65–69 year olds was about 148 per 100 000, whilst the death rate at this time for 50–54 year olds was about 78 per 100 000 – almost half as great.

With the introduction of screening in 1988, the death rate for both age groups fell. There were still fluctuations, but the overall trend was a continuous drop right through to the year 2000. By 2000, the death rate for 50–54 year olds had fallen to about 50 per 100 000, a difference of 28 deaths per 100 000 from its peaks in 1976 and 1987.

The graphs in Fig 9.25 show that the earlier breast cancer is diagnosed, the longer the patient is likely to live. If a tumour is diagnosed at the earliest stage (stage 1), 80% of patients will still be alive 10 years later. In contrast, if the tumour is diagnosed at stage 4, 80% of patients will be dead within 3 years, and 10 years after the diagnosis only about 5% will still be alive.

Chapter 10

10.1a i The younger the mother, the more likely she is to have smoked in the year before or during her pregnancy. Women who are 35 and over are almost three times less likely to have smoked than women under 20.

ii Without further information, it is not possible to put forward reasons with any confidence. It is possible that, as a woman gets older, she becomes more aware of the potential harm that smoking could do to her baby, and so finds the motivation to give up smoking. Another possibility is that older women are more likely to have planned to get pregnant, and therefore give up smoking before their pregnancy begins; younger women are perhaps more likely to become pregnant without planning it, and therefore have not predicted the need to give up smoking. Yet another possibility is that the type of young women who smoke are perhaps more likely to become pregnant without planning this to happen. More data would be needed before any of these hypotheses could be considered further.

iii The trend shown by the data about the percentages of women who smoked throughout pregnancy quite closely matches that for the percentages of women who smoked in the year before or during pregnancy; the younger the woman, the more likely she is to smoke throughout pregnancy. This supports the suggestion that as a woman gets older, she becomes more aware of the potential harm that smoking could do to her baby, and so finds the motivation to give up smoking. It also makes the 'unplanned pregnancy' hypothesis in (ii) less likely. However, the numbers in all age groups are now much smaller. About half of women aged 35 and over who smoked before pregnancy found the willpower to give up once they knew they were pregnant. But in under 20 year olds the proportion giving up is smaller, at about 40%.

b i 36% of these women smoked in the year before or during pregnancy
$(36 \div 100) \times 1397 = 503$

ii 45% of smokers gave up smoking.
The number of smokers was 503.
$(45 \div 100) \times 503 = 226$

c Smoking decreases the supply of oxygen to the growing foetus, both by reducing the amount of oxygen which can be carried by haemoglobin (because carbon monoxide combines irreversibly with Hb) and by inhibiting the development of blood vessels. Babies born to smokers are, on average, of lower weight than those born to non-smokers. Smokers are also more likely to have a miscarriage than non-smokers. There is also some evidence of increased ill health in babies born to women who have smoked – even if the mother remains a non-smoker.

10.2a The crown-rump length of many babies of known age would have been measured, using ultrasound scanning an electronic caliper. The mean length for all babies of a precisely known particular age would have been calculated and then plotted onto the graph.

b From the graph, the mean age of a foetus with a crown-rump length of 53 mm is about 12 weeks. Ros now knows how long she has been pregnant, and so can predict approximately when her baby will be born.

c From the graph, a baby of 10 weeks would be expected to have a crown-rump length of about 30 mm. This matches the measurement of Fauzia's foetus, and suggests that it is growing normally.

10.3a After the substitution of A by G:
   AUG GAC UCC UGC UAA A
   After the deletion of G:
   AUG GAU UCC UGU AAA
   After the insertion of A:
   AUG GAU UCU CUG CUA AA

b For the normal DNA:
   methionine – aspartate – serine – cysteine – end
   After the substitution:
   methionine – aspartate – serine - cysteine – end
   (that is, no change)
   After the deletion:
   methionine – aspartate – serine – cysteine – lysine
   (that is, no 'stop' signal)
   After the insertion:
   methionine – aspartate – serine – leucine – leucine

10.4a The karyotype is from a male, as the sex chromosomes are X (the larger one) and Y (the much smaller one).

b i This person has two X chromosomes and one Y. He has Klinefelter's syndrome.

ii The diagrams should show that, when a cell in the mother's ovaries was dividing by meiosis, both X chromosomes went in one direction, rather than one going into one daughter cell and one into the other. (You do not need to know any details of meiosis, so your annotated diagram can be very simple – it need not show any other chromosomes, for example.) This XX cell then became a female gamete, and was fertilised by a sperm carrying a Y chromosome. The resulting zygote had two X chromosomes and one Y.

c Chromosomes can be seen directly under the light microscope. They are large enough to be seen clearly, and their lengths and the positions of their centromeres can be seen if the chromosomes are stained. This means that changes in the lengths, centromere positions or numbers of chromosomes can be identified by looking at them.

Genes, however, cannot be seen directly in a light microscope. A gene is part of a molecule of DNA, and – though DNA molecules can be seen using an electron microscope – no detail of their structure can be picked out visually. A change in a gene involves a change in the sequence of bases, and this can only be identified by more complex tests, for example using a prepared piece of DNA called a 'gene probe'. So point mutations cannot be identified by looking at the chromosomes in a cell.

Chapter 11

11.1a i The mean weight of boys increases with age from 0 to 2 years (24 months). The mean weight at birth is 3.3–3.4 kg, and the mean weight at 2 years is 12.6 kg. This represents a mean increase per year of 4.6–4.7 kg. The rate of growth is greatest in the first 3 months (accept up to 6 months), slowing gradually after that.

ii The mean weight of boys increases with age from 2–20 years. The mean weight at 2 years is 12.6 kg (read from the top graph, but possibly 12–13 if you have read from the bottom graph) and at 20 years it is just over 70 kg. This represents a mean increase per year of about 3.2 kg. However, the rate of growth is not the same throughout these years. It gradually increases between 2 and 10 years, but the rate of growth shows an increase between the ages of about 10 and 16. After this, the rate slows once more, but the graph has still not completely levelled off at 20 years old, indicating that growth has still not completely stopped.

iii The pattern of growth for girls between the ages of 0 to 2 years is very similar to that of boys. Birth weights are virtually the same for both, but by 2 years old the average weight for girls is about 12.1 kg, 0.5 kg less than that of boys. This represents a mean increase of 4.4 kg per year. The rate of growth is greatest in the first 3 months (accept up to 6 months), slowing steadily after that.

iv The pattern of growth for girls between the ages of 2–20 years is similar to that for boys. Up to the age of 10 years, there is no difference between them. The increased rate of growth for girls begins at a slightly earlier age than for boys, does not last so long and is not so steep. The graph is still rising slightly at age 20, suggesting that growth is not yet complete.

b The overall patterns of growth for boys and girls are very similar. They both have a rapid period of growth in the first 3 months, and then a second high rate of growth at puberty.

Up until about 10 years of age, there is little difference between the mean weights for boys and for girls. However, the increased rate of growth for girls begins about 1–2 years earlier than for boys, so there is a brief period between about 10–12 years of age when girls have a greater mean weight than boys. The steeper and longer growth spurt which boys experience at this time results in their mean weight at age 16 being greater than that of girls, and this difference continues right through until the age of 20.

Activity 11.1

1.

Year	Growth rate / kg yr^{-1}
1	6
2	3
3	2
4	2
5	2
6	2
7	3
8	3
9	4
10	4
11	4
12	5
13	4
14	3
15	3
16	2
17	1
18	1
19	1
20	1

Growth rate is shown to nearest whole number.

2. You could draw a line of best fit, or join each point to the next with a ruled, straight line.

3.

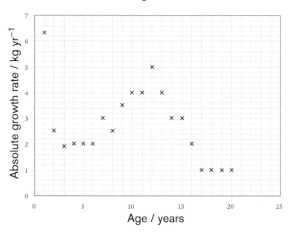

Growth rate curve for girls

4. Growth rate is at its highest in the first year.
5. Though the highest rate in adolescence on the graph is shown at 12 years, the period around this, from about 10 to 13 years, shows a higher rate than most of the years before and all the years after.
6. The original data being used for these graphs are averages calculated from measurements of thousands of people. The increase in growth in adolescence – the adolescent growth spurt – starts at different times in different people, so the average 'smooths out' this growth spurt.
7. A falling rate of growth is not the same as falling growth (getting smaller). Growth rate is the increase in weight, for example, in a period such as a year. A lower growth rate means that there is a smaller increase in weight in a year.
8. An absolute growth rate curve shows clearly when the rate of growth is increasing or decreasing, whereas this is not immediately obvious in a growth curve. In an absolute growth rate curve the adolescent growth spurt is much easier to identify.

Activity 11.2

1.
2.

Year	Relative growth rate
1	1.91
2	0.26
3	0.16
4	0.14
5	0.13
6	0.11
7	0.15
8	0.11
9	0.14
10	0.14
11	0.12
12	0.14
13	0.10
14	0.07
15	0.06
16	0.04
17	0.02
18	0.02
19	0.02
20	0.02

3. Relative growth rate declines with age. There is a

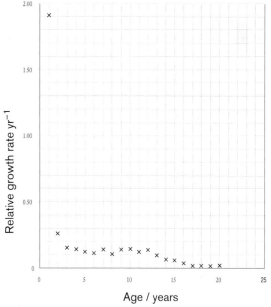

Age / years

rapid decrease from 2 to about 4 years, and it then fluctuates until about 13 years, when it falls once more.

4. In the absolute growth rate curve the adolescent growth spurt looks very pronounced. However, when this growth spurt is measured against the mass of the body at the time, as shown in the relative growth rate curve, it is seen to be much less than

the relative growth rate of the first year after birth. This may be a fairer representation of growth rate.

11.2a An absolute growth curve has time (or age) on the x axis and weight or height on the y axis. The slope of the curve indicates the rate of growth.

b An absolute growth rate curve has time (or age) on the x axis, and rate of change of weight or height on the y axis.

c A relative growth rate curve has time (or age) on the x axis, and relative growth rate on the y axis. Relative growth rate is calculated by finding the change in weight or height in one year, and dividing that by the weight at the beginning of the year.

Chapter 12

12.1 You could answer this question in prose, or as a comparison table. If you write it as prose, then make sure that you do compare one with the other, rather than just writing about the virus and then about the bacterium.

Bacterium *Mycobacterium tuberculosis*	virus HIV
is cellular	is not cellular
has a cell membrane	has an envelope
has cytoplasm	no cytoplasm
much larger than the virus	much smaller than the bacterium
contains DNA	contains RNA
metabolic reactions occur within it	no metabolic reactions
does not contain reverse transcriptase	contains reverse transcriptase
no capsid	has a capsid made of protein
metabolic activities can take place even when not inside a cell	no metabolic activity unless inside a cell

12.2a B lymphocyte
   b neutrophil
   c pathogen
   d antibody
   e macrophage
   f antigen

12.3 Viruses enter body cells, where they hijack the cell's machinery to reproduce themselves. If a cell is infected by a virus, it cuts up some of the virus molecules and puts them in its cell surface membrane. T lymphocytes respond to antigens in the cell surface membranes of other cells, so they will recognise when a cell is infected by a virus. T helper lymphocytes then secrete cytokines, which alert other cells to respond. T killer lymphocytes bind to the cell that is infected by the virus and kill it.

B lymphocytes, however, respond by secreting antibodies. These will not reach viruses that are safely inside a body cell. Antibodies cannot cross membranes.

12.4

	B lymphocyte	T lymphocyte
appearance	relatively small cell, with nucleus almost filling the cell	exactly like B lymphocytes
where in the body they are first formed	bone marrow	bone marrow
where in the body they mature in childhood	bone marrow	thymus gland
how they respond to contact with their specific antigen	divide to form a clone of plasma cells that secrete antibody, and also memory cells	divide to form clones of T helper cells that secrete cytokines, and T killer cells that destroy cells displaying the antigen

12.5a Ribosomes, then endoplasmic reticulum, then Golgi body. The results show that the radioactivity was found first in the ribosomes, then ER, then Golgi. As the radioactivity in ribosomes declines, it rises in the ER. As it declines in the ER, it rises in the Golgi body.

b At the ribosomes, the labelled amino acids would have been used to make protein molecules. The ribosomes are attached to the membranes of the endoplasmic reticulum, and the proteins move into the cisternae of the endoplasmic reticulum as they are made. Pieces of the ER then break off to form small vesicles, containing the proteins. These vesicles travel to the Golgi, where they fuse with the Golgi membranes. In the cisternae of the Golgi, carbohydrates will be added to the protein molecules to convert them to glycoproteins.

c This suggests that all of the proteins made on the ribosomes moved into the cisternae of the ER. However, not all of these proteins were transported to the Golgi. Some of them might have gone straight into the cytoplasm of the cell.

Another possibility is that the radioactivity of the amino acids decreased over time.

d The amino acids might have been taken up by phagocytosis. The cell would have formed a vacuole containing a droplet of the liquid surrounding it, containing these amino acids.

They could have been taken up by active transport, through a protein channel in the cell surface membrane.

e Small vesicles would pinch off from the Golgi body, and travel to the cell surface membrane. They would then fuse with this membrane, emptying the contents of the vesicles outside the cell. This is an example of exocytosis.

Chapter 13

13.1 An antibody is a glycoprotein produced by B lymphocytes, and secreted into the blood in response to the presence of a specific antigen. Antibodies help to destroy pathogens.

An antibiotic is a substance that destroys, or slows the growth of, pathogenic bacteria but does not harm human cells. It is produced by another organism, often a microorganism.

Resistance is the ability of an organism to withstand a chemical which destroys other similar organisms. For example, bacteria may become resistant to a particular antibiotic. Often, the resistance is due to the bacteria's ability to destroy or modify the antibiotic.

Immunity is the ability to destroy a pathogen within the body before it is able to multiply and cause illness. For example, a person may become immune to measles after having the disease. The specific groups of B cells and T cells that recognise the measles antigen proliferate, and memory cells are produced which remain in the blood for a long time. This enables the immune system to destroy the virus very quickly if the body is invaded again.

13.2a Antibiotics kill bacteria, not viruses. Influenza is caused by a virus.

b The more antibiotics bacteria are exposed to, the more likely it is that a resistant strain will be produced.

13.3a It is not a person who becomes resistant to antibiotics – it is bacteria that become resistant. The sentence could read:

If antibiotics are over-used, populations of bacteria may evolve that are resistant to these antibiotics.

b The presence of antibiotics does not cause bacteria to mutate. There is already variation amongst the bacteria, and some of them may already have a gene that makes them resistant to the antibiotic.

13.4a Fig 13.10 shows a general downwards trend in the number of deaths from TB in England. Previous to 1945, this is likely to be due to better living conditions and better hygiene, so that fewer people got TB. It may also be due to better treatment of TB patients, so that fewer of them died.

When antibiotics were introduced in 1945, the death rate decreased at an even greater rate. Antibiotics could cure many cases of TB, so fewer people died from it.

Fig 13.11 also shows a downward trend, which is steepest between 1950 and 1970, flattening off after that. The introduction of the BCG vaccination in 1950 is almost certainly responsible for almost all of this drop in cases. The continued use of antibiotics during this time will also have contributed. The levelling off from 1970 to 1990 may mean that we have reached the limit that can

be achieved using currently available drugs and vaccines.

b Fig 13.10 shows deaths from TB, while Fig 13.11 shows new cases.

c Fig 13.12 shows that the incidence of TB has increased steadily since 1988. This may be due to the evolution of antibiotic-resistant strains of the bacterium that cause TB. This would mean that people with the disease are difficult to treat, so their disease lasts for longer and they are more likely to pass it to someone else. The increase in HIV/AIDS is also a reason for this increase in cases of TB.

13.5a i These two species of bacteria may be closely related (in evolutionary terms) and may have similar antigens, so that our immune system reacts in a similar way to both of them.

ii It may be difficult to produce an attenuated strain of *M. tuberculosis* that is harmless but still elicits a strong immune response.

b The Heaf test is used to determine whether a person has previously had contact with *M. tuberculosis*, as this determines what should happen next. If there is no response, they are given the BCG vaccination.

c A strong response to the Heaf test suggest that the person has had previous contact with the bacterium, and may actually have the disease. A chest X-ray can show whether the lungs are affected.

13.6 Attenuated is a term used to describe a weakened, but still living, form of a pathogen. It can be used in a vaccine to elicit the same immune response as the normal form would do, but without causing disease.

A retrovirus is one that contains RNA, rather than DNA. HIV is a retrovirus. Once the RNA is in a host cell, a DNA copy is made of it.

The Heaf test injects a small quantity of tuberculin into the skin. The degree of response by the immune system to this test gives a pointer to whether or not the person requires the BCG vaccination.

MMR stands for measles, mumps and rubella. This triple vaccine is given to children at 13 months, and then a booster is given just before starting school.

A booster vaccination is a second, or sometimes third, dose of a vaccine. This increases the initial response to the antigen in the vaccine, and ensures that the number of memory cells does not decrease too rapidly.

13.8a 'Not at risk' is a term used to describe people whose life-styles or past illnesses mean that they are unlikely to become infected with HIV.

b The main purpose of Phase 1 is to test the safety of the vaccine. Phase 2 will only be conducted if

Phase 1 has found that the vaccine is safe. Now further information can be sought without risking the health of people who are already at risk.

c Phase 3 involves very large numbers of people, and considerable organisation and funding. This takes time to organise. Also, it is useful to run Phase 3 over a longer period of time because this increases the number of people who become exposed to HIV, making it more possible to collect information about whether the vaccine is effective or not.

13.9a The general trend for mumps and rubella is downward: there have been progressively fewer notified cases between 1992 and 2002. However, for both diseases there have been outbreaks when the numbers suddenly increase and then decrease again, within the period of about 1 year. This happened for rubella in 1994, and for measles in 1993 and 1996.

There is no real increase or decrease for mumps, where the number of notifications simply fluctuates slightly throughout the entire time period.

b The MMR controversy decreased the percentage of children who were vaccinated against measles, mumps and rubella. This controversy really took off in 1998. It might be expected that this could lead to outbreaks of these infections, but there is no real evidence for this on the graph, except possibly the rise in the number of notifications for mumps between 1999 and 2002.

13.10a Many parents may not take a child with whooping cough to see a doctor, so no-one in the medical profession knows about it. Another possible reason is that the illness may be mis-diagnosed. A third possibility is that a GP who is supposed to notify the disease does not do so.

b The low rate of notification means that the numbers on the graph represent only a very small sample of all the children who had whooping cough. If the sample is small, it makes it less certain that the results are typical of all the cases. Perhaps people only took children with a really bad form of the disease to a doctor, so it is changes in bad cases of whooping cough that are shown on the graph, rather than changes in all cases.

c The number of notifications fell overall between 1940 and 2000, although there were major fluctuations during this time. Peaks occurred in 1941, and on three occasions between 1947 and 1955. The highest peak was in 1941, when more than 200 200 notifications occurred. There were smaller peaks in 1977 and 1982, with around 60 000 cases on each occasion. By 2000, the number had fallen to practically zero.

d The graph shows that vaccination against whooping cough was being given to more than 90% of children in 2000. This is almost certainly the cause of the number of cases falling to zero at this time.

e The percentage of children being vaccinated fell sharply between 1976 and 1977, and this is probably the cause for the two peaks that occurred during this time.

13.11a The distribution of these diseases is extremely similar. Both are especially common in sub-Saharan Africa and in Eastern Europe, India and China.

b HIV/AIDS decreases the number of T lymphocytes, weakening the ability of the body to mount an effective immune response against this virus and other pathogens. This allows other infectious diseases, including TB, to take hold.

13.12a The low takeup of the vaccine meant that quite large numbers of children had no immunity against measles.

b Once people knew that there was a measles epidemic, they were alert to the possibility that they or a child might get it. They may have thought that symptoms which they would normally not worry about could be measles.

d People who were children before the measles vaccine was introduced would have been exposed to the live virus, so they had measles when they were young. Others would have been vaccinated against it when they were children.

Glossary

absolute growth – an increase in size, measured as height, weight or another parameter, for example 3 kg

absolute growth rate – the growth that occurs in unit time, for example 3 kg per year

activation energy – the energy which needs to be put in before a reaction will take place; enzymes lower activation energy

active immunity – immunity achieved by the body's own production of antibodies and memory cells; it may be the result of past infection with the disease, or of vaccination with attenuated pathogens or toxins

active site – the part of an enzyme to which the substrate temporarily binds; it has a specific shape which can only bind with one or a few different substrates

active transport – transport which requires an input of energy from a cell

acute – sudden onset and lasting for a short time

adenine – one of the four bases found in a DNA molecule; it is a purine

adipose tissue – tissue in which the cells contain fat globules; adipose tissue is an energy store, and also helps with heat insulation beneath the skin

agglutinate – clump together

aerobic respiration – the complete oxidation of glucose to make ATP; it requires oxygen

AIDS – an acquired immune deficiency syndrome caused by infection with HIV

allergens – substances which can cause an allergic response

allergic response – an inappropriately large response by the immune system to a substance such as pollen or dust mite faeces

alveoli – air sacs within the lungs, where gas exchange takes place

amino acid – a molecule with a central carbon atom to which are attached an amino group, NH_2, a carboxyl group, COOH, a hydrogen atom and a variable group known as an R group; amino acids link together to form protein molecules

amino group, a group of atoms, NH_2, found in amino acids

amniocentesis – the removal of a small amount of amniotic fluid using a hypodermic needle inserted through the wall of the mother's abdomen; cells from the foetus can be tested for genetic abnormalities

amnion – a membrane surrounding the developing foetus in the uterus

amniotic fluid – a fluid secreted by the amnion, which protects the developing foetus from mechanical shock

ampicillin – an antibiotic derived from penicillin

anaemia – an illness in which the blood does not contain sufficient haemoglobin

anaerobic respiration – the incomplete oxidation of glucose to make ATP; no oxygen is used

anaphase – the stage in mitosis in which the chromatids of each chromosome are pulled apart as their centromeres break, and are then pulled to opposite ends of the cell

angina – pain felt in the left upper body, resulting from atherosclerosis in the coronary arteries

angioplasty – opening a blocked blood vessel using a device threaded through the affected vessel

antenatal – before birth

antibiotic – a substance which kills bacteria but does not harm human cells

antibiotic resistance – the ability of a bacterium to survive despite exposure to an antibiotic

antibody – a glycoprotein molecule secreted by plasma cells derived from B lymphocytes, which destroys or neutralises antigens within the body

anti-coagulant – a substance which stops blood from clotting, for example sodium citrate, heparin

anticodon – a sequence of three bases at one end of a tRNA molecule; this sequence determines the amino acid which it can pick up, and also the mRNA codon with which it can bind at the ribosome

antigen – a chemical that is recognised as foreign by the body's immune system

antigen-presenting cell (APC) – a cell such as a macrophage, which places molecules from a pathogen or other antigen in its cell surface membrane, where they may be encountered and recognised by B or T lymphocytes

antioxidants – substances which 'mop up' free radicals in the body, which may help to prevent damage to cells; vitamin C is an example of an antioxidant

antithrombin – a protein which inhibits thrombin

antitoxin – a substance which can neutralise or destroy toxins

arteriole – a small artery, which carries blood between an artery and capillaries

artery – a thick-walled vessel with a relatively narrow lumen which carries blood away from the heart

artificial immunity – immunity achieved by vaccination with attenuated pathogens, or by injections of ready-made antibodies

asthma – a condition in which the immune system overreacts to the presence of certain substances in the air, causing the bronchioles to narrow and breathing to become difficult

atherosclerosis – narrowing of the lumen of the coronary arteries by fatty plaques, preventing adequate blood flow to the cardiac muscle

ATP – an energy-containing molecule made by respiration; it is the immediate energy source for all cells

atrio-ventricular node (AVN) – an area of tissue in the septum between the atria, which delays the electrical impulse from the atria briefly, before it passes to the Purkyne tissue

atrio-ventricular valves – the valves between the atria and ventricles, which allow blood to flow from the atria to the ventricles but not back the other way

atrium – one of the two upper chambers of the heart, which receive blood from the veins and pass it on to the ventricles

auto-immunity – a condition in which the lymphocytes attack the body's own cells

B lymphocyte – a white blood cell which forms plasma cells after contact with a specific antigen; the plasma cells then secrete antibodies

bacillus – a rod-shaped bacterium

background radiation – the ionising radiation that we are exposed to every day, from the normal environment

bacterium – a prokaryotic organism; bacteria are single-celled, and have no membrane-bound nucleus or other membrane-bound organelles

bases – a short-hand version of 'nitrogenous bases', the carbon-nitrogen ring compounds found in nucleotides

BCG – vaccination against tuberculosis

benign – a benign tumour stays in one place and does not shed cells which grow into tumours in other parts of the body

bicuspid valve – the valve between the left atrium and left ventricle; sometimes called the mitral valve

bilayer – a double layer, for example the two layers of phospholipids in cell membranes

biparietal diameter – the width of the widest part of the head; it is used to check that brain development in a foetus is normal

blastocyst – the ball of cells formed by repeated divisions of the zygote in the first few days after fertilisation

blood clot – a structure which forms when a blood vessel is damaged; it is made of fibres of fibrin in which red cells and platelets are trapped

blood film – a thin layer of blood on a microscope slide

blood group – a characteristic determined by a group of antigens found on red blood cells

blood pressure – the pressure exerted by the blood on the walls of the blood vessels

booster – a second or third vaccination, which increases immunity by eliciting a secondary response

bradycardia – a slow heart rate

breathing movements – movements caused by the contraction and relaxation of the intercostal muscles and the muscles in the diaphragm, which move air into and out of the lungs

broad-spectrum – a broad-spectrum agent, for example an antibiotic, acts against many different species of organism

bronchiole – a small tube branching from a bronchus and leading to the alveoli

bronchitis – an inflammation of the bronchi usually as a result of infection

bronchodilators – drugs which can relax the muscle in the walls of the bronchioles, thus relieving an asthma attack

bronchus – one of two tubes which branch from the trachea and carry air into the lungs

buffer – a buffer solution remains at a particular pH, despite the addition of small quantities of acids or alikalis

cancer – a disease in which there is uncontrolled division of cells

capsid – a structure formed from proteins which surrounds the DNA or RNA in a virus particle

carbohydrates – molecules whose general formula is $C_2H_{2n}O_n$; the smallest ones are sugars, and these may link together in long chains which form polysaccharides

carbon monoxide – a gas produced during incomplete combustion; it is present in cigarette smoke and prevents haemoglobin from carrying oxygen efficiently by combining irreversibly with it

carboxyl group – a group of atoms, COOH, found in amino acids and fatty acids

carcinogen – something which can cause cancer

cardiac arrest – a heart attack; the cardiac muscle stops contracting and relaxing, so the heart stops beating

cardiac cycle – the series of events which take place in the heart during one heart beat

cardiac muscle – the type of muscle found in the heart

cardiac output – the volume of blood leaving the left side of the heart per minute

cardio-pulmonary resuscitation – restoring heart beat and breathing movements to a person in whom they have stopped; often known as CPR

cell cycle – the sequence of events during which a cell grows and divides

cell surface membrane – the membrane around the outside of a cell; sometimes known as the plasma membrane

cell wall – a relatively thick structure which lies outside the cell surface membrane of a plant cell or bacterium; it is made of cellulose and pectin in plants, and of peptidoglycans in bacteria

cellulose – a polysaccharide made of many beta glucose molecules linked together to form fibrils; used to form the cell walls of plant cells

centriole – an organelle found in animal cells which organises the development of the spindle fibres during mitosis

centromere – the part of a chromosome at which the two chromatids are held together

CHD – coronary heart disease; illness caused by the build-up of plaques in the coronary arteries, reducing the supply of blood to the heart muscle

chemotherapy – destroying cancerous cells using drugs which affect them more than other cells in the body

chloroplast – an organelle found only in plant cells, which contains chlorophyll to absorb sunlight, and where photosynthesis takes place

cholesterol – a molecule related to lipids; it is needed for cell membrane formation; too much cholesterol in the blood increases the risk of heart disease

chorionic villus sampling – the removal of a small sample of tissue from the chorionic villi in the placenta; the cells can be tested for any genetic abnormality

chromatids – two identical strands of DNA attached to one another by a centromere, making up a chromosome

chromosome mutation – a change in the number or size of the chromosomes in a cell

chromosomes – structures made from a molecule of DNA and of proteins (histones); in humans there are two sets of 23 chromosomes in each cell

chronic – a chronic disease is one that lasts for a long time

chronic pulmonary obstructive disease (COPD) – a condition of the gas exchange system caused by various diseases, such as emphysema, where insufficient air flows through the system

cilia – microscopic extensions from the surface of an epithelial cell; they can wave in synchrony, which moves fluids across their surfaces

ciliated cells – epithelial cells with numerous cilia on their surfaces

cisternae – small membrane-bound interconnecting channels, making up some organelles e.g. endoplasmic reticulum

clone – a group of genetically identical cells or organisms

closed blood system – a blood system like that of humans, in which the blood is carried inside vessels

codon – a sequence of three bases in an RNA molecule which codes for one amino acid

cofactor – a substance which needs to be present before an enzyme-catalysed reaction can take place

colostrum – the first milk secreted by a new mother; it is especially rich in antibodies

competitive inhibition – the inhibition of an enzyme caused by another molecule competing with the substrate to bind with the active site

complementary base pairing – the pairing between A and T, and between C and G, in a DNA molecule; in RNA, uracil replaces thymine

complementary therapy – treatments involving procedures which are not part of mainstream medicine, e.g. acupuncture, reflexology

concentration gradient – a condition in which a substance is more concentrated in one place than in another

condensation reaction – a chemical reaction in which two molecules link together while losing a molecule of water

COPD – see chronic pulmonary obstructive disease

coronary arteries – arteries carrying oxygenated blood to the cardiac muscle in the heart wall

coronary bypass – an operation in which a piece of a blood vessel taken from somewhere else in the body is used to provide a new route for blood to flow to the heart wall, avoiding a blocked artery

coronary heart disease (CHD) – illness caused by the build-up of plaques in the coronary arteries, reducing the supply of blood to the heart muscle

coronary thrombosis – a blood clot in a coronary artery

crown-rump length – the length of a foetus from the top of its head to the base of the spine; it is used to check that growth in the uterus is proceeding normally

CT scan – computer assisted tomography scan; X rays are used to built up a 3D image of the body, using computers

culture medium – a substance containing nutrients and other factors in which cells can be grown

cytokine – a substance secreted by T cells which affects the behaviour of other cells of the immune system

cytokinesis – the part of the cell cycle during which the cytoplasm splits to form two new cells

cytosine – one of the four bases found in a DNA molecule; it is a pyrimidine

deep vein thrombosis (DVT) – a blood clot which has formed inside a vein, often in the deep-lying veins in the legs

defibrillation – using electric shocks to restart a heart which has stopped beating

deforestation – the removal of forests

deletion – a point mutation in which one base pair is removed from a DNA molecule

denatured – an enzyme is denatured if the shape of the molecule is permanently altered; high temperatures or large pH changes can denature enzymes

deoxyhaemoglobin – haemoglobin which has not combined with oxygen

diabetes – usually used to mean 'diabetes mellitus', a condition in which the control of blood glucose level by insulin is not working correctly

diaphragm – a dome-shaped sheet of tissue which separates the thorax from the abdomen; contraction of its muscles pulls it flatter, which increases the volume inside the thorax and helps to draw air into the lungs

diastole – the phase of the heart beat when the muscle is relaxing

diastolic pressure – the pressure exerted by the blood in an artery as the heart muscle relaxes

differential growth – the growth of some parts of the body at different rates than others

diffusion – the net movement, as a result of random movement of molecules or ions, of a substance down its concentration gradient; it is a passive process

diploid – a diploid cell contains two complete sets of chromosomes

disaccharide – a carbohydrate made of two sugar units

disulphide bond – a strong bond between sulphur atoms which are present in the R groups of cysteine molecules; disulphide bonds often hold together the different polypeptide chains in a protein molecule

diuretic – a drug which stimulates the kidneys to produce large amounts of dilute urine

DNA – deoxyribonucleic acid; a polynucleotide which carries genetic information in the form of a code using the sequences of the four different nucleotides in its molecules

DOTS – directly observed treatment course; a procedure used for ensuring that a TB patient takes their drugs at required times over the whole course of the treatment

double circulatory system – a blood system like that of humans, in which the blood travels through the heart twice in one complete circuit of the body

DTP-Hib – the vaccination against diphtheria, typhoid, pertussis (whooping cough) and Hib

electrocardiogram – a recording of the heart's electrical activity; often known as an ECG

electrolytes – ions such as sodium, potassium and chloride, dissolved in water

electron microscope – a microscope which uses electron beams instead of light rays to view a magnified image of an object; it has a much greater power of resolution than a light microscope

electronmicrograph – a photograph made by using an electron microscope

embolism – a blood clot or fragment of fatty plaque which has broken away from the site of its formation and been carried in the blood

embryo – the developing baby in the first 10 weeks after fertilisation

embryonic stem cells – stem cells obtained from a very young embryo

emphysema – a condition in which the walls of the alveoli break down, severely reducing the surface area available for gas exchange

endoplasmic reticulum – a network of membranes in the cytoplasm of a cell, which enclose spaces called cisternae

endothelium – the tissue lining the blood vessels

envelope – two membranes which surround an organelle; nuclei, mitochondria and chloroplasts have envelopes

enzyme – a protein which acts as a catalyst, that is, it increases the rate of a reaction without being changed itself

epidemiology – the study of the patterns of the incidence and prevalence of disease in populations

epithelium – a tissue which covers the surface of an organ

equator – the midline of a cell during mitosis (or meiosis), where the chromosomes are lined up at metaphase

erythrocytes – blood cells containing haemoglobin, whose function is oxygen transport; also known as red cells

erythromycin – an antibiotic made by a fungus

ester bond – the type of bond which links fatty acids to glycerol in a triglyceride molecule

ethambutol – an antibiotic used to treat TB

ethnobotany – the study of the uses made of plants by local populations

eukaryotic – a eukaryotic cell contains a nucleus bound by an envelope, and also numerous other membrane-bound organelles; animal and plant cells are eukaryotic cells

expiratory reserve volume – the maximum volume of extra air, over and above the tidal volume, that can be breathed out with one breath

extrinsic proteins – proteins which are attached to the surface of a membrane

facilitated diffusion – diffusion across a cell membrane, where the diffusing substance is insoluble in lipids and has to pass through with the aid of transport proteins e.g. a protein-lined pore; it is a passive process

Fallopian tube – the oviduct; the tube leading from an ovary to the uterus

fatty acids – molecules made of hydrocarbon chains and a COOH group

fibrillation – a fluttering movement of the heart muscle, rather than rhythmic beating

fibrin – a fibrous protein whose long molecules help to form the framework of a blood clot

fibrinogen – a soluble protein found in blood plasma which is converted to insoluble fibrin when blood clots

fibrous proteins – proteins with long molecules, usually insoluble in water

fluid mosaic – a term used to describe the structure of a cell membrane; it is fluid because the molecules in it can move, and it is a mosaic because of the patterns formed by the protein molecules dotted around in the membrane

foetal alcohol syndrome (FAS) – a syndrome in a child which is linked to excessive alcohol consumption by the mother during pregnancy; the child may have learning difficulties and health problems

foetus (fetus) – the developing baby from 11 weeks after fertilisation

folic acid – a vitamin found in dark green vegetables; it is important for a mother to have a good intake of this vitamin right at the start of her pregnancy, as this greatly reduces the chance of the baby having spina bifida

foramen ovale – a small hole between the left and right atria; it is present in all babies but should close at birth

forced expiratory volume per second (FEV_1) – the volume of air that can be expired in the first second of a forced expiration

frame shift – the result of a deletion or insertion, in which all subsequent triplets in a DNA molecule are altered

free radical – a highly reactive chemical which can oxidise others, for example nitric oxide

fully permeable – able to let almost any molecule or ion pass through

gas exchange – the diffusion of oxygen from the alveoli into the blood, and of carbon dioxide from the blood into the alveoli

gene – a length of DNA that codes for the synthesis of a polypeptide (or protein)

genetic code – the three-letter code by which information is contained in a DNA molecule; a group of three bases specifies an amino acid to be added to a growing polypeptide chain during protein synthesis

genome – the complete set of genetic information contained in an individual organism or a population

globular proteins – proteins whose molecules curl into a ball-shape, often soluble in water

glucose dehydrogenase – an enzyme that catalyses the removal of an atom of hydgrogen from a glucose molecule

glycerol – an organic alcohol with the formula $C_3H_8O_3$

glycogen – a polysaccharide made of many alpha glucose units; the molecules are branched; it is used as an energy storage molecule, especially in liver and muscle cells

glycolipid – a molecule which contains a lipid component and a carbohydrate component (chains of monosaccharides)

glycoprotein – a molecule which contains a protein component (chains of amino acids) and a carbohydrate component (chains of monosaccharides)

glycosidic bond – a C–O–C bond linking sugar units together in a disaccharide or polysaccharide

goblet cells – epithelial cells which secrete mucus

Golgi apparatus – a stack of curved cisternae; proteins synthesised on ribosomes are converted to glycoproteins and packaged here

grana – stacks of membranes inside a chloroplast, where chlorophyll is found

growth – a permanent increase in size

growth factor – a substance which affects the growth of cells in culture

guanine – one of the four bases found in a DNA molecule; it is a purine

haemocytometer – a special slide used for counting cells, for example blood cells; it has a chamber of known depth ruled with microscopic grid lines, thus allowing the cells in a sample of known volume to be counted

haemoglobin – a red pigment found in red blood cells; it transports oxygen and carbon dioxide between lungs and body cells

haploid – a haploid cell contains one complete set of chromosomes

Heaf test – a preliminary test carried out to check for immunity against TB before giving the BCG vaccination

heart block – a condition in which electrical impulses are not able to spread through the walls of the heart in the normal way

heart rate – the number of heart beats per minute

heart-lung machine – a machine which pumps and oxygenates a patient's blood while their heart is stopped to allow surgery to be carried out

hepatitis – a disease of the liver, caused by a virus

hexose – a sugar containing six carbon atoms

high-density lipoprotein (HDL) – lipoproteins containing a lot of protein and relatively little lipid

histones – proteins which are found in chromosomes in association with DNA

HIV – the human immunodeficiency virus, which causes AIDS

HIV positive (HIV+) – infected with HIV, but not necessarily showing any symptoms of AIDS

homologous chromosomes – two chromosomes of the same kind in a diploid cell; they contain the same genes at the same loci, and have their centromeres in the same place

human immunodeficiency virus – the virus which causes AIDS

hydrogen bonds – relatively weak bonds between partly charged groups; for example, in water, hydrogen bonds form between the slightly negatively charged oxygen atoms in one molecule and the slightly positively charged hydrogen atoms in another

hydrophilic – able to associate with water; hydrophilic molecules have charges on them which interact with the charges on water molecules

hydrophobic – not able to associate with water

hypertension – high blood pressure

hypotension – low blood pressure

immune response – the response of the body to invasion by a foreign organism or substance; it involves B and T lymphocytes

immunity – having antibodies and memory cells in the body which can react quickly to their specific antigen, so preventing development of disease

immunoglobulins – antibodies

immunosuppressant drugs – drugs which damp down the body's immune response, so allowing an organ from another person to be transplanted

implantation – the process in which the blastocyst becomes attached to the lining of the uterus

incidence – the incidence of a disease is the number of new cases occurring in a given period of time

incubation time – the time period between infection by a pathogen and the first symptoms of disease

infectious disease – a disease which can be caught from another person or from an animal; infectious diseases are caused by pathogens

inhibitor – a substance which reduces the rate of an enzyme-catalysed reaction by reducing the ability of the enzyme to catalyse the reaction

insertion – a point mutation in which an extra base pair is inserted into a DNA molecule

inspiratory reserve volume – the maximum volume of extra air, over and above the tidal volume, that can be breathed in with one breath

insulin – a polypeptide hormone that is released by the pancreas when blood glucose levels are too high, and that brings about action by liver and muscle which reduce levels

intercostal muscles – muscles between the ribs, which contract and relax to raise and lower the ribcage during breathing

interferon – a substance (cytokine) secreted by T helper cells, which helps other cells of the immune system to destroy cells attacked by viruses; it has also been used to treat cancer

interphase – the longest stage of the cell cycle, during which the cell carries out its normal activities such as protein synthesis, and when DNA replication occurs

intrinsic proteins – proteins which are embedded in a cell membrane

ionic bond – a strong bond caused by the attraction between a negatively charged ion and a positively charged ion

ionising radiation – radiation which can dislodge electrons from atoms, which may damage DNA and cause mutations; X-rays, alpha rays and gamma rays are examples of ionising radiation

isoniazid – an antibiotic used to treat TB

isotonic drinks – drinks containing solutes in similar concentrations to those in body fluids

karyotype – an image produced by photographing the chromosomes in a cell and arranging their images in pairs

keratin – a fibrous protein found in the dead, protective layer of cells on the surface of the skin, and in hair and nails

keratinocytes – stem cells in the skin

Klinefelter's syndrome – a condition resulting from having the genotype XXY; the person is male, but will probably be infertile

Kupffer cells – phagocytic cells (macrophages) in the liver

Leishman's stain – a type of Romanowsky stain, used to show up the different types of leucocytes in a blood film

leucocytes – white blood cells; their function is destroying cells which are foreign to the body, such as bacteria

lipids – substances whose molecules contain an alcohol and fatty acids, for example triglycerides and phospholipids

lipoprotein – a tiny ball of lipids and proteins, transported in the blood

Listeria – a bacterium which can cause food poisoning, and which is especially harmful to pregnant women

low-density lipoprotein (LDL) – lipoproteins containing little protein and a lot of lipid

lumen – the space in the centre of a tube, for example in an artery

lumpectomy – an operation in which a lump (tumour) is removed from a breast

lymph – the fluid inside lymphatics; it is formed from tissue fluid

lymphatics – blind-ending vessels containing valves, which transport tissue fluid back to the blood stream

lymphocyte – a type of leucocyte; unlike phagocytes they become active only in the presence of a specific antigen that matches their specific receptors or antibodies

macrophage – a type of leucocyte; it is a large cell and destroys bacteria and other foreign material by phagocytosis; also known as a monocyte when in the blood

magnification – the number of times larger that an image is compared with the real object

malignant – a malignant tumour sheds cells which settle in other parts of the body and produce new tumours

maltose – a disaccharide made of two glucose units

mammography – X-rays of the breasts, normally done to detect and screen for early stages of cancer

mass flow – movement of a liquid in which it all moves together, like water in a river

mastectomy – an operation in which a breast is removed, to remove a cancer; usually, some of the lymph nodes under the arm are also removed, as these may also contain cancerous tissue

MDR-TB – multi-drug resistant TB; TB caused by antibiotic-resistant strains of *Mycobacterium tuberculosis*

meiosis – a type of cell division in which a diploid cell divides to form four haploid cells, each genetically different from each other and from the parent cell

melanoma – a malignant and very agressive cancer in the skin, visible as a spreading red to black patch with an irregular, notched border

memory cells – cells formed from B cells or T cells following exposure to their specific antigen; memory cells remain in the body for a long time afterwards

messenger RNA (mRNA) – RNA formed by transcription of DNA in the nucleus, which then travels to a ribosome where it controls the sequence of amino acids as a polypeptide is built

metaphase – the stage in mitosis in which the chromosomes are moved to the equator of the cell by the spindle fibres, which are attached to their centromeres

methicillin – an antibiotic derived from penicillin

microorganism – an organism too small to be seen with the naked eye, for example bacteria and viruses

microtubules – long, thin tubes of protein found in most cells; during mitosis, they form the spindle, which moves the chromosomes around within the cell

mitochondrion – a relatively large organelle in which aerobic respiration and the synthesis of ATP occur; mitochondria have two membranes around them, sometimes known as an envelope

mitosis – the part of the cell cycle during which the chromosomes are separated equally into two daughter cells; mitosis produces two daughter cells which are genetically identical to each other and to the parent cell

MMR – the vaccination for measles, mumps and rubella

monoclonal antibodies – a group of identical antibodies; 'tailor-made' monoclonal antibodies have been used to try to destroy cancerous cells

monosaccharide – a carbohydrate made of a single sugar unit

mortality – the number of deaths per 100 000 of the population

MRI scan – magnetic resonance imagining; images of the inside of the body are built up using differences in magnetic field strength

MRSA – methicillin resistant *Staphylococcus aureus*

mucus – a substance made from glycoproteins; it coats the inside of the digestive system and protects it from attack by acids and enzymes; it traps particles in the air being inhaled into the lungs

mutation – an unpredictable change in the genetic material of a cell

Mycobacterium tuberculosis – a bacterium which causes tuberculosis

myocardial infarction – the loss of blood flow to part of the cardiac muscle in the heart; it is usually caused by a coronary thrombosis

myogenic – a property of cardiac muscle; its contraction is initiated within the muscle itself, not by impulses from a nerve

narrow-spectrum – a narrow-spectrum agent, for example an antibiotic, acts against only one or a very few species of organism

natural immunity – immunity achieved by having a disease, or by a baby receiving antibodies from its mother across the placenta or in breast milk

neutrophil – the most common type of leucocyte; it has a lobed nucleus and destroys bacteria and other foreign material by phagocytosis

neutrophil elastase – a enzyme secreted by neutrophils which hydrolyses elastin in the lungs

nicotine – the addictive substance in tobacco

non-competitive inhibition – the inhibition of an enzyme caused by another molecule binding with the enzyme at a position other than its active site, which causes the shape of the active site to change

notifiable disease – a disease which must be reported to the health authority whenever a new case is seen by a health worker

nuclear pore – a gap in the envelope around the nucleus; mRNA can pass through here

nucleolus – a darkly-staining area within the nucleus where DNA is being transcribed to rRNA

nucleus – a large, darkly-staining structure found in most cells; it is bound by a double membrane (envelope) and contains the cell's DNA

oncogene – a gene formed when a proto-oncogene mutates; oncogenes allow cells to divide uncontrollably, and this can result in cancer

open heart surgery – surgery on the heart in which the chest cavity is opened

optimum temperature – the temperature at which an enzyme-controlled reaction takes place at its maximum rate

organ – a part of the body made up of different tissues, which performs a specific function

organelle – a discrete structure within a cell, for example a mitochondrion

osmosis – the diffusion of water down a water potential gradient, through a partially permeable membrane; it is a passive process

oviduct – the tube leading from an ovary to the uterus; also known as Fallopian tube

oxyhaemoglobin – haemoglobin which has combined with oxygen

pacemaker – the sino-atrial node; its inbuilt rhythm of beating sets the pace for all the muscle of the heart

palisade mesophyll cells – the cells within a leaf which contain the largest concentration of chloroplasts and where most photosynthesis takes place

partially permeable – able to let some molecules or ions through but not others

passive immunity – immunity achieved by receiving ready-made antibodies

passive transport – transport which requires no input of energy from a cell; diffusion, facilitated diffusion and osmosis are methods of passive transport

pathogen – an organism, usually a bacterium or virus, which causes disease

peak expiratory flow rate (PEFR) – the maximum rate at which air can be forcibly expelled from the mouth

peak flow meter – an instrument used to measure the peak expiratory flow rate

pectin – a substance found in plant cell walls which helps to hold the cellulose fibres together and one cell to another

penicillin – an antibiotic made by the fungus *Penicillium*

peptide bond – a CO–NH bond which links amino acids together

pentose – a five-carbon sugar, e.g. ribose

PET scan – positron emission tomography; images of the inside of the body are built up by picking up differences in the metabolic activity in the tissues

pH – a measure of acidity or alkalinity; a pH of 7 is neutral, a pH below 7 is acidic and a pH above 7 is alkaline

phagocyte – a type of leucocyte which destroys bacteria and other foreign material by phagocytosis; neutrophils and macrophages are phagocytic cells

phospholipids – lipid molecules containing a phosphate group; the phosphate group is hydrophilic and the fatty acid tails are hydrophobic; this causes the phospholipids to form a bilayer in water, as in cell membranes

photosynthesis – the process by which green plants absorb energy from sunlight and use it to combine water and oxygen to form glucose

placebo – a 'dummy' treatment that is given to one group of subjects so that their response can be compared with those given an experimental treatment or drug

placenta – an organ formed partly from the foetus's tissues and partly from the mother's, in which substances are exchanged between the foetus's and mother's blood

plaque – atheromatous plaque is a damaged and rigid area of an artery wall where tissue, cholesterol and lipids build up

plasma – the liquid part of blood

plasma cell – B lymphocytes differentiate into plasma cells after coming into contact with their specific antigen; plasma cells then secrete antibodies

platelets – special fragments of cells carried in the blood plasma, which are involved in blood clotting

pluripotent – able to divide into cells which can differentiate to form all other types of cell

point mutation – a mutation involving one base pair in a DNA molecule

polio – poliomyelitis, a disease caused by a virus

polypeptide – a chain of amino acids

preconceptual – before fertilisation (conception)

prevalence – the prevalence of a disease is the number of people with the disease in a population at a given time

primary response – the response of the immune system following the first exposure to a particular antigen

primary structure – the sequence of amino acids in a polypeptide or protein; it is determined by the sequence of bases in a DNA molecule

product – the substance formed by an enzyme-catalysed reaction

prokaryotic – a prokaryotic cell does not contain a membrane-bound nucleus or any other membrane-bound organelles; bacterial cells are prokaryotic

prophase – the first stage in mitosis, in which the chromosomes appear and the nuclear membrane and nucleolus disappear

proto-oncogene – a gene which helps to regulate cell division

pulmonary circulation – the part of a double circulatory system in which deoxygenated blood is pumped to the lungs and then flows back to the heart

pulse – the regular expansion and recoil of an artery, as a result of the heart beat, which can be felt from the surface of the body

Purkyne tissue – tissue found in the septum of the heart, along which electrical impulses pass to the base of the ventricles

pyrazinamide – an antibiotic used to treat TB

quaternary structure – the structure of a protein molecule formed by the combination of two or more polypeptide chains

radiation therapy – destroying cancerous cells using ionising radiation

receptor molecules – molecules in the cell surface membrane which have a specific shape that allows other molecules to slot into them; receptor molecules are proteins or glycoproteins

red cells – blood cells containing haemoglobin, whose function is oxygen transport; also known as erythrocytes

reduction division – the first division in meiosis, in which homologous chromosomes are separated, resulting in a halving of the chromosome number

relative growth – the change in size measured in relation to the original size, for example 20 g per kg

relative growth rate – the change in weight in one year divided by the weight at the beginning of that year

repressor gene – a gene which inhibits cell division

residual volume – the volume of air which remains in the lungs after breathing out the maximum possible

resistance – bacteria are said to be resistant to an antibiotic if they are able to survive and breed despite exposure to the antibiotic

respiration – metabolic reactions which take place in all living cells, in which substrates such as glucose are oxidised, releasing energy which is used to make ATP

respiratory arrest – stoppage of breathing movements

respiratory pigment – a coloured substance which carries oxygen or carbon dioxide, for example haemoglobin

respiratory substrate – a substance which can be used in respiration to form ATP

retrovirus – a virus containing RNA; HIV is a retrovirus

reverse transcriptase – an enzyme which catalyses the formation of a complementary DNA strand using RNA as a template

Rhesus antigen – an antigen found on red blood cells; problems can arise if a Rhesus-negative mother is carrying a Rhesus-positive foetus, and she will normally be given an injection of anti-Rhesus antibodies to prevent these from happening

ribosome – a small organelle made of rRNA and protein; the site of protein synthesis

rifampicin (rifampin) – an antibiotic used to treat TB

RNA – ribonucleic acid; a polynucleotide which carries genetic information in the form of a code using the sequences of the four different nucleotides in its molecules

Romanowsky stain – a stain used to show up the different types of leucocytes in a blood film

rough endoplasmic reticulum – endoplasmic reticulum to which ribosomes are attached, where protein synthesis takes place

rubella – an infectious disease caused by a virus; a developing foetus can be seriously harmed if its mother contracts this disease

Salk vaccine – vaccination against polio, which can be taken by mouth

saturated fats – fats in which the fatty acids contain as much hydrogen as they can; there are no double bonds between the carbon atoms

secondary response – the response of the immune system following a second exposure to a particular antigen

secondary structure – the regular shape taken up by a polypeptide chain, such as an alpha helix or beta sheet

selective agent – a factor which decreases the chance of survival of one variety of an organism, and so selects other varieties to survive

selectively permeable – able to let some molecules or ions through but not others

semi-conservative replication – the formation of new DNA molecules in which each molecule contains one old strand and one new one

semilunar valve – a half-moon shaped valve such as those in the entrances to the pulmonary artery and aorta

septum – the part of the heart separating the two chambers on the left from those on the right

serum – blood plasma from which all the clotting factors have been removed

sickle cell anaemia – a genetic disease caused by a faulty gene coding for haemoglobin, in which haemoglobin tends to precipitate when oxygen concentrations are low

sino-atrial node (SAN) – the heart's pacemaker, situated in the wall of the right atrium

smooth endoplasmic reticulum – endoplasmic reticulum with no attached ribosomes; it has many functions, including the synthesis of steroid hormones

soda lime – chemical which can remove carbon dioxide from the air

sodium-potassium pump – a group of transporter proteins found in cell membranes, which use ATP to move sodium ions out of the cell and potassium ions into it

soluble – able to dissolve in water

specific heat capacity – the quantity of energy which must be put into a particular mass of a substance in order to raise its temperature by a certain amount

spectrin – an extrinsic protein found inside red blood cells, which helps to hold them in shape

sphygmomanometer – a device which measures blood pressure

spindle – the structure formed by microtubules (spindle fibres) during mitosis; the spindle is organised by the centrioles

spirometer – an instrument used to measure and record the depth and frequency of air movements during breathing

squamous epithelium – an epithelium made up of thin cells fitting closely together, for example in the alveoli

staining – adding a dye to a sample on a microscope slide, so that particular structures will show up clearly

Staphylococcus aureus – a normally harmless bacterium found on the skin, which may cause infections in people with weakened immune systems

starch – a polysaccharide made of many alpha glucose molecules linked together; used for energy storage in plant cells

statins – drugs which lower cholesterol level by inhibiting one of the enzymes in the liver which catalyses the production of cholesterol

stem cell – a cell which is capable of dividing and forming new cells which can differentiate into specialised types of cells

steroids – molecules derived from cholesterol; oestrogen and testosterone are examples of steroids

stethoscope – an instrument used to listen to the sounds of the heart during the cardiac cycle

streptokinase – an enzyme used to treat DVT

streptomycin – an antibiotic made by a fungus

stroke volume – the volume of blood leaving the left ventricle during one heart beat

substitution – a point mutation in which one base pair is altered to another in a DNA molecule

substrate – the substance on which an enzyme acts; for example, starch is the substrate of amylase

sugar – a carbohydrate made of one or two monosaccharide units; sugars are soluble and taste sweet

surfactant – a substance secreted by some of the cells lining the alveoli, which acts like detergent and reduces surface tension, stopping the alveoli from sticking shut

systemic circulation – the part of a double circulatory system in which oxygenated blood is pumped to the body and then flows back to the heart

systole – the phase of the heart beat when the muscle is contracting

systolic pressure – the pressure exerted by the blood in an artery as the heart muscle contracts

T helper lymphocytes – T lymphocytes that secrete cytokines, so increasing the activity of other cells in the immune response

T killer lymphocytes – T lymphocytes that attach to their specific antigen when it is presented by another cell; they then kill the cell to which they have attached

tamoxifen – a drug used to treat breast cancer

telophase – the stage in mitosis in which the two groups of chromosomes form two new nuclei

tertiary structure – the shape formed by the twisting of a polypeptide or protein molecule on top of its secondary structure; globular proteins have a roughly ball-like shape, while fibrous proteins have long, thin molecules

tetanus – a disease caused by the soil-living bacterium *Clostridium tetani*

thermography – making images of the body by recording differences in temperature; warmer areas may indicate increased metabolic activity associated with cancers

thrombin – an enzyme formed from prothrombin, which catalyses the conversion of fibrin to fibrinogen when blood clots

thromboplastin – a mixture of proteins released by damaged tissue which stimulates blood clotting by catalysing the conversion of prothrombin to thrombin

thrombosis – a blood clot that has formed inside a blood vessel

thymine – one of the four bases found in a DNA molecule; it is a pyrimidine

tidal volume – the volume of air moved into and out of the lungs with each breath

tissue – a group of similar cells which together carry out a specific function

tissue culture – growing cells or tissues in the laboratory, in a culture medium

tissue fluid – the fluid filling the spaces between cells within the body tissues; it is formed from blood plasma

toxin – a poisonous substance; a chemical which can harm the body

trachea – the windpipe

transcription – the formation of an mRNA molecule by building it up against one of the strands of part of a DNA molecule

translation – the building of a polypeptide chain, using the base sequence on an mRNA molecule to determine the sequence in which amino acids are added to the growing chain by tRNA

transmission – the way in which an infectious disease is passed from one person to another

transport (carrier) proteins – assemblages of protein molecules in the cell surface membrane that allow or help molecules or ions to pass through the membrane

tricuspid valve – the valve between the right atrium and right ventricle

triglycerides – substances whose molecules consist of a glycerol 'backbone' to which three fatty acids are linked by ester bonds

tuberculin – a preparation made from tuberculosis-causing bacteria, which is used to make the BCG vaccine

tuberculosis – an infectious disease, usually of the lungs, caused by *Mycobacterium tuberculosis*

tumour – a lump formed by dividing cells

turgid – a condition in which a plant cell is full of water, pushing out on its cell wall

Turner's syndrome – a condition resulting from having the genotype XO; the person is female but is infertile

ultrasound – sound with a higher frequency than we can hear

ultrasound scan – making images of the internal organs of the body using ultrasound waves

ultrastructure – the fine structure of an object; usually applied to cell structure, where the ultrastructure is the detailed structure of the organelles and other structures within the cell

ultraviolet light – light with a shorter wavelength than can be detected by the human eye; ultraviolet light can damage DNA in the skin and cause cancer

unsaturated fats – fats in which at least one of the fatty acids has double bonds between at least one pair of carbon atoms

vaccination – injection with a weakened (attenuated) pathogen, in order to elicit an immune response which will confer immunity

vein – a thin-walled vessel with a relatively large lumen, containing valves, which carries blood towards the heart

ventilation – the process of moving air into and out of the lungs

ventilation rate – the volume of air moved into and out of the lungs per minute

ventricle – one of the two lower chambers of the heart, which receive blood from the atria and pump it out into the arteries

venule – a small vein, which carries blood between capillaries and a vein

vesicles – small membrane-bound structures in a cell, with no internal structure

virus – a non-cellular particle containing a strand of either RNA or DNA surrounded by a protein capsid; viruses are unable to reproduce on their own and can only do so inside a living cell

vital capacity – the tidal volume plus inspiratory reserve volume plus expiratory reserve volume; the maximum volume which can be moved in and out of the lungs with one breath in and one breath out

water potential – the tendency of water to move out of a solution; pure water has a water potential of zero; adding a solute to it decreases its water potential

zygote – a diploid cell formed by the fusion of two haploid cells during fertilisation

Index

ABO blood grouping 18
absolute growth 212–213
actin 162
activation energy 50
active immunity 231
active site 49
active transport 33
acupuncture 180
acute illness 132
adenine 146
adipose tissue 110
aerobic respiration 13
agglutination 18
AIDS 65, 221–223, 247–248, 255
alcohol 190
allergen 135
alpha helix 22
alveoli 128–129
amino acids 21
amino group 21
amniocentesis 203–204
amnion 185
ampicillin 236
anaemia 7
anaphase 162–164
angina 74
angioplasty 81, 85
antenatal care 186–188
antibiotic resistance 238–239
antibiotics 138, 236–240
antibodies 12, 18, 180, 226, 232, 244
anti-coagulants 63
anticodon 154
antigen-presenting cells 225, 227
antigens 18, 226–230
antioxidants 118, 171
antithrombin 56
antitoxin 231
APCs 225, 227
aromatherapy 180
arteries 95–96, 98
arterioles 95–96
artificial immunity 231
aspirin 56, 77, 79

asthma 132, 135–136
atherosclerosis 74, 115
ATP 13, 33, 149
atria 69
atrio-ventricular node 89
atrio-ventricular valves 69–71
auto-immune disease 226
AVN 89

B lymphocytes 226–227, 229
bacteria 219–221, 236–238
bases 146
BCG vaccination 245
benign tumour 167, 171
beta agonists 136
beta-lactamase 238
bicuspid valve 69
bilayer 28, 111
biosensor 38
biparietal diameter 194
blastocyst 141, 185
blood circulation 94
blood clotting 46–53
blood groups 17–19
blood plasma 18, 36–37
blood pressure 99–104
blood staining 3
blood storage 60, 64
blood transfusion 18
blood vessels 95–97
body fluids 36–38
bone marrow 141
bradycardia 90
breast cancer 168, 173–174, 178–179
breathing 120–121
bronchioles 128
bronchitis 133
bronchodilators 136
buffer 63

calcium ions 47, 63, 191
cancer 167–182
capillaries 95–96, 98
capsid 221

carbohydrates 42–45, 191

carbon monoxide 192

carboxyl group 21

carcinogen 134, 169–173

cardiac arrest 76–78

cardiac cycle 70–71, 88–89

cardiac muscle 69

cardiac output 72

cardio-pulmonary resuscitation 77

cell count 8

cell cycle 160–161

cell division 159–166

cell structure 6–10

cell surface membrane 10, 11, 14

cell wall 15

cellulose 15

centrioles 162

centromere 160

cervical cancer 171

CHD 73–78, 112, 114–118

chemotherapy 138, 178–179

chest X-ray 256

chlorophyll 15

chloroplast 15

cholesterol 28, 106, 111

chorionic villus sampling 204–205

chromatids 160–164

chromatin 11, 13

chromosome mutation 199–201

chromosomes 13, 160–166

chronic illness 132

chronic obstructive pulmonary disease
        132–134

chylomicrons 112

cilia 127

cinchona tree 259–260

cisternae 12

clonal selection 227, 229

clone 227

CNS 204–205

codon 154–155

cofactors 63

collagen 95–97

colorimeter 24

competitive inhibition 57

complementary base pairing 148, 150, 153, 155

complementary therapy 180–181

condensation reaction 21, 44, 107, 147

condensation, of chromosomes 162

conservation 262–263

COPD 132–134

coronary arteries 70, 82

coronary bypass surgery 82, 85

coronary heart disease 73–78, 112, 114–118

coronary thrombosis 74

crista 13

crown-rump length 194

CT scan 177

culture medium 142

cytokines 180, 228–229, 247

cytokinesis 160–161, 163

cytosine 146

deep vein thrombosis 55

defibrillator 77–78

deforestation 261–262

degenerate code 197

deletion 197

denaturation 61

deoxyhaemoglobin 25

diabetes 115–116

diaphragm 120–121

diastole 70

diastolic blood pressure 102

diet 215

diet, in pregnancy 189–191

differential growth 215–216

differentiation 141–142

diffusion 30

diffusion, facilitated 31

diploid cells 166

disaccharides 43

disulphide bonds 62

diuretics 115

DNA 13, 145–153, 157, 196–198

DNA replication 150, 160

DOTS 239

double bond 108

double circulatory system 94

double helix 148

drugs, from plants 259–263

DVT 55

ECG (electrocardiogram) 88
electrolytes 41
electron microscope 10
ELISA test 256
embolus 115
embryonic stem cells 141, 143
emphysema 133
endoplasmic reticulum 11, 12
endothelium 95–96
envelope 13, 15, 221
enzyme inhibitors 56–57, 236
enzymes 48–51, 61–63
epidemiology 171–174, 252–253
epithelial tissue 126–129
epithelium, ciliated 126–128
epithelium, squamous 128–129
erythrocyte 6
erythromycin 237
Escherichia coli 236
ester bond 107
ethnobotany 260
eukaryotic cells 3, 219–220
expiratory reserve volume 122
expired air resuscitation 121

facilitated diffusion 31
fats 106–112
fat-soluble vitamins 110
fatty acids 28, 106–110, 217
FEV$_1$ 124, 134
fibrillation 78, 90
fibrin 47
fibrinogen 47
fibrous protein 23, 48
foetal alcohol syndrome 190
foetal growth 183–194
folic acid 186, 191
foramen ovale 82
forced expiratory volume 124, 134
frame shift 197
free radicals 171

gas exchange 126
gas exchange system 120
gene mutation 196–198
gene 151

genetic code 146, 151
genome 157
global warming 262
globular protein 23
glucose dehydrogenase 38
glucose 42–43
glycerol 106–107
glycogen 43, 44
glycolipid 12, 29
glycoprotein 12, 29, 127
glycosidic bond 44
goblet cells 127–128, 133
Golgi apparatus 11, 12, 14
granum 15
growth factors 142
growth patterns 211–214
guanine 146

haem group 23
haemocytometer 8
haemoglobin 21–27, 198
haploid cells 166
HDLs 112
Heaf test 245
health promotion 181
heart attack 75–78
heart block 90
heart disease 68–79
heart structure 69–70
heart surgery 80–85
heart transplant 84–85
heart-lung machine 82
heparin 63
hepatitis 65
hexose 42
HIV/AIDS 65, 137, 171, 221–223, 247–248, 255
hole in the heart 82–83
human genome 157, 207
human papilloma virus 171
hydrogen bonds 61, 62, 148, 153
hydrophilic groups 25, 28, 110
hydrophobic groups 28, 62, 110
hypertension 102, 115
hypotension 100, 102
hypothermia 76

immune response 224–233, 244
immune system 224–226
immunity 230–232
immunoglobulins 232
immunosuppressant drugs 84
immunotherapy 180
implantation 185
incidence 174
incubation time 248
infant growth 209–216
infectious disease 218–263
insertion 197
inspiratory reserve volume 122
insulin 115–116
intercostal muscles 120–121
interferon 180
interphase 160
ionic bonds 62
ionising radiation 169
iron 23, 191
isotonic drinks 41

Kaposi's sarcoma 223
karyotyping 204–205
Klinefelter's syndrome 199–200
Kupffer cells 225

LDLs 112
Leishman's stain 3
leucocyte 11
lipids 106–112, 191
lipoproteins 111–112
liver 43
lumpectomy 178
lung cancer 132, 134, 168, 172, 175, 179
lung tissue 129
lymph 36–37
lymphatics 36–37
lymphocyte 6, 11, 222, 226–229
lysosomes 225

macrophage 6, 221, 225
magnification 5
malignant tumour 167
maltose 43, 44
mammography 176

mass flow 94
mastectomy 178
meiosis 165–166
membrane structure 28–29
membranes, movement across 30–34
memory cells 227–228
menopause 173
messenger RNA 153
metaphase 162–164
metastasis 167
methicillin 236
microtubules 162
mitochondria 11, 13, 14
mitosis 160–165
mitral valve 69
monoclonal antibodies 180
monocyte 6
monosaccharides 42
mortality 174–175
MRI scan 177
MRSA 240–242
mucus 127–128, 133
mutation 168–169, 196–201
Mycobacterium tuberculosis 137–138, 219–221, 239, 245, 255
myocardial infarction 74–76
myogenic contraction 89

natural immunity 231
neutrophils 5, 225
neutrophil elastase 133
nicotine 192
non-competitive inhibition 57
non-disjunction 199
notifiable diseases 253
nuclear pore 11, 13
nucleolus 13, 14
nucleotides 146–147
nucleus 11, 13, 14

oestrogen 173, 179, 200
oncogenes 168
open heart surgery 82–84
opportunistic disease 223
organelle 10
osmosis 30, 236

oxygen transport 25
oxyhaemoglobin 25

pacemaker 89
palisade cell 14
palisade mesophyll 13
pathogens 219
peak expiratory flow rate 124–126
peak flow meter 122, 125
PEFR 124–126
penicillin 236, 238
pentose sugar 146
pepsin 63
peptide bond 21
PET scan 177
pH, effect on enzyme activity 63
phagocytes 225
phagocytosis 6, 225
phospholipids 28, 110–111
phosphorus 191
photosynthesis 14, 15
pigment 15, 21
placenta 185
plaque 74
plasma cells 227, 229
plasmids 238–239
plasmin 56
platelets 6, 47
pluripotent cells 141
point mutation 196–198
polynucleotides 146–148
polypeptide 21, 155
polysaccharides 43
polyunsaturated fat 108
pre-conceptual care 186
prevalence 175
primary response 230
primary structure 22
prokaryotic cells 219–220
prophase 162, 164
prostaglandins 79
prostate cancer 168, 174
protein synthesis 153–156
proteins 21–23, 29, 191
prothrombin 47
proto-oncogenes 168

pulmonary circulation 94, 101
pulse 102
purine 146
Purkyne tissue 89
pyrimidine 146

quaternary structure 23
quinine 259–260

R groups 21, 62, 198
radiation therapy 178, 179
radiation, background 169
radiation, ionising 169
rainforest 259–263
receptor molecule 12, 226
red blood cells 6
reduction division 166
relative growth rate 214
repressor genes 168
reproductive organs 184
residual volume 122
respiration 13, 126
respiratory distress syndrome 131
respiratory substrates 42
retrovirus 221
reverse transcriptase 221
reversible inhibition 56
Rhesus factor 19, 189
ribose 150
ribosomes 12, 155–156
RNA 13, 150, 153–156
Romanovsky stain 3
rough endoplasmic reticulum 11, 12, 14
rubella 186

SAN 89
SARS 251
saturated fats 108
scab 48
scanning 176–177, 194, 203
screening 65, 256–257
secondary response 230
secondary structure 22
secretion 12
selective agents 238
semi-conservative replication 150

serum 48, 64

sex chromosomes 199

sickle cell anaemia 198

sino-atrial node 89

skin cancer 170, 171, 223

smoking 115, 133, 136, 172, 192

smooth endoplasmic reticulum 11, 12, 14

soda lime 123

sodium-potassium pump 33

sphygmomanometer 102–103

spindle 162–164

spirometer 122–124

Staphylococcus aureus 240–242

starch 15

statins 109, 112

stem cells 140–144

steroids 111, 136

stethoscope 56, 77, 92

streptomycin 237

stroke volume 72

substitution 197

sugars 42–43

surface area 130

surfactant 131

systemic circulation 94, 100

systole 70

systolic blood pressure 102

T helper cells 228–229

T killer cells 228–229

T lymphocytes 223, 226–229, 247

tamoxifen 178

TB 137–139, 220–221, 239, 245–246, 255–256

telophase 162–164

tertiary structure 23

testosterone 200

thermography 176

thrombin 47–49

thromboplastin 47

thrombosis 55, 74

thymine 146

tidal volume 122

tissue culture 160

tissue fluid 36–37, 96

toxins 230

transcription 153

transfer RNA 154

translation 153, 154–156

translocation 199

transporter proteins 10, 31, 33

tricuspid valve 69

trypsin 63

tuberculin 245

tuberculosis 137–139, 220–221, 239, 245–246, 255–256

tumour 134, 167

tunica externa 95–96

tunica intima 95–96

tunica media 95–96

turgor 15

Turner's syndrome 199–200

ultrasound scan 176, 194, 203

ultrastructure, of cells 10–16

ultraviolet light 169

umbilical cord 185

unsaturated fats 108

uracil 150

vaccination 231, 243–249

vaccine 180

valves, heart 69–71, 83

valves, in veins 97

veins 95–98

ventilation 120–121

ventilation rate 122

ventricles 69

vesicle 12

viruses 171, 219, 221–222, 228

vital capacity 122

vitamin A 191

vitamin D 191

vitamins 171

vitamins, fat-soluble 110

warts 171

water potential 31–32

water, functions in the body 36

X-rays 176